SAMFOW:
The San Joaquin Chinese Legacy

SAMFOW:
The San Joaquin Chinese Legacy

By Sylvia Sun Minnick

金山三埠

Foreword by Thomas W. Chinn, Founding President,
Chinese Historical Society of America

Panorama
West Publishing
Publishers of Fine Books
Fresno, California 1988

Library of Congress Catalog Number 87-063495
ISBN 0-944194-09-5
Paper 0-944194-10-9

Distributed by:

Heritage West Books
2632 Pacific Avenue
Stockton, CA 95204

*This book is dedicated to my children
and my friends' children*

Contents

Foreword

This is a story of a California Central Valley county that harnessed the bounty of its environs—and Stockton, an early supply town which eagerly strived to be listed among the giants in metropolitan communities. Moreover, it is a story about people—Chinese and white—living together, dependent upon each other, and ultimately enduring because of their interdependence.

Perhaps the most unusual aspect of Chinese American history has been the lack of Chinese historians to record the story of our experiences in California until quite recently. History itself has produced this situation. Shortly after the first Chinese immigrated to California, an anti-Chinese movement gathered momentum and its philosophy became encoded in many state and local laws which greatly restricted the Chinese. This ensured that writers were largely able to gloss over the role they played in American life. As the anti-Chinese movement passed from talking to violent action, many Chinese moved from isolated rural areas where they were at risk. They relocated in large urban communities where, they hoped, there was strength in numbers. Their security meant keeping silent and maintaining a low profile. Ironically, that low profile eventually grew to overshadow the opportunities for Chinese people to voice their stories as caution and discretion ruled their lives and precluded focusing attention upon themselves.

Early historians of the Chinese in the United States such as Mary Coolidge and Gunther Barth recognized the importance of recording the Chinese presence, and each produced classic histories like Coolidge's *Chinese Immigration* (1904) and Barth's *Bitter Strength: A History of the Chinese in the United States 1850-1870* (1964). Carey McWilliams, in his social history, *Brothers Under The Skin* (1943), made a particularly important point when he stated: "It would be impossible to trace the history of the Chinese in this country without at the same time writing the history of California from 1850 to 1900."

With the formation of the Chinese Historical Society of America in 1963, in San Francisco, the first concrete steps were taken to record the Chinese side of the story. This step in turn gave rise to the Society's publishing a compendium of all the bits and pieces of source material, formal and informal research and other cultural resources for Chinese history in one place. *A History of the Chinese in California: A Syllabus* appeared in 1969, and it was our fondest hope it would help provide the foundation for further work in our history. It is now in its sixth printing.

Only recently has Chinese history as written by Chinese emerged from its long silence. Works such as those of Betty Lee Sung recounted the Chinese in America as a whole, while Ping Chiu narrowly focused on economic facets of Chinese labor. Yet, in light of the growing interest in social history, these and other recent Chinese American works have revealed enormous gaps in our knowledge, particularly with regard to the lives of individual Chinese. Ultimately, they raised more questions than they answered, and these questions nagged: What were the lives of the early Chinese pioneers like? Is city experience the norm or the exception? How did these individuals think? What motivated them? What did they experience and what were their legacies to our own generation?

It is, thus, a great personal pleasure for me to write the introduction to this book, for in these pages lies the initial culmination of my hopes for Chinese history in California: the first work detailing the lives of Chinese in a small geographical area from the earliest time to the present by a Chinese historian of ability and insight. Yet beyond this, the book is doubly unique: it sets a standard for other young Chinese historians, and holds wide-ranging implications for future interpretation of the Chinese experience in America.

The greatest strength of this book is the fact that it is a well-conceived, contextual history, placing the Chinese story within the matrix of previously written white California history. It is also groundbreaking, in that, within its pages, Minnick subtly delineates the interpretational and ideological flaws of some previous works. She further explains why some of these biases occurred—the inability of early Chinese and white settlers to understand the language, habits and beliefs of each other. Backed by sound archival research, Minnick has also provided a plethora of information on Chinese customs and traditions as practiced by the early Chinese in the community; explanations of the lifestyles and folkways of a people which has been at arm's length from the curiosity-seeking white America. Her writing has nothing in it of the demagogue; no strident or judgmental qualities intrude upon the reader. It is a simple, straightforward recounting of what happened. It is not really a Chinese history, but a Chinese history about white/Chinese interactions. It will fascinate all who dare to consider the work on the cutting edge of ethnic research, and entertain those who are simply interested in the subject.

Most of all, this is a true story of America and the basic experience of the Chinese in San Joaquin County, California reoccurred in hundreds of communities with a significant Chinese population.

The first Chinese in this country had envisioned themselves only as sojourners in a foreign land. Yet the courage and hardiness which impelled the first Chinese to embark for America gave some a chance to experience the meaning of freedom as they took root in this country. The immigration and assimilation stories of other ethnic peoples have been told frequently. Now, the story of the Chinese, as it unfolds in these pages and, hopefully, in future writings, further legitimizes their role as equally important contributors to the American way of life and as integral partners in our future.

Thomas W. Chinn
Founding President
Chinese Historical Society of America

Acknowledgements

I began my investigation on the Chinese in San Joaquin County ten years ago; in some ways it seems like only yesterday. Now that the final touch of the book is at hand—the important task of listing contributors and supporters has become an overwhelming experience. Memories are flashing through my mind: thoughts of laughter, camaraderie, warm moments, sad occasions, tears at funerals and quiet reflections about people, places and activities which went into making this book truly a people's history.

Many, many members of the Stockton community, both Chinese and white, became so interested in this project they devoted countless hours and days patiently answering all my questions. Sometimes I would return years later when some other leads required their assistance. When they were in doubt as to the accuracy of their answers, they made telephone calls to their friends and dug deep in their closets and old photograph albums for evidence. By the time I prepared the final draft of this manuscript I felt embarrassed that I had taken so long; yet these friends' faith in me never wavered. I am deeply grateful to John Fong, Donald Lee, Elsie and Johnnie Chang, Esther Fong, Earl Jann, John and Leona Wong, Sam Louie and Glenn Kennedy for helping recall the Stockton of their youth; to Harry Chin for his energy and willingness to accompany me at a moment's notice to the most obscure places to translate documents.

I am saddened by the passing of James R. Chew, Wee Poy Wong, and Louie Yee Pai; during the investigative period, each of these Chinese gentlemen drew me into his own world, filled with his life experiences in the old Chinese community.

This research has truly been a community effort: staff members of the San Joaquin County Historical Museum, Haggin Museum, Stockton Public Library, Stockton Rural Cemetery, Stockton Community Development-Renewal Division and CalTrans District 10 Office have given unselfishly of their time and office spaces so I could pry into the recesses of their archives.

There were also friends who served as readers of my various drafts, giving me a wealth of ideas, helping scrutinize those sections which needed rethinking or revisions and supporting the project each step of the way. In this category I am grateful to Jim Shebl, Todd Ruhstaller, John and Jane Cambus, Bill Strobridge, Margaret and Ben Sah, Ron Limbaugh and Eugene Itogawa. I thank Thomas W. Chinn for tucking me under his wing, and Diane Spencer Pritchard, a true friend and colleague, who gave so much time and effort toward the completion of this project.

The greatest appreciation goes to Richard, my mentor, friend and loving husband, whose encouragement, patience and active participation helped make this book preparation memorable and pleasurable.

—S.S.M.

Photographs and graphics courtesy of:

The Ah Tye Family Collection
Haye B. Chan
Ruth Pon Chew
Harry S. Chin
Chinese Association of Stockton
Chinese Historical Society of America,
  San Francisco
Milo Chun
Mary Wong Fong
Hy Gorre
Hugh E. Hayes, Jr.
Earl Jann

Sam Louie
Herbert Ng
Pacific Center for Western Historical
  Studies, University of the Pacific,
  Stockton
Alice Perry
Tod Ruhstaller
San Joaquin County Historical
  Museum, Lodi
Neil Starr
Stockton Greater Chamber of Commerce
Stockton Record

Introduction

As Louie Yee Pai stepped off the *SS Siberia*'s gangplank onto the San Francisco pier in 1909, his immediate thoughts centered on the questions immigration officials commonly asked newcomers to the United States. Other Chinese pushed past the tall, lanky eighteen-year-old and lined up for disembarkation; those who were returnees were out of the holding area in a matter of hours and headed uphill toward San Francisco's Chinatown.

New arrivals, however, underwent intensive questioning. Yee Pai's mind and speech became one as he recalled the answers his father had grilled into him weeks before and even up to the day of his sailing.

Louie Yee Pai and his brothers, as obedient sons, followed the footsteps of their father, Louie Seun Hawk, who arrived in California in the 1880s. A typical sojourner, Seun Hawk saved his money while working in California's Central Valley and periodically returned to his wife and family in his native Guangdong village. As each of Seun Hawk's sons came of age, their father prepared him for his transpacific crossing.

In each Chinese family the first emigree carried with him the burden of the entire family's dreams and desperate hopes. With additional and repeated crossings by other family members, the weight of financial burdens lessened and dreams became realities. In time the transoceanic pattern was perfected; contacts on both sides of the ocean eased the way for families, clans, friends, fellow villagers and even entire districts. The system, a series of social connections and networks, extended beyond the San Francisco docks. It penetrated California's coastline through the interior and even branched beyond to other western states. Yee Pai's 1909 journey was a personal adventure; his route was used by countless others who were to follow.

Drawn initially by the California gold rush, men from the Guangdong Province of Southern China found many avenues by which to pursue their golden dreams when the elusive shiny metal became more difficult to procure. Adaptable to various work techniques and accepting of the most frugal of living conditions, these humble men were appreciative of the work they found. To them there was no comparison between limited opportunities here and the impossible conditions in their own homeland.

The Chinese experience on the West Coast was a series of phenomena. California in the mid-nineteenth century was a young and burgeoning state. She had too much to accomplish in too short a time span; too many dreamers and too few workers. Her labor pool had little variety, particularly in the ethnicity of her laborers. Only one group was large enough and willing enough to provide the muscle power—the Chinese.

Being the first and, of course, the only work force meant the Chinese played a major role in developing a series of procedures by which employers and workers, from totally alien cultures, could agree and benefit. They set the pattern for hiring agricultural workers and negotiated the means to fulfill the workers' daily needs. Eventually, the Japanese, followed by the Filipinos, replaced the Chinese in the field. And while employers' and workers' cultures and languages continued to be dissimilar, the efficiency of matching laborers to work needs continued. Few of these later Asian workers ever realized their work routine had been stamped from a Chinese mold.

In the mid-1880s power-hungry unions and union leaders found the quiet, industrious Chinese perfect scapegoats for their campaigns to instill economic competition among restless, idle, blue-collar workers. Politicians' need to bask in the limelight and newspaper editors' quests for readership added to the anti-Chinese hysteria at both the state and local level. A series of exclusion acts directed at restricting Chinese in 1882, 1888 and 1892 serve as shameful landmarks in the annals of United States law. Individual cities and counties, seeking to reinforce these edicts, passed their own anti-Chinese ordinances.

Discriminated against in both word and action, Sinophobes hoped the Chinese would hastily retreat home. Yet, the Chinese continued to traverse the Pacific despite overt racism. In their wisdom, the Chinese realized they were not the problem but the visible victims of aggravated socio-economic growing pains of the west.

Without a doubt the Chinese are a patient people, for they rode the tide of prejudice until they were no longer its primary focus. And all the while they continued to add strength to their human bridge, taking a little of the western ways back to their villages while increasing their bloodline in this country. More importantly, they hybridized two cultures in this new world into what we recognize today as the Chinese American lifestyle. And as such there lies a common beginning for thousands of Chinese American families.

In the scope of major historic events, the Louie family's pattern of migration and their ability to establish a foothold in this country might be considered insignificant but when compared to the total account of the Chinese people's experience in America, they were no different from other early pioneering families.

Until recently the Chinese story within the context of a larger community study has been almost non-existent. If mentioned at all, their social history has been painted with large, but stereotypical strokes. Regional histories have been that of white history. Quite understandably, local writers needed to consider their readership as subscriptions provided for most of the funding. Obvious problems other than the lack of interest in the Chinese existed. An examination of a distinct ethnic group required an access into

Eighteen-year-old Louie Yee Pai began his adventure in 1909 when he left his South China home and joined his three brothers in the truck gardening business in Stockton. San Joaquin County was to remain his home for seventy-two years.

Many young sojourners left their families behind when they went to seek their fortune and, when successful, were able to send money to relieve the financial burden of those still at home.

that subculture, and, too often, because of their past experiences, the Chinese were less than willing to provide full disclosures, fearing exploitations and immigration problems.

Language disparity and even customs within the Chinese culture itself created a number of stumbling blocks for those wanting to gather information on the Chinese. Transliteration, a common problem for all immigrant groups whether they entered the United States from eastern or western portals, increased the variation in spelling of common names. As such the variety in Chinese surnames sometimes led one to believe there was no correlation among a number of families and clans when, in fact, kinship ties did exist. For example: persons with the last name of Chin, Chinn, Chen or Chan use the same character in the Chinese language and are members of the same family association. Conversely, other common family names such as Wong, Wang or Hwang may actually be members of either the "big stomach" Wongs or the "three stroke" Wongs, depending on how the individual writes "Wong" in Chinese.

Chinese, like westerners, often have a sequence of three names: first, middle and surname. However, it is not unusual for the Chinese to have more than one set of names. In fact, the Cantonese custom dictates that the male may frequently have three or more sets of first and middle names, each given to him during his various passages in life: At birth he receives a childhood or "milk" name; if and when he enters school he is given a "book" name; at marriage he officially forsakes his childhood name and takes on his generation name according to the clan schematic for all males born in his generation. Additionally, scholars and businessmen, when so inclined, chose professional names.

The multiple name system and clan relationship became further complicated when Chinese, desperate to enter the United States after the passage of the Chinese Exclusion Law, resorted to buying affidavits stating they were, on paper, sons of Chinese residents in this country. Once in America these "paper" sons were obligated to continue the ruse, and their children, as a practical course, have perpetuated the paper name.

There was yet another anomaly associated with the Chinese in public documents: early records listed most Chinese as "Ah Fook, Ah Sin, Ah Wey" and so forth. Westerners did not realize the "Ah" was only a guttural expression used to address and describe individuals informally, such as "Oh, Charles" could be interpreted as "Ah, Chuck." Additionally, the name following the "Ah" was actually the individual Chinese's nickname or his common name, for example Bob instead of Robert.

Ignoring the task of tracing individual names in western archives, historians have documented a generalized story of the Chinese, often concentrating on political issues and economic development fostered by the Chinese presence. Only recently have a few books focused on the Chinese within a regional context, and these monographs have treaded gingerly, if not apologetically, on any negative facet of the Chinese character. In the last twenty years it has seemed easier to write Chinese and ethnic history by fanning an angry flame, delineating the victims and the exploiters and cursing the ignorance and insensitivity of the times. By limiting evidences which show that perhaps not everyone was against the Chinese, authors have unmercifully condemned entire communities and have, themselves, continued to exploit the Chinese. Such books have done the Chinese pioneers a great disservice; the Chinese plight was often belabored, suggesting they were a helpless lot and devoid of spirit. In the same vein their accomplishments appeared to be the result of Confucius, patience and supernatural strength. Additionally, many historians have skirted any discussion on Chinese social activities, fearing that they may be branded insensitive and accused of stereotyping if words such as opium, prostitution and gambling were mentioned one time too many. Consequently, the Chinese came across as one dimensional: money-hungry workoholics.

This book has two major objectives, a duality of historical responsibilities: to document the Chinese within San Joaquin County's social history and to develop a holistic understanding of the Chinese experience within that context. Because of these stated tasks this book's format differs from the usual histories written within the framework of sequential chronologies. The first five chapters focus on dovetailing the Chinese, as an entity, into the mid-nineteenth century gold rush history and within the development of San Joaquin County and its major city, Stockton. Rather than apologizing for the abrupt shift in context in the second half of this book, I invite the reader to take a daring plunge into a macro examination of social areas important to the Chinese, for only then can one understand their bi-culturism and the dynamics of their inner community. Major chronological events became only secondary to evolutionary developments within the various topics of religion, education, women, social institutions and so forth.

Regional history, by definition, focuses within a definitive geographical perimeter. This book's title, *Samfow*, means "third city" in the Cantonese dialect. Early Chinese referred to Stockton as the third major town, with San Francisco as "Dai Fow" (the big city) and Sacramento "Yee Fow" (second city). Stockton was important for it served as the gateway to the Southern Mother Lode and the great San Joaquin Valley. However, this regional history of the Chinese is not confined to a town's city limits. Their adventures covered a much greater geographical territory; more specifically, an area that is bounded by two mountain ranges—the Diablo range to the west separating the San Joaquin communities from the influences of the San Francisco Bay Region and, to the east, the Sierra Nevadas and the gold rush story. After decades of breathing, working and living among other citizens of the county, one might say the Stockton Chinese of San Joaquin County are unique and that they differ from the Bay Area Cantonese. Yet, their story is not an anomaly nor is it a limited regional experience. Similar settlement patterns, continuance of customs, folk ways and organizations and societal clan networks occurred elsewhere in other California communities, western states and other western countries.

Instead of massaging and manipulating data extrapolated from censuses and other public documents to prove hypotheses, I used these statistics sparingly as representative examples of visibility and movement within the Chinese community. Often times numbers, tabulations, charts and maps have served as key instruments to depict the Chinese, thus suggesting only masses of hard-working, almost non-descriptive laborers. But they were a people who laughed, cried, fought and loved in their own Chinese quarters. They gambled, joined fraternal organizations, got married, had children and lived full lives. They aided each other, used subterfuge when necessary and, when called upon, rallied around civic efforts. Some became community leaders, others did not. A few individuals deviated from the community norms, other were endowed with inner strength.

Even though there was, at times, a preponderance of sentiments against them, the Chinese maintained a stable community and viewed themselves with balanced perceptions. Louie Yee Pai was one individual. Although his father, Louie Seun Hawk, returned to the native village to live out his twilight years in 1898, Yee Pai carved a niche for himself in this community. As a young man he worked with his brothers in a truck garden and peddled the vegetables they grew; eventually he owned a thriving delicatessen in Stockton. He became active in his clan association, at one point serving a term as its president. With his wife he raised five children and later saw grandchildren and great-grandchildren deepen his roots in this county. A resident of Stockton for seventy-two years, Yee Pai witnessed many changes in this city and within the Chinese community.

There is a personal urgency in writing this story. When I arrived in Stockton in 1961 her Chinatown had become the core habitat of the local derelicts. Second and third generation Chinese Americans living in the suburbs returned to the downtown area only during working hours. Within a few years redevelopment and freeway construction wiped out all semblance of the old Chinese world. The passage of the 1965 Immigration Act which abolished the national-origins quota and the lifting of the Bamboo Curtain in the 1970s have infused the number of Chinese newcomers to California and to Stockton. However, for those who are interested in this area's Chinese heritage, many of the old community leaders are no longer around to tell of their life experiences, including Louie Yee Pai who, at the age of ninety-two, died in 1983. Additionally, white old-timers who could recall the old Chinese vegetable peddlers and family cooks of their youth are also passing quickly with time.

I wrote this book to capture the total Chinese experience in one California county and in a community that became a city representative of all America's people.

Gum Shan

In the mid-nineteenth century, thousands of young Chinese men stared fixedly at the horizon beyond their village and, with trepidation and excitement, envisioned a sojourn to foreign lands. The reasons for their travel were many. Some felt the weight of their family's financial strain pressing on their shoulders. Others felt only relief at the prospect of escaping from the devastations in China. Many were simply exhilarated by the thought of a voyage and the opportunity to prove their abilities as fortune hunters. Those who journeyed eastward followed a dream across the Pacific Ocean to the gold-filled mountains of the California Sierra.

Actual immigration to the western world came only after thoughtful discussion in family council where heavy reliance was placed upon success stories told by fellow clansmen and other villagers. The Cantonese Chinese knew great wealth could be amassed in foreign lands by those willing to work. In preceding centuries, the more adventuresome young men periodically left Guangdong Province in South China and sailed southward, often settling in Malaya and Dutch East Indies. Other travelers from the neighboring province of Fukien founded settlements in Formosa, Borneo, the Sulu Archipelago and the Philippine Islands. News of California's gold discovery, quickly followed by that of Australia two years later, served as the impetus for many to gather their courage and venture toward their destiny— for dreams of gold overshadowed the miseries of circumstance and surrounding.

The decision to leave the homeland seemed both difficult—and easy. The ease came because the whole family accepted the responsibility that it was a sound decision. Although the young man would be missed, there would be one less mouth to feed. But the young Chinese would later experience a profound loneliness, a condition he could not fathom at the moment with so much family nearby.

Chinese families tended to be large; normally several generations lived under one roof. Surrounded by family, relatives and clansmen, children were reared together in extended families and taught the importance of solidarity, and they were expected to follow family dictates as defined in centuries-old Confucian teachings. Thusly, a Chinese developed a sense of belonging to a series of interrelated, interlinking and interdependent units composed of his family, his father's clan and lineage, his village, district and language group.

Climatically, the subtropical, temperate Guangdong area of South China is typhoon-ridden in the summer months. Seasonally, summers begin in April and end in October; the thermometer may reach 100 degrees Fahrenheit in the shade. Winters last through January, and the spring rains of February and March fill the Pearl River Delta's navigable streams to flood stage. Were it not for the periods of flooding, followed by droughts and subsequent famines, the temperate climate might have tempted the native to remain. Historian Ta Chen reported that in the 227-year period between 1369 and 1596 A.D., the Guangdong Province suffered a drought every 28.4 years, while famine struck the same area every 13.1 years. Between 1832 and 1875, the mountain heartland of the Chungshan District, famous for its fruit orchards, experienced six droughts, ten floods, twenty typhoons and four snowfalls.[1]

Being so closely tied had its advantages; a support network was a comforting thought although it did increase the pressure for one to succeed. On the other hand, these young men felt there was no reason to falter because uncles and cousins who had left Guangdong Province earlier, established businesses in foreign countries that served as links to the homeland; thus, all the mechanics of keeping the umbilical cord connected to one's family was in place and functioning. Logistically, the port cities of Canton, Hong Kong and Macao, gateways to dreams, lay in one's own backyard.

THE IMPETUS TO LEAVE

Emigration seemed the only solution to many problems in South China. In the mid-nineteenth century, China, and more particularly Guangdong Province, suffered not only from a series of natural and social disasters, but from the oppression of a decaying feudal system as well.

The nearly 2,000 square mile Toishan District in Guangdong Province lies between 800 and 1,000 feet above sea level. The terrain is rocky, and by 1853 the meager farms produced only enough food to feed its population of 680,000 for four months of the year. Wherever possible, farmers concentrated on growing rice, sweet potatoes, peanuts, vegetables and small livestock, but with the scarcity of land and poor soil conditions, many abandoned agricultural work and sought other occupations to feed their families. Some journeyed to the cities and became peddlers, shopkeepers, merchants; others with skills became carpenters, fish farmers, or basket-weavers. For many, competition became too difficult, and living in the

Major provinces of China and selected districts within Guangdong Province.

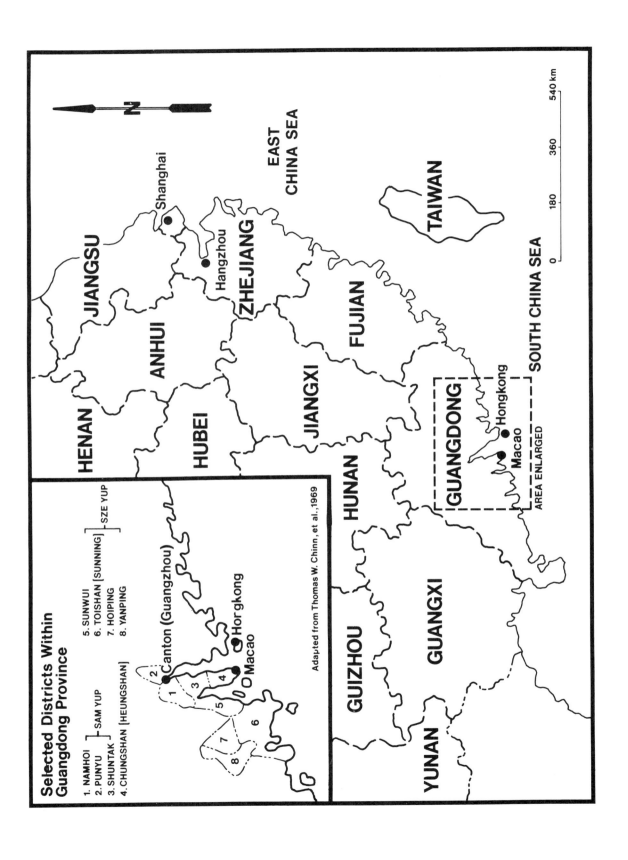

Selected Districts Within
Guangdong Province

1. NAMHOI
2. PUNYU ⎤ SAM YUP
3. SHUNTAK ⎦
4. CHUNGSHAN [HEUNGSHAN]

5. SUNWUI
6. TOISHAN [SUNNING] ⎤ SZE YUP
7. HOIPING ⎥
8. YANPING ⎦

Adapted from Thomas W. Chinn, et al.,1969

Canton (Guangzhou)
Hongkong
Macao

GUANGDONG

HENAN

JIANGSU

ANHUI

HUBEI

ZHEJIANG

JIANGXI

FUJIAN

HUNAN

GUIZHOU

GUANGXI

YUNAN

Shanghai

Hangzhou

TAIWAN

EAST
CHINA SEA

SOUTH CHINA SEA

Hongkong
Macao

AREA ENLARGED

N

540 km

360

180

0

OCCIDENTAL & ORIENTAL STEAMSHIP COMPANY.

GENERAL OFFICERS.

LELAND STANFORD, President, San Francisco, California.
C. F. CROCKER, Vice-President and General Manager, San Francisco, California.
D. D. STUBS, Secretary, San Francisco, California.
T. H. GOODMAN, General Passenger Agent, San Francisco, California.

JAPAN and CHINA LINE.

Steamers leave Wharf, cor. First and Brannan Sts., at 2 p. m., for

YOKOHAMA AND HONGKONG,

Connecting at YOKOHAMA with Steamers of the MITSU BISHI COMPANY for Hiogo, Nagasaki, Shanghae, and other Japanese and Chinese Ports, and at HONGKONG with Steamers for East Indian, Australasian and European Ports.

SAILING SCHEDULE, 1883.

FROM SAN FRANCISCO FOR HONGKONG.	STEAMER.	FROM YOKOHAMA FOR SAN FRANCISCO.
Thursday, January 18th.................	ARABIC..............	Saturday, March 10th.
Tuesday, January 30th................	OCEANIC	Friday, March 23d.
Saturday, February 10th	COPTIC..............	Tuesday, April 3d.
Tuesday, March 6th	GAELIC	Friday, April 27th.
Saturday, March 17th.................	BELGIC	Tuesday, May 8th.

PASSAGE RATES AS FOLLOWS, SUBJECT TO CHANGE:

PAYABLE IN U. S. GOLD COIN.	* First-Class or Cabin.	European Steerage.	Chinese Steerage.	Distances from San Francisco.
San Francisco to Yokohama, Japan	$250 00	$ 85 00	$51 00	4,800 miles.
" Hiogo, "	268 00	98 00	58 00	5,100 "
" Nagasaki, "	285 00	111 00	63 50	5,550 "
" Shanghae, China	305 00	125 00	71 00	6,000 "
" Hongkong, "	300 00	100 00	51 00	6,400 "
" Singapore, India	380 00	....	......	7,850 "
" Penang, "	400 00	....	......	8,250 "
" Calcutta, "	450 00	....	......	9,900 "

CHILDREN under 12 years of age, one-half rates; under five years, one-quarter rates; under one year, free.

SERVANTS accompanying their employers will be charged two-thirds of cabin rate, without regard to age or sex, and will be berthed and served with meals according to ship's regulations.

250 lbs. Baggage allowed each adult first-class or cabin passenger; 167 lbs. each servant; 150 lbs. each European Steerage; 100 lbs. each Chinese steerage; proportionate to children. Excess Baggage charged for at ten cents per lb.

* **Round-trip Tickets to Yokohama and Hongkong,** good for twelve months, will be sold at a reduction of 12½ per cent from regular rates.

An allowance of 20 per cent on return passage will be made to passengers paying full fare to Yokohama or Hongkong, or vice versa, who re-embark within six months from date of landing, and an allowance of 10 per cent to those who return within twelve months.

* **Round-trip Tickets** from San Francisco to Yokohama and return, good for three months from date of arrival at Yokohama, $350.

Families, whose fare amounts to four full passages, will be allowed seven per cent reduction on cabin rates to Yokohama or Hongkong.

Exclusive Use of State-Rooms can be secured by the payment of half-rate for extra berths.

Prompt attention paid to telegraphic reservation of state-rooms or berths. Cabin plans on exhibition and passage tickets for sale at the

C. P. R. R. CO'S GENERAL OFFICES,

Room 74, cor. Fourth and Townsend Streets, San Francisco, Cal.

overcrowded urban areas presented new and even more rigorous hardships than in the country.

Along with the certainty of natural disasters, there was no escape from the social and political problems caused by man. In 1851, the Taiping Rebellion, a grass-roots, quasi-religious uprising under the leadership of Hung Hsiu-Ch'uan, a self-proclaimed Chinese messiah, began in South China and swept northward, spreading death and destruction in its wake. This bloody movement called for agrarian land reforms and an end to the decadent, corrupt rule of the Manchu dynasty. By 1864, when the Ching government finally suppressed the rebellion, the death toll had reached an estimated twenty-five million.

Even as the Taiping Rebellion began to affect other parts of China, another destructive civil disturbance began in the heart of Guangdong Province. Animosity between the Hakka people, invaders from the northeast, and the Punti, natives or long-established residents of the region, flared into violence in 1854, ultimately devastating the Toishan, Chungshan, and Yeungkong districts. The Punti-Hakka feud, which lasted fourteen years, left thousands homeless as village after village was destroyed.

This civil strife, with its attendant social dislocation and distress, caused many thousands to migrate from the Pearl River Delta region. The seaport towns of Canton and Hongkong became release valves and jumping-off centers for thousands of young sojourners seeking a solution to hunger and want for themselves and their families.

GOLD!

The waning days of 1848 proved propitious for those who would seek their fortunes. In San Francisco, the Mormon store proprietor Sam Brannan shouted news of the gold discovery at Sutter's Mill on the American River. Chum Ming, a Chinese merchant who arrived in that city in 1847, became the first of his race to join the gold rush. Ming sent word of California's el dorado to fellow villager Cheong Yum in Guangdong Province; the excited Yum spread the news further before he too departed for the California gold mountains. By 1849, 323 Chinese arrived to capitalize on the fortune to be had. The next year 450 other countrymen followed.[2]

Meanwhile, on the other side of the world, 120 Chinese landed in Sydney, Australia, in December 1848. They were part of a large imported workforce which included men from India and Malaya. White Australian settlers, unable to harness the energy of the aborigines, needed an abundant supply of cheap, tractable, industrious workers as pastoralists, farm laborers and

Transoceanic advertisement of the Occidental and Oriental Steamship Company, a major competitor of the Pacific Steamship line, lists ports and passage rates. Steerage fees and baggage limitations were less for Chinese than for European passengers.

Astute merchants, knowing their countrymen's needs, stocked their stores amply with imported native food products, clothing, medicines, herbs and fresh produce.

domestic workers. In the spring of 1851 gold was found in the Victoria District, and one of the first to hear the news was Louey Ah Mouy, a Sydney merchant catering to Chinese needs. Louey quickly dispatched an enthusiastic letter to his home village in the Toishan District, and in early 1852 the first major party of Chinese reached Australia's goldfields. The following year nineteen members of that party returned to their village, flaunting gold and telling of their good fortune. To them can be assigned the cause of a great Chinese migration to Australia.[3]

THOSE WHO CAME

Almost without exception, the Chinese who entered California and the Victoria District goldfields in Australia in the mid-nineteenth century came from twenty-four districts of the Guangdong Province. Greatest in number were the three major dialect groups, the *Sam Yup, Sze Yup*, and *Heungshan* people. These would ultimately have the greatest influence in California. The Hakka people, scattered in many districts of Guangdong, served as a fourth but minor immigrating group. The people of each district, distinctive because of their dialect and location in Guangdong Province, brought with them specialized skills, each making major contributions to the growth and prosperity of California. Among these immigrants of the gold-rush period, at least a third became the service network for their countrymen.

The Sam Yup or three dialect districts of Namhoi, Punyu and Shuntak, comprised mostly of urban merchants and skilled craftsmen, opened the first Chinatown shops and businesses in San Francisco. Perceiving the material needs of the immigrants, the Sam Yup softened the cultural shock experienced by so many upon disembarkation. Their stores, stocked with Chinese food, herbs and other sundries, reassured the new arrivals their diet, health and personal needs would be met.

The Sze Yup Chinese, coming from the four dialect regions of Sunwui, Toishan, Hoiping and Yanping, were the most numerous of any Chinese language group. Asian-American historians estimate that for every ten Cantonese, seven were Sze Yup people, and of these seven, four came from Toishan district alone. Their occupations lay in both urban and rural activities. The Heungshan people from the Chungshan (heartland mountain) district, followed agricultural, orchardist or fishing pursuits.

While the number of Hakka who migrated to California was quite small, they were well represented in Hawaii. In the Australian goldfields the Hakka presence was sizable; but, even there, the Hakka were again overshadowed by the large numbers of Sze Yup, Sam Yup and Heungshan.

CROSSING A MIGHTY OCEAN

Whether embarking on a voyage for goldmining or for other enterprises, all immigrants faced universal problems associated with adjustment in a new environment. Thus, when people with different lifestyles, practices, languages, customs and traditions are placed in competition for a limited resource, it is natural that conflicts arise. And there was yet one further distinguishing difference among California gold miners: whites who headed for the goldfield generally risked only personal investment. The Chinese with the same goal risked the investments—and future—of many.

For practical and economic reasons, wives and families did not accompany the sojourner. Most Chinese who emigrated intended their stay to be a temporary one. The short-range goal was to make money abroad, and send enough home to relieve the financial burden. Nearly all intended to return to China to care for their elderly parents. Others who planned to stay longer did so with the intent of accumulating enough money to buy property in China and retire to the homeland to spend their twilight years.

There were various methods of actually funding the voyage. Some Chinese paid their fare themselves or with resources pooled from other family members. There were also other means by which even the very poor were able to secure passage. For instance, under the credit ticket system, Chinese companies in the United States advanced up to 97 percent of the passage fee through their company agents in Chinese ports. This system required the traveler to put up a personal or collateral security equal to the price of the passage fee, or forty dollars U.S. At times relatives or friends served as collateral; even women under the age of thirty-six were considered as marketable security. The sojourner-debtor was expected to repay the passage debt from future earnings.

For a brief period in the early 1850s and 1860s other Cantonese companies, based both in California and Hong Kong, operated a contract labor system which actively recruited workers. These laborers were expected to work a specific period of time in payment for their passage. The flow of immigrants under this system was controlled by those in California and the worker-volume depended on the companies' ability to find employment needs. When no work was available the number of ticket offers declined.[4]

By comparison, Chinese who entered Melbourne, Australia, heading for the diggings were termed "free" immigrants despite the fact that 70 percent were bound by contract or credit ticket to Chinese businessmen or clansmen who provided the twenty-seven to thirty pound ($131-146 U.S.) passage fee, The immigrants received rations, their keep, and a small wage; however, all gold they obtained during their first year in Australia belonged to their creditors.[5]

Between 1850 and 1859 tickets to America cost from thirty to fifty dollars, and, in 1865, steerage accommodation from Hong Kong to San Francisco rose to fifty-five dollars and fifty cents. As the volume of eastbound passengers increased, the price stabilized at forty dollars in gold. With increased competition among the shipping lines as well as the tendency to overcrowd ships eastward bound, the vessels sailing back to the Orient attracted few passengers and the price of a ticket plummeted to thirteen dollars.[6]

Ticket price, accommodations, and the number of sailing days fluctuated according not only to the type and size of the ship, but also to the shipping companies' policies. The sleek clipper ships of the 1840s and early 1850s raced across the Pacific, but both holds and passenger spaces were severely limited, making passage costs prohibitive for most Chinese customers.

Aboard the large steamships, early travelers were packed into the holds. Often these overcrowded steerage sections housed three tiers of bunks, usually only stretched canvas over a wooden frame approximately six feet by thirteen and a half inches in size, which provided headroom of only seventeen to twenty-four inches. Amenities as well as provisions were minimal for the duration of the voyage, and fatalities were frequent. On board the *Libertad*, health conditions were so bad that on one trip in 1854, a fifth of the passengers died of scurvy or ship's fever. As a general rule, sailing vessels took between forty-five and ninety days for the crossing, depending upon weather conditions. Seasickness would be only the first of many illnesses the Chinese would endure in his voyage; complaining provided no solution as all passengers were at the mercy of the sea and the ship's captain, whose sole purpose was to ferry as many for the least expenditure of money as possible.[7]

Even when accommodations were adequate and passengers reasonably healthy, other dangers existed. Foremost was fire. Confined to the wooden vessel and with no possible escape, fear among the passengers and crew spread faster than the flames. One accident in 1872, which resulted in the deaths of fifty-three Chinese passengers, occurred when hay stored in the steerage section caught fire and the passengers panicked and jumped overboard. Two years later there was a far greater tragedy when a ship leaving Hong Kong harbor burst into flames and 391 of the 429 Chinese aboard perished along with twenty-three of the ship's officers and crew members.

By 1867, when the Pacific Mail Steamship Company began its routine overseas run from San Francisco to the East, shipboard conditions had improved considerably. The reputation of this company for passenger concerns and reliability preceded its trans-Pacific trade, for in the early 1850s the Pacific Mail Steamship Company held a contract to carry the U.S. mail from the east coast to the west coast via the Panama route. For the California-China passage, the company placed four large wooden, paddle-wheel steamers, the *America, China, Japan* and *Great Republic*, into service. When Chinese crews were hired as stewards to cater to first-class passengers, owners of the line noted an immediate saving in wage and food costs. The Occidental and Oriental Steamship Company, a major competitor of the Pacific Mail Steamship Company, soon hired Chinese as firemen, cooks, waiters and servants to serve on its line.

The Pacific Mail luxury steamers carried up to 250 first-class passengers, and from 1,200 to 1,400 in the steerage section. A special galley prepared food for the Chinese passengers and even wealthier Chinese merchants traveling first class preferred eating in the steerage section where the food was more to their taste. The sojourners' fears were further allayed when they saw their countrymen serving as crew members. By 1874 the luxurious old paddlewheelers and sidewheeler vessels were rapidly being replaced by the screw-propelled, iron-hulled steamships. Within five years, the Pacific Mail's last surviving paddlewheeler, *China*, made her final voyage.[8]

LAND OF GUM SHAN

Upon arrival in *Dai Fow* (the "big city"—the Chinese name for San Francisco), interpreters and representatives from the various *hui kuens* (associations) were at the embarcadero to greet the new arrivals. Although differences in dialects among the Chinese passengers made communications virtually impossible during the voyage, most quickly recognized the shouts and screams of individuals on the pier trying to catch the attention of travelers hailing from the various locales of Guangdong Province. This first contact, coming as it did in an accustomed dialect, brought quick acknowledgement and also uplifted the spirit of each newcomer.

Those Chinese entering via the credit ticket or contract labor system held a ticket which contained their name, home district, names of the headman and sponsor, and date of their ship's arrival. This information was matched with the sponsoring company's docket. New arrivals had their papers processed, then piled into wagons and headed for Tong Yen Fow (city of the Chinese or Chinatown). Those who preferred to shake off their sealegs walked the short distance from Brannan Street up Clay Street clutching their meager possessions: a rolled-up mat, a box of tea, a few articles of clothing, and still tucked into the breast pocket of their jacket, the ragged and well-creased piece of paper listing the names and addresses of relatives, friends or fellow villagers in America.

Here in San Francisco's Chinatown, in the area surrounding present-day Portsmouth Square, the Chinese found an ambience similar to their homeland: the aroma of Chinese food filtering from the restaurant kitchens, the native sausages tied in bundles and slabs of pork suspended on meat hooks in front of grocery stores. Other shops carried vegetables, hardware, wicker baskets and sun hats stacked in neat piles, and clerks unpacked newly-arrived imported packages of dried fish, shrimp and other meat products from the nest of straw in the packing crates.

Chinatown bustled with activity wherever one looked: merchants tended their businesses, traders hurried between shops checking on merchandise, restaurants and gambling houses hawked for customers and pushed those who had nearly finished their meals out the door to make room for new arrivals. There was a sea of Chinese faces. Men wore the familiar dark-colored pajama trousers and loose-fitting, front-buttoned overshirts. Some trotted briskly down the streets as they carried their wares suspended from their shoulder poles. Brightly-painted wooden placards written in familiar characters hung over doorways, announcing agents and consultants ready to sell information and maps to specific areas in the California hinterland, gold or work opportunities supposedly being plentiful in these locations. Herb shops did a thriving business selling medication to those who became ill on the long sea voyage, and temple attendants sold incense and punks to new arrivals who felt the desire to thank their gods for a safe passage. As the newcomer wandered through Chinatown, its sights and sounds were so similar to his homeland that these reminders gave him a sense of inner peace even though he was in a strange new land.

The young Chinese knew he could not spend many days in San Francisco. His lodging at the hui kuen center was only temporary and soon another would need his cot. Also the few dollars he had were rapidly depleted with meals and incidentals, and he needed to start inland where he was destined to make his fortune. Many new arrivals stayed only long enough to get their legs landworthy and their stomachs back to normal, an average of two or three days. Others, with a burning desire to get to the business at hand, did not even stay that long.

THE ROUTE TO EL DORADO

After consulting with his district association and perhaps looking for others who were interested in pooling resources to work a claim, the sojourner gathered his necessities and once again headed for the docks. From there many types of vessels—sailing ships, sidewheelers and paddle-wheelers—traveled to the inland ports. Those traveling to the northern mines purchased a ticket to Sacramento. To reach the southern Mother Lode regions one boarded ships destined for Stockton, gateway to the southern mines.

The distance via the inland waterways between San Francisco and both inland port cities was almost identical. After sailing through the Carquinez Straits and passing California's first state capitol at Benicia, the ships parted course at Sherman Island, at the juncture of the Sacramento and San Joaquin rivers. The route to Stockton, almost due east, skirted the northern boundaries of Contra Costa County, and from there it was a short distance before one reached that city's head of navigation. For those bound for Sacramento, the ships continued on a northeasterly course and followed the Sacramento River until it met the American River.

Sacramento, *Yee Fow* (City Number Two in Chinese), was so called not only because of the town's size, but also because it was the second stop en route to the goldfields. Chinese stepping off the boats, heading east lured by the gold, passed other Chinese heading west to find quarters before winter set in, as well as some who were disheartened because gathering gold was harder than anticipated.

A large Chinese settlement existed only a block from the Front Street harbor. The quarter resembled a scaled-down San Francisco Chinatown with the same sights, sounds and smells associated with Chinese living. Sacramento's early Chinese settlers were in service-oriented occupations: traders, merchants, restaurateurs, laundrymen, and peddlers.

The Chinese presence in Sacramento was very noticeable; the special state census of 1852 listed 804 Chinese—794 males and ten females. Their settlement, dubbed "Chinadom" by the white populace, was located on I Street, between Second and Sixth streets, close to the harbor and the main business section of town. I Street itself was a levee road; both sides of the street lay on low ground, and the north bank backed onto Sutter Slough, which extended from the American River levee to I Street and from Sixth Street to the American River at its mouth; the high water runoff from the Sacramento River filled it, and the slough also received the overflow from the nearby American River. With so many Chinese in that vicinity many Sacramentans

An 1870 view of Sacramento by Augustus Koch with an aerial view of the Sacramento River traffic. Sutter Lake (center) was often referred to as "China Slough" or "China Lake," for Sacramento's Chinatown lay at its I Street bank (right).

called the area "China Slough" or "China Lake."[9]

There were several indications that Yee Fow would remain a viable Chinese community. For instance, in early 1851 the Sze Yup Association purchased a building on I Street between Fifth and Sixth streets to serve as a temporary shelter for its transient brothers including those needing a place to stay when ill. Secondly, a gambling house, halfway down I Street toward Fifth Street, had a 100-seat room in the rear of the building set aside for theater entertainment that included puppet shows and Chinese opera troupe performances on special holidays. However, the most important function of all Chinatowns, wherever located, was to provide supplies and services to other Chinese. Newcomers noticed there were more contacts between the Chinese and the white community here than in San Francisco.[10]

As the newcomers struck up conversations with the more experienced who had traveled to the mines, they realized they were no longer hearing second- and third-hand stories of mighty discoveries, but were getting real accounts of mining techniques and the physical and social conditions existing less than fifty miles away.

After purchasing necessary picks, shovels, pans, baskets and poles and assembling their supplies, the Chinese eagerly made their way to the foothills and, at long last, to the mountain streams lined with gold.

MINING

The Chinese were primarily engaged in placer mining and used tools such as the Long Tom and rocker or cradle. Instructions for using the rocker were simple. It involved shoveling auriferous dirt from a nearby riverbed or stream into a hopper at the top of the machine, then flushing water through a series of sieve-like boxes in the unit. While the water flowed the length of the machine, the miner gently rocked the device, dividing earth from gold; the heavier metal stuck to riffles in the box and was then removed. The inexperienced quickly became adept in this simple but tedious process.

In a few short years placer mining depleted the surface gold and different techniques were employed to penetrate the earth farther, in search of a rich vein. Quartz mining became the next accepted method, followed by hydraulic mining and then dredging. By the time placer mining ended most Chinese had already begun to look elsewhere for other work opportunities. A few remained in the goldfields and found employment in quartz mines and stamp mills owned by white companies.

CHINESE CAMPS AND CHINESE QUARTERS

There were two types of Chinese habitations in the goldfields: Chinese camps and Chinese quarters in mining towns. The former, the more numerous, was located generally on the bank of a stream. The camps, consisting of up to six men in a tent, served as convenient shelters for the men doing the actual digging. These camps, inhabited by kinsmen, clan or fellow vil-

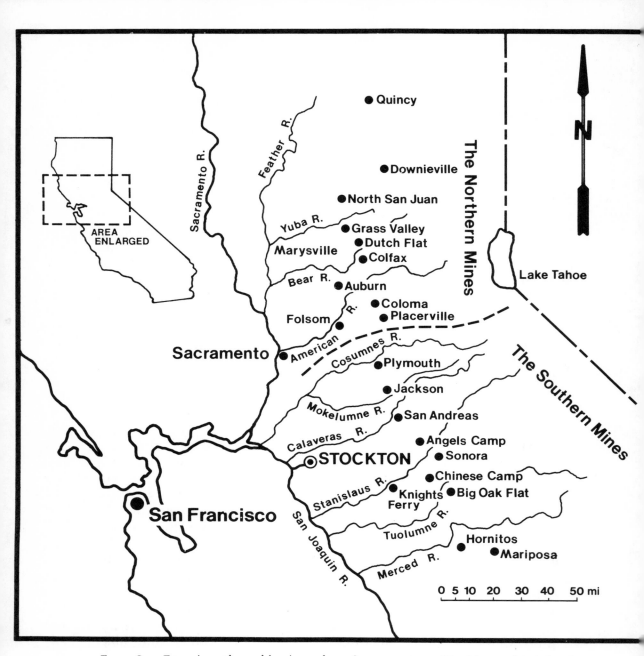

From San Francisco the gold miner chose Sacramento or Stockton as his inland port city depending on his choice of the northern or southern mines. Both cities served as the supply centers between the gold mining foothill communities and the Bay Area metropolis.

lagers, maintained their distance from other Chinese groups. Those from Toishan encamped away from the Heungshan diggings, and both kept their distance from the Hakkas.

Numbers of Chinese in mining camps fluctuated according to the gold's availability and the social and political conditions in the region. Visitors to the mining areas noted many Chinese camps throughout the Mother Lode. For example, traveler J. D. Borthwick described the conditions at Mississippi Bar on the Yuba River: "There were about 150 [Chinese] living in a perfect village of small tents, all clustered together on the rocks . . . " Other historians have cited 200 Chinese at Mormon Bar and 400 at Horseshoe Bar on the American River, while "a whole bevy" inhabited Weaver Creek in Placerville. These and other descriptions provide us with clear images of the numbers and appearance of Chinese encampments.[11]

In all mining camps a routine developed. At the crack of dawn, the white miners, after a hearty meal of coffee and hardtack or ship's bread and salt pork, began their pick and shovel work which ended only when daylight faded. On Sunday, work was suspended out of respect for the Sabbath and to attend to housekeeping chores. The day was also spent visiting, reading or writing to loved ones of their experiences.

Chinese miners maintained essentially the same routine, and while their meals were different because of their culture, they too changed their routine on Sunday. Their day of rest was used for housekeeping, settling accounts, butchering fresh meat and socializing among their own. Unlike some white miners who could read and write, most Chinese in the mines were illiterate, and their quiet times were spent singing songs or reciting poetry they had learned in their childhood. These activities evoked memories of their loved ones and a homeland far away.

The Chinese did not recognize Sunday as a day of religious activity. To them, their gods were available every day and at all hours to hear their prayers. Some Chinese erected wayside shrines made out of makeshift materials. One was recently found strapped around an old oak tree in an abandoned mining area in Mariposa County. Unlike the more elaborate altars associated with formal Chinese temples, this five-foot-high structure with Chinese characters etched in the wood on both front panels has stood the test of time. A small drawing of a deity, or several Chinese characters associated with ancestor worship written on a piece of paper was affixed to the altar. A small tin can filled with sand or dirt held the supplicant's offering of two or three sticks of punk and incense. The miners' prayers were mostly for good luck, the universal hope of all gold seekers.[12]

The territorial separation that existed among various groups of Chinese was also exhibited by men of other nations. Intense competition for gold and the differences in language, habits and customs served as natural barriers. Each miner, regardless of race, had a singular purpose—gold. No one intended to hate his neighbor, but human nature, being as it is, fostered

This abandoned wayside shrine was found strapped to an oak tree in the Southern Mother Lode. Chinese miners offered incense, joss candles and simple offerings to their gods; their prayers asked for safety and success in their venture.

competition and bigotry. The Chileans, Peruvians and Sonorans stayed in close proximity, the French isolated themselves from other Western Europeans; the Irish, Cornish, English and Australians came closest to blending in with the Americans although their speech patterns remained distinctive. Men of each nationality started to the mines in clothing that was a part of their homeland; the French berets, blouselike shifts and wide pantaloons stood out as much as the Sonoran serapes or the pigtails and the shapeless dress of the Chinese. All had derogatory and rather descriptive names for others; Sawnies, Paddies, Jonathans, Cousin Jacks and Keskydees (a term for the French miners who often repeated, "Qu'est-ce que se dit?" when attempting to understand questions) were but a few names used for Blacks, Irish, English, Cornish and French miners.

Prior to 1852, when the number of Chinese in the mining region was minimal, they were regarded as a curious lot and were generally tolerated. But with the increased Chinese mining population after 1852, they were chased out of the rich claims and relegated to isolated regions or areas that had already been mined out. The Chinese were willing, however, to rework patiently those tailings abandoned by previous argonauts for they felt the earlier miners had worked the earth too quickly and carelessly.

Although their mining locations and campsites were not the best and their high visibility generated animosity among other miners, the Chinese closeness yielded immeasurable benefits. There was companionship and cooperation. The commonality of bonding, mutual investment and trust was far more valuable than gold itself.

Even in the most remote mining areas the Chinese had little difficulty obtaining food items in keeping with their diet such as rice, dried fish and shrimp, and tea. Chinese merchants in nearby mining towns played a major role in these gold seekers' life. Aside from providing the necessary supplies and food, the storekeeper was a vital link in the Chinese network. Oftentimes a shareholder in the nearest Chinese diggings, the merchant held the group's yield in safekeeping until it could be safely transported to San Francisco; at times, he financed the miners' needs and kept an account of their debts. His store served as a message and postal center for the highly transient Chinese, ready to move their camps at a moment's notice when a new strike was announced or when the surface dirt offered up its last speck of gold.[13]

By the mid-1850s, one of every five miners was Chinese and major mining towns such as Marysville, Oroville, Auburn and Weaverville boasted as high a percentage of Chinese in their population as San Francisco. Even smaller towns witnessed a proportionate increase in the number of Chinese stores and businesses ready to serve the miners' needs.

Chinese quarters of many mining communities were generally situated in the oldest part of town and/or located alongside the nearest waterway, some distance from the more prosperous residents of the community. Frequently they adjoined the fandango and "red light" districts. It did not bother the Chinese that his place of business was next to a bordello or saloon for he was uncritical of his neighbors' livelihood; in fact he welcomed their patronage. In time of natural disaster such as the frequent floods or fires, the Chinese and their neighbors aided each other.

The Chinese in the Mother Lode communities promoted their own forms of entertainment. Gambling houses operated for those with a few nuggets, prostitutes were brought in to service a chain of mining towns, and every so

Sonora in Tuolumne County exhibited the ambience of an international community in the early years of the gold rush, c.1850.

often opera troupes and other Chinese performers toured the Mother Lode circuit.

Yet the Chinese life was not peaceful, for their critics were many. The criticisms usually were about the noise, vice and filth within the Chinese quarters. However, in all fairness, such charges could also have been leveled at the other quarters in every mining community.

Unfortunately, the highly critical, moralizing comments aimed at the Chinese in local newspapers after 1852 lent a false note to the overall excitement, gaiety, color and flavor so prevalent in the early California gold mining frontier. For instance, in the southern mining region, Sonora, a town initially settled by Mexican miners, quickly took on an international flavor common to most Mother Lode towns. An article in the San Francisco *Alta California* of 1850 captured some of that flavor:[14]

> Sonora is nearly as large as Stockton, and far ahead of it for gold, gals, music, gambling, spreeing, etc. It's a fast place, and no mistake. Every Sunday there is either a horse race or a bull bait and any number of fights and rows . . .

With different nationalities coming together, selective words from the various tongues crept into the language of all. In describing the town of Hornitos, south of Sonora in Mariposa County, "The stage house is the 'Progresso Restaurant,' the bakery is a 'panderia,' the hotels invite the traveler in both Spanish and English, while Sam Ting or Too Chang equal the 'lavado y planhado.'" Other words such as arrastra, piojos and frijoles were understood by all.[15]

Aside from food and language each nationality adapted to clothing and mining techniques introduced by others and considered practical: the French exchanged Parisian dress for flannel shirts, wool trousers and rough boots. Local Indians used to wearing a minimum of clothing found shirts and trousers more practical, while the Chinese traded in their impractical cloth-soled shoes for boots, and the Americans took to using bandannas to cover their faces from dust and to wipe their brows.

BEGINNING SIGNS OF PREJUDICE

When placer mining began to fail the scramble for gold created a natural cleavage between men of different skin color and cultures. The first to feel the political sting of the white miners' actions were the dark-skinned foreign miners, Chileans, Mexicans and Peruvians. Passage of a Foreign Miner's Tax of twenty dollars per month in 1850 and its enforcement quickly forced most of the Latin miners from the region. At this time there were comparatively few Chinese in the mines and of these, many worked productive areas and were able to pay the high tariff. As the Latin miners disappeared from the gold regions, county officials noted with alarm the rapidly-shrinking revenues which were used to support county functions.

Even valley towns such as Stockton felt the effects of this decrease in revenues, and many counties successfully lobbied for repeal of the stringent law. In 1852 a modified miner's tax of three dollars per month was reinstated to appease the local governments and placate those still hostile to the Chinese. For some years the tax fluctuated between three dollars and six dollars per month, depending upon the amount of clamor against the Chinese and the counties' dependency on this source of funding. The income derived was indeed substantial: in one month alone, the miner's tax in Sacramento County amounted to $1,200. When the tax was increased to six dollars per month, many Chinese abandoned the mines; when it was subsequently decreased to four dollars, one source claimed: "Sacramento's I Street almost became completely deserted as the Chinese again headed for the hills."[16]

While taxes were a political form of harassment, physical violence endured by the Chinese occurred randomly, and as the years progressed, more frequently. Frustrated, and often liquor-filled, white miners began simply to roust them from their diggings. Chinese miners fleeing from such wrath often fled to nearby mining towns in the hope that local law enforcement and the proximity of more civilized, level-headed citizens would serve to dampen the violence. In some towns, such hopes were vain, and the persecutors became encouraged by their successes. Beginning around 1860 and lasting well through the 1880s, violent white citizens joined by workingmen and lumbermen in small Mother Lode towns and surrounding areas took to driving out the Chinese miners. In addition, they also called for eviction of local Chinese laundrymen and restaurant workers, even though these individuals did not participate in any sort of mining activity and their businesses were considered necessary to the growing communities. Many of those who acted in violence had been patrons of the Chinese businesses. In many instances angry mobs burned down the Chinese sections of towns giving no thought to the lives or property of others. The furor in the mining communties waxed and waned; like dominoes, when one community struck out against its Chinese, residents in the neighboring towns did likewise within a matter of days.

The anti-Chinese experience in the California goldfields, however, was not an anomaly. In the Australian goldfields the coming together of men from different nations created much the same animosity. However, there the Chinese miners underwent a far more devastating experience than that of their cousins in California.

CHINESE EXPERIENCES IN THE AUSTRALIAN GOLDFIELDS

At the time the California miner's tax was in effect, the Australian fields were just coming to life. As mentioned previously, in 1852 the first major party of Chinese miners arrived in Sydney, and in 1853 nearly five thousand Chinese disembarked at the ports of Melbourne and Sydney. Other argonauts from England, Russia, Denmark, Italy, Germany, France and America also aggressively pursued their golden dreams, and the Australian goldfields exhibited much the same international flavor as those of California.

The Australian anti-Chinese movement began within two years of the first gold strike in Victoria District. While whites resented the Asian surface miners' system of cooperatives and their efficient work gangs, the difference in language, dress and habit were purportedly key reasons for their persecutions. Hundreds of Chinese were killed in pogroms from Bendigo and the Buckland fields in Victoria to Lambing Flats in New South Wales.

These episodes of violence may be comparable to the experience of Chinese miners in California, but the Australian laws were far more punitive than the relatively simple California tax. The government imposed a ten-pound (forty-nine dollars U.S.) head tax on each Chinese arrival. Additionally, under the Chinese Protectorate System, a paternal colonial practice, Chinese were prohibited from mining in the same areas as whites and were required to live in isolated compounds or villages administered by governmental bureaucrats. Herded into one of these internment camps, each Chinese was forced to pay a yearly one-pound "protection fee." By the end of the 1850s, placer mining in the Victoria District ended, and with continued government restrictions, the flow of Chinese to Australia ebbed.[17]

Displaced from the placer mines by force and by changing mining techniques, the confirmed Chinese miner found other parts of the world opening up new strikes just when the California and Victoria fields were closing. Following the initial boom and speedy collapse of the strike on the Fraser River in British Columbia in 1858, the pace quickened again with the discovery of gold in the Cariboo Mountains and the Kootnai area of the Purcell Mountains in the early 1860s. These were quickly followed by other discoveries on the upper Columbia in 1865. In 1871, when British Columbia entered the Canadian Confederation, its population included 10,000 whites and 4,000 Oriental settlers. Yet wherever gold strikes were made, the white-Chinese conflict repeated itself time and time again.

In California today there is little evidence of the many Chinese gold camps, largely due to the temporary nature of the shelters. Yet a number of sites of early Chinese quarters exist in the old mining towns such as Angel's Camp, Fiddletown, Chinese Camp, and Folsom. The Chinatown of Folsom, a small town just east of Sacramento, was once located on Reading and Leidesdorff streets and included numerous shops, grocery stores, a slaughterhouse, family and district association buildings, a joss house, and even a charity house, sponsored by the Sze Yup Association, for the sick and elderly. Today only one store from the early Chinatown remains.[18]

Chinese temples in Weaverville, Oroville, Marysville and Mendocino, now tourist attractions, remain extremely important to California's heritage. These few houses of worship are the only surviving examples of the many temples which once dotted the California Mother Lode. Columbia, Knight's Ferry and Coulterville had sizable Chinese populations, but now show no sign that the Chinese had influenced and colored their lives. Some old-timers in these communities can still recall elements of the Chinese past.

BUT THE RUSH CONTINUED...

Despite rumors filtering back to the Guangdong Province that the easy way of gold-gathering had ended and that racism had given way to violence, the Chinese impulse to immigrate did not cease. Even when the Chinese government forbade emigration on penalty of death, the hopefuls still gambled they could make a fortune in California. Many believed there was no choice. Even if all the placer gold had been removed from the California mountains before they arrived, most Chinese felt they had a distinct advantage for they were willing to adapt and work in any laboring capacity. They hoped to receive higher wages abroad and chose to take that chance rather than remain at home to compete in the already saturated employment market.

Once in California, the agrarian-oriented Heungshan and Toishan Cantonese headed for the coastline and the central valley, seeking to work the earth and to fish the waters of the California shores. Instinctively, they realized the Delta region of the great Central Valley was as close as they could come to finding conditions and climate similar to those of their native homeland.

With the commonality of local dialects, the companionship of kin and fellow villagers, and their camaraderie in making room for one more, the Chinese sojourners eased through the transition from their homeland, and all they held dear, into an all-male society in a land that still offered golden opportunities.

CHAPTER ONE ENDNOTES

1. Gunther Paul Barth, *Bitter Strength: A History of the Chinese in the United States* (Cambridge, 1964), p. 19. Ta Chen, *Chinese Migrations with Special Reference to Labor Conditions* (New York, 1923), p. 10. Henry Townsend Walker, Jr., "Gold Mountain Guests: Chinese Migration to the United States, 1848-1882" (unpublished doctoral dissertation, Stanford University, 1976), p. 8.

2. Thomas W. Chinn, H. Mark Lai, and Philip P. Choy, *A History of the Chinese in California, A Syllabus* (San Francisco, 1969), p. 9.

3. Kathryn Cronin, *Colonial Casualties: Chinese in Early Victoria* (Victoria: Carlton, 1982), p. 16.

4. Walker, "Gold Mountain Guests," p. 13.

5. Cronin, *Colonial Casualties*, pp. 19-21. *Annual Statistician-1876* (San Francisco, 1876), p. 162.

6. Robert A. Weinstein, "North from Panama, West to the Orient: the Pacific Mail Steamship Company," *California History*, Spring 1978, pp. 50-52. *Stockton Daily Independent*, April 12, 1876.

7. Chinn et al, *Chinese in California*, pp. 16-17.

8. Weinstein, "North from Panama," pp. 46-53.

9. John C. Jenkins, "Sutter Lake or China Slough," *Golden Notes*, December 1966, pp. 1-3. *San Joaquin Republican*, February 2, 1853.

10. Mary Praetzellis and Adrian Praetzellis, *Archeological Study of the IJ-56 Block, Sacramento, California: An Early Chinese Community* (Sonoma, 1982), p. 17. Brienes, West and Schultz, *Overview of Cultural Resources in the Central Business District, Sacramento, California, 1981* (Sacramento, 1981), p. 61. William K. Willis, *History of Sacramento County, California with Biographical Sketches* (Los Angeles, 1913), p. 198.

11. Stephen Williams, *The Chinese in the California Mines 1848-1860* (Stanford, 1971), p. 40.

12. The wayside shrine found abandoned in the mining area of Mariposa County is permanently exhibited at the San Joaquin County Historical Museum in Micke Grove Park, Lodi, California.

13. George H. Tinkham, *History of San Joaquin County, California with Biographical Sketches* (Los Angeles, 1923), p. 93.

14. Rodman W. Paul, *California Gold: The Beginning of Mining in the Far West* (Nebraska, 1947), p. 111.

15. John Walton Caughey, *The California Gold Rush* (Berkeley, 1948), pp. 191-95.

16. Cheryl L. Cole, "Chinese Exclusion: The Capitalist Perspective of the Sacramento Union, 1850-1882," *California History*, Spring 1978, p. 13.

17. Cronin, *Colonial Casualties*, pp. 41-44, 56-59.

18. Interview with Mabel Chan, Folsom, 1983.

Charles Weber's Community

2

Gold was the catalyst which brought the Chinese to California but they soon recognized the difference between the elusive metal and golden opportunities. Their presence dovetailed with the young state's need for a workforce in the 1860s to construct massive railroad lines, followed by reclamation and agricultural developments. San Joaquin County offered work in these activities, and when all three areas of employment no longer required their great number, it was the spirit of the land that continued to hold the Chinese's attention.

One must see the land as it was to understand the role the Chinese played in transforming the Central Valley into an agricultural wonderland. Only then can one comprehend the visions of the early white settlers and the Chinese's willingness to give of their energies. With bone and muscle, they moved the earth, built the levees and rearranged the Delta in the western portion of the valley. Ultimately the time and effort expended on these herculean tasks became rich investments for those who participated.

San Joaquin County is located in the north end of the San Joaquin Valley and at the heart of the great California Central Valley. The county is flanked on both sides by mountain chains. The foothills of the majestic Sierra Nevada lie to the east, and to the west the Mount Diablo range separates San Francisco bay cities from less populous valley towns. The county measures 1,370 square miles in size, or approximately 926,720 acres.

Three major rivers—the Mokelumne, Calaveras and Stanislaus—flow westward across the county and enter the San Joaquin River, a major waterway which courses through the western portion of the county in a northwesterly path. The Stanislaus River serves as the county's southern boundary. The Mokelumne, which flows through the northeastern part of the county, divides Sacramento and San Joaquin counties in the northwest and its tributaries fill to overflowing during fall and winter months. The Calaveras River, whose source also lies in the foothills, enters the county at its eastern border and crosses the valley just above Stockton; its minor rivulets connect into the town's five transverse sloughs, all terminating at the Stockton channel, an inlet of the mighty San Joaquin River. Sloughs, tributaries and channels of these waterways snake across the land, creating a

Seemingly tranquil, the French Camp Slough teemed with activity in the 1820s and 1830s. French fur trappers and American explorers headquartered here in the summer months as there was an abundance of elk, deer and beaver in the vicinity.

microcosm of various geographic phenomena. A delta of swamp and overflow land surrounds the confluence of the San Joaquin and Sacramento rivers. Together these two rivers form two sides of the Delta triangle whose many streams and inlet offshoots create a pattern of myriad islands, waterways and coves. These two river systems merge at Suisun Bay and pour through the Carquinez Strait into San Francisco Bay until, at last, it reaches the Pacific Ocean.

Winter rain and spring snowmelt spill water into the arterial drainage of the county from east to west; the peak flows are from January to June. During the dry season, the pulsing tide from San Francisco Bay sends a reverse flow of water into the Carquinez Strait, forcing the westward river flow back into numerous sloughs and channels. During heavy rains the channels overflow their banks and flood immediate areas. In early years, respite from flooding came only during the dry months of summer and fall. The constant wetting and drying state of the river banks encouraged an abundant growth of willow, cattail, tule, and wild blackberry bushes at the river's edge, which was itself well-shaded by a variety of valley oak, cottonwood and walnut trees. In the depth of the water, beavers actively built their homes in the smaller streams while man feasted on an astonishing variety of fish and shellfish.

Early explorers and travelers to the area left numerous detailed accounts of the county in its virgin state. Deer, elk, antelope and bear roamed the land at will; a carpet of tall grasses and wildflowers grew on the valley floor and gave a parklike appearance to the homes of smaller wildlife species. Squirrels and other ground animals subsisted on acorns supplied by numerous oak groves, and the skies were often dark with the passing of uncounted numbers of birds and waterfowl. Flocks of ducks and geese flying in their V-formations entered the county en route to their winter quarters to feed among the tules. Numerous waterfowls such as mallard, teal, widgeon, spoonbill, canvasback and woodduck made the land a hunter's paradise from mid-October to mid-March. It has been estimated that more than 100 million birds crossed the county in their seasonal migrations. Yet all paradises have their drawbacks, and in San Joaquin County hordes of voracious mosquitoes were the only defect in an otherwise picturesque Eden.[1]

San Joaquin County boasts a sub-tropical climate and winter temperatures seldom drop below thirty degrees Fahrenheit. A blanket of heavy fog protects the area from the colder temperatures and snow found in the neighboring foothills from late November to February. The thermometer may rise above the 100-degree mark in summer, but low humidity makes the intense, dry heat bearable. And, almost predictably, much-welcomed ocean breezes rush through the Delta to cool the land following three or four days of high temperatures.

The seasonal extremes of hot, dry summers and damp, foggy winters, uncomfortable at times, were preferable to the threat of severe winter rains and accompanying melting snowpack of the Sierra. When both heavy rains and runoffs occurred in one season, rivers and minor waterways overran their banks and caused devastating floods.

Damaging floods occurred often; for instance, between 1852 and the 1950s some parts of San Joaquin County were completely inundated every three or four years. The earliest pioneers could recall the crippling spring floods of 1852, 1878, 1881, 1886 and 1982, as well as others of the early twentieth century. But the worst disaster was the great flood of 1861-62 when heavy rains, combined with runoff from the Sierra foothills, flooded an area nearly three hundred miles long and twenty miles wide. During this disaster the water of the Sacramento basin surged past Stockton and raised the town's water level twelve feet above the previous high tide mark. The flooding was so great that no reversal of current occurred on the flood tide in the Carquinez Strait for three weeks. The ocean of water west of Stockton was so deep steamboats traveling between Stockton and San Francisco could navigate directly to Antioch across usually dry fields and orchards. Not until the turn of the century did the construction of dams in neighboring eastern foothill counties mitigate the nearly annual plight of many San Joaquin residents.

THE FIRST PEOPLE

The earliest settlers in the county were Indians from two distinct language groups, the Yokuts and Miwok. Using major waterways to mark their territory, the Miwok-speaking Mekelkos, Lalas, and Machacos settled in the area around the Mokelumne River, and the Calaveras River divided them from the Yokut-oriented Hachicumne, Chilamne, and Passasime groups. It is generally believed that the Yachicumne occupied a large settlement in Stockton.

In the late eighteenth and early nineteenth centuries only Spanish explorers and priests entered the Central Valley. The first was Lt. Gabriel Moraga, who is credited with naming both the San Joaquin River and valley. During the 1820s exploration into the area turned into a lucrative fur trapping enterprise. In 1827 Jedidiah Smith, an American fur trader and explorer, was first to trap in the county, and Alexander R. McLeod of the British Hudson's Bay Company followed two years later. Between 1833 and 1843 French Canadian fur trappers under Michel La Framboise established an annual rendezvous south of Stockton in the area called Los Campos de Los Francais.

In the early 1840s, entrepreneur John Marsh, an American from Missouri, and John Sutter, a German-Swiss and founder of Sacramento, purchased land grants from the Mexican government with the intention of developing permanent settlements. Marsh's parcel was located at the eastern base of Mount Diablo, while Sutter's land lay at the junction of the Sacramento and American rivers. Both wrote home about the natural beauty of California and encouraged overland immigrant parties to stop at their establishments. Many did so; one group, the Bidwell-Bartleson party, left Saint Louis, Missouri, in May 1841 and arrived at Marsh's ranch five months later. In the party was twenty-seven-year-old Carl David Weber, son of a Lutheran minister from Steinwenden, Germany, who immigrated to America five years earlier. When the main body of the Bidwell train moved to San Jose, Weber journeyed north to Sutter's Fort where he found work as overseer of Sutter's store in the winter of 1841. Sutter encouraged Weber to put down roots in northern California and, to serve that end, acted as Weber's sponsor, guaranteeing his protege's good character to the Mexican government.

CHARLES MARIA WEBER AND STOCKTON'S DEVELOPMENT

The story of Weber's life is extremely interesting in itself, quite apart from the crucial role he played vis-à-vis the Chinese in Stockton, and deserves some attention.

After leaving Sutter's Fort in 1842 he dabbled in a number of ventures in

*German immigrant and Stockton founder Charles M.
Weber played a benefactor's role in the development of
the Chinese legacy. At his death in 1881, 200 Chinese
mourners participated in his funeral procession.*

the San Jose area, including a commercial partnership with San Jose
merchant William Gulnac, a naturalized Mexican citizen originally from
New York. Remembering Sutter's suggestion that settlers alter their names
to identify more closely with local customs, Weber chose the name "Charles
Maria."[2]

Both Gulnac and Weber were interested in owning property in California, a prerequisite for which was Mexican citizenship. This Weber applied
for and received in February 1844. In the interim, Gulnac petitioned
Governor Micheltorena for a land grant, and in 1843 received the El Rancho
de Campo de los Franceses, an eleven-league grant aggregating 48,747 acres.
The grant lay east of John Marsh's land and commenced on the east side of
the San Joaquin River. The Weber-Gulnac partnership eventually dissolved over a dispute between the two men, and in the spring of 1845 Gulnac
sold the grant to Weber for "two hundred dollars, half in silver and the other
half in goods."[3]

One condition of Mexican granted land was that it be settled and
developed within a fixed period of time. At the time of Gulnac's possession

Campo de los Franceses had perhaps five settlers and attrition soon reduced even this number to zero. When Weber received ownership, only forty-five days remained in which to "settle" the land. Luckily, enforcement of Weber's deadline was suspended by the Bear Flag Revolt and subsequent acquisition of California by the United States in 1846.

Weber was deeply involved in the Mexican-American War, and at one point General Jose Castro imprisoned Weber (now a Mexican citizen) for refusing to organize a local militia unit to fight American occupation. Weber remained imprisoned until Commodore Robert F. Stockton, military commander of California, rescued him. Impressed by this young naval officer, Weber named his settlement—previously known by the unglamorous epithets of Slough Town and Tuleburg—after the commodore.

With peace at hand, Weber began actively to develop his land grant in the Central Valley. In August 1847 he hired Jasper O'Farrell and Walter Herron to survey a block of lots in his settlement bounded by Weber Avenue, Center, Main and Commerce streets, with the Stockton channel as the focal point. That year a large wagon train stopped at El Campo de los Franceses, and Weber enticed these people to settle, offering large parcels of land at low prices. As further incentives, he gave new residents seed, horses, and agricultural equipment and even threw in a city lot in Stockton.

At the beginning of 1848 Charles Weber's little village was a modest settlement of tule and log houses, but the gold discovery of January 1848 provided the vital spark the town needed to make an indelible imprint on the map. Within a few months schooners and boats of different configurations crowded into Stockton's natural harbor, etching the skyline with ships' masts. A sea of canvas tents and framed dwellings dotted the head of the channel as hundreds of miners poured through town on the way to the upper Stanislaus, Mokelumne and other streams of the rich southern mining region.

The first ships to Stockton were propelled by sail, but passage on such crafts was slow, uncomfortable and monotonous, for it often took ten to fifteen days to travel from San Francisco. However, by mid-1849 woodburning steamers plied the Sacramento and San Joaquin rivers, offering rapid, regular service and reducing travel time to Stockton to a mere seven to twelve hours. Thirteen large seagoing vessels including the bark *San Jose*, the schooner *Invincible*, and brigs *Progresso* and *Susannah* were among hundreds of watercraft which regularly transported freight and passengers.

Freight prices varied from thirty to forty dollars per thousand board feet for lumber, while first-class passenger cabins sold for twenty-five cents and steerage was a bargain at ten cents. Although the water voyage was the easiest way to reach Stockton, it was dreary. The serpentine route of endless curves stretched ahead interminably, and the walls of thick tules which lined the banks effectively prevented any real view of the scenery beyond. Ships entering the San Joaquin River toward dusk, out of necessity, anchored for the night along the river to avoid getting lost in the maze of channels. When this happened, passengers were doubly irritated, for not only was their journey to the gold country postponed by a day, but their night on the river was one of continuous torment from giant mosquitoes who unmercifully punctured helpless victims even through thick covering.

Although the majority of miners arrived in Stockton by boat, those who could not afford passage eagerly came on foot. Some, with a little money to spend, bought a horse or mule to carry their tools and belongings. Others simply strapped their baggage on their backs and followed the route through the Livermore Pass to the Pescadero Crossing of the San Joaquin River, then onward to French Camp and finally to Stockton.

Weber momentarily succumbed to gold fever also, and in 1848 he organized the Stockton Mining Company. While his partners prospected, Weber set up a temporary store at various mining locations. When placer mining in the area surrounding Weber's store played out, he simply moved it, lock, stock and barrel, to a new location. However, in September 1848, Weber withdrew from the mining venture, for he fully realized his fortune would come with the development of his land—the natural debarkation and forwarding port for the goldfield traffic.

In autumn 1848, Weber bought the *Maria*, a thirteen-ton vessel, loaded it with provisions bought in San Francisco and sailed to Stockton to stock his store there. The *Maria* also received the first contract to carry the mail between San Francisco and Stockton on her regular run, in addition to provisions. A year later Weber bought the brig *Emil* and its entire cargo. When the *Emil* arrived in Stockton he dismantled the ship, sold the provisions and used the lumber from the vessel for several of his many building projects.

To encourage even further growth, Weber advertised heavily in the San Francisco *Alta California*, from June 14 to September 27, 1849, stating that Stockton was "... now and always has been the depot for supplying the different mines of the Mokelumne, Calaveras, Stanislaus and Merced."[4]

By the end of 1848, Stockton was home to 1,000 permanent residents, and by the following May the population had doubled. During the winter months miners and other speculators descended from the hills to wait out the cold and snow that otherwise would have stranded them in the rugged mountains, and it was during this season that the town's population swelled to almost twice its usual size. Stockton also became the center for those wanting to exchange their gold dust, desiring entertainment, or requiring other supplies. Prices became exorbitant and building materials scarce; for a time lumber cost a dollar a board foot and laborers received sixteen dollars a day. Houses were erected by driving posts into the ground and simply stretching canvas or muslin between them. Some people salvaged lumber from grounded ships to build frame houses; others used the ships as floating stores. Within a few months, Stockton's inland port was

choked with abandoned vessels as crew members also headed for the goldfields.

Accounts of the town's appearance between 1849 and 1851 are numerous, and many travelers described the activity and bustle of the booming community. When James Carson arrived on May 1, 1848, he wrote:

> ... The tall masts of barges, brigs, schooners were seen highpointed in the blue vault above, while the merry yohos of the sailors could be heard as box, bale and barrels were landed on the banks of the slough.[5]

In 1849, William S. McCollum, a contemporary of Carson, wrote more precisely of the approach to Stockton:

> Our first evidence that we were nearing the new city in the wilderness was a discovery through and above the trees of masts of some thirty brigs and schooners. The harbor is a deep bay or arm [slough] of the river, four miles long and generally about 300 yards wide.[6]

Stockton had not only "...become the mart of trade connected to the southern mines," but was destined to become one of the larger towns in the interior of California.[7]

And the city continued to grow rapidly; numerous frame and canvas commercial buildings were spreading from the head of the Stockton channel across the town. The original O'Farrell and Herron city survey soon proved too limited for the rapidly-expanding population, and in the spring of 1849 Weber commissioned Major Richard P. Hammond to resurvey the town in a grid pattern of Weber's own design, measuring one mile square. Hammond's survey, which became the basis for the future city, also segregated seventeen blocks as public lands and parks. Lots Weber sold in 1847 for three hundred dollars, and even those he had given away freely, escalated to ten times their cost within three or four years, while titles changed as rapidly as the prices.

When McCollum returned to Stockton a few months after his initial arrival, he found a town whose ambience closely resembled San Francisco's, where business boomed, prices soared, crime ran rampant, and whose population had increased to 5,000 individuals. Yet just at the point where the embryonic community could no longer sustain the frenzy, the more stable, responsible pioneers gradually assumed civic leadership and began to give shape to community life.

In the spring of 1850 Stockton began groping toward a local government, and on July 23, 1850, preceding even statehood for California, achieved incorporation. By this time the provisional legislature empowered San Joaquin County to levy a tax to build a county courthouse, elect a Court of

The advertisements in an 1857 newspaper suggest that Stockton's growth was imminent.

Sessions, and set a fee schedule for business licenses. In August 1850 Stockton elected her first set of municipal officials: Samuel Purdy became mayor; C. M. Leak, recorder; George D. Brush, treasurer; C. Edmundson, assessor; and Henry C. Crabb, city attorney. Seven aldermen also were elected: Charles Weber, W. H. Robinson, J. W. Reins, James Warner, B. F. Whittier, Hiram Green and George A. Shurtleff.[8]

Fletcher C. Andrews, a twenty-four-year-old native Virginian, became the first harbormaster. Andrews was responsible for all ships and shipping controls in the channel. He saw that ships anchored in the port were charged ten dollars a day; those abandoned or considered permanently anchored were towed to Mormon Slough, the inlet south of the civic center, and burned. The French brig *Susanne*, converted to a prison ship, was also moored in the Mormon Slough.

CRIME IN EARLY STOCKTON

Such a massive population influx contained all elements of society, so it is hardly surprising that as early as 1850 Stockton residents were victimized by such criminal elements as the "Hounds" and the "Sydney Coves" or "Sydney Ducks." These ruffians' stay in San Francisco and other bay area communities had been shortlived, for residents, tired of their depredations, forced these undesirables from their towns. Many moved upriver to Stockton. With their arrival, the murder, robbery and extortion rates rose significantly, and many businessmen, harassed into paying protection money, considered vigilante action. In June 1851 Stockton's leading citizens organized the Stockton Vigilance Committee, which soon became so powerful that three committee members regularly met all boats to inspect the passengers for undesirables. As an example of their zeal, when eight known Sydney Ducks arrived on a morning steamer from San Francisco, a meeting was quickly called and 170 law-abiding citizens stood ready to run them out of town. Stocktonians developed a suspicious nature toward any rabble rousing element because of their vigilante experience. Consequently, when outside anti-Chinese forces called for the removal of all Chinese in the mid-1880s, the town's reaction naturally was ambivalent.[9]

Stockton's growth rate continued to be phenomenal, and Weber's little town soon took on big-city aspects. For example, Weber built the Corinthian Building, so-called because of the Corinthian columns supporting the balcony, to house offices, bachelor quarters and a theater. There were two newspapers in town, the *Stockton Journal* and the *Stockton Daily Argus*. The Stockton House, built at a cost of $100,000, was the principal hotel. Its weekly rates, including board, ran about twenty-five dollars. Other lodging houses charged fifteen dollars a month, while cottages for the few families in the downtown area rented for thirty dollars a month. Most of the thriving businesses and mercantile houses such as Davis & Smith, Capen & Co., and Underhill Bros., were within the business district bounded by

Center, Hunter, Main and Levee (later Weber Avenue) streets. The city also had three churches for those of Presbyterian, Methodist and Catholic faiths. The embarcadero was the center of activities, and the Chinese settlement lay only a half a block away. To the south near Main and Center streets could be found " . . . a rendezvous of fandango houses, Spanish fondas, and houses of general ill-repute."[10]

Even prior to California's admission to statehood Stockton had elected her first set of municipal officials. Her first city seal incorporated the essence of the environment: a tule elk, grassland, watercraft in the Delta and the Sierra Nevada on the horizon.

THE CHINESE QUARTER IN STOCKTON

As in the early years of booming mining camps, the first contact in Stockton between men of different nations was one of curiosity, tolerance and civility; everyone attended to his own business and single-mindedly pursued his own dreams. Thus, the first appearance of Chinese in the city drew no particular public notice until March 23, 1850, when a local newspaper reported that a boat resembling a cross between a Chinese junk and Portuguese schooner had arrived at the Stockton harbor. The article further stated that the vessel had been financed by four Englishmen. Their $20,000 Macao-built investment carried thirty-five Chinese who had contracted to work for two years in the mines at Wood's Creek, some three and a half miles northwest of Tuolumne City. The Chinese even posted bond guaranteeing their intent to fulfill their contract. Their two-year enterprise failed, however, because the white employers sold the mine and the Chinese force reportedly vanished from the site.[11]

To the Chinese, Stockton was *Sam Fow*, third city, indicating it was the third stop on the way to the mines. There were many reasons Chinese gold-seekers might travel to Stockton: the southern mines were rich, steerage fee was low, the voyage was relatively short, and the Chinese quarters were less than a block from the pier. And, perhaps best of all, prospective miners simply headed due south, over a bridge, and were soon away from the bustling activity of town and on the way to the diggings.

Another article appeared on May 21, 1851, referring to a group of 100 Chinese passing through to the Mother Lode. The editor of the *San Joaquin Republican* indicated the Chinese, as a whole, had apparently made a favorable impression upon the town: "The Chinaboys are amongst our best citizens. They are generally honest and industrious and very seldom figure in a police report. Such men are always welcome. We would like to exchange every Sydney man in California for a Chinaman."[12]

Although the local papers noted Chinese passing through Stockton on their way to the goldfields, the townspeople became aware of their actual numbers in the months when the Chinese, like other miners, drifted back into town. In November 1851, under a small heading entitled "China Invasion," another newspaper article stated: "Chinese are crowding upon us of late in a manner that looks decidedly belligerent. Stockton is fast becoming the Pekin [*sic*] of California."[13]

The Chinese who wintered in Stockton were accustomed to patronizing the services and accommodations offered by other Chinese from their native districts. As with many other communities in California, the early Stockton Chinese residents were mostly Sze Yup, Heungshan and a handful of Sam Yup.

Geographically, Stockton's first Chinese settlement was bounded by Channel Street between El Dorado and Hunter streets, and included Bridge Place, a small alley paralleling Channel Street. Their quarter was conveniently located near the head of the Stockton channel, with easy access for incoming and departing vessels, and just around the corner from Hunter Plaza, heart of the business district. The first documented Chinese businesses were two restaurants on the waterfront catering to both the white and Chinese trade.[14]

The San Joaquin County census of 1850, its first, listed fifty-three Chinese men, but no Chinese women. Additional information showed the men were mostly traders, stewards and cooks. There was one hotel keeper and one barber. The latter two men may have had exclusively Chinese clientele.[15]

The first Chinese quarter consisted of a former French hotel, several one-story shacks that had been places of business, and a house on the corner of Hunter and Channel Street which served as a hotel. In the 1850s the Chinese from the Heungshan District erected a wood-frame joss temple. Their house of worship, at 120 North Hunter, was midway between Channel and Weber and faced Bridge Place.[16]

These Channel Street residents tried to stay out of the limelight, but as their numbers increased and most were confined to the small downtown area, the Chinese community quickly became the focus of white criticism. Again, much like the complaints heard in the mining towns, their objections were to the overcrowding, the filthy living conditions, the nightly gambling and noisy merrymaking of Stockton's Chinese. Yet, white citizens also gambled and were equally loud in their saloons, chief of which was the El Dorado Saloon on Weber and Center streets only two blocks away. away.

By 1854 Stockton was maturing and becoming more stable. A state asylum for the insane was built in 1853 on land once owned by Captain Weber, and also in 1854 the newly-completed courthouse on Weber Avenue next to Hunter Plaza adequately housed both city and county officials. In March of the same year the closing of several fandango houses south of Main Street gave people less than tolerant of different cultures cause to focus on the Channel Street Chinese settlement. One such citizen was Abraham C. Bradford, a young Virginian who held a number of public offices simultaneously during the town's developmental years.[17]

Bradford thought it would be in the best interest of the city if he used his influence as editor of the *San Joaquin Republican* to call attention to the hovels on Channel Street. In an editorial dated September 18, 1854, he subtly suggested that the Chinese quarters be washed in the same way San Francisco and Sacramento had cleansed their Chinese sections—by the simple act of dousing. No sooner had this suggestion been printed than, late on the night of September 19, 1854, rowdy individuals tried to wash the Chinese settlement by using a fire engine pump and drawing the water from the channel. The following day, Stockton's other newspaper, the *Daily Argus*, accused the *Republican* of instigating the irresponsible act. In mock anger, Editor Bradford responded:

> A word from the *Republican* moved a city to such deeds of outrage. We never before knew our own influence ... Those who attributed to us such motives are wrong, we never counselled [*sic*] violence, we only spoke to warn the authorities to remove the evil. The Chinese in the location where they were attacked are a nuisance, they are an eye-sore, they are almost in the heart of town upon a thoroughfare adjoining our public schools where girls and boys pass and repass every day ... Not withstanding all this, we never counselled violence ...

Although surprised by the dousing, the Chinese thereafter kept a wary eye out for any further attempts at harassment and took to posting guard to protect their property.[18]

It should be noted that this Channel Street Chinese quarter was not an isolated settlement; the neighborhood was actually a commingling of different nationalities, cultures and political beliefs. It was located near the head of the channel where foot traffic associated with the embarcadero, nearby businesses and hotels never ceased. On Bridge Place, between El Dorado and Hunter streets, in the very heart of the Chinese quarter, stood the Hotel de Mexico, built in 1849 by Colonel Frank Cheatham, a southern gambler who later became a general in the Confederate Army. It was purportedly a center for Confederate sympathizers in pre-war years. Some believed the hotel also housed the underground workings of corrupt city politicians as well. The Hotel de Mexico was later replaced by the Philadelphia House.

One block to the west, at the corner of Channel and Center Street, stood the New York Hotel started in 1850. D. W. Lockwood, its owner, was at one time questioned extensively by the Stockton Vigilance Committee on the suspicion that he harbored Sydney Ducks. Within twenty years this hostelry was converted into a planing mill, then a steam laundry, and by the 1870s, Chinese moved into the building, much to the displeasure of the city Board of Health. It eventually burned to the ground.

Another hotel, the Stockton House, considered one of the prominent hotels in town, was also close to the Channel Street Chinese quarter. Located on El Dorado between Channel Street and Bridge Place, the Stockton House looked directly at the Stockton harbor. Entertainment offered at this establishment ranged from the sublime to the sensational: in 1851 it held the first ball attended by Stockton's high society; two years later, visitors gathered in its lobby to view what was purported to be the pickled head of notorious bandit Joaquin Murietta and the hand of the outlaw Three-fingered Jack preserved in a container of brandy.

The neighborhood also served as heritage centers for two other immigrant groups. On Miner and Hunter streets, one block to the north, people of the Jewish faith built their first synagogue in Stockton. Completed in 1852 at a cost of $35,000, the building held up to two hundred worshippers.[19]

In 1856 German immigrants built their Turnverein Hall on Hunter Street, adjoining the Chinese joss temple on the south side. Here in Stockton, two major immigrant groups, the Chinese and Germans, coming from opposite sides of the world not only transplanted their social institutions but maintained these facilities in an amazingly close proximity. The Turnverein Society's objectives were mutual aid and fellowship, important factors in sustaining cultural continuity and similar in many ways to the functions of the Chinese district and family associations. The hall served as a gathering place where men practiced gymnastics and women organized

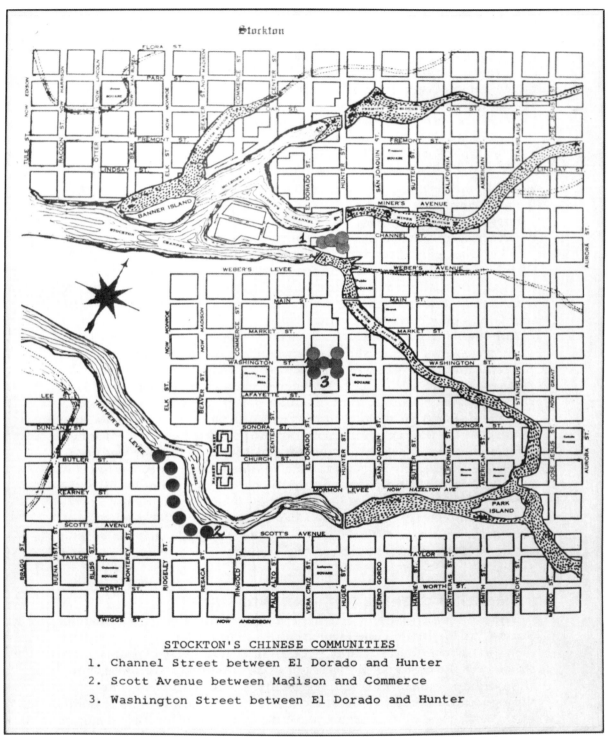

STOCKTON'S CHINESE COMMUNITIES

1. Channel Street between El Dorado and Hunter
2. Scott Avenue between Madison and Commerce
3. Washington Street between El Dorado and Hunter

These are the locations of the Chinese communities in the city of Stockton prior to the 1890s. Also visible are the many sloughs and inlets that cut through the city.

dances and amateur plays. In later years, during the height of anti-Chinese
campaigns, the hall was often rented by those denouncing the Chinese
presence in Stockton. In retrospect, it was ironic to have heated arguments
against the Chinese rage just on the other side of the Chinese temple walls.
Yet even in such times the Chinese felt fairly confident their temple was well
protected, for should some arsonist attempt to destroy their house of
worship, the Turnverein Hall also would be damaged. They were well
aware that the Germans, a major political and social force in Stockton,
would be understandably unhappy should their hall suffer the same fate as
the joss temple.

Fires remained a constant hazard for the canvas tents and wood-framed
buildings of early Stockton, and major fires occurred in 1849, 1851 and 1855.
The 1862 fire, which began with the explosion of a lamp, swept through the
Channel Street Chinese section and quickly destroyed many of the one-story
shacks, although the joss temple escaped the flames. A few white property
owners questioned why the fire trucks took so long to arrive when the fire
station was only two blocks away.

Although the Channel Street settlement was not totally demolished,
many were forced to seek shelters elsewhere in town. Until the time of the
fire, two groups of Chinese existed in the Channel Street quarters: the
Heungshan and Sze Yup. They shared the same section of town, but did not
share the same buildings. Both maintained separate cooperative systems
and the disparity in dialects further widened the gulf between the two
groups. There was a certain amount of distrust based on tales of wrongs
done each other in earlier mining days, although this rivalry was not so
much life-threatening as it was a game of one-upsmanship. Because any
relocation from Channel Street would have to be done by one group or the
other, it was the Sze Yup Cantonese who chose to move farther south and the
Heungshan who remained in the Channel Street area. This outcome reflected a certain pragmatic acceptance by the Sze Yup, a tacit recognition
that most Heungshan activities centered around their joss temple on Hunter
Street.

STOCKTON'S CHINESE HOUSE OF WORSHIP

The joss temple did play an important role in the lives of the Channel
Street Chinese. In 1881 the Heungshan launched a campaign to replace
their first wood-framed temple with a more substantial two-story brick
structure. Funding for the project came from local support, various Heungshan organizations, other Chinese temples, and wealthy businessmen
throughout California. Without architectural plans, contractors or building expertise, the Chinese set about constructing a sturdy brick and mortar
building which has endured for more than a hundred years.

Although the building specifications differed slightly from those used by
white contractors in those years, the Chinese, guided almost completely by

JOSS HOUSE WHERE CHINESE HELD FORTH ON
EAST SIDE OF HUNTER STREET BETWEEN
WEBER AVENUE AND CHANNEL STREET.
1895

WOLLNER'S
GROCERY

S. SINAI

A Ralph Yardley sketch of the two-story, brick Heungshan Joss Temple on Hunter Street built in 1882.

common sense alone, completed construction in 1882. Building costs amounted to $7,000, and another $5,000 was spent for interior furnishings of the sanctuary and altar, housed on the second floor. The temple had an overhanging balcony which faced Hunter Street and extended along the width of the building. Sleeping quarters were located both upstairs and on the ground floor, where an herb shop and a doctor's office occupied the front of the building while a garment factory was located at the rear. Behind the building in an open courtyard, a few leantos were used as both storage and isolation quarters for the sick and dying. The courtyard served several other functions as well. In the evenings Chinese residents sat there chatting, eating a meal or engaging in card games and other entertainment. In this open area they grew green onions, parsley, scallions and other vegetables in the small garden and hung fish and bok choy on lines to dry for future use.[20]

Money for the elaborate second-floor sanctuary was well spent. The main deity, Kwan Kung, the red-faced god of war and the most powerful god in the Chinese pantheon, sat on an elevated platform at the east end of the main room, facing west toward China. The arms of the imposing, eight-foot-high statue spanned four feet. Alongside sat other lesser deities, surrounded by ornately-carved pillars and wooden stands, peacock feathers, wax candles and urns of sandalwood incense; bright highlights of red, gold and silver gilding glistened, reflecting light on walls, ceilings, and even in mid-air. The names of more than one hundred contributors were deeply etched in a thick marble slab measuring three feet by four feet, which hung on a side wall.

In the spring of 1882 the nation's attention was focused on potential passage of the Chinese Exclusion Law. Stocktonians' awareness of the issue did not overshadow their enthusiasm for the activities of the local Chinese. The consecration of the Heungshan temple drew extensive front-page coverage in both Stockton newspapers. A three-day celebration began on March 27, 1882, and visitors arrived from Sacramento, San Francisco, and even so far away as San Jose. A Chinese band led a procession of Chinese dignitaries north from Washington Street up to the temple, where an aged priest addressed the large crowd from the balcony. Celebrants were then guided to the back courtyard to witness a fireworks display which officially marked the opening of the new building. When the noise subsided, three chief priests and nine attendants preceded the crowd upstairs to the sanctuary, where they performed their rites among prostrate worshippers in elaborate surroundings. On the lower floor, visitors partook of a large banquet which included a whole roast pig and many other delicacies. According to the newspapers, this celebration was not limited to the Chinese. Many whites visited the temple during this opening, and attendants stood ready to impart information to the curious. Conspicuously-placed placards stating "Hands Off" and "Positively No Admittance" helped guide those visitors in the protocol of the temple.[21]

The Heungshan population of Channel Street began to dwindle in the early twentieth century and by 1920 only two laundries and the temple could still be found in the area.

OTHER CHINESE SETTLEMENTS IN THE STOCKTON AREA

It is possible to isolate two factors which gave impetus to the development of two other Chinese settlements within Stockton. First, the Channel Street quarter was seriously crowded, for the Chinese population of Stockton increased by more than 300 percent between 1850 and 1860. Secondly, the great fire of 1862 mentioned previously destroyed most of the possible housing for Chinese within the Channel Street area.

During the mid-1860s, many newly-arrived Sze Yup Chinese from Guangdong's Toishan District joined their relocated Sze Yup brethren in settling four blocks farther south on Washington Street, between El Dorado and Hunter. The Washington Street area was only two blocks south of the business district and the Hunter Plaza, and still only a short walking distance from the head of the Stockton Channel. As one historian noted: "There was good money in renting buildings to Chinese tenants and parties with capital erected one-story buildings for them on Washington Street . . . they were soon filled." Some of the property owners of Washington Street had no qualms renting to the Chinese; many of them were also new immigrants from northern Italy who purchase property in that area for income investment. To these people the Chinese made ideal tenants. They were fairly desperate for housing, did not ask much of the landlords, particularly regarding maintenance, and they paid the relatively high rents on time.[22]

Other property owners on Washington Street intended to keep their neighborhood a select residential area and strongly objected to Chinese neighbors and particularly their commercial enterprises. One of the strongest objections was that they gave little attention to sanitation and lacked neighborhood pride. Their dwellings became dirty hovels shortly after they occupied a place. The whites' arguments should be viewed from both cultures' differing perceptions of quality of life and priorities. The white felt his residence was permanent, whereas the Chinese looked upon his austere, minimal quarters as but a temporary situation to be abandoned upon his return to China. Additionally, some landlords lacked pride in the upkeep of their property and felt it unnecessary to plow any profits back into their investments. To them there seemed little need for property improvement when the income from rents was virtually guaranteed.

Charles G. Hubner was one white neighbor who felt his property value was declining due to his Chinese neighbors. Hubner, a second-year member of the Stockton City Council, described as an "honest, plain-spoken Hollander [and] capitalist," lived on Lafayette Street, one block south of Washington; his back yard adjoined the back property line of the Chinese quarters on that thoroughfare. On numerous occasions he voiced his displeasure about the Chinese in his neighborhood and argued for their eviction. Unlike many who simply complained, Hubner acted on his feelings by actively searching out other areas in town where the Chinese might be relocated.[23]

In the summer of 1867, while looking for a likely relocation spot, Hubner noted several Chinese who were engaged in fishing the Delta living near the south bank of Mormon Slough. The Chinese had apparently moved here surreptitiously and squatted illegally, for the land actually belonged to Captain Charles Weber.

THE MORMON SLOUGH SITE AND VILLAGE

The Mormon Slough area was ideal for those who used the Delta water-ways to eke out a living. Beginning near Bellota at the Calaveras River, the slough, located at the confluence where foothill tributaries drained, cut across the entire southern portion of the city and entered the Stockton channel. The land south of the slough was low lying and, as with most Delta areas, was subject to annual flooding.

The area around the slough, however, was blessed with a plentiful supply of fish, clams and blackberries. The pulsing tide of the Pacific flushed the westward riverflow back into the slough, and the ebb tide created soft, thick mudbars—an ideal environment for freshwater clams. Two varieties of clams were found in the slough's silty soil, and harvesting these delectable mollusks merely required plunging one's arms to a depth of a foot or more and scooping. This activity often resulted in at least a dozen clams for each attempt. In the 1860s and 1870s residents of the area recalled that local Indians came seasonally to harvest the clams and cooked them over open fires in old cans or discarded buckets in the area just west of Commerce Street. The gradual filling of the slough and the diversion of the water into the main channel has eliminated this natural condition for further clam cultivation.[24]

Councilman Hubner knew city founder Weber had previously donated land to churches and public parks and asked him to set aside some of the land south of the Mormon Slough for the exclusive use of the Chinese. Weber, however, deferred his answer. He had been plagued in the early 1850s by squatters who built on some of his most valuable town properties. Although he was ultimately successful in evicting them, the lawsuits and attorney's fees were costly. With regard to the Chinese squatters along Mormon Slough, however, Weber felt they were not troublesome and allowed them to continue their occupation. The fact that he employed a large number of Chinese in his various enterprises helps explain his tolerant attitude. Weber did not feel it necessary, however, actually to set aside the entire area simply because of Hubner's request. An astute businessman, Weber suggested an alternative. He told Hubner that Block 9, bounded by

PICKING WILD BLACKBERRIES ALONG THE SAN JOAQUIN RIVER

BLACK BELLIES

THE CHINESE PEDDLER

The Chinese captured the local market for the blackberries that grew naturally along the San Joaquin River banks, harvesting them as soon as they ripened.

Commerce and Madison streets and adjacent to the Chinese fishing village, was vacant and that he was willing to sell the property to Hubner if he (Hubner) wished to construct some tenement houses and rent them to Chinese.

Reacting positively to the suggestion, Hubner approached Police Chief Jerome Myers and Officer Bernard McMahan, a patrolman assigned to the Washington Street area, with a partnership proposition. The officers were somewhat less than enthusiastic, for they did not believe the Chinese could be induced to move from Washington Street. But they agreed to help solicit subscriptions for the project from people living in the neighborhood who had voiced displeasure with their Chinese neighbors. The rest of the community assumed the project merely a speculative venture to enrich Hubner, Myers and McMahan, and wanted no part of it. Myers and McMahan ultimately reneged on the deal and the housing project became Hubner's sole investment. It remained devoid of community support, and prior to completion of the several structures, the buildings were even set afire. Although beset by these sorts of difficulties, Hubner eventually completed his building project and proceeded to the next step of his relocation plan: populating the buildings. To this end, he placed the following advertisement in the *Stockton Daily Independent* on December 13, 1867:

> To citizens of Stockton, Celestials, Caucasians and of African descent
> . . . to lease for a long term two spacious houses centrally located.
> Chinese tenants preferred; offer protection guaranteed and premises
> duly watched by police and constabulary at a small consideration.
> Application for lease to be made to honorable Board of Common
> Council of the city of Stockton.
>   Signed, The Proprietor.

Although a number of Chinese moved into his units, there was little noticeable reduction in the Washington Street Chinese population. In 1868 Hubner abandoned the project when he moved from the neighborhood upon his election to the state assembly and soon thereafter sold his Lafayette Street property.

The Chinese living in the Mormon Slough area capitalized on all the opportunities offered by the waterway and surrounding land. Fish were plentiful; sunfish, chubs, suckers and Sacramento perch, of no interest to white fishermen, provided a ready industry to Chinese who used the slough's banks to dry their catch. Later these fish were salted and packed for the ready market in the Mother Lode or prepared for San Francisco's export market to China. The heart of the Chinese fishing industry in San Joaquin County could undoubtedly be pinpointed by the smell of fish drying in the hot Stockton sun. Chinese fishing skiffs also sailed down the slough through the Stockton channel to the deeper waters of the San Joaquin River. There they fished with set nets, a more effective method of industrial fishing. Many Chinese occupied themselves in this manner: the 1870 census showed 106 Chinese fishermen in Stockton, and ten years later the census revealed only a slight reduction, to 91.[25]

The Delta waterways also carried many other Chinese working as farm laborers and those on reclamation projects to various Delta islands where their labor was much in demand.

Immense patches of blackberry vines grew along the banks of the San Joaquin River, and at one time berry-picking was a favorite summer activity for many of Stockton's citizens. When blackberry season rolled around, during the 1850s and early 1860s, city-wide contests were held in which enthusiastic boating parties departed in search of the thick rambling bushes on the river's edge. It was not long before the Chinese turned even this activity into an industry. One early Stocktonian recalled that in early summer " . . . half of the Chinese population in that area would be upriver picking blackberries while the other half was cantering about town selling from house to house . . . The price was generally ten cents a pound, but when the market was glutted the price dropped to twenty-five cents for three pounds." Intensely industrious, the Chinese picked the blackberry vines clean long before the whites found time to organize the annual sporting event.

The stretch of land at the northwesterly curve of the slough was undeveloped, and the Chinese seized the opportunity to turn a portion of that area into a vegetable garden. In summer, when the dry ground needed water, they devised a pump to carry water from the slough across the banks to the plot, which lay at a lower elevation. Two Chinese provided the peddle power to operate an ingenious mechanism constructed of a series of wooden paddles affixed to a strip of canvas which conveyed the water through a rectangular wooden trough. This ancient form of irrigation was a common sight in China, but in California the contraption and its operators fascinated many western passersby.

One further Chinese industry in the Mormon Slough area should be noted. Around 1860, one Chinese laundry began using the slough water for washing clothes. Here laundrymen would set slab tables up just above the water's edge, then immerse themselves to the waist for the actual cleaning process. The various items of apparel were first placed in a basket and suspended in water to soak and thereby loosen the soil. Then they were spread on the tables and scrubbed with soap, dipped in water again, and finally wrung into a club and pounded against the table. The process of soaking, soaping, thrashing and rinsing was repeated until the laundryman was satisfied with his results. This rough treatment often damaged the porcelain buttons used to fasten shirts and dresses and could cause the loss of unhappy customers. To save their business, many Chinese laundrymen advertised that they would removed these buttons before the washing process and resew them when the clothing was clean.[26]

For over three decades the Mormon Slough Chinese settlement thrived

OLD "CHINA TOWN" ON THE SOUTH BANK
OF THE MORMON SLOUGH NEAR THE CORNER
OF WHAT IS NOW WEST CHURCH AND SOUTH
MONROE STREETS. ABOUT 1900.

A Ralph Yardley sketch of the Chinese fishing village at Mormon Slough. Cartoonist Yardley drew upon his memories of several decades and, as in this case, his dates were not always accurate. This Chinese settlement ended in the early 1890s, not at the turn of the century.

and evolved into a virtual industrial complex, particularly the fishing industry. Removed from the actual scene of political activities associated with anti-Chinese attitudes found in downtown Stockton, this settlement provided a relatively safe and often picturesque haven for many Chinese families. Their houses were shacks built of refuse lumber, discarded boxes and scraps of tin. There were no ordered streets or lanes. Some of the paths in the settlement took sharp and unexpected bends leading to dead ends, back yards or directly to the tules.

The Mormon Slough settlement had several distinct advantages over the quarters in Stockton, the principal one being plentiful open space. Here one could raise animals and vegetables both for sale and for the family table. And even by current standards the Chinese here ate well. Many foods we today consider gourmet items were readily available to Chinese palates south of town. For instance, many varieties of ducks fed on ponds in the tules which lay practically on the doorsteps of Chinese residents. In 1893, a newspaper reporter wandered into the Chinese settlement and noticed each house maintained a number of elevated pigeon cotes, which suggests the Chinese ate delicate-tasting squab or young pigeon regularly. Chickens and goats roamed the yards, there were plentiful fish in the river and clams in the mudbars, vegetables grew in profusion in truck gardens, and an edible tuber resembling the potato could be found growing at the water's edge. Without question the Chinese fare was varied and substantial.[27]

Only rising channel waters and annual floods presented danger to the inhabitants of the low-lying Mormon Slough region, which was almost perfect in every other respect. In winter, each household tied a boat to the outside door to insure safe evacuation at a moment's notice. A common question among those who lived north of the slough was, "Is the slough roaring today?" This referred to the fact that in certain seasons the slough waters ran dangerously high and swiftly. With the exception of the wagon bridge on Center Street and the footbridge at El Dorado, which washed away periodically, the Mormon Slough region was totally isolated from the main part of town, and area residents were unable to hear town alarms heralding danger from flood.

The Chinese and the few white families families farther east along the slough kept small rowboats available for evacuation during such disasters. And Mormon Slough was indeed prone to such flooding, which generally arrived at night. The interior of the makeshift Chinese dwellings would fill to some three feet deep, and with no facility to pump out the water, residents waited patiently until the water abated. Familiar dirty watermarks on the walls of these shacks were mute evidence to the wrath of nature.

Predictably, not all the Chinese moved from the Washington Street neighborhood for a variety of reasons. At the time Hubner's buildings were completed, the Chinese population had again increased, from 139 in 1860 to 1,619 in 1870, far more than both the Mormon Slough settlement or

Hubner's housing together could readily accommodate. Additionally, the remoteness of the Mormon Slough settlement made living there impractical for many Chinese involved in restaurant, laundry, domestic and other service work in Stockton's downtown area. Even though the slough area was a good place to raise a family, it was an area which could neither cater to the wants of a bachelor society nor accommodate the transient lifestyle of the many laborers who lived in Stockton only seasonally.

When white industries such as the Stockton Woolen Mills and the California Paper Company moved into the Mormon Slough neighborhood, many Chinese worked in these companies until the mid-1880s when political pressures forced owners to release their Chinese help.

OTHER POCKETS OF CHINESE

Towards the end of the nineteenth century the dynamics and cohesiveness of the fishing village declined as political events and further assimilation of western lifestyle changed these people's attitudes. Moreover, in 1893, the Weber estate sold the Mormon Slough land to the Buel Land and Lumber Company. Much to their distress, the sale forced Chinese families to relocate and fishermen to abandon their industry.

One might assume a total eradication of the Chinese occurred; however, an examination of the 1900 census shows small groups of Chinese settled even farther south of the slough. In the area bounded by Harrison, Edison and Jefferson streets, the 1900 enumerator found a small cluster of Chinese, and he made the notation: "China Camp." In later years historian Glenn A. Kennedy noted the existence of a settlement east and across the Santa Fe roundhouse near Edison and Anderson, in the same area as that of the 1900 "China Camp." A tall bamboo thicket fence surrounded and helped isolate this compound, which also was guarded by many barking dogs.[28]

There were other isolated Chinese settlements in the south part of town. One reportedly was a gambling establishment barely on the outskirts of town, just beyond the jurisdiction of the local law. Two other legitimate groups were a hog-raising operation and a slaughterhouse. The hog-raising group lived in the triangle formed by French Camp Turnpike, Clay and Madison streets. The Chinese slaughterhouse was on the old Garwood Ferry Road (later Eighth Street), across McDougal Canal and just off the French Camp Turnpike. The stench accompanying both operations necessitated these businesses be located some distance from the sensitive noses of city-dwellers.

The Washington Street Chinatown, originally founded to serve the needs of early sojourners, served their descendants as well into the 1960s. The notion of relocating the main Chinese settlement from the center of town to the Mormon Slough area arose on a number of occasions in the 1870s and 1880s. Some disgruntled whites, including several newspaper editors, supported this alternative as an out-of-sight, out-of-mind solution to their prejudices against Chinese. But despite all their numerous tribulations, the core of Stockton's Chinese citadel remained on Washington Street for over a hundred years. Only the construction of a crosstown freeway and local redevelopment caused the physical relocation of a people whose lives had played an integral role in Stockton's history.

CHAPTER TWO ENDNOTES

1. Clotilde Grunsky Taylor, *Stockton Boyhood, Being the Reminiscence of Carl Ewald Grunsky Which Covers the Years from 1855 to 1877* (Berkeley, 1959), pp. 2-3, 69-70.

2. To his contituents, Weber also was known as the "Captain," for he held a Mexican commission and had participated in a skirmish against Governor Micheltorena's troops marauding near San Jose in 1844.

3. George P. Hammond, *The Weber Era in Stockton History* (Berkeley, 1982), p. 46.

4. Hammond, *Weber Era*, p. 95.

5. James Carson, *Recollections of the California Mines* (Stockton, 1852), p. 14.

6. William S. McCollum, *California As I Saw It: Pencillings by the Way of its Gold and Gold Diggers! and Incidents of Travel by Land Water* (Los Gatos, 1960), p. 128.

7. E. Gould Buffum, *Six Months in the Gold Mines: From a Journal of Three Years' Residence in Upper and Lower California 1847-8-9* (Philadelphia, 1850), p. 155.

8. F. T. Gilbert, *History of San Joaquin County, California With Illustrations Descriptive of its Scenery* (Oakland, 1879), p. 26.

9. George A. Tinkham, *History of San Joaquin County, California With Biographical Sketches* (Los Angeles, 1923), p. 105.

10. Hammond, *Weber Era*, p. 111.

11. *Stockton Times*, March 24, 1850.

12. *San Joaquin Republican*, May 21, 1851.

13. *San Joaquin Republican*, November 15, 1851.

14. *San Joaquin Republican*, May 17, 1851.

15. *1850 Census of San Joaquin County* (Stockton, 1959).

16. Tinkham, *History of San Joaquin County*, p. 161.

17. Among the offices Abraham Bradford held were county clerk, city clerk, and assistant chief of Weber Engine No. 1 Volunteer Firemen; in later years he became

district judge of the Southern San Joaquin Valley District. (Tinkham, *History of San Joaquin County*, p. 157.)

18. It was only partially true that school children trespassed near the Chinese settlement. Stockton's first public education system housed boys and girls in separate locations. Boys were taught in classrooms in the McNish Building on Hunter and Channel Street in the vicinity of the Chinese quarters. Girls attended four blocks away at the Presbyterian Church's Academy Building at Market and San Joaquin streets. By 1856 the school board relocated the boys to a two-story building at Sutter and Market. The decision to change classroom location came not because of the possible negative Chinese influence but because the Grand Jury found the pupils were too distracted by the hogs, cows and chickens fed in pens next to the school building by owners of the Magnolia House, one of Stockton's respectable hotels, on El Dorado and Channel streets. (Tinkham, *History of San Joaquin County*, pp. 161 and 228; *San Joaquin Republican*, September 18 and 22, 1854; *Stockton Daily Argus*, September 20, 1854.)

19. Tinkham, *History of San Joaquin County*, pp. 157-58.

20. Taylor, *Carl Grunsky*, p. 84.

21. *Stockton Daily Evening Herald*, March 27, 1882; *Stockton Daily Independent*, March 27, 1882.

22. Tinkham, *History of San Joaquin County*, p. 161.

23. Tinkham, *History of San Joaquin County*, p. 162.

24. Taylor, *Carl Grunsky*, pp. 59 and 78.

25. Taylor, *Carl Grunsky*, pp. 58-59.

26. Taylor, *Carl Grunsky*, pp. 82-84.

27. *Stockton Daily Independent*, September 26, 1893.

28. *Stockton Daily Independent*, July 27, 1893. Glenn A. Kennedy, *It Happened in Stockton 1900-1925* (Stockton, 1967), p. 41.

White Men's Vision and Chinese Muscle

3

The Chinese presence in Stockton, however strong, cannot compare to the Chinese deeds in San Joaquin County. The muscles of a highly adaptable Chinese army reclaimed the mosquito-infested swamplands of the Delta and transformed the flat valley floor into grazing and workable farm land. With equal energy they laid vital transportation links in the county, connecting the region with the major consumer and shipping areas of Los Angeles, Sacramento and San Francisco. Without Chinese involvement, development of the county's resources would have been greatly delayed. As Stockton's development has been previewed, so too must the county townships be described and placed in context to demonstrate the magnitude of the Chinese contributions.

As mentioned before, the San Joaquin River and valley were named by Spanish explorer Gabriel Moraga; two decades later much of this county was divided into land grants by various Mexican governors of California and given to Mexican citizens to further Mexican settlement plans. Four land grants existed within the boundaries of San Joaquin County: El Pescadero, located in the southwestern part of the county and given to Pio Pico in 1844; El Campo de los Franceses, Charles Weber's grant, purchased from William Gulnac; Los Moquelemos, in northeastern San Joaquin County, granted to Andres Pico in 1846; and a small portion of the Thompson grant, primarily located in Calaveras County, straddled the southeastern border of the county.

The division of the state into townships, ranges and sections was one of the initial chores of state government following statehood in 1850. In Northern California, surveyors used Mount Diablo, the highest peak of the Diablo range, to locate the east-west baseline of the central part of the state, and they platted San Joaquin County into the standard measurements of six-mile squares for townships and one-mile squares for sections. However, the Court of Sessions (board of supervisors) ignored the surveys done by the government as they laid the pattern for nine townships. For a period of eight years, from 1853 to 1861, county leaders drew and redrew boundaries as each township was created in an attempt to achieve a delicate political-geographic balance. They noted the natural river boundaries, counted the

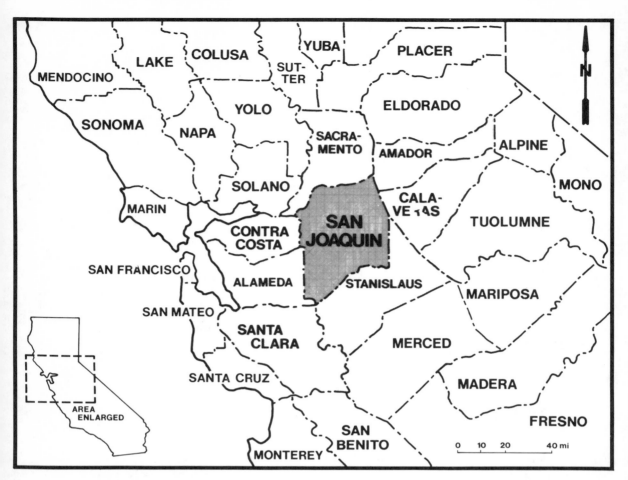

California counties contiguous to and surrounding San Joaquin County.

number of inhabitants in outlying hamlets, carefully skirted all federal lands, and tried to appease the demands of their constituents. Often, too, during those years, local leaders disputed with neighboring counties over county boundaries, as the state legislators, forced by great lobbying efforts, shifted and reshifted county lines. In 1879 the state legislators adopted the present San Joaquin County boundaries.[1]

A brief description of the townships would be helpful to our story. The first three townships, created in 1853, were Castoria, Elkhorn and ONeal. Two others, Elliott and Liberty, lying in the northeast and north central section of the county, attracted many Chinese workers in the early years but rejected them during the height of the 1880s anti-Chinese campaigns. Two townships, Dent and Douglas, played lesser roles in our Chinese story because these areas were sparsely populated and had correspondingly fewer Chinese inhabitants. The northern portion of Tulare township and Union township, in the northwest section of the county, were mainly swamp and overflow marshlands when their boundary lines were drawn. But both had changed by the 1880s; reclamation increased their land mass, agriculture

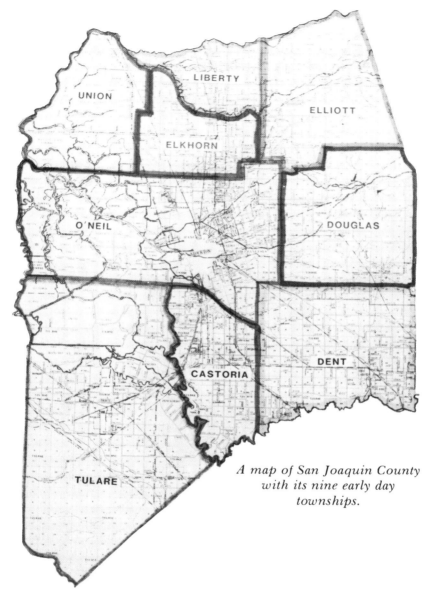

*A map of San Joaquin County
with its nine early day
townships.*

became the primary industry, and, particularly in Union, the Chinese were the predominant residents.

Census reports in the late nineteenth century showed the Chinese lived and worked in all nine townships. They became more familiar with some than others as they traversed the land looking first for gold and then for work. For instance, they knew crossing the Castoria area was expensive. The township was between Stockton and the Southern Mother Lode mines, and because two major rivers (the San Joaquin and Stanislaus) formed two sides of the township, ferry service was a necessary and lucrative business, particularly during the gold rush. The first ferry to cross the San Joaquin River, Doak and Bonsell's Ferry, was established in 1849 near the present-day Mossdale Wye. Ferry traffic across this river is an excellent gauge for estimating the number of miners headed for the southern mines: the crossing charge was three dollars for man and horse, eight dollars for a wagon—and, in 1850 alone, the daily ferry receipts ranged from $500 to $1,000.[2]

The Chinese learned that in various townships the people's attitude and temperament differed, perhaps dictated by the terrain. One such area is ONeal township, which encompassed all the Campo de los Franceses grant. Stockton's city limits laid in its eastern half and the Delta islands in the western portion.

ONeal's history, apart from Stockton, is that of small communities which grew around the numerous landings along the San Joaqin River and its tributaries. These towns, sponsored by Delta landowners, served share-cropping tenants and generally consisted of warehouses, a saloon or two, a post office and a few stores. Residents relied on river traders to bring in mail, merchandise, and news of the outside world. In essence, these delta people lived in a small-town, river-oriented atmosphere, more concerned about tides, crops and changes in seasons than in the pressing issues on the state and national scene. In contrast, the Stockton metropolis to the east flourished in political and social activities as expected of a hub city and county seat.[3]

As a rule, early towns in San Joaquin County survived because they played a key role in the transportation network. Stockton and Lockeford were inland ports; French Camp and Linden began as mere stage stops. Others such as Tracy, Lathrop and Lodi were fortunate to have railway officials plant a depot in their communities. Although the Chinese played a major role in the early years of these towns, history shows that few remained to enjoy the fruit of their labor.

There are a number of county communities that are important to our story, however. In Elkhorn township, the town of Lodi, one-half mile south of the Mokelumne River, was surveyed in 1869, and it began to grow rapidly after the Central Pacific built a depot there on the Stockton-Sacramento line. The town received a continuous trickle of people relocating from the nearby communities of Woodbridge, Galt, Liberty and Acampo, attracted to employment in such industries as the Lodi Mill and Warehouse Company, and the Lodi Land and Lumber Company.

Unlike the varied nationalities who made up Stockton's citizenry, Lodi ethnicity has been dominated by Germans from North Dakota. While the town was progressive in agriculture and business, its civic spirit in a large part reflected the provincial, conservative traits associated with German heritage. The community remained homogenous well into the twentieth century, penetrated then only by the Japanese who may have had some sort of understanding with the dominant society. The Chinese experience in Lodi was particularly unpleasant in the mid-1880s during the anti-Chinese campaigns.

In contrast to Lodi, the town of Holt, in ONeal township, named for

An unknown artist in 1884 captured Chinese reclamation workers closing a foot levee break on the San Joaquin River four miles south of Stockton. The Mount Diablo range is silhouetted in the background.

Benjamin Holt, developer of the Holt "Caterpillar" tractor, deserves special recognition. Instead of calling the town by its name, the Chinese, in their Cantonese dialect, called it the "thirty-five cent rail station," meaning that to find it, one went to the Santa Fe Railway Station in Stockton, plopped down the correct change and was automatically handed a ticket for Holt by the agent.

Fairly secluded in the backwaters of the Delta, Holt became a lively entertainment center where gambling houses and bordellos abounded. As testimony to the red light activities, Dean DeCarli, former mayor of Stockton and raised in Holt, wrote that the "five o'clock train from Stockton would bring prostitutes out to the men at Holt." The town's popularity was widespread, and even immigration officials in San Francisco knew of its existence. The somewhat unsavory reputation of the Thirty-five Cent town included incidents of shootings and killings among Chinese tong members at the height of the tong wars between 1910 and 1925.[4]

And Terminous, on Potato Slough, just off the Mokelumne River, at one time was the second largest Chinese settlement in the county, after Stockton.

WHITE MEN'S VISIONS AND CHINESE MUSCLE

The sheer size of San Joaquin County demanded manpower to develop its resources. Whites brought capital and business expertise to the land, but many hands were needed to work its acres, and numbers were a commodity only the Chinese could supply. Come they did: from the mines of the north and south as well as from China itself, hundreds of Chinese headed for San Joaquin County.

Historians and journalists alike have written about the Chinese work habits, often remarking on their similarity to the Puritan ethic with its emphasis on industry, reliability, thrift and intelligence. For example, Mary Coolidge, in her book *Chinese Immigration*, stated:

> The Chinese' ability to cook, sew, and wash which white laborers seldom do to satisfaction is an advantage to the employer and to the Chinese in the homeless life he leads. His native thrift and moderation in pleasure and vice enables him to endure with less danger of degeneration from the effects of intermittent employment.[5]

Early forty-niner James Carson, for whom Carson Hill in Calaveras County is named, wrote a series detailing the geography and potential of the San Joaquin Valley for the *San Joaquin Republican* in 1852. In his story of March 3, Carson envisioned cotton and sugar cane cultivation in the valley, or its transformation into "one vast vineyard and orchard." To accomplish these goals, the visionary Carson suggested:

> . . . We have amongst us several thousand of the inhabitants of China; a great many of them are intelligent men, from whom much reliable information can be obtained in regard to the introduction of the tea plant into California, and the value of our tule land for the cultivation of rice . . . These emigrants are, as a class, the best people we have amongst us—they are sober, quiet, industrious, and inoffensive . . . Those of them [white] who understand the civil institutions of the United States adore them . . . thousands of these men [Chinese] are ready to become citizens of the U.S., settle down and turn our waste lands into beautiful fields as soon as proper inducements and protection is afforded them; and no better class of men could be chosen to develop the agricultural resources . . . than the Chinese who are amongst us.[6]

No greater testimonial could be given to the Chinese character and their potential for the Central Valley's future. And Carson was not alone in his opinion. Other white civic and political leaders realized the importance of the Chinese work force. These men, often of conservative German or Yankee backgrounds and new immigrants in the county, were the first to come into contact with the Chinese here. They hired them as domestics in their homes and as laborers to develop their farm properties. Because of these relationships and ties, they were able to evaluate the abilities and shortcomings of the Chinese and thus eventually played a crucial role in the county's anti-Chinese tensions of the 1880s.

The Workers' Accommodations

The Chinese had no trouble finding work, but living accommodations was quite another story. They were frugal and their needs simple, but they learned that work and living accommodations had to go hand in hand; otherwise, they not only faced language difficulties but their living expenses would exceed their actual earnings. Therefore, groups of laborers consolidated into large work units and, regardless of project or location, functioned under similar communal living arrangements.

Most preferred working alongside relatives or fellow villagers, enjoying the brotherhood and solidarity afforded by the contract labor system. Gathering together in groups of up to twenty individuals, Chinese laborers worked on railroad or reclamation projects or as seasonal farm workers. Generally the men in these work clusters hailed from the same district or village, spoke the same dialect, and were clan-related, if not also by blood. They found work through their family association meeting halls or from stores frequented both by laborers and labor contractors. Through this word-of-mouth employment system, the men were guaranteed work without worry about bed and board expense and thus could afford to send money home to China.

The labor contractor served as interpreter and business manager for the work unit, and although he, himself, did not live with the men, he saw to their needs. He hired a cook to satisfy their diet and arranged for social entertainment, which included forms of gambling and visits by prostitutes to the work camps. His wages came from several sources: his negotiated fees from the employer, the room and board charges he collected from the laborers, commissions paid to him by "entertainers," and rebates he might receive from Chinese merchants who sold food and supplies to the group. The contract labor system worked well for many decades, even as the nationality of the work force gradually changed from Chinese to Japanese and then to Filipinos.

As a rule, the Chinese opted for simple oral agreements rather than lengthy, legal contracts they could not understand and distrusted. Once committed, large groups of laborers tenaciously devoted their total energies to complete the job at hand. Sometimes the projects were shortlived, perhaps only one season or even less. Wherever needed, a large labor force of Chinese was there to lend its strength, and the importance of the work accomplished is amply demonstrated in numerous locations throughout the county.

In collective farming and truck garden cooperatives they also lived together and had a cook attend to their needs. These cooperative units generally numbered from seven to fifteen men per work unit, according to census records. A cook and/or boss served as the interpreter; frequently that individual's name headed the group's listing in the census. Authority, however, was reserved for the senior partner, who often was the oldest member of the group.

White farmers hired anywhere from one to five Chinese as ranch hands or farm laborers. The more self-assured Chinese and those with a smattering of English shared chores and living quarters with other Chinese and white workers. According to census data, there was a greater natal diversity among these men than among those working under the contract labor or cooperative systems. Even though they hailed from the Guangdong Province, their differences in regions, customs and dialects kept dialogue between these men at a minimum, and while the farmer knew there were dissimilarities, his only interest was in their productivity. The Chinese working in such commingled units received a rapid and intensive training in the dominant society's culture by dealing with the white farmer and other hired hands. In the broader perspective the Chinese not only learned western farming methods and operation of agricultural equipment, but sometimes advised their employers on Chinese horticultural techniques.

TRANSPORTATION
Railroads: Main and Feeder Lines

In the 1860s, as in many parts of California, local leaders realized the need for improved transportation to connect San Joaquin County with the rest of the nation. The inland waterways, particularly the San Joaquin and Mokelumne rivers, played important roles in initially populating and supplying the county, but the transfer of goods by overland routes was always expensive and costs continued to escalate. Additionally, overland freighting was at the mercy of the elements, and seasonal flooding insured that the more isolated communities were virtually cut off from civilization as teamsters were unable to use the muddy, impassable roads. Railroads would provide the perfect answer.

Simultaneously with the Chinese involvement in the Central Pacific transcontinental connection, other Chinese in California were busy building local and feeder lines connecting many of California's early cities.

The Stockton-Copperopolis Railroad Company, formed in 1865, was the first railroad project initiated in the county. Company founders intended to capitalize on the Civil War's need for copper and proposed to haul this mineral from Copperopolis in Calaveras County to Stockton and then ship the material east via railroad. This plan required a direct line from Copperopolis, a small town some forty miles due east, to Stockton. Local politics, material shortages and other problems delayed completion. By the time the first locomotive pulled into a Stockton waterfront shed in December 1870, conditions had changed: the war was over and the demand for copper thus sharply reduced, and the needed track was still fifteen miles short of its goal. The California Pacific Company bought the line.

The Stockton-Visalia Railroad Company was formed in 1869 to compete

INTERESTING TO
HUNGRY TRAVELERS!

A FIRST CLASS

REFRESHMENT SALOON

AND

RESTAURANT

HAS BEEN FITTED UP AT THE

Railroad Depot in Stockton,

*Where Meals or Lunch of every variety are
served promptly, and ample time is
afforded to enjoy the food.*

Those who appreciate

Good Eating and Drinking !

*Can always get their money's worth at
this Saloon.*

H. A. BLOSS, - - *Proprietor.*

**All the Finest Brands of WINES, LIQUORS and
CIGARS on hand.**

Passengers provided with Lunch for their trip without vexatious delay.

*This advertisement draws attention to the amenities at the railroad
depot in Stockton in the 1870s and 1880s.*

with the San Joaquin Valley Railroad line, a subsidiary of the Central Pacific. Its chief goal, to build a line from Visalia to Stockton, fell prey to many of the same problems that had plagued the Stockton-Copperopolis Railroad Company, and it eventually defaulted. And, like its predecessor, it was acquired by the California Pacific Company. Yet, the California Pacific's ascendancy also was shortlived, and in 1888, Leland Stanford's Southern Pacific Railroad (formerly the Central Pacific) acquired all its holdings.

Most local accounts of county railroad history focus on the shortlived regional companies, local politics, and the struggle against Central Pacific's domination; few acknowledge the role of the Chinese and their contribution to the county railroad development. From the late 1860s on, there were enough county railroad projects to keep large numbers of Chinese employed.

In 1869, while Chinese railroad workers witnessed the driving of the golden spike at Promontory, Utah, symbolically linking the two sides of the nation, other Chinese in San Joaquin County worked for the Central Pacific's subsidiary, the Western Pacific Railroad. The most difficult problem in constructing the entire transcontinental railroad was the bridging of the Carquinez Straits between Sacramento and Oakland. Therefore, company officials decided to run the line from Sacramento through Stockton to Oakland. The Sacramento-Stockton leg of the transcontinental route was completed in August 1869, and the line from Stockton to Oakland in September. The final railroad bridge across the San Joaquin River at Mossdale was completed on November 10, 1869, exactly six months after the premature ceremony at Promontory. Thus, it was in San Joaquin County that the final link, the "ocean to ocean" connection, occurred.

The exact number of Chinese engaged in railroad construction in this county is difficult to determine, for many projects criss-crossed the county at various times, and there is a lack of data on day-labor work. Yet, the 1870 census offers a viable clue, as it listed 138 Chinese railroad workers. The Chinese role in railroad development in this county was of paramount importance since no other nationalities contributed any appreciable number of railway construction workers. In 1870 alone, there were 101 Chinese working on local lines in ONeal township, and the thirty-seven in Liberty township were busily building the Sacramento-Stockton connection for the Central Pacific.

By 1880 the county had ninety miles of tracks laid: fifty-seven belonging to the Central Pacific and San Joaquin Valley lines and thirty-three miles of the Stockton to Oakdale line. At the Central Pacific's terminal point in Lathrop, where the company's line radiated to the small towns of Wickland, Banta and Ellis in neighboring Tulare township, twelve Chinese kept the tracks and complex around the main junction in prime condition. In 1879 construction of a southwest leg of the Central Pacific got underway with sixty-one Chinese laborers helping to connect Tracy to Grayson in Stanislaus County.

Supervised by one contractor, the Chinese workers were divided into two crews, twenty-seven in one and thirty-four in the other. A cook and the overall contractor were part of the larger unit, according to the census report. They cut timber, shaped the ties, constructed embankments, hauled gravel for ballast and, eventually, laid the ties and rails.[7]

It was faster and cheaper to build railroad lines in the valley than in the mountains. The county's terrain and its adjacent waterways made supplying work crews and projects much easier, ensuring that more work could be done with fewer laborers. While it has never been established precisely how many workers were used to build the Central Pacific's eastbound lines across the Sierra Nevada, a frequently quoted number is ten thousand or more. Speculative as this number might be, it is in vivid contrast to the fewer than two hundred Chinese who were constantly employed in railroad construction in San Joaquin County—despite the vast amount of tracks.

Highways and Byways

Aside from railroad construction, local Chinese also built roads and gravelled turnpikes. In 1878, eleven Chinese worked at the gravel pit in Peters, a major borrow site for turnpike material twelve miles east of Stockton. And like others arrested for legal transgressions and housed in the county jail, Chinese served on chain gangs building public roads and maintaining city streets.[8]

The 1879 state constitution and subsequent legislation prohibited Chinese from working on municipal projects, and Stockton, itself, enacted similar laws relating to the Chinese. Yet despite these legal prohibitions, Chinese on regular work crews—not on chain gangs—continued to pave many of the city streets when the contractors were not able to obtain other day laborers. Still other evidences of Chinese working on the county's road system in the nineteenth century can be found in overseers' reports to the board of supervisors.[9]

RECLAMATION

In 1852, the state surveyor-general identified swamplands in California of which approximately half a million acres were in the Sacramento-San Joaquin Delta. By 1871 practically all Delta swamp and overflow lands were in private hands, and the responsibility for improvements in the Delta islands and surrounding areas had been transferred to the local county board of supervisors, under whose jurisdiction reclamation districts were formed.

The Delta tule land or islands are flat regions whose surface elevation was at or a little below ordinary high tide. The island soil was so light that it floated. The soil was composed of silt and decayed vegetable matter (peat)

CHINESE SCOWS DREDGED SAND FROM THE BED
OF THE SAN JOAQUIN RIVER WEST OF STOCKTON
SAND WAS USED IN BUILDING CONSTRUCTION

UNLOADING
AT LINDSAY POINT

RALPH O YARDLEY

For the Chinese, the San Joaquin River provided a bounty other than fishing and river transport; those who were involved in construction projects found the sand from the river an ideal building material.

and had a natural and vigorous growth of reeds or tules and cattails. In the fall the cattails and tules died out and added another layer to the organic matter. On the outer perimeter of the islands the natural levees had belts of willow, oak, sycamore, cottonwood, walnut or alder trees, and at the river's edge, blackberry and wildrose thickets clung to the banks. This growth surrounding individual islands served as natural erosion protection but were no match for unusually heavy snowmelts and spring runoffs. Man added two other problems: the surging waves caused by steamers and other river traffic hammered against the banks and caused soil erosion, and, when placer mining gave way to hydraulic mining techniques, the rivers and streams from east to west were choked with mining debris and sand. This raised the channel elevation and constricted water flow, thereby causing the water to spill over onto the adjacent land. Geographic historian John Thompson estimated that between 1860 and 1914 more than 800 million cubic yards of mining debris passed into the delta. The federal government's concern was only for the channel navigability of the rivers, leaving the state legislators to take the brunt of the complaints from farmers and residents of the lowland towns who were frequently flooded out by rising river waters. Finally, by March 1878, the office of state engineer was created to correct the level of the main channels, control debris and organize drainage districts.

Prior to this time, purchase of Delta lands and initiation of reclamation projects was done by developers, foreign investors and individual land-owners. Between 1860 and 1880, one of the largest of these entrepreneurial groups was the Tideland Reclamation Company, owned by George C. Roberts. Scotsman Morton C. Fisher, who entered a joint venture with the Glasgow-California Land and Reclamation Company, controlled another. The reclamation of Roberts Island in ONeal township was a major project of these two companies. Seldom did a local landowner have sufficient capital to finance an entire reclamation project; however, Assemblyman Ross C. Sargent and his brothers sank enormous sums into reclaiming Staten Island in Union township.

In 1872, the Tideland Reclamation Company initiated the first major reclamation project in San Joaquin County. It constructed levees completely around Union Island; however, these levees lasted only four years before forty-five miles were destroyed by winter flooding. Levee breaks and washouts became perennial problems. Ross Sargent experienced much the same difficulty with his Staten Island project, which also commenced in 1872. He girdled his island with a five-foot-high embankment, only to see it washed away the following spring. It was rare that a levee remained intact for more than a year or two, and additions to already-existing levees were constantly being made to compensate for rising water levels caused by ever-increasing amounts of mining debris clogging the channels.

In theory, the height, strength and width of levees were estimated to withstand rainfall of the same level as that of the preceding season. The reality was that major floods often weakened the levees so that after a season or two even those thought able to withstand the strongest, highest surge of water merely crumbled away under the latest aquatic onslaught. John Thompson estimates that there was no "three-year period that passed between 1852 and 1911 during which some improved land was not inundated." Even today, despite foothill dams to check flood waters, periodic levee breaks result in the flooding of some Delta islands.[10]

By the mid-1870s reclamation had become a large-scale production which required large amounts of capital, for massive infusions of money made possible the use of mechanical earth-moving equipment such as clamshell diggers, dredgers and ditchers. By 1875, both the *Samson* and *Goliath*, gigantic floating steamshovels, were used to level parts of the islands where men and animals could not reach. In December 1878 a timber bulkhead was built around Staten Island to strengthen previously-constructed levees. The 9,194-acre island eventually cost $257,000 to reclaim, or around twenty-eight dollars an acre. The original purchase price was only one dollar per acre. Of this island's land size, levees covered 510 acres while 8,700 acres became productive farm lands.

In the 1870s local citizens focused their attention on major reclamation projects in four locations: Staten and Bouldin islands in Union township and Roberts and Union islands in ONeal and Tulare townships. The documentation and written histories of these massive earth-moving tasks have focused primarily on white pioneers' efforts: their personalities, costs involved and the actual technical phases of reclaiming. The role of Chinese labor is briefly mentioned as performing the "shovel and wheelbarrow" work and often described in inanimate terms, no different from the horses and mules used to pull the scrapers. Some writers were able to infuse life and animation in describing large mechanically-powered machinery, but dismissed the spark of human spirit and the drip of sweat mirrored in the leathery faces of the laborers.

Modern writers of Asian American history have at times repeated and overemphasized one bit of evidence regarding Chinese involvement in Delta levee projects, when the figure of 1,000 Chinese is used in connection with the Union Island project. However, this figure may have been taken out of context and misapplied both with regard to number and location, for the reclamation projects on Roberts and Union islands occurred simultaneously.

The original citation from which the figure was taken appeared in the September 11, 1876 issue of the *Stockton Independent* in a story describing the importation of 100 Chinese to Roberts Island by W. R. Fisher, agent for the Glasgow-California Company. These laborers were needed to complete the last six-mile gap left unfinished in 1875. J. F. Whitney, principal owner of the island, stated he hoped the upper section would be enclosed within six weeks' time and suitable for planting the following year, and that the lower

The San Joaquin Delta contains over one thousand miles of waterway, and Chinese truck gardeners, whose farming acreages were often accessible only by water, developed their own navigational routes and shortcuts.

section would be completed in two years. During this interview, Mr. Fisher was quoted as saying he had brought in 100 Chinese the prior week and would import as many as were needed " . . . even a thousand if necessary to get the job done."[11]

Another incident may also provide further evidence of exaggerated numbers of Chinese laborers in reclamation projects. In 1878, at the height of the Union Island project, its superintendent realized he had an excess of Chinese laborers, for 200 Chinese had descended on his land hoping for employment, when rumors circulated in Stockton's Chinatown that work was available. At the time, however, only forty men were actually needed, and the Chinese foreman was ordered to discharge the remainder.

Angered because they were not hired, the disappointed Chinese threw the foreman into the river and drove the white superintendent, Gen. T. H. Williams, and his staff off the island. Fleeing to Stockton, General Williams sought the help of Sheriff Thomas Cunningham. The following day, Cunningham and a dozen deputies, armed with Henry rifles and warrants against twenty-five Chinese ringleaders, swept into the area and made some arrests. Unfortunately, ten of those arrested were not the men listed on the warrants, necessitating a second expedition, led by Constable Ben Kohlberg, to locate the rest of the ringleaders. Kohlberg and his deputies surrounded 142 Chinese still loitering around the project site and forced the reluctant foreman to identify the correct troublemakers. Following this incident, the Chinese dispersed and no other major employment problems occurred on the project.[12]

The previous incidents should in no way negate the notion that many workers were needed at different times on the Union, Roberts and Staten islands projects—often on short notice. At such times, word of mouth was an excellent method to hire a large work force. Another was to contact local Chinese merchants who served as the contractor-interpreter and use their stores as hiring halls. Besides the merchants, a Chinese Intelligence Office (an employment office) situated at the embarcadero served as an intermediary between the developer and the Chinese merchants.

Once hired and under the direction of a Chinese foreman, work gangs were assigned to various portions of the levee. Using packed soil, they filled and levelled sections of the levees and reseeded the embankments in some areas to strengthen the compacted mounds of dirt. Sometimes the Chinese worked in waist-deep water and muck or battled the ravaging tides that hammered against the levees. The employers sometimes provided the hand tools and wheelbarrows to haul the dirt. Other times it was the Chinese headman who furnished the equipment. Chinese laborers were paid either a flat rate of a dollar a day or for the amount of earth moved, between nine and twenty-five cents per cubic yard. Generally the Chinese received approximately thirty dollars a month, from which they paid their room and board. White laborers employed as mule team drivers and carpenters received between thirty and thirty-five dollars per month and their room and board. The turnover rate for skilled white workers was high, for many of them came simply to acquire a stake and once they accumulated a few dollars they departed. Ironically, although the whites drove the teams which pulled the scrapers, it was the Chinese who developed tule shoes for the animals which prevented them from becoming bogged down in the mire.

Because the projects were relatively shortlived and those applying for work so plentiful, day labor pay for the Chinese never substantially increased over the twenty years of ongoing projects. A sampling of pay receipts for Chinese laborers on Roberts Island in October 1884 indicated day laborers received one dollar for one day of work, two dollars and twenty-five cents for two days of work, five dollars for four days' work, and ten dollars for eight days of work. Each Chinese laborer signed a receipt for his pay next to the dollar amount. Some wrote their full name in Chinese, others just their surnames, while the illiterates signed with the universal "X."[13]

Full-scale reclamation in the Delta lands had not begun when the 1870 census was taken, and the 1880 census listed forty-one Chinese as reclamation workers in Union township, none in ONeal or Tulare townships. This 1880 figure may seem minimal, but both the Roberts and Union Island projects in ONeal township had been completed by 1878, as had the Staten Island project. Eighty percent of the acreage on Bouldin Island was also in a productive state by 1880. Additionally, with the increased use of heavy mechanization and improved dredging equipment, by the 1880s the need for Chinese muscle, so imperative at the beginning of these projects, no longer existed. Yet depiste the undenied cost effectivness of modern equipment, it should be remembered that the Chinese provided the manpower when the Delta swamplands were first reclaimed.

As an additional note, in Union township particularly, Chinese laborers must be given a lion's share of the credit for doing the physical work to develop this township. In Staten and Bouldin islands reclamation yielded a combined 13,000 acres of rich farmlands.

AGRICULTURE

Until the Delta was reclaimed, most of the farmlands in San Joaquin County were used for grazing and wheat farming. In 1869, 72 percent of the 250,000 acres of fenced land were under cultivation: 117,000 in wheat and the rest in barley, hay and orchards. In 1883, after completion of the major reclamation projects, San Joaquin County raised the largest wheat crop in the world: 3,414,920 bushels. In that year the county also produced 1.2 million bushels of barley, 20,000 bushels of oats and thousands of tons of fruit and vegetables. By the 1920s the county's concentration on wheat had changed to production of barley, potatoes, onions and grapes, and the county ranked fourth of all counties in the nation in agricultural production, and first in California in barley, corn and wheat.

Historians have estimated that in 1870 the Chinese supplied one-tenth of the state's agricultural work force and by 1880, one-third. Carey McWilliams has suggested that not only were Chinese ideal farm laborers and stoop production workers, but that "the transition from wheat to fruit acreage in many areas would have been delayed for a quarter of a century had it not been for their [the Chinese] presence. They were a vital factor in making the transition possible, and by and large, it is correct to state that in many particulars the Chinese actually taught their overlords how to plant, cultivate and harvest orchards and garden crops."[14]

The Chinese moved in to work the Delta islands as soon as the land was ready for cultivation, and as early as 1869 they farmed Roberts Island on the San Joaquin River side, even before reclamation efforts were in full swing. By 1875 they cleared the land just west of the Stockton harbor near Rough and Ready Island and cultivated plots where they raised onions, beans and blackberries as far south as the Pescadero-Grant line in Tulare township. Other groups of Chinese began farming Staten Island in 1881, then moved on to Bouldin Island in 1884. Census material from 1870 to 1900 shows that farm labor work, including truck gardening, became the largest occupation for Chinese. In 1870 the census indicated 197 Chinese employed as farm workers or farmers, 704 in 1880 and 956 by 1900.

Partnerships in these endeavors varied. In some units all participants had the same surname. Other units were a combination of several family names, all members of the same clan organization. Only rarely did these farming cooperatives include people from different districts, and frequently they had the same surname or belonged to the same family association. In addition to lineage bonding, these farming units shared a commonality of techniques and expertise in growing specific crops.

Consistently Staten and Bouldin islands in Union township attracted the largest number of farm workers, but there were also smaller groups in ONeal, Tulare and Castoria townships. While some were employed by white farmers and ranchers, other Chinese worked in groups as tenant farmers either on leased plots or as contracted sharecroppers. American-born settlers tended to be owner-operators engaged in animal husbandry, wheat and fruit growing, while the Chinese, Italian and Portuguese tenant farmers were closely identified with garden or truck farming.

Various combinations of sharecropping and tenant lease agreements existed. Sometimes a white entrepreneur would lease the land and have Chinese work it for him; on other occasions, the Chinese themselves leased in a company's name or as a family enterprise. These lease agreements were generally oral. During the 1870s, owners usually received 30 to 50 percent of the crop if they provided seed, feed, teams and implements, while a tenant's responsibility included paying the laborers and laborers' boarding expenses. In addition to the crop agreement, there was an additional maintenance agreement for those subleasing in the Delta. Owners were responsible

Chinese truck gardeners began growing fresh produce in the Delta as soon as reclamation projects were completed. They became noted for their onion, potato, asparagus and, in later years, celery production, c.1940.

for maintenance of the levees, digging and maintenance of the main irrigation canal and excavation of seepage ditches near the levees. Tenants were required to maintain the seepage and drainage ditches and put in irrigation laterals.

Chinese had leased plots ranging in size from six to fifty acres by 1875. Farther east toward Stockton, Chinese truck gardens were so plentiful their harvest glutted the San Francisco market, and the price of potatoes dropped to fifteen cents a sack before the market could recover. The local Chinese proved to be formidable competitors against the Chinese farmers of the Bay Area and the Santa Clara Valley.

By the 1880s, the division in territory, crop specialization and farming expertise between the Heungshan and Toishan Chinese was fairly obvious. Each, accustomed to the traditional farming methods acquired over many centuries, transplanted its knowledge and practices into the Delta lands of California. Additionally, the imaginary county line through the Delta separating Sacramento County from San Joaquin County also served to delineate the Heungshan from the Toishan through distinctly different farming methods and types of crops. From Courtland, Sacramento County

north, the Chinese from the Heungshan District were mainly orchardists—
even today Courtland prides itself on its Chinese-owned pear industry.
South of Rio Vista the Toishan Chinese, accustomed to stoop labor, produced row crops such as potatoes, onions and asparagus, and, by the turn of
the century, celery.[15]

The twentieth century added another dimension to Chinese involvement
in county agriculture. As a natural progression, canneries, devoted to
canning asparagus, tomatoes and fruit, sprouted along the rivers. Soon this
became a multi-million-dollar industry, and as they had been foremost in
the fight to tame the Delta waters, the Chinese became the major cannery
work force.

Whatever the Chinese grew—fruit, garden vegetables, potatoes or onions
—they used the river route to deliver their produce to the head of the
Stockton channel for transshipment to San Francisco or Los Angeles.
Stockton's inland port with accessible railway connections had become as
much an integral part of Chinese livelihood as they had become the
mainstay of the county's economy.

Other Day Labor Work

A look into the first fifty years of census data for San Joaquin County
heralds other areas where, as day laborers, Chinese brickmakers and woodcutters also played important roles in the county development.

When fires swept through sections of towns in the early 1850s destroying
flimsy canvas tents and wooden shanties, local ordinances required rebuild-
ing be done with fireproof material; the most common was brick. The
county's heavily forested riverbottoms, rich clay soil and available Chinese
manpower provided abundant raw materials for successful manufacture of
quality brick. Stockton was soon informally dubbed "brick city" as tall
commercial buildings and numerous houses silhouetted the skyline in
yellow, red and vitrified black colors of heat-hardened moist clay. One of
Stockton's earliest brickyards, owned by John Doak, owner of the Doak &
Bonsell Ferry, opened its doors in 1850. Other brickyards soon developed on
the outer fringes of the city and in smaller towns such as Lockeford, Woodbridge and Tracy, where the Chinese became deeply involved in the manufacture of this building material.

A labor-intensive activity, brick making required considerable expertise.
While one group of laborers mixed the proper water-to-clay combination
and placed the mixture into wooden forms or molds, other groups prepared
the kiln and fired the brick. Kilns operated twenty-four hours a day during
the firing process, which could take from a week to a month, depending on
the number of bricks formed around the kiln and type of wood fuel used.
Oak wood kept the fire hotter and burned longer than sycamore or elm. The
brick industry also depended heavily on woodcutters to keep them supplied
with fuel for their kilns—as did other local industries.

Woodcutting became a lifelong occupation for many Chinese, as wood served as the basic energy resource in homes, industries and transportation from the 1850s to the 1890s. In railway transportation wood was used to build trestles, lay the ties and fuel the locomotives.

Today, as we use electricity created from hydroelectric power dams, gas pumped from the depths of the earth, and experiment with wind, solar and nuclear power, we envision woodburning fireplaces and stoves almost as a luxury. And as we now consciously attempt to conserve our energy resources, we must envy early pioneers who simply assumed the natural resources of San Joaquin County were infinite.

We tend to forget that until recently wood served as the basic energy source for everyday needs such as cooking and heating, as well as for some modes of transportation such as river steamers and the railroads. In addition to fueling the brick kilns, wood also was used in railroad construction as ties and trestles and to operate the locomotives. In industry, wood was used to run power plants and mills. The abundance of oak and sycamore trees in the overflow land along the waterways of the county supported numerous lumber companies in the area. One such was the Lodi Land and Lumber

Company, situated on the Mokelumne River a mile north of Lodi, which in 1879 had a sawing capacity of 40,000 board feet per day.

Woodcutters were thus an important category, and the Chinese had been working in this occupation since the earliest period of the county's growth. In the 1880 census alone eighty-five Chinese were employed as woodcutters. Almost singlehandedly in this endeavor, they changed the face of the county from the heavily-timbered region of early days to one more closely resembling a savannah. Chinese woodcutters cleared the riverbottoms and tenaciously grubbed stumps from the flat farmlands. This tedious job, so necessary to homes, farms and industries provided industrious Chinese with a lifetime career.

CHINESE ENTERPRISES

While we may assume the Chinese worked for both white and Chinese employers in numerous labor intensive occupations, in fishing and mining the Chinese formed independent work forces which did not rely upon the white economy. Both the 1870 and 1880 census showed ONeal township, particularly the Mormon Slough area of Stockton, contained large groups of Chinese fishermen (108 and 93 respectively), and their fish-curing and packing industry in Stockton rivaled those of their countrymen in Monterey, San Francisco and Marin County.

On the whole, Chinese fishermen were hindered by numerous fishing restrictions and inconsistent laws instigated by competing fishermen of other nationalities. For example, during the short four-year period between 1860 and 1864, Chinese fishermen were forced to pay four dollars a month for a fishing license, in a levy quite similar to the Foreign Miner's Tax. Then, in the 1870s, legislation was passed prohibiting the use of set nets, and later gill nets were added to that restriction. In addition, for a time the Chinese were permitted to keep only large fish, yet a subsequent law required them to throw the large fish back and keep only the small ones. In 1879 a California law prohibited aliens ineligible for naturalization, which of course included the Chinese, from obtaining a fishing license. The inconsistencies and absurdities of these laws serve to support the theory that they were simply measures aimed at forcing the Chinese from the fishing industry. Fighting injustices such as these took time, interested and able attorneys, and large sums of money—all of which the local fishermen lacked. Therefore, they depended on their city cousins to challenge these laws, and, in time, the courts ruled they were unconstitutional.

The prejudice endured by Chinese fishermen was much more overt in the Bay Area and other coastal towns where their chief competition came from Italians, Greeks and Portuguese. In comparison, the San Joaquin County Chinese fishermen's lot was less troublesome, and the county's waterways provided a variety and abundance of fish which almost guaranteed daily success. Whites who fished the Delta enjoyed it only as a sport but did not

EVERY HUNTER
HAD A DUCK
BOAT

CHINESE
SAND SCOWS

THE TIN
HOUSE

JAMES HIGGINS

FISH HARRY   SUGAR FOOT
                    JOE

C.N.
THOMPSON

THE OLD STEPS
AT THE HEAD OF
THE CHANNEL

ME LONG

POTATOES

ONIONS

THE CHINESE WERE
THE PRINCIPAL FARMERS
OF THE DELTA AND HERE
THEY MARKETED THEIR
PRODUCTS

Chinese Delta farmers used the waterway and Stockton's inland port to ship their produce to market via rail and steamer connections ideally located at the head of the Stockton channel.

make it their livelihood. Only on occasions when the local constable wished to show his authority did the local Chinese pay fines for using set nets.

The abrupt disappearance of Chinese fishermen in the 1900 census resulted from the sale of the Weber land to a local lumber company in 1893. Once forced to leave the south bank of Mormon Slough where they had squatted for almost forty years, these fishermen saw it was time to re-evaluate their occupation. By then also the fishing industry no longer proved as lucrative: their Mother Lode market dried up as other Chinese abandoned the mining towns, fishing restrictions had become more diffi-cult to circumvent, and the locals no longer had access to large open areas to dry and process the fish. Social changes also placed other demands on these men.[16]

In comparison, however, the Chinese worked as fishermen longer than they did as miners. The majority of the Chinese abandoned the mines when placer mining techniques gave way to hydraulic mining. By employing a small number of men to operate pressurized monitors, high financiers took goldmining out of the hands of thousands of individuals and placed the industry in the realm of major corporations. The last of the Chinese miners sought out little known areas, worked over tailings and abandoned sites in the most remote regions of the back county. Even with patience their reward became less and less as the years rolled by. In 1870, according to the census, only thirty Chinese considered themselves miners. By 1880 the last three Chinese miners in the county were living in Elliott township on the fringe of the foothills, hoping to dredge out the last bit of gold. And the 1900 census showed no Chinese employed as a miner or fisherman.

URBAN OCCUPATIONS AND ACTIVITIES

In urban living, the laundrymen and cooks' residential patterns were similar to those of the rural laborers. The 1880 census provides the best analysis of laundry work units and indicates laundry crews varied in size from four in small towns such as Woodbridge, Lodi and Lockeford, to as many as fifteen in one laundry in Stockton. Maintaining the same familial ties as the collective farming units, laundry workers often were also blood relatives, had the same surnames or were fellow villagers. In addition, these laundrymen frequently shared the same crowded living quarters behind the laundry.

The "closeness" associated with Chinese living was also due to the scarcity of lodging facilities available to them. Ranch hands might be given a bed in the bunkhouse, but, in town, white landlords preferred to rent their rather limited number of rooms to whites. Even when landlords were not racially selective, the Chinese would not seek lodging, thinking the room and board rates to be more than he could afford. Moreover, he foresaw communication and dietary problems if he lived in western boarding houses. Consequently, the Chinese preferred to seek shelter among their own no matter how crowded the living arrangements.

Census studies of Chinese in small rural communities suggest that Chinese sharing living quarters and working together in one occupation were generally related; those residing together but working at different jobs were often not related and there was some sort of boarding arrangement. Laundrymen and those in truck gardening frequently made room for fellow countrymen. For example, in Lodi in 1880 Sam Gun ran a washhouse in partnership with his brother and uncle. Four other Chinese lived with Gun: a laundry worker, a gardener and two woodcutters. A woodcutter listed among laundry workers might suggest the individual was not only a boarder, but may well have been hired to provide fuel for the laundry. However, in Gun's case, two woodcutters are one too many and suggest that one or both were employed elsewhere. For Sam Gun and those like him, the rent charged boarders was minimal, satisfaction was gained from helping a countryman and, of course, the extra money was always welcome.

Chinese involvement in the cooking industry was certainly not a new phenomena in this county. Cooking was the single largest urban occupation; the number of cooks exceeded the numbers of laundrymen and merchants. The first two Chinese businesses in Stockton were two restaurants on the embarcadero and, for more than a century, many generations of Stocktonians have been acquainted with, if not weaned on, meals prepared by the Chinese.

Types of cooks could be categorized accordingly: commercial cooks who worked in restaurants, saloons and hotels; domestic cooks in homes, who often doubled as servant or caretaker; and lastly, the ranch cooks who fed work crews. On the farm or feeding a large white work force, the ranch cook easily learned to serve up meat, potatoes, biscuits and gravy. In the better restaurants and private homes, these eastern culinary artists often duplicated and improved upon original recipes. Cooks, above all other types of workers, had the greatest opportunity to interact with whites and familiarize themselves with western culture, and many became quite adept in English.

On the whole, Chinese cooks were undemanding and willing to work long, late hours. Their frugal nature prevented food waste, and they were willing to accept low wages. Some who doubled as domestic servants in large households earned the respect of the entire family and were often treated as surrogate members. Many worked in the homes of the wealthier English, German, midwestern and southern families in the county. However, the more affluent southern Europeans such as Italians and Portuguese did not hire the Chinese in their homes. One reason may be that the early Italian immigrants came from locations where their women traditionally took charge of food preparation and, in America, these women, unaccustomed to hired help in the home, maintained control of the kitchen.

As with all other Chinese groups, the Chinese cooks shared lodging with others to defray expenses even though they worked in different locations. Other times cooks slept in the back storerooms of restaurants. When times were hard and jobs scarce, they relied heavily on each other for word of employment opportunities. The 1900 census listed two places in Stockton where a number of cooks lodged together. In one, twenty-two lived in the back of Lee Yuen's store at 101 East Washington Street. Lee, a Toishan merchant, provided fellow villagers shelter whenever asked. In the other, five cooks took temporary lodging at the old Heungshan Temple on North Hunter Street. The manner in which these Chinese grouped together underscored their dependency on clan and district members and suggests that even as late as the turn of the century Heungshan and Toishan mutual aid and network systems were still viable.

Among the more unusual and enterprising occupations of urban Chinese were those of peddlers, scavengers and rag pickers. The 1870 census listed one rag picker and thirteen scavengers among Stockton's Chinese. Investigation suggests that rag pickers may have been the forerunners of today's industrial rag companies, and those so occupied probably rummaged through discarded clothing and cloth materials to salvage what they could for profit. After being cleaned and packed into usable bundles, the rags were reused by blacksmiths, men in wheel manufacturing companies and other industries where axle grease or other oily substances presented problems to hand and power-driven machinery. Unused rags were unraveled and their fibers mixed with wood fiber for papermaking. Even today quality writing paper has a high rag content. Rag picking, though humble, was a profession found in many California towns, but Stockton's one Chinese rag picker was fined two dollars each time local police found him at work. They also placed a two-dollar fine on Chinese scavengers for transporting garbage. These work-related fines, at times, discouraged and confused the Chinese, who saw others in the community doing the same type of work. And, understandably, by 1880 the rag picking and scavenging industries no longer interested them.

From the 1880s to this author's recollection of only a decade ago, Chinese peddlers have been a familiar sight on many Stockton streets. Census data list five Chinese peddlers in 1870, eighteen in 1880 and fifteen in 1900. Enumerators may not have caught up with all the peddlers in each decade, for in 1893 the *Stockton Independent* noted at least fifty Chinese peddlers were paying license fees for that occupation.[17]

Senior citizens can still recall the old Chinese peddler clad in blue cotton trousers and woven bamboo hat, trotting around town balancing hundred-pound baskets of fruit and vegetables on both ends of his flexible bamboo shoulder poles. For those who lived too far from the downtown market or housewives occupied with children and housework, the Chinese peddler became a godsend. The sight of the peddler in the neighborhood evoked the

Local cartoonist Ralph Yardley captured the essence of the old Chinese peddler.

A multi-level, horse-drawn vegetable wagon used by Chinese peddlers at the turn of the century.

same pleasure as seeing the postman making his rounds. These peddlers plotted their routes to include homes where friends or relatives worked as cooks or domestics. Quite naturally, the cook would suggest to the mistress of the house to buy from this particular peddler rather than from others. And, as expected, the peddler would repay his friend in goods or services at a later date. In actuality, the peddler served as a town crier and local gossip.

These peddlers made indelible impressions on children, and the warmest recollection comes from the writings of local historian Glenn Kennedy as he described the relationship these peddlers had with their customers:

> He was past middle age, with a full round face, little silver-rimmed glasses with thick lenses, a gray moustache of not too many long hairs on either side and dressed as Chinese were expected to dress in those days. Over his shoulder was a long pole and hanging by small ropes from either end was a five-gallon oil can with the top removed. In one was freshly caught and cleaned catfish, each layer separated with a wet cloth. The other, at times, was filled with something special, like blackberries which grew along the levee near his house. We looked for him when Friday came, the kids ran out to say hello to him, the old family dog wagged her tail when she saw him coming. He put down his pole and cans, and seated himself on the back stairs. It seemed as if he had come just for a friendly visit. And when someone had a headache, he reached down into his pocket and brought out a little vial about three inches long, which held not too many drops, and as it was tenderly rubbed into

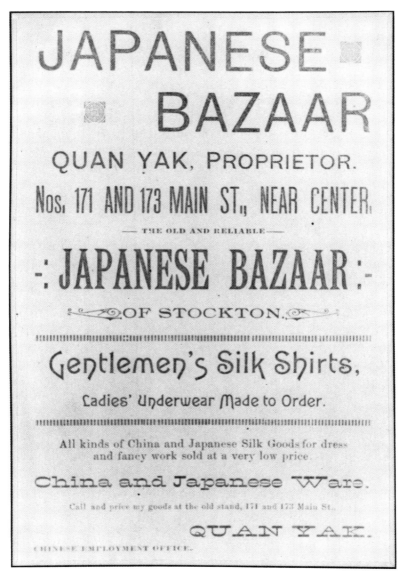

JAPANESE BAZAAR

QUAN YAK, PROPRIETOR.

Nos. 171 AND 173 MAIN ST., NEAR CENTER.

— THE OLD AND RELIABLE —

-: JAPANESE BAZAAR :-

OF STOCKTON.

Gentlemen's Silk Shirts,

Ladies' Underwear Made to Order.

All kinds of China and Japanese Silk Goods for dress
and fancy work sold at a very low price.

China and Japanese Ware.

Call and price my goods at the old stand, 171 and 173 Main St.

QUAN YAK.

CHINESE EMPLOYMENT OFFICE.

*Catering to the white community, Mr. Quan Yak also provided an
avenue for his customers to hire Chinese employees for domestic
and farm work.*

the forehead, the headaches seemed to just fade away. No one can
remember how many years we had our Friday morning chat with one of
the grandest persons anyone had ever known.[18]

By the turn of the century, many peddlers turned to using horsedrawn
wagons to get around. They picked up their vegetables at Go Sam's produce
market on Weber Point in the early morning before the rest of the town
arose, and reached residents living in the outer limits of town by mid-
morning. The younger wagon peddlers carefully skirted the foot routes

reserved for the old peddlers. Until recently pickup trucks loaded with vegetables continued to pass slowly through the old neighborhoods as the Chinese descendants of the old foot peddlers literally followed the routes of their fathers. Today, however, even the auto-driven vegetable peddlers have become a thing of the past, and the recollections of the old Chinese peddlers would have been dimmed were it not for a few memoirs.

OTHER RESIDENTIAL PATTERNS

A sense of naivete and community color came through in the censuses during the latter decades of the nineteenth century. For example, in 1870 there were thirty-six prostitutes, forty gamblers and two opium dealers, but in 1880, only twenty-two prostitutes were listed in the census despite the fact that the Chinese male population had increased 22 percent, creating greater demands for feminine charms. Even more startling is the fact that the 1880 census shows no Chinese listed as gamblers. The trend to reword or obscure certain occupations also occurred in the 1900 census. This time all the prostitutes and opium dealers seemed to have disappeared along with the gamblers. However, it did list twenty-two female housekeepers in their twenties and thirties. Some of these women might have been more appropriately classifed as sexual professionals. While there were undoubtedly some actual housekeepers on the enumeration, logic suggests that the two female housekeepers listed as residing with twenty-two males at 129 East Washington Street in Stockton, the several housekeepers living with one merchant, or the three female housekeepers living at 143 East Washington who lived by themselves may have been prostitutes. Local residents of Stockton have been aware that gambling and prostitution continued to thrive in certain areas of Stockton well beyond the 1940s.

As we discuss various urban residence patterns some attention must be given to those Chinese who were incarcerated institutionally. In 1877, the founders of the Woodbridge-based Nevada Insane Asylum and Sanitorium, Drs. Asa Clark and Samuel Langdon, moved their sanitarium to Stockton and changed its name to the Pacific Asylum. This private facility continued to house inmates of neighboring western territories in its new forty-acre complex on South Center Street and French Camp Toll Road. The 1880 census showed this facility held 125 wards, eight of whom were Chinese (one female and seven males). Unfortunately, there is no indication as to the date these inmates entered the institution. By 1888 the asylum, renamed Clark's Sanitorium after the death of Dr. Langdon, changed from caring for the insane to become a private health sanitorium for the wealthy, and, not surprisingly, no Chinese was in residence there according to the 1900 census.

While the listing of Chinese in the Pacific Asylum was only a one time occurrence, there was a consistent number of Chinese housed in the State Insane Asylum in Stockton. Located on California Street between North

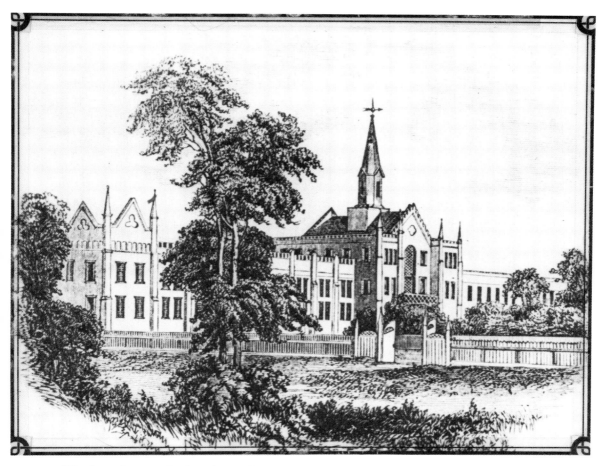

The State Insane Asylum located on California Street in Stockton was California's first public mental institution. Built initially for those who succumbed to "gold fever," the hospital housed inmates of all nationalities including the Chinese.

Street (Harding Way) and Park Street, this first public mental insitution was established in 1853 primarily for those who became afflicted with gold fever. In the ensuing years its residents exhibited a wide range of mental and physical disabilities. Although no census indicates the date the first Chinese entered the facility, in 1870 there were thirty Chinese inmates (twenty-eight males and two females); in 1880 thirty-seven Chinese resided there (thirty-three males and four females). By 1900 the number of Chinese housed in the asylum rose to ninety-two, only one of whom was female. Unfortunately, in contrast to the voluminous records relating to white inmates' origins, former occupations, marital status and so forth, little is known about these Chinese residents. Perhaps the language barrier or lack of interest on the part of asylum officials account for the lack of information on the Chinese.[19]

It is possible that improved administrative procedures accounted for the large increase in numbers of Chinese individuals being committed to the Stockton Asylum during the 1890s. Yet it is equally possible that many Chinese were committed by officials who could not understand the Chinese and therefore thought them demented. Interestingly, five years after the 1880 census, during the height of the anti-Chinese campaign, the number of Chinese committed to the asylum almost doubled, from thirty-seven to sixty-five. This increase strongly suggests covert activities between city leaders and asylum officials to effectively remove some Chinese from the Stockton streets.

Undoubtedly, the Stockton asylum on California Street provided valuable services to many requiring special care, as well as those families unable to shoulder the financial burden of mentally deficient family members. While information on specific care of inmates is nearly absent, some insight can be gained from a newspaper clipping concerning both the positive aspects of the institution and the dependent nature of the Chinese. The article noted that one Lung Foy appeared before a local court for a minor offense. Foy explained to the magistrate he had been discharged from the state asylum on April 15, 1886, and sent to San Francisco for deportation to

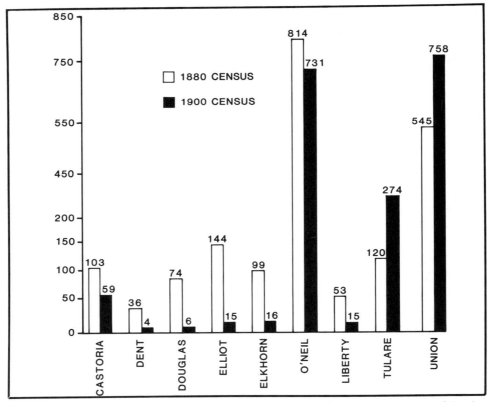

Chinese in the 1880 and 1900 censuses show a major reduction in six townships by 1900 because of the success of the 1882 Exclusion Law and successful anti-Chinese campaigns in these areas. The increase in three townships can be attributed to isolation and Chinese concentration on agriculture.

China. Instead he made his way back to Stockton, committed an arrestable offense, and asked Police Judge James G. Swinnerton to recommit him to the asylum. Foy evidently preferred to stay in the institution rather than starve in the outside world. But, since Lung Foy showed no evidence of insanity the judge felt he could not recommit the man and even dropped the minor charges.[20]

THEIR PRESENCE IN THE TOWNSHIPS

Charting the mercurial presence of Chinese in each township shows clearly the demographic shifts which occurred in response to the county's various stages of development and as the results of national, state and regional efforts to exclude the Chinese.

Briefly, the 1850 census (the earliest count of the Chinese in San Joaquin County) listed fifty-three Chinese males and no females; in 1860 there were 139 Chinese. The 1870 census listed an astonishing increase to 1,619, a jump of more than 1,016 percent over the previous decade. By 1880, when the county's numerous reclamation and transportation projects were in full swing, the Chinese workforce numbered 1,989—the highest of the nineteenth century. Ten years later this number declined to 1,676, and most historians concur that passage of the 1882 Exclusion Law was the major cause of the decrease.[21]

At this juncture, some explanation of the 1882 Exclusion Law should be given, for it played a significant factor in the Chinese story. Initially, this legislation suspended entry of new Chinese laborers for ten years. Those Chinese fitting ten other categories such as merchants and their families, teachers, students, seamen and those laborers who had previously resided in the United States and were merely returning from a visit to China were still allowed to enter the country.

Toward the end of the 1880s immigration laws relating to the Chinese became increasingly more stringent and complex, and September 1888 saw further restrictions, particularly against laborers. Henceforth only laborers with a wife, child or $1,000 in assets in the United States were permitted to return to this country. Yet even this slim loophole was closed when, on October 1, 1888, the Scott Act slammed the door to all returning Chinese laborers, regardless of family or property in this country. More than twenty thousand Chinese laborers with valid certificates permitting re-entry were stranded in China, and some six thousand already en route to San Francisco were refused admission when they disembarked.[22]

A second exclusion law, the Geary Act of 1892, extended prohibition of Chinese immigration to the United States for another ten years, and the efficiency of the two exclusion laws was clearly reflected in the total Chinese population count in the United States by the turn of the century.

Only two of the fifty-eight counties in California—Contra Costa and San Joaquin—showed an increase in their Chinese population, while adjacent

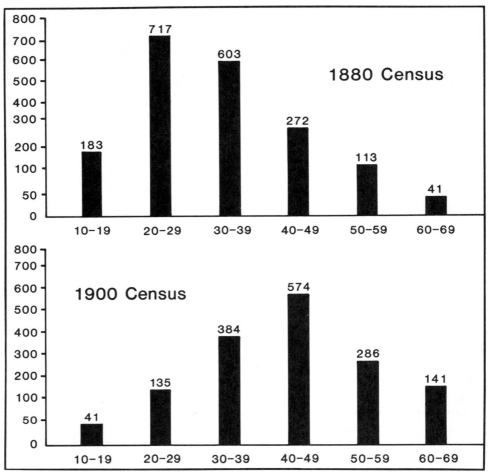

In spite of the 1882 Exclusion Law and normal attrition Chinese who were in their twenties in the 1880s continued to be the largest age group in 1900.

Sacramento County declined 26 percent, San Francisco dropped 46 percent and Stanislaus County to the south lost 44 percent of its Chinese citizens.

As San Joaquin County entered the twentieth century, seven of the nine townships saw substantial decreases in their Chinese population. Only Union township and the reclaimed delta islands of Tulare township showed an increase in their Chinese numbers. A look at individual townships will best demonstrate where the losses and shifts occurred.

In 1880 thirty-six Chinese lived in Dent township, but only four, all ranch cooks, were located there twenty years later. Douglas township suffered an even larger reduction in numbers, from seventy-four to six. In addition, the remote community of Farmington no longer had its ten-worker Chinese laundry nor did any Chinese continue to work in cooperative farming or woodcutting activities in the Douglas area.

Elliott township figures tell a similar story. There 144 Chinese raised hogs, cut wood, framed and worked as cooks in 1880. By 1900 this number had been reduced to fifteen—all three miners, two groups of hog raisers, two of Lockeford's laundries and many woodcutters had disappeared.

In Liberty township, the Chinese population dropped from fifty-three in 1880 to fifteen in 1900. Those who remained formed three sets of collective farming groups numbering seven, five and three workers, and none worked for white farmers.

In Elkhorn township, the number declined from ninety-nine to sixteen. Castoria township reduced its number of Chinese almost by half, from 103 to fifty-nine. Those who remained formed nine small farming units, and an additional seven Chinese cooks were listed as working for white farmers.

The increase in Tulare township's Chinese population to 242 in 1900 was a result of the additional acreage put into production in the southern Delta, as well as the maturation of the town of Tracy, the shipping center of the township. Most of the new farmland was leased to Chinese for truck gardening. A "China Camp" on Victoria Island showed two farming groups totaling thirty workers; they were but two of the total twenty-eight farming crews enumerated in the township. Fifteen Chinese involved in urban occupations located their businesses in Tracy, according to the 1900 census.

Union township was a Chinese phenomena. In 1870 only fourteen Chinese were in the marsh and swampland township; they were working for four white farmers. As soon as Staten and Bouldin islands were reclaimed most of their acreages were leased to Chinese tenant farmers. A brief statement in the *History of San Joaquin County - 1879* alluded to these Chinese as it mentioned, "... the land was cultivated by good tenants, forming a community of two hundred."[23]

In 1880 the census listed 545 Chinese living in Terminous, a small hamlet on Potato Slough. Most worked in farming, woodcutting, brickmaking and reclamation activities. There were also three merchants, eight clerks, two butchers, a hotel cook, a shoemaker, a saloon keeper, a doctor, a boat builder and three labor contractors. The number and diversity of these service-oriented individuals and their clusters in the census suggest that this all-male community was a Chinese rather than a white community. In addition, the sole laundryman in the whole township lived in a ten-man farming unit. A lack of Chinese laundries also meant a lack of white residents, or at least those who could afford to let someone else do their washing. Chinese laundries depended on the white man's trade, for the Chinese could not, themselves, afford the luxury of having their clothes laundered by others. Furthermore, they gave little thought to their appearance when most of their waking hours were spent working the soil.

An 1880 enumerator assigned to Union township proved most diligent when it came to getting information about the Chinese. Instead of simply recording "China" as country of origin, he extracted names that to him may have sounded strange, but, in his tenacious way he phonetically transposed his findings onto the data sheet. Some of the Chinese gave their district associations, others stated they were either Heungshan or Sze Yup. Although the enumerator was not able to get village breakdown on all 545 residents, his information revealed that 105 (20 percent) of the residents were Heungshan Chinese and the remainder Sze Yup. The only minority group among all the Chinese were two businessmen from the Sam Yup-speaking Shuntak district. The doctor, saloonkeeper and shoemaker were Sze Yup, but individuals from both districts were in the retail business, each catering to his kinsmen's needs. Obviously, when given a choice the Chinese preferred doing business with their fellow villagers, and the Sze Yup and Heungshan businessmen benefitted from this traditional separation.

In the mid-1880s when other Chinese were fleeing from the violence and hatred fomented during the anti-Chinese period in the western states, including the smaller communities in San Joaquin County, Union township experienced an increase in its Chinese population, for here they were safely tucked away in a sparsely populated, obscure area of the county.

Over the years the community of Terminous changed. In 1880 no females were listed, but by 1900 the families of some merchants were living in the area. While these females, wives and children numbered only nine, they were clearly a forerunner of the future for the once all-male society.

By 1894 asparagus had been added to the agricultural cornucopia of Union township. Six years later, 3,000 acres of the 6,000-acre Bouldin Island were given to asparagus cultivation, and by 1901 two canneries were in operation there to service the crops of the area.

By 1900 the Chinese population of ONeal township outside Stockton city declined. Reclaimed Delta lands had by then added new farming acreage to ONeal's western sector, but instead of the large, intensive farming units found in Union township, most farm plots in ONeal were small and operated by limited partnerships. Of the 136 living in the outlying farming areas, 80 percent were farm workers.

CENSUS-BASED CONCLUSIONS

Censuses filled in many aspects of the Chinese story in this county which otherwise would have been conceptual, lean and less meaningful. Those enumerators' markings of over a hundred years ago, at times resembling only hen-scratches, as seen in microfilm reels, bear testimony to the breadth and depth of Chinese participation in the development of California.

One unexpected facet of the census kaleidoscope began to manifest itself when the Chinese legacy was examined. Although the Chinese were adaptable and had the perseverance to succeed, their employers also deserve recognition. In each census period the names of many leading residents of the county from all occupations and walks of life appeared repeatedly and consistently as employers of the Chinese.

Labor historian Carey McWilliams, in *Brothers Under the Skin*, concluded that the white/Chinese relationship became symbiotic rather than social. And although this was so, the faith white employers placed in their

Chinese help and the efforts they expended in their defense during times of conflict when the Chinese themselves were voiceless and defenseless demonstrated a compassion for the Chinese and a recognition of their value despite the wide social gulf that separated the two races. They did share the common goal and pleasure of turning a virgin land into one of growth and productivity. In the final analysis, this partnership paid dividends: both groups received immediate financial remuneration, and the county received the lasting benefits of this unique and durable relationship.

CHINESE BY OCCUPATIONS, SAN JOAQUIN COUNTY, 1880

Laborers, Unskilled

Farm labor	575	
Truck gardening	78	
Hog raiser	18	
Woodcutter	85	
Railroad	73	
Brickmaker	47	
Reclamation	41	
Woolen mill	19	
Paper mill	7	
Unspecified	112	

Private industry

Fisherman	93
Miner	3

Urban Occupations

Merchant	28
Clerk and bookkeeper	13
Contractor	11
Interpreter, intelligence officer	4
Doctor	4
Druggist	2
Opium Dealer	8
Saloon Keeper	1
Prostitute	23
Hotel, roominghouse manager	5
Butcher	3
Tailor	8
Shoemaker	3
Barber	9
Peddler (fruit and wood)	18
Carpenter, boat builder	3
Brazier maker	1

Semi-skilled

Cooks:

Commercial	116
Domestic	104
Work crew	62
Servant	32
Gardener	8
Laundry worker	239

CHINESE BY OCCUPATIONS, SAN JOAQUIN COUNTY, 1900

Laborers

Farmer and farm laborer	957
General/day laborer	304
Sheepherder	1

Urban Occupations

Merchant	97
Clerk	21
Cigar dealer	3
Restaurant proprietor	11
Contractor	1
Peddler	15
Tailor	2
Ironer	1
Dressmaker	1
Barber	4
Physician	1
Housekeeper	19
Steamboat runner	1

Semi-skilled

Cooks:

Commercial	103
Domestic	37
Work crew	32
Waiter	11
Laundry Worker	107
Gardener	6

CHINESE IN UNSKILLED AND SEMI-SKILLED OCCUPATIONS BY TOWNSHIPS SAN JOAQUIN COUNTY, 1880 CENSUS

| Township | Unskilled | | | | | | | | | | Semi-skilled | | | | | | Total Chinese Population in Township |
| | Farm Labor | Truck Garden | Hog Raiser | Woodcutter | Brickmaker | Railroad | Reclamation | Woolen Mill | Paper Mill | Unspecified Labor | Cook | | | Servant | Gardener | Laundry | |
											Commercial	Domestic	Work Crew				
CASTORIA	70					12						5	7	2		7	103
DENT										21		15					36
DOUGLAS	26			2						2	2	14	17			11	74
ELLIOTT	73		18	21							3		10			14	144
ELKHORN		8		38							4	25	2		2	18	99
O'NEIL	14			1				19	7	76	105	41	7	28	4	180	814
LIBERTY	8			12	23					4		2		2	2		53
TULARE	25					61				8	1	2	6			8	120
UNION	429			11	24		41			1			13			1	545

CHINESE POPULATION AND OCCUPATION COMPARISON CHART SAN JOAQUIN COUNTY BY TOWNSHIPS, 1880-1900 CENSUSES

| Townships | Population | | Farming | | Cook | | Laundry | |
	1880	1900	1880	1900	1880	1900	1880	1900
CASTORIA	103	59	70	50	12	7	7	2
DENT	36	4	21	--	15	4	--	--
DOUGLAS	74	6	26	--	33	6	11	--
ELLIOTT	144	15	91	10	13	2	14	2
ELKHORN	99	16	8	3	31	4	18	8
O'NEIL	814	731	14	109	153	138	180	93
LIBERTY	53	15	20	15	--	--	--	--
TULARE	120	274	25	244	9	24	8	--
UNION	545	758	429	525	14	7	1	2
Total	1,987	1,878	704	956	282	192	239	107

CHAPTER THREE ENDNOTES

1. George A. Tinkham, *History of San Joaquin County, California With Biographical Sketches* (Los Angeles, 1923), p. 64.

2. F. T. Gilbert, *History of San Joaquin County, California With Illustrations Descriptive of its Scenery* (Oakland, 1879), p. 129.

3. ONeal township was named for John W. ONeal, an early pioneer and politician of the county. There are two other spellings of his name—O'Neil and O'Neill—found in various county maps and local documents. A dispute as to the correct spelling continues to rage among local historians. Some speculate because ONeal was a Southerner that after the Civil War he used O'Neil to disguise the use of his original name.

4. Tongs, in this instance, refer to members of particualr Chinese fraternal societies whose primary interests in the 1870s to the 1920s were territorial control of gambling, prostitution and opium. (Dean De Carli, *Holt Station, Holt School, Peterson School* [Stockton, n.d.], p. 1. Interview with John Fong, Stockton, 1985.)

5. Mary Robert Coolidge, *Chinese Immigration* (New York, 1909), p. 128.

6. *San Joaquin Republican*, March 3, 1852.

7. F. T. Gilbert, *History of San Joaquin County*, pp. 104, 128-30.

8. *Stockton Daily Evening Herald*, October 9, 1878.

9. J. Witse, overseer of the road district in Elliott township, listed all the Chinese in his section who chose to work two days on county roads in lieu of paying the county's assessed road tax of four dollars. Apparently the Chinese preferred to work the two days to pay off this indebtedness rather than give up four days' real wages at the normal rate of one dollar a day. (J. Witse, Overseer of District Road No. 32, Elliott Township, Report to the Board of Supervisors, May 1878, San Joaquin County Historical Museum.)

10. John Thompson, "The Settlement Geography of the Sacramento-San Joaquin Delta, California" (unpublished doctoral dissertation, Stanford University, 1957), p. 43.

11. *Stockton Daily Independent*, September 11, 1876.

12. *Stockton Daily Evening Herald*, March 21-23, 1878.

13. Roberts Island Reclamation Pay Receipts, County Probate Receipts Collection, Haggin Museum, October 1884.

14. Carey McWilliams, *Brothers under the Skin* (Boston, 1946), pp. 67-70.

15. George Chu, "Chinatown in the Delta; The Chinese in the Sacramento-San Joaquin Delta, 1870-1890," *California Historical Society Quarterly*, March 1970, pp. 22-30.

16. *Stockton Daily Independent*, July 26, 1893.

17. *Stockton Daily Independent*, August 16, 1893.

18. Glenn A. Kennedy, *It Happened in Stockton 1900-1925* (Stockton 1967), p. 39.

19. The Pacific Asylum contracted with Nevada, Arizona and New Mexico to house their inmates while these states were still territories. The Stockton Insane Asylum, the first state insane asylum in California, began in 1853; the largest number of wards at a given time in this facility was 1,361 in October 1875. When Napa Insane Asylum opened its doors the following month, Stockton's population was reduced by almost half. Renamed the Stockton Developmental Center, the state hospital still exists at the same location. The Pacific Asylum's doors closed in the 1920s and its grounds are now used for Edison High School. (Gilbert, *San Joaquin County*, pp. 73-75.

20. *Stockton Daily Independent*, April 28, 1886.

21. My personal tabulation of the 1870, 1880 and 1900 census of Chinese in San Joaquin County differs from the work of Chinn, Lai and Choy, *Chinese in California: A Syllabus*.

22. The 1882 Exclusion Law limited Chinese immigration but a Chinese who had lived in this country and returning after a home visit would report to immigration authorities upon his return to the United States the birth of a son or his wife's pregnant state. This formal declaration of his procreation or prospective progeny created a legal avenue for his child to one day enter this country; by law the child was due the same entry status as his father. Often Chinese men would offer the reserved admission slot to other Chinese who otherwise had no legal means to enter America and were willing to pay the price of being someone's son "on paper." It was a ruse, but the men were so desperate to immigrate they were willing to accept whatever scheme was offered to gain admission.

23. Gilbert, *San Joaquin County*, p. 133.

Building Blocks
to Relationships

4

Men from many nations flowed into Stockton in its early years, and all exhibited the same intense desire for financial gain. Some, already half-crazed with delusions of riches, moved on in search of gold; others stayed. Filled with hope and endowed with abilities in their respective fields, bankers, blacksmiths, merchants, restaurateurs and others sought to make lives for themselves and their families in this port city. While these business people offered their services to all, they gave preferential treatment to their own countrymen or those who spoke their language.

Few newcomers savored their first international encounters. Most paid little attention to those who looked different: men with long hair braided into queues, or others who wore serapes or buckskins. Shouts of "ola," "ca va," or "shalom" were only muddled sounds for ears trained to words and inflections of their own native tongues. With opportunities so abundant, no one cared how a neighbor amassed his wealth. Competition in business came not from foreigners in the same occupation but from others of each businessman's own culture.

Each race carved out a particular niche for itself within Stockton's business community, and the families of each lent distinctive flavor to the neighborhoods. Soon the cultural traits of the Germans, English, Blacks, Hispanics, Jews and Chinese, as well as the regional traits of Yankee and Southerner, were established in Captain Weber's new settlement. Elements of these diverse cultures all seeded themselves elsewhere in the county. In time, traditions including festivals, religious holidays, and specific ethnic traits of the population formed the social environment of the county.

When their businesses settled to an even keel and their livelihood was fairly secure, men found time to appraise their environment in the larger and more permanent context. It was then that they took note of their own neighborhood and those of other foreigners who also had made Stockton their home. The dissimilarities in lifestyles became topics of discussion and comparison within each ethnic group. Ethnocentrism, the judging of another society's customs and ideas in the context of one's own culture, was an attitude shared by all pioneers, and those of San Joaquin County were no exception. The pioneer's cultural baggage consisted of folkways, traditions and customs of his native land, and the perpetuation of these practices gave purpose to his life. The greater the deviation from what individuals were accustomed to, the more difficult it was to accept.

And, yet, during this special time in Stockton's history, first steps were taken to mold the town into a truly American city. Residents observed customs and traditions of foreign countries; they learned the meanings behind religious and ethnic celebrations; and they witnessed the mundane daily activities of various ethnic groups. It is at this juncture we explore some of the encounters and contacts between the early whites and Chinese, two races with contrasting cultural backgrounds. Some of the actions and reactions were self-serving and produced short-range effects to the overall relationship between the two groups. Time and familiarization proved to be the cohesive elements that formed the basis of tolerance, understanding and respect: social conditions that subsequent generations believed to be a natural part of their heritage.

THE TWO-WAY MIRROR

As the Chinese immigrant came and settled in San Joaquin County, his main concerns centered around work and a place to stay. To that extent he relied heavily on help from his family associations, fellow villagers and other established mutual aid networks. To him, a Chinese world had been transplanted from Guangdong Province onto the Central Valley floor. The customs, diet and habits within the Chinese quarters were familiar and comforting. But, here also in this new land, the sojourner found that his life was neither simple nor routine. He was, after all, an integral part of the larger community, one that was totally foreign and controlled by the white man. The Chinese enshrined the essential differences between the Chinese and white worlds with a colloquial term for white man, "Lo Fon," or "old foreigner," signifying that the white and his ways were foreign to the Chinese. The vast differences between people cut both ways, and it is perhaps ironic that while the Chinese bemoaned the foreignness of the white world in their Cantonese dialect, the whites also took note of the alien characteristics among the Chinese.

Some whites understood the Chinese need to maintain his diet and his desire to continue traditional practices. But could a Chinese describe to a meat-and-potato eater the sensual excitement which occurred on one's palate as garlic, ginger and soy sauce passed through the lips? Such unfamiliar tastes, and the smell of dried fish, squid and shrimp, were so alien that they offended white olfactory senses. Yet in the same context, the sauerkraut eaten by Stockton's German citizens displeased the Chinese nostrils.

Many whites were unaware of the circumstances which brought the Chinese into their midst, for the political and natural devastation in China remained a topic of discussion for the most part only among the Chinese.

And only the Chinese knew that his decision to emigrate without family could result in a lifetime of loneliness in an all-male society. But there were other differences between the whites and Chinese that went beyond food and personal circumstances.

Whites who came made a commitment to the new land, but the Chinese who came planned only a short sojourn. And while the Chinese system of communal living and pooling of their resources seemed logical in low-income circumstances, the fact that they sent money back to their families in China brought back to many whites bitter memories of tyranny and famine in their own homelands. Even the thought of returning Chinese bones to their native villages presented an unfathomable foreignness to the white belief that once a person was buried he should be left to rest in peace.

Conversely, westerners baffled the pragmatic Chinese. Obviously anti-Chinese whites were easy to spot, particularly those who believed the Chinese should be isolated in a community of their own. Yet while the Chinese did not expect to be embraced with open arms, they did hope for quiet acceptance. The peacemakers and a few seeking simple solutions to ease the tension in the community earnestly believed that if the Chinese were assimilated they would be less rejected. Missionizing whites used this argument to Christianize a few Chinese in the 1870s. According to theory, once a person was baptized, an automatic western-oriented transformation would occur. And if the Chinese were lucky, his distinctive features would hardly be noticed.[1]

Tom Hing, a Chinese peddler, found merit in this theory and, perhaps even more importantly, reasoned that baptism might increase his business profit. Hing became a Methodist, but his understanding of the finer points of his new faith was clearly colored by his Chinese mentality. One warm summer Sunday the local police arrested and jailed Hing for peddling his wares through Stockton. Imprisoned, Hing loudly expressed his indignation, stressed that he was a member in good standing at the local Methodist Church, and requested his pastor be called. When the minister arrived, he admonished the prisoner for violating Stockton's blue laws, to which Hing retorted that since Jesus Christ had healed on a Sunday, he, Hing, ought to be allowed to work on that day also. Obviously there was still much Chinese reasoning in Hing's thinking.[2]

BASIS FOR CULTURAL MISUNDERSTANDINGS

In fairness and for historical accuracy, we must acknowledge that some whites had an inherent prejudice against the Chinese. While this attitude was not unanimous, those who had such resentments learned through observations and personal dealings and, of course, were influenced by others. As a race, the images the Chinese projected both attracted and repulsed the dominant society. Chinese work ethics and industry ranked among their positive attributes. But there were other things about the

Chinese that whites found distasteful and even contemptible. Additionally, bigotry often colored each group's perception of the other. In areas where whites felt they had a set of standards and principles, they assumed the Chinese lacked concern for these same values. Thus, when whites believed their laws and ordinances were enacted for the common good, they resented Chinese circumvention or legal challenges of these laws.

In court and in simple intercourse whites emphasized the importance of truth and honesty. Westerners' perception of honesty required a straight-forward answer, and they often believed an individual trustworthy until proven otherwise. Chinese, on the other hand, believed frankness and honesty to be rude and that trustworthiness was proven only through time and deeds. This clearcut difference between the two cultures created an atmosphere in which the veracity of the seldom-concise Chinese was often doubted. Few realized that the Chinese weighed several factors before he formulated an answer to any question: he considered the immediate situation, the questioner's objective, his own personal circumstances and the possible consequences of his answer. Whereas Chinese thinking is often structured along pragmatic lines, he places great importance in the per-ceived results; in contrast, whites prefer to "tell it as it is" and "let the chips fall where they may." All these considerations suggest the Chinese to be situation-motivated and his responses to be somewhat colored, yet the Chinese found nothing wrong with this type of reasoning.

While vast misconstrual of the Chinese code of manners may have produced real or perceived difficulties in business, in matters of law it became extremely difficult to impanel unbiased jurors or find officers of the court willing to accept the Chinese word. In criminal cases involving Chinese, defense attorneys consistently questioned potential jurors about their attitudes toward the Chinese. Some stated blatant bias; other claimed impartiality. All who claimed they were not prejudiced were then asked their general feelings about the crime in question. (Seldom would anyone admit that he had no opinion on or was in favor of robbery, burglary or murder.) Such highly subjective questioning may have attempted to guar-antee an impartial jury, but it also quickly depleted venires, lengthened trials and raised court costs. For instance, during jury selection in the case against Ah Gan, charged with selling lottery tickets in Stockton, the county prosecuting attorneys Charles W. Miller and George F. McNoble and defense lawyer W. B. Nutter exhausted two lists of potential jurors in two days. Only after questioning thirty citizens (a high number in light of the small population) did both sides believe there were enough jurors with diverse opinions to see that justice would be done. But, of course, even if a Chinese were proven innocent, his reputation had been damaged by the court experience.[3]

In time, with enough experience facing law enforcement officials, the Chinese were labeled "wily" and "clever." Not intended as a compliment,

Interaction between Italians and Chinese began in the early years of Stockton's growth and continued for several generations. Earl Jann remembered when his father, Louie, and uncle, Tim, would make monthly visits to Jack Solari at his ranch on Foppiano Lane and Solari Road, c.1922.

these words referred to the Chinese's abilty to think on their feet. When a Chinese was accused of breaking a law, his glib and sometimes transparently false defense fueled white contempt despite the fact that this instinct for self-preservation is a common human characteristic.

The initial reaction to an arrest led the Chinese to either feign ignorance of the law, suggest analogies or similar circumstances that fell within those legal limits, or even insist that no crime had been committed, based on strict interpretation of the law governing the violation. This last was possible because local laws were often ambiguous, particularly if written in reaction to a specific circumstance in order that many similar potentially illegal situations could be lumped within the violation.

When all explanations failed the Chinese then sought the best legal defense money could buy. Only when they felt that their situation was desperate or when they had exhausted all legal avenues would the Chinese resort to unethical means. As an example, in one incident in 1885 the

Chinese employed tactics which showed poor judgment and duplicity. After being pressured by the *Stockton Independent* to clean up Chinese gambling, local police arrested nine Chinese men. Two made bail, but seven remained in jail for trial. On September 10, Joseph La Rose Phelps, editor of the *Independent*, claimed a strange Chinese visited his office and offered to pay him to stop his newspaper's crusade. In his editorial Phelps reported the attempted bribe and implied the Chinese gambling community was behind this action, and further, that it paid $220 monthly to local police and that graft pervaded the district attorney's office, too, for its employees appeared reluctant to draw up additional warrants against the Chinese. Phelps never denied his anti-Chinese stand, and two incidents less than twelve days later lent credence to his accusations.[4]

On September 24, 1885, Chow Gum of San Francisco came to Stockton and requested to see City Attorney Frank Smith on behalf of the seven defendants. At this meeting, Chow was immediately arrested and arraigned on charges of attempting to bribe a public official. His bail was set at $2,000 and his trial held over until a later date.

Meanwhile, another strategy was instituted toward the same goal. One Ah Lee, a naturalized citizen living in Saint Louis, Missouri, was paid to come to California and testify as a character witness on behalf of the seven prisoners. The Chinese community had assumed that as Lee was a naturalized citizen, his word would bear more weight in court. However, on the stand Lee admitted he did not know any of the defendants and came because of the generous offer by some of Stockton's Chinese.[5]

The Chinese concept of health and sanitation appalled many whites. The Chinese appeared to know little and care even less about the westerner's concern for general hygienic conditions, and the manner in which the Chinese dealt with illness and death greatly concerned local health officials. During the latter part of the nineteenth century, a single county hospital built in 1857 served those inflicted with contagious diseases and the seriously ill. The Chinese generally did not use this facility, for the hospital was limited in bed space, and also the language barrier served to prevent Chinese from seeking admission. In reality, however, the Chinese were not oblivious to the sick and dying, but simply dealt with health care problems in their own way.

Even though there was a housing shortage and living space presented a problem, they managed to furnish rooms or screen off areas for the terminally ill in their district association headquarters. Many lonely sojourners were grateful for the accommodations; a small cot or a space in a corner was far better than no shelter at all. More importantly, the Chinese knew his countrymen would take care of his remains when death came. That in itself provided peace of mind.

Some whites found such arrangements distasteful and unacceptable. In 1874 Ben Kolhberg, a local constable with anti-Chinese sentiments, and

L. M. Cutting, a local insurance agent, filed a joint complaint with the city council. They reported that two buildings, one at the corner of Channel and Hunter and the other the Heungshan Joss Temple, were being used for hospital purposes and demanded that "legal proceedings be taken to stop this nuisance at once." The two testified they saw "at least eight Chinese in bed in one house and, although no actual count was taken at the other facility . . ." they saw numerous sick Chinese there as well. Subsequent investigation by the city health committee revealed only three incapacitated individuals. It is possible many of the sick had been temporarily moved to other locations.[6]

City leaders faced a dilemma: if the city provided some alternatives for the critically ill Chinese, the expense would tax the city coffers. Apparently they chose not to deal with the issue, and in 1878 a newspaper article claimed the Heungshan building was an area where the "old and despondent went to end their life." The actual amount of attention the city gave to Chinese health conditions at the temple was probably minimal, as is evidenced by the fact that when a coroner went to the temple to remove a body on September 12, 1878, he found another corpse in a state of decomposition. Three days later he returned to remove yet another dead Chinese and found a fourth individual near death. As the bodies were being removed, Dr. Moon Ho, caretaker of the facility, requested they be given a proper burial in the Chinese section of the Rural Cemetery.[7]

It puzzled white citizens that the Chinese, sick and well alike, were untroubled by dead bodies in their midst. But considering their circumstances and their pragmatic nature, it is understandable why they de-emphasized the matter of dying. The Chinese considered death but a transitional, temporary phase; what counted in the end was to have one's bones placed in final rest in one's own country.

BEHIND THE INSCRUTABLE FACE

Wealthier community members often judged the Chinese by the cooks and domestics in their employ. They and others who did business with the Chinese found that beyond the inscrutable faces and the subservient facades were complex individuals with strong principles. Quick to ire, particularly in situations that might cause him to lose face, the Chinese had an almost uncontrollable temper. However, his fit of rage was short, but his memory was long. Others who had the opportunity to deal with the Chinese over a period of time saw their acquaintanceship evolve into sustained friendship. In the company of trusted friends, that reserved exterior dissipated and his friendliness and calculative honesty, characteristics of his race, became obvious.

Local businessmen found Chinese merchants willing to meet them more than halfway regarding agreements or problems. The Chinese paid their bills without quibbling and their relationships remained stable. Freight companies and shipping lines such as Wells Fargo and Company and the Pacific Mail Steamship Line actively courted Chinese patronage and attempted to overcome language barriers by use of interpreters. If none was present, company officials resorted to phrase books to transact their affairs.

The Chinese believed in mixing business with pleasure, and some whites learned that Chinese generosity and hospitality knew no bounds. This characteristic puzzled and delighted many in the white society whose own social circles were inhibited by racial barriers. Civic leaders, business associates and other friends partook of special Chinese festivals, celebrations and elaborate banquets. On other occasions they were given gifts such as paintings, carvings, vases, scrolls and other items which epitomized Chinese culture and symbolized generosity and goodwill. The more skeptical whites interpreted such magnanimous gestures as a form of bribery. But, in reality, the Chinese simply relished eating and believed meals to be happy experiences that should be shared. Hosting meals which coincided with special events and propitious occasions gave them a feeling of magnanimity, a sentiment which extended to giving gifts as well. The Chinese believed gift giving placed the giver on a par with the recipient, and frequently the Chinese gave more than they got in return.

A PUBLIC DISPLAY OF GENEROSITY

Twice a year the Stockton Washington Street Chinatown took on an expansive air in which Chinese friendliness and hospitality were amply demonstrated. During Chinese New Year and the Harvest Moon Festival, businesses along Washington Street were festively decorated. Chinese and men of other nationalities from nearby communities and the Mother Lode towns flooded into Stockton's Chinatown to participate in the feasting and entertainment.

The Moon Festival, an agricultural celebration similar to Thanksgiving, fell in mid-September when, according to the lunar calendar, the moon reached the highest point in the heavens. On the Chinese calendar, the festival occurred on the fifteenth day of the eighth moon, which in China coincided with the rice harvest. In Stockton celebrations, the Chinese community set aside three days for feasting and relaxation. Priests came from the Chinese temples in San Francisco to the Heungshan Temple to bless the harvest, and local merchants imported opera troupes to entertain the masses at an outdoor stage erected in the middle of the Washington Street block. And Stockton's own weather contributed to the pleasure of the festival; on warm autumn nights the cool Delta breeze gently nudged the candle-lit lanterns that hung from awnings and balconies as the golden-red glow illuminated the surroundings with a soft radiance. Traditionally, the festival ended with a huge bonfire on the third day of the fete. According to an account in the *Stockton Evening Herald*:

> The Chinese celebration had much ado and trappings. Musicians and priests with equipment were brought in from San Francisco. Now Chinatown will not take on a resort-like atmosphere until their New Year. There were as many curious and interested whites as there were Chinese. The Chinese were well-behaved, orderly and not drunk or riotous, however, there were white drunks about Chinatown . . . [8]

White citizens found the gaiety in Chinatown during Chinese New Year even more difficult to resist than that of the Moon Festival. With Christmas and regular New Year already only memories, the festivities associated with any type of celebration lifted the human spirit in that otherwise cold, foggy and often rainy season when farmers and laborers remained inactive and business slackened. Chinese New Year's Day fell on the second new moon after the winter solstice and, by custom, the celebrations lasted two weeks or longer. Whites knew that the holiday fell anywhere between late January and early March; the exact time was unknown until their Chinese domestics requested their annual vacation or the dates were given by Chinese friends. Not unexpectedly, Chinatown's population increased substantially during New Year as boardinghouses and hotels crammed lodgers into their facilities. Even gambling halls turned gaming tables into temporary sleeping bunks during the wee hours of the morning. As a public service, local police posted warnings to visitors venturing into the Chinese quarters for a look-see: ladies should not wear jewelry or other finery and men were asked to guard their wallets as "these gatherings normally drew a number of Chinese and white pickpockets."[9]

From the mid-1870s onward local newspapers diligently covered the New Year celebrations in Chinatown. Even during the 1880 decade, when public sentiment ran strongly against the Chinese, reporting of these celebrations never waned. Some articles suggest the reporters' enthusiasm as they wrote about the ambience:

> The Chinese seem to be a very free, hospitable and generous people. Their quarter is visited daily during their celebrations by white people who wanted to take a look at what is going on, and the Chinese establishments are always open to them. Cigars, drinks, candies and so forth are passed to the visitors by smiling Celestials, and all is hospitality and good will. Especially is one with whom the Chinamen are acquainted well treated. Many American ladies have visited Chinatown since the celebration opened. In all the stores and the other places there is a tray wheron cards or rather folded slips of red paper are deposited by visitors, the slips bearing the visitors' names. These trays are well filled with red papers. When a Chinaman receives a visitor he first offers him a small cup of tea, then a cigar and then anything else that is about that the visitor desires.
>
> Although the Chinese have intoxicating liquors which they hand out to visitors, they rarely drink anything intoxicating themselves, tea being their favorite beverage . . .

> . . . Chinatown at anytime is an interesting place. A day or two before
> the opening of the celebration a MAIL reporter took a trip through the
> quarters to note the preparation being made by the Chinamen for their
> New Year's. The spirit of expectancy that filled them was very apparent
> and they talked enthusiastically of the "heap big time" they were going
> to have.[10]

Whites who attended family association dinners during Chinese New
Year reveled in food, drink and merriment; some even tried their luck in the
gambling houses normally off-limits to them.

While the Chinese attempted to bridge the cultural gap with their celebrations, their use of firecrackers reflected a spirited desire to cling to
traditional ways. Few whites ever became accustomed to the unexpected,
heart-stopping eruptions that shattered the senses. To the Chinese, firecrackers were no different a noise maker than the tooting horns and pistol
shots during American New Year, or the use of fireworks on Independence
Day—all were expressions of jubilation and celebration. But white merrymaking was relatively shortlived, while the Chinese continued to express
their excitement for two weeks or longer. From the midnight incendiary
eruption on the eve of Chinese New Year until each clan/family association,
business, house and shop had the opportunity to hold its observance,
periodic explosions filled the air and the pungent aroma of burnt sulfur
filtered down the street. And, in keeping with tradition, no banquet began
during the observance of the new year without the release of twenty to thirty
strings of firecrackers.

Noise in the Chinese sector eventually became a bone of contention
among those of anti-Chinese sentiment, and complaints about the noise
became as traditional as the New Year celebration itself. To appease all
parties the police attempted to place restrictions and limitations to the
fireworks permits granted the Chinese. Local law enforcement, as a rule,
was for once in sympathy with the Chinese, for there was no real harm in the
noise; thus firecracker-firing restrictions seemed a reasonable compromise
between all factions. Several incidents, however, suggest that the Chinese
occasionally ignored the restrictions.

For instance, during the height of the 1886 anti-Chinese fury, Police Chief
Ben Rogers signed a permit allowing the Chinese to discharge their firecrackers only in the Chinatown Washington Street area and at the Heungshan Temple on Hunter Street, beginning February 2 at 7:00 A.M. and
ending February 8 at 5:00 P.M. Within this time span the fireworks could be
exploded only between 5:00 A.M. and 7:00 P.M. of any day, and none would
be allowed on Sunday, February 7. Chief Rogers' hope was that neighbors
would be subjected to only seventy hours of the aggravating noise.

Two days after the permit began, a *Stockton Weekly Mail* article noted
that Henry Lagomarsino, who lived near the Chinese quarter, complained
to his councilman that he had been ill and was kept awake all night by the

noise of firecrackers. A nearby female resident lodged a similar complaint as well. E. L. Colnon, editor of the *Stockton Weekly Mail*, and attorney James Budd, later to become governor of California, took their crusade against firecrackers to Police Judge Charles H. Clements. These three in turn called on City Attorney Frank Smith, but Smith stated that since a permit had been issued, no illegality had occurred.

Police Chief Ben Rogers walked in on the group by chance, whereupon they launched into their tirade and asked what he had done about the situation. Rogers responded that he had been "busy that morning checking to see how many in the neighborhood were really as sick as the paper had previously reported." It was only because of Colnon and Budd's persistence that Rogers revoked the permit several days later. He gave as an excuse that Chinese New Year was not a national holiday, and the revocation took effect close to the expiration date of the original permit. This revocation did not, however, set any real precedent, for in succeeding years the Chinese were able to gain their firecracker permits and continue their tradition.[11]

In 1893 Police Chief I. H. ("Ike") Robinson told the Chinese who applied for the annual permit that while it would be granted "they [the Chinese] could not have a little fun of that kind after nightfall for other people in that neighborhood wanted to sleep if they did not." The Chinese heeded Chief Robinson's words from sunset until midnight of the first day of the celebration when, their enthusiasm at the breaking point, they set off many of the firecracker strings they had stored in anticipation of the event. The police were called, but the Chinese gleefully continued firing the strings from roofs and windows throughout the quarter, and muffled sounds reaching the street indicated explosions from within the buildings. Nearly all Chinatown joined in the noisy sport and it was not until after 3:00 A.M. that the disturbance ceased. Arrests were made, and the next morning five Chinese faced the local magistrate and were speedily convicted of disturbing the peace. The Chinese acknowledged the offense but pleaded ignorance of the law. Four paid the fine and reassured the fifth that his time in jail would be short since they would raise the money to bail him out. One Chinese, Ah Jake, received the relatively stiff fine of thirty dollars, for the magistrate knew he had been among the group personally forewarned by the police chief.[12]

These incidents appear comical when placed in today's perspective, yet one cannot help but cheer for the Chinese in their spirit to perpetuate a sense of cultural continuity. The opening of Chinatown with its bazaar-like atmosphere and the hospitality they displayed were indeed outward expressions of good will. Their simplistic eagerness to show a side of Chinese culture that paralleled customs and values found within the white society indicate a pride in their own heritage and demonstrate a quest for tolerance from those who appeared to have none.

FISCAL OBLIGATIONS

White civic leaders may have rarely understood the Chinese, but they did recognize them as an important, integral part of the economic community with great ability to influence the county's physical development and economic well-being. All community members had certain fiscal obligations to the county which usually took the form of local taxes and assessments, and the Chinese were no exception. A look into the fees and fines that the Chinese paid provides an added dimension to the white/Chinese interdependence.

The Chinese in California could neither become citizens nor participate in the elective process, for, despite their numerous contributions, they were aliens. As county residents, however, they were expected to contribute to the public coffers which funded public works, fire and health measures, law enforcement, court expenses, public education and other local improvements requiring city or county monies. They realized that their tax money went toward improvement of the community as a whole rather than toward their own gain. But research suggests that when it came time to collect from the Chinese some local authorities' practices were less than praiseworthy.

Merchants, businessmen and even peddlers paid a license fee to stay in business. The lucrative revenue-generating ordinance enacted in 1850 set a fee schedule according to the type of permit and the length of time for which it was issued. The more frequently the license needed to be renewed the greater the cost. For instance, a livery stable owner would pay twenty dollars for a two-month license, or forty-five dollars for six months, or seventy-five dollars for a full year. Similarly, a blacksmith paid either seventy-five dollars every six months or one hundred dollars a year for his operating license. Chinese filing for operating licenses found their permits issued for shorter terms and were required to renew them more frequently.

The most common business licenses issued to Chinatown residents were a thirty-dollar-two-months' license to operate a store, one for twenty dollars to operate a saloon and another for twenty dollars to operate a draying business. A hotel or butcher shop paid seventy-five dollars every six months, although a restaurant paid only ten dollars for three months. The Chinese peddler's license fee was three dollars per month, an amount which required that the blackberry peddler sell thirty pounds of the fruit each month just to pay the fee. In 1893 the peddler's rate was increased sharply to seven and a half dollars per month, although this was applicable only to Chinese peddlers. City officials reasoned that Italian peddlers needed incentive to compete with the Chinese. Fees for laundry operations fluctuated: in the mid-1880s the rate was often regulated by the amount of anti-Chinese agitation. Frequently, officials also added a sanitation and fire inspection charge on top of the fee.[13]

Seldom did the Chinese complain about their business licenses. The license and its receipt served as evidence to legitimize their merchant status and therefore were useful in easing travel restrictions between their home-land and their San Joaquin County residence.

POLL TAXES

The poll tax, once used in southern states to disenfranchise blacks, was a head tax. State legislation of 1850 authorized the counties to add an additional amount above the state-imposed tax. The Court of Sessions immediately used the assessment to raise funds for local revenue, with a large portion of the money earmarked for public education. This county's head tax remained two dollars per person per year until it was abolished in 1914. Taxes were due by June 30 to county collectors, and late collection charges for delinquent payments increased the amount by one dollar. Collectors were paid on commission and were thus quite diligent in their work. During the spring and summer months when the annual tariff was due, these men fanned out to all work locations and collected at the job sites.

All males in the county between the ages of twenty-one and fifty were subject to this tax, except American Indians. In contrast to the payment of fees for a business license, the Chinese saw no advantage to paying the poll tax, for most Chinese were single and the children of those who were married generally lived in China and could not attend local schools. The assessor's men scoured the fields in the Delta and remote farmlands looking for taxpayers, and the Chinese tried to avoid them. When they did pay, it seemed reasonable to circulate the tax receipts among fellow countrymen to spare them the expense, if not also to circumvent the collectors whenever possible.

An enterprising Chung Yaw made the poll tax his business by collecting a dozen or so of his countrymen's receipts and renting them out, at fifty cents each, to other Chinese who had not yet paid the assessment. Chung ran his business from the deck of the *T. C. Walker*, a local steamboat which ran between San Francisco and Stockton. Often only one step ahead of the tax collector, who frequently boarded the ship to beat the bushes for potential taxpayers, Chung would slip receipts to his customers as he circulated around the ship, then collect both receipts and "rent" money at the end of the voyage. Chung made between three and six dollars per trip. County officials eventually got wind of Chung's system and began to mark the receipts so none but the actual owner could use the receipt. Chung was apprehended and served a jail term for his clever scheme; he later found other means of livelihood.[14]

In the mid-1880s anti-Chinese sentiment gave new impetus to collection methods. Rather than direct collection in the fields, the assessor's men sought out Chinese in Stockton's gambling halls, at the railway depots and at the docks. They hoped to catch all Chinese heading in or out of San Joaquin County. Chinese carrying large boxes or suitcases or those richly dressed were prime candidates. If a Chinese was unable to show a tax receipt upon request, the assessor collected on the spot and imposed the extra dollar late payment. If a Chinese refused to pay, he was hauled to jail and given a choice of serving time or paying a fine, and even then if he chose jail he had to pay the poll tax upon release. Visiting Chinese who stopped in Stockton merely en route to other locations often found themselves paying the poll tax which, under these circumstances, substituted as a transit fee for non-resident Chinese. Gamblers resented the tax collector peering over their shoulders when lady luck was beckoning. But, if the gamblers refused to pay, the collector threatened to close down the gambling hall.[15]

Tax evaders were fined thirty dollars or fifteen days in jail while the use of another's poll receipt brought a severe fine of thirty dollars or fifteen days on the chain gang.[16]

A random survey of the assessor's poll tax rolls indicates the largest number of Chinese who paid the tax worked in Union and ONeal townships, coinciding with census data of large work units in these areas. Elkhorn, Elliott and Liberty townships were other substantial collection points. The 1886 county tax records showed taxes collected only in Stockton and the amount collected totaled more than the number of individuals listed. This strongly suggests that many Chinese were charged the delinquent fee and the tax collectors received substantial commissions for their efforts.[17]

INVOLUNTARY CONTRIBUTIONS

License fees and poll taxes were but two ways Chinese aided the local coffers. Payment of fines for completely discriminatory ordinance violations passed by bigoted civic leaders to restrict the Chinese and their way of living also increased community funds at the expense of the Chinese. Under the guise of health and fire safety protection, local police, fire and health officials issued citations, made arrests and jailed Chinese for work-related infractions, their housing conditions and recreational activities. Despite the quiet lives they tried to live and the low profiles they tried to keep, Chinese frequently found themselves violating one ordinance or another. For instance, they were fined five dollars or ten days in jail for violating fire ordinances such as cooking without a kitchen range or cooking in a room without proper ventilation. In 1885, at the close of his November court, Police Judge Nathaniel Milner turned over ninety dollars collected from the Chinese for violation of this one ordinance alone. The money placed in the city treasury was earmarked for the fire department's charitable fund. Actually, the white property owners should have been cited for failing to provide adequate facilities for their Chinese tenants.[18]

During the nineteenth century only a small number of property owners were willing to rent to Chinese in San Joaquin County. Transient Chinese who quartered in Stockton during winter and in periods of unemployment felt the housing shortage and took whatever sleeping accommodations they

In the Justice Court of the City of Stockton,
STATE OF CALIFORNIA.

The People of the State of California

_vs_

Ah Chung

FOR THE CRIME OF

Transporting garbage

STATE OF CALIFORNIA,
COUNTY OF SAN JOAQUIN } ss.

I hereby certify that **Lee Yuen** *was in attendance before this Court as a* **Chinese** *interpreter in the above entitled criminal action on the* **96th** *day of* **Feb** *19 02 on a subpœna duly issued out of this Court in said action: and for said services the Court orders that he be allowed the sum of* **$1.50** *Dollars, to be paid by the* **City of Stockton**

Dated Stockton, **Feb 96th** *1902*

W M Washington
Justice of the Peace of the City of Stockton.

This authorization to pay Lee Yuen for interpretation services suggests the Chinese were arrested and tried for a variety of occupation-related offenses.

could find. When possible, clan members and relatives made room for their visiting kin. Chinese hotel managers also rented bunk beds by the hour, and two to four in a room was considered common. Compaction in Chinatown during special holidays became so severe that gaming tables and opium bunks were converted into sleeping spaces. The lack of bed spaces became a Catch-22 problem for the Chinese as well as the fire and health officials.

In an attempt to remedy the situation, a law was passed regulating the number of persons in a sleeping area. This statute, initially copied from a San Francisco ordinance, required a minimum of 500 cubic feet of air per person.[19]

Occasionally police raids roused men from their sleep and hauled them before the judge for violating this law. The magistrate invariably handed down the sentence of ten dollars or ten days. These bedroom raids became extremely popular in many cities. In neighboring Sacramento, the police chief there, at one point, had to call a halt to his sweeping campaign to nab air ordinance violators. It seemd the Sacramento jail was more crowded than the Chinese tenements, and the police chief stood in violation of the ordinance.[20]

Stockton Chinese arrested for this infraction generally paid the fine without protest. In one case, however, four Chinese fell victim to a midnight raid and contested the arrest. They believed their sleeping room measured seventeen feet by eleven feet and thus contained an adequate volume of air. These men hired Deputy County Surveyor Georg A. Atherton to measure the room's air capacity; he found it to be 3,000 cubic feet, and so swore in court. Police officers who had made the arrest claimed the room was much smaller and concluded the Chinese must have removed a subceiling to enlarge the room. The explanation apparently seemed reasonable to the judge, who found the Chinese guilty.[21]

Paying fines for work-related infractions became an accepted condition for the Chinese, particularly when Mother Nature and one's occupation became incompatible. For instance, in the fall and winter months the fog crept into the San Joaquin Valley and lingered for months on end. Chinese laundrymen, accustomed to meeting deadlines, found the damp, overcast weather a hindrance to their business and some laundries took to burning coal in tin cans inside the shops to dry the clothes, despite ordinances prohibiting such fire hazards. The fine for this violation was ten dollars or ten days. Paying the fines cut into the overall profit, but it was clearly better than losing one's customers, as one would if in jail.[22]

Also cutting into profits were the two-dollar fines associated with violation of Stockton's blue law prohibiting peddling on Sunday. Rag-pickers and scavengers also were fined two dollars when caught transporting garbage and cast-off garments. The same individuals were caught and fined for the same violations time and time again, but found it more expedient in the long run to pay the fines than to halt work. Only threat of a jail term caused some Chinese to give thought to lying low for a while.[23]

As restrictive as these occupation-oriented ordinances appear, they were more reasonable than the laws enacted against Chinese recreational activities. For many Chinese in a predominantly male society, living a frugal, stringent lifestyle, gambling, opium smoking and the enjoyment of prostitutes were the only social and psychological outlets available. While gambling and prostitution have always been with us, the tightly-corsetted thinking of Victorian white society saw Chinese pursuit of these vices as hedonistic. Curiously enough, the laws pertaining to prostitution, opium and gambling were so technically written the Chinese and their defense attorneys became familiar with all the loopholes.

Of the three vices, prostitution received the least attention from local authorities. Stockton's bordello area was centered in the Washington Street Chinatown; its buildings were owned by prominent members of the community. Even though there were infrequent arrests, ordinances governing this vice mandated that prostitutes be fined twenty dollar, landlords renting rooms to prostitutes seventy-five dollars, and owners and managers of bordellos three hundred and sixty dollars.

At the height of the anti-Chinese movement in Stockton, *Weekly Mail* editor E. L. Colnon suggested an ordinance to remove all houses of ill-repute as a way to abate the Chinese from Washington Street. His rationale was that gambling halls and opium dens also would depart. Less than two weeks following this suggestion, Stockton witnessed the first and only arrest of a Chinese prostitute. Her name was Ah Toy and she lived in a semi-respectable part of town on the east side of El Dorado between Market and Washington. The report claimed she attempted to bribe the police. She may well have been successful, for there is no further reports of Ah Toy in later newspapers.[24]

Colnon's ordinance was never written, let alone passed, possibly because some leading activists of the anti-Chinese campaign were also handily collecting rent from the prostitutes. One such landlord was J. A. Morrissey, who also served as a delegate from San Joaquin County to the 1886 Anti-Chinese Convention in Sacramento.[25]

Only one arrest and conviction of a male Chinese brothel owner has been found. In March 1910 a jury found the gentleman guilty of running a bordello. Because the owner was blind, the judge thought he would apply judicial mercy by giving the defendant the choice of paying a $360 fine or serving 180 days in the county jail. The accused chose jail; he reasoned his business could function without him, so why pay out good money unnecessarily.[26]

Opium provided another major bone of contention between the Chinese and the local constabulary. Its importation was not illegal until 1908. Duty was one dollar per pound on crude opium and ten dollars per pound for prepared opium. Under the U.S. Treasury jurisdiction, the customs collector in San Francisco collected the tax when the narcotic entered the country. To circumvent paying the higher import duty the Chinese generally shipped the narcotic in its crude form and had it cut and prepared locally with the final product's quality equalling the imported merchandise.[27]

Authorities knew opium was a mild sedative used by the Chinese for both medicinal purposes and relaxation. However, the campaign against smoking opium began when police found evidence of use not only by Chinese but by the general population as well, including women and children. During several raids, police found white men and women, Mexican youths and blacks indulging in the narcotic, and more importantly, the sites raided were city-wide, not just in Chinatown.

In one raid, Mexican youths were discovered smoking opium on West Washington Street, at the westernmost city limits. In a raid on a Market Street location, police found Frances Floyd, a black woman, operating a house where opium was offered. Floyd was not smoking the drug herself, but a white man was found stretched out on a bunk in a euphoric state. The most frequent raids were made during the anti-Chinese period. However, the local sheriff made occasional forays into Holt Station (just west of

Completed in 1893, the old jail on Channel and San Joaquin streets, dubbed "Cunningham Castle," at one time had separate facilities for Chinese prisoners. They were housed in one section of the basement where the local sheriff provided them with a gas stove so they could prepare their own Chinese meals.

Stockton) as late as 1912 in quest of opium smokers.[28]

The fine assessed an offender depended on where the person was arrested. If one were nabbed on the outskirts of town or south of the Mormon Slough (considered removed from the public areas of town), the fine was the usual ten dollars or ten days. But if one were arrested downtown, the fine escalated sharply to twenty dollars or twenty-five days in jail for the first offense, and twenty to twenty-five dollars for the second and subsequent convictions, without the alternate jail term choice. Offenders were fined equally, white, Chinese, or others. Poorer Chinese often opted for jail since they could not well afford the fine, but the courts learned incarceration did not necessarily prevent subsequent arrests for opium smoking. In fact, some Chinese looked forward to the few days' rest in jail, and for such repeat offenders the judge soon learned to mete out twelve days on the chain gang.[29]

Gambling in one form or another occurred in Stockton's Chinatown from the 1860s to the 1940s. Because of numerous defense installations in and about Stockton, the U.S. armed forces' concern about personnal demoralization forced the gambling industry to close during World War II. Yet during its heyday, Stockton's reputation for this pastime was known literally from sea to shining sea, and many of the Guangdong villages were familiar with the town's reputation. But there are two ways of looking at everything—the local Chinese considered gambling an industry, not a vice. Gambling establishments provided a livelihood for owners, dealers and other personnel, as well as an excellent income-generating source for the city treasury. Relationships between Stockton's city fathers, police headquarters and Chinese gamblers were as colorful as they were complex, and could fill a chapter by themselves. When sufficient complaints were filed or when a zealous newspaper felt inspired to clean up Chinatown, the local law enforcement agency, at least temporarily, made arrests and closed down gambling halls.

City officials found it particularly difficult to suppress local citizens' zest for lottery games, and the twice-a-day drawings attracted both Chinese and whites. However, city leaders became concerned when housewives and young boys began to show interest in this game of chance. Restaurants sold tickets under the counter and women bought them from enterprising peddlers or lottery runners fairly regularly; needless to say, husbands often resented their wives' use of household funds to indulge in the sport.[30]

The lottery companies of Stockton's Chinatown were so successful that individuals in the white and Mexican communities sponsored their own games, patterned after the Chinese ones. During one clean-up campaign in 1899, Julius Cohn and Will Goodfriend were arrested for selling "Little Louisiana" and Mexican lottery tickets. Their arrest occurred immediately following the incarceration of two Chinese, Ah Chuck and Ah King, but while the two whites were released on their own recognizance, the Chinese had to post $100 bail each. Attorney William B. Nutter, however, was able to obtain an acquittal for the Chinese. Those with less luck learned a lottery conviction resulted in a seventy-five-dollar fine.[31]

Raids on gambling halls were not limited to Stockton; every community in the county had its own gambling ordinances. County Sheriff Thomas Cunningham, although basically sympathetic to the Chinese, instigated

A bill to the county from Dr. George A. Shurtleff in 1863 certifying the mental state of two Chinese whom the courts or police thought were demented.

some raids, even on remote farmhouses where he knew the Chinese were running fan tan games. He made numerous arrests in the Lodi and Lockeford area during his three decades in office.[32]

Bail for employees and patrons of gambling houses was high: $500 for dealers and $100 for visitors. While this seems an excessive amount, the gambling establishments usually made bail for employees and, as a gesture of goodwill, for the patrons as well. When convicted, employees were fined $75 to $200 for the first offense and $500 for subsequent arrests. Customers arrested for the first time paid a far lesser amount, $20 or ten days in jail; any subsequent arrest increased the fine to $100. It was not uncommon for habitual gamblers to give police a different name for each arrest, in the hope they would go unrecognized as prior offenders and thus minimize the fine. Although the fines were fairly stiff, the judges did take the offender's circumstances into account. Joseph La Rose Phelps, the *Stockton Independent* editor and quite an anti-Chinese fanatic, once accused Police Judge Milner of being too lenient when the judge released two Chinese from a group of seven arrested for gambling violations. However, Judge Milner merely felt the two he released were too old to serve jail terms and too indigent to pay the fine, and simply exercised judicial discretion.[33]

OTHER PEOPLE'S MEAL TICKET

While the taxes, fees and fines the Chinese paid went toward the benefit of the entire community, it should be noted that other members of the community also profited from the fiscal misfortunes that befell the Chinese. For instance, during the early years in Stockton, policemen arresting Chinese for civic violations were paid a bounty of two or two and a half dollars for each arrest—in 1855 arresting five Chinese earned a good day's wages. This practice was essentially head-hunting and placed the Chinese in a merciless position. They became the law enforcers' meal tickets. Even when the police finally received a monthly salary of seventy-five dollars in the 1880s, the pressure against Chinese arrest did not ease. Politically astute law enforcement officials realized wholesale arrest of Chinese was a positive image-enhancer, particularly during times of extreme anti-Chinese sentiment.

Coroners and medical examiners collected directly from the county treasury each time they attended a Chinese. George A. Shurtleff, M.D. (former mayor of Stockton, county sheriff and superintendent of the state insane asylum) charged five dollars each time he examined and certified a Chinese to be insane. Other doctors responding to medical emergencies among the Chinese were paid by the county when the Chinese patient could not pay. For instance, on April 9, 1863, both Dr. John Rathbone and Dr. William Belville responded to a fracas between two Chinese men over a woman. Dr. Rathbone submitted a bill for five dollars to the county for "watching one day and night with one Ah Sec stabbed by Thomas Thome alias Gee Ho." Dr. Belville's bill for forty dollars covered surgery he performed on the woman, who was stabbed during the dispute.[34]

Chinese interpreters also made a good living from their countrymen's troubles. To qualify as a court interpreter, a command of the English language and fluency in both Heungshan and Sze Yup dialects was necessary; few Chinese could qualify for the position. Yet while the pay was low, only three dollars a day, the position was extremely prestigious. Those who became court interpreters had great influence in the Chinese community, for they served as the major link between the Chinese, the whites and the white judicial system. Among the Chinese were two who served with distinction for many years.

The first, Dr. John Ho, was a Heungshan herbalist whose office was located in the joss temple half a block from the courthouse. He was followed by Lee Yuen, a Toishan merchant whose business was located on Washington Street. Other Chinese also held interpreter positions but were dismissed when it was discovered they either colored the interpretation to the benefit of their own countrymen or succumbed to bribery.

INCIDENTS OF ASSAULTS

The Chinese learned to be wary not only of police officials looking over their shoulders, but from attacks by ruffians as well. While Stockton's Chinese were never physically chased out of town or experienced concerted mob assaults as in other California communities, incidents of harassment and individual attacks did occur. Easily identifiable by both features and dress, the Chinese were also victimized by negative publicity in which Chineseness was often equated as weakness. Thus, intolerant, ignorant, insensitive members of the larger community in search of cheap entertainment fell upon unsuspecting Chinese individuals.

In such assaults the Chinese were often victims of surprise attacks. For example, a Chinese walking near the Pacific Tannery on Fremont Street one evening was assaulted and thrown over the bridge into the slough. "When he was rescued he was more scared than hurt," stated the *Evening Herald*, and was unfortunately unable to identify his assailants because of darkness.[35]

In another incident, a Chinese rowing his boat across Mormon Slough was shot in the back. Despite his injury, he was able to help identify his two attackers, Patrick Cassidy and William Lonnigan. The young men claimed they had only been shooting blackbirds in the slough, but the police judge apparently doubted their story, for each was fined $1,000.[36]

While that fine was rather steep, another incident suggests that fines for such crimes varied. Two Chinese peddlers riding in their vegetable wagon down Center Street were stoned by a couple of boys in their teens. The judge fined these boys only twenty dollars or twenty days in jail, a small judgment considering one of the peddlers was severely injured.[37]

Law enforcement officers, while accustomed to arresting Chinese for various infractions, also expended energy apprehending people who attacked the Chinese, for assault was one crime not tolerated in San Joaquin County. For instance, one April day in 1885, following an attack on two Chinese pedestrians in Lodi, the local constable gathered a citizens' posse and chased the three young white offenders across the county line. One was caught in Elk Grove, Sacramento County, and at his trial was found guilty and sentenced to ninety days in jail.[38]

It is important to note that these acts of violence were never condoned. Moreover, when the local newspapers reported these incidents the articles invariably included a public admonishment such as in the case of the Chinese thrown over the bridge:

> It is about time that something should be done to prevent attacks upon the unprotected and unoffensive Chinese by parties who take advantage of every opportunity they observe to commit some outrage upon this class of human beings.[39]

DOMESTIC BONDING

To depict the Chinese merely as victims of history and society would be to commit a great disservice to these people who, without knowledge of language and customs, were able to adjust to life in an alien land and eventually command respect from many citizens. Those Chinese who adapted to the white men's ways—and they were numerous—did so not to infiltrate community dynamics, but rather to ease their own adjustment into the larger community. Chinese cooks and servants in white households paid close attention to the finer points of white lifestyle. They eagerly noted certain routines, food preferences, habits, holiday customs, familial relationships and other cultural practices. Even though some may have thought they knew all there was to know, the nuances and interpretations of western laws and regulations escaped some of these men from the Guandong area.

For example, few Chinese clearly understood the concepts of private property and public property. To them public properties such as roads, bridges and parks were accessible for everyone's use. Thus, with the best of intentions, a group of servants working in homes near the center of Stockton, decided to give their employers' carpets a good spring cleaning one day in May 1886. To accomplish this, they took the rugs to the pedestrian bridge on Hunter and Fremont and there hung them over the bridge railing and proceeded to beat them thoroughly. Irate passersby soon objected to the pollution and commotion in the area and insisted these servants be arrested for creating a public nuisance. While they were not arrested, the Chinese did receive a thorough admonishment. Most, however, could not understand what they had done wrong.[40]

In time the reputation of the Chinese as outstanding cooks and domestics outstripped that of other nationalities. And while their responsibilities in a normal household appeared nearly endless, so too did their employers' praise. A letter to the editor of a local newspaper in 1876 best describes the value of Chinese help. The writer, who signed herself simply "Martha," related her circumstances and experiences in employing servants. Martha, her husband and two young sons arrived in California in 1850 and became farmers in San Joaquin County. In 1854, when her husband became disabled, she sought household help while she assumed control of the farm responsibilities. Martha searched for appropriate servants from as far away as Stockton and San Francisco and offered a salary of as much as fifty dollars a month, including room and board. Her first servant was a white widow who was heavy on her feet and light with her fingers, but the main objection to the widow was that she just could not cook. The widow was followed by a Paiute woman, then by an Irish woman with an alcoholic husband. And finally, in 1866, Martha hired her first Chinese and felt the household burden lifted from her shoulders:

> What a blessing he was; he made bread, coffee, broiled steaks with no fuss nor noise. [He] stayed nearly a year and left for higher wages. Since then I have hired strictly Chinese and seldom one I could not trust. The one I now have has been here nearly two years, he is about eighteen and is a good plain cook, washer, ironer . . . he churns, takes care of the pigs

The Wee[...]

ndependent.

APRIL 15. 1876.   NO 6[...]

A WOMAN'S PLEA FOR CHINESE LABOR.

Eds. Independent: The time seems to have come when one can speak or write a few words in favor of Chinese labor without the risk of being black-boarded, blackguarded, and, it might have been, mobbed, and, with no claim upon the attention of your readers; except that I have been a housekeeper since 1829, in California since 1850, I propose to tell some of my trials in the hiring of domestic or house servants, going only as far back, however, as 1854, when I hired my first house servant on my farm. My family consisted of myself and husband (an invalid), two boys, one 10, the other 14 years of age, and three men employed on the farm. For all these I had to cook, to wash for my own family, churn, prepare butter for market, with the many other employments that fall to the lot of the farmer's wife, besides supervising all the out-door work. I sought for help in vain, in Stockton and in San Francisco, offering as high as $50 per month, for I found myself wholly unable to accomplish all I had to do. One of the men found a recent arrival willing to come for that price, and I hired her. She was [...]

NEW GOOD[...]

LARGEST AS[...]

H. Marks, Mer[...] Street, has just r[...] with the largest ment of goods in to Stockton. Ger[...] ionable suits fro[...] reasonable terms.

FROM REV. SYL[...] FORMERLY F[...] TI[...]

Dear Sir—It [...] you to be inform[...] of the "Peruvia[...] daughter was b[...] last Spring, and continued very distressed her[...] the same debili[...] 1st of September[...] taking the Syr[...] proved, and sh[...] rivacity; and [...] she is restored[...] led, she appe[...] she has for [...] opinion that i[...] tained in the "[...] to her case, an[...] me[...]

"THE HEATHEN CHINEE"

A farmer writes to the Chronicle as follows:

First Fact—The Chinese are doing a great quantity of work in this State.

Second Fact—If they did not do it, it would not be done W—, in Tuesday's Chronicle, says: "Let the fruit men give the boys a chance." We have tried it. At San Jose the owners of the fruit-dry ing factory determined to give the work of preparing fruit to the boys. The first day a boy threw a peach pit at another boy; that boy threw one back; then all the boys threw at each other, and they kept it up until they were all sent away, and the heathens were taken to fill the place. It is an old saying that "A boy is a boy, two boys are half a boy, and three boys no boy at all." It is true. No man can run a business with the boys of California.

It is said that wages are reduced by the Chinamen. This is a grand mistake. We pay higher wages than are paid in any other State in the Union. The fact that a great deal of cheap labor is secured, enables farmers and others to pay white men more than they could do otherwise. As well say that horses do a great deal of work simp[...] boarding [...]

Black[...] the black[...] sively in [...] grower, a[...] zee, which [...] ber, bring[...] other tim[...] States. T[...] Indiana, S[...] and over a[...] Southweste[...] in Ohio at[...] ced out by[...] furniture m[...] the tempera[...] Southwest[...] nut for th[...] great wealt[...] little furnit[...] It was cons[...] too light. [...] fencing, an[...] in the West[...] in a post an[...] walnut. Gr[...] for furniture wood was [...] coloring, and[...] preferred to [...] of black wal[...] tree [...]

"A Woman's Plea for Chinese Labor" and "The Heathen Chinese" are two of several articles from local white employers defending their Chinese help in the late 1870s when California's anti-Chinese leaders prepared themselves for the Second Constitutional Convention which enacted many anti-Chinese measures in the new constitution.

and poultry, herds stock, harnesses the horse and buggy, handy with carpentry tools and paint brush . . . in fact very quick to learn anything. He can kill and dress a hog and take care of the meat and lard as any professional butcher. He is honest, and I give him money to take care of the household and I pay him twenty dollars a month . . . Will anyone tell me how I can replace him and how except by one of his countrymen?[41]

To charges that the Chinese drained the local economy, Martha responded:

One of the objections raised against them [the Chinese] is that they send their money to China. I know that this boy buys boots, hats, shirts, socks, etc. in Stockton . . . the money I pay him comes back to me in part. I sell my wheat to Mr. Sperry; he grinds it into flour for shipment to China and the money for which it is sold comes back to purchase my next crop . . . I find my China boy honest and with principles that would do credit to a Christian.

Although wages paid Chinese domestics were often less than those paid servants of other nationalities, their responsibilities frequently exceeded those of their predecessors. Pictures of cooks and servants in family albums bear witness to the bonding that developed between these Chinese and the families they served. One such album now in the archives of Stockton's Haggin Museum belonged to the family of George West, a local viticulturist whose estate and vineyard, El Pinal, lay along West Lane just south of the Calaveras River. Their Chinese cook's likeness, framed for posterity in an oval mounting, was prominently displayed among pictures of family members.

Local historian Glenn Kennedy recalled with affection the family cook of his youth:

Among the front pages were two pictures of a Chinese. In one he wore sort of a black pilgrim-type hat, typical of Chinese of that day, with a folding fan in his held up right hand, a white jacket coat, dark trousers, and a big broad smile. In the other picture he was wearing his light-colored trousers, his shirt sleeve undershirt, his long white apron, with his queue bound around his head. Yes, he was the family cook. No, not a blood relative, but he did belong in that album, for he was to us like a part of the family.[42]

The Asa Clark family provided perhaps the most lasting tribute ever given to a Chinese cook. Research shows Clark first hired Chinese cooks sometime during the 1880s, and the 1900 census listed a thirty-year-old Chinese, Tom Wah Att, working as the family cook at the time Dr. Clark was superintendent of the Stockton Insane Asylum. Tom moved with the family into the Charter Way Pacific Sanitorium when the doctor acquired that institution. Dr. Clark passed away in 1912, his wife, Mary, in 1915 and

The George West family's cook attended to the family's meals as well as to those of the ranch hands who worked at the Wests' El Pinal vineyards.

Tom Wah Att in 1920. Instead of letting the Chinese community handle the arrangements whereby Tom's remains would be buried in the Chinese section of the Rural Cemetery, the Clark children ordered Tom cremated and placed his ashes in the Clark family plot. In common with so many of his countrymen, Tom never married and the Clarks became his only family. Today a headstone similar to those of other family members marks his grave. However, the marker reads W Y A T T, instead of Wah Att, for that was the name the family came to call him. The epitaph on the line below reflects the respect they accorded their long-time cook, reading simply, "A Friend."[43]

Truly, the loyalty and concern domestics felt for their charge were genuine feelings; their interests in their families served as avenues to express what otherwise would have been pent-up emotions of loneliness for their own loved ones in the homeland. And in the case of Tom Wah Att, his love for the Clark family was returned in kind.

Tom Wah Att, nicknamed Wyatt, was a servant-cook for the Asa Clark family. Upon his death in 1920 the Clark family chose to bury him in the family plot. The simple epitaph, "A friend," speaks of the deep loving relationship between the cook and the family he grew to love.

A discussion of white and Chinese relationships cannot be complete without the mention of influential leaders in the community whose efforts made life more tolerable than it otherwise would have been for the Chinese. Heading this list would be Captain Charles M. Weber, founder of Stockton, and County Sheriff Thomas Cunningham. Through Weber's generosity, the Chinese settlement south of Mormon Slough proved a safe haven for almost forty years. From time to time Weber himself employed Chinese in his many business endeavors. At Weber's death in 1881, 200 Chinese mourners took part in his funeral procession, and their high visibility left no doubt that they deeply respected the good captain.[44]

For almost thirty years, from 1871 to 1899, Thomas Cunningham served as county sheriff and keeper of the jail located at San Joaquin and Channel

In the 1880s, in spite of warnings from anti-Chinese agitators, San Joaquin County Sheriff Thomas Cunningham retained two Chinese in his employ: a male servant to help him raise his children and a cook to interpret and cook for the Chinese prisoners in the county jail.

streets. Cunningham was extremely popular in the county, even among the prisoners. Widowed early, Cunningham used a Chinese to care for his three young children. Through the cook's influence, Cunningham developed an awareness of Chinese habits and lifestyle, and during his administration he routinely housed Chinese prisoners in a separate section of the jail with a special Chinese cook to act as their interpreter as well as to provide for their dietary needs. The cook earned extra money by running errands for these prisoners and even purchased brandy or gin for those with a few dollars to spare.[45]

Some white businessmen with Chinese customers hired a Chinese in order to further their business interest with these special clients. For instance, D. C. Oullahan, an Irish liquor distributor, made it a policy always to employ at least one Chinese.

Frank Hatch, another white employer, demonstrated an exceptional understanding of the Chinese way of life. Hatch, a blacksmith, migrated to California in 1860 and moved to Stockton in 1873. When he set up his shop, he hired a Chinese, Ah Kay, as an assistant, not realizing Ah Kay had a violent temper. Periodically Ah Kay was arrested for creating disturbances in gambling houses when luck was not going his way. In one instance in 1885, Ah Kay, angered by a store proprietor, seized a number of china plates and threw them at a crowd which had gathered to watch the spectacle. He was arrested and brought before the judge, and his employer appeared in his behalf for the umpteenth time and once again pleaded for leniency, stating Ah Kay was by nature impulsive and hot-tempered. Hatch paid the fine, Ah Kay received a dressing-down from the judge, and the pair headed home together—until the next time.[46]

In many relationships involving Chinese and white, human feelings and personal experiences bridged the cultural differences between them. And a

Shading his face with a fan, Henry, the family cook, patiently waits for his picture to be taken by Glenn Kennedy, c.1900.

surprisingly high number of relationships did exist based on the following census data:

EMPLOYERS WHO HIRED CHINESE AS COOKS, SERVANTS AND RANCHHANDS:

Townships	1870	CENSUS YEARS 1880	1900
Castoria	13	13	6
Dent	15	16	4
Douglas	20	25	6
Elkhorn	17	25	6
Elliott	9	16	2
Liberty	17	10	0
Tulare	4	12	13
Union	4	16	21
ONeal	17	37	10
Stockton	51	42	25
TOTAL	167	212	89

In 1870 the number of whites who hired Chinese in this county numbered 167 and by 1880 had increased to 212. While the number of white employers dropped in 1900 to 89, this figure reflects the effects of the exclusion laws and the anti-Chinese pressure of the mid-1880s rather than dissatisfaction with their Chinese help.

In 1885-86, during the height of the anti-Chinese campaign, Chinese served as domestics in the households of a striking list of leading citizens who were capitalists, farmers, bankers, educators, physicians, hotel keepers, ministers, lawyers, judges and many others of varied occupation and class. The list reads like a Who's Who in San Joaquin County, and includes Benjamin Bours, Dr. Dean Locke, and Captain William Moss, among others.[47]

CONCLUSION

The Chinese was by no means docile or passive, nor was his life among the whites simple. He used his instinct to survive, and despite the accusation that he was clever and wily, many whites learned that the Chinese was basically open and friendly when given the opportunity. He was loyal to his employer and generous to other whites he knew. Historical records reflect that close white/Chinese relationships were numerous, and the effects of these relationships touched upon the well-being of all Chinese in the community. Even during the worst years of turmoil and bigotry, it seemed the God of Fortune smiled on the Chinese as these relationships were challenged—and strengthened—through the decades.

CHAPTER FOUR ENDNOTES

1. *Stockton Weekly Mail*, March 31, 1885.

2. *Stockton Weekly Mail*, August 22, 1885.

3. *Stockton Weekly Mail*, January 26, 1885; *Stockton Evening Mail*, January 21, 1893, November 21, 1899.

4. *Stockton Daily Independent*, September 10, 1885.

5. *Stockton Daily Independent*, September 10, 11 and 25, 1885.

6. *Stockton Daily Independent*, March 3, 1874.

7. *Stockton Daily Evening Herald*, September 13, 1878.

8. *Stockton Daily Evening Herald*, August 14, 15 and 17, 1878.

9. *Stockton Weekly Mail*, August 15, 1885.

10. *Stockton Weekly Mail*, February 6, 1892.

11. *Stockton Daily Independent*, February 4 and 5, 1886.

12. *Stockton Weekly Mail*, February 16, 1893.

13. F. T. Gilbert, *History of San Joaquin County, California With Illustrations Descriptive of Its Scenery* (Oakland, 1879), p. 27. *Stockton Daily Independent*, August 16, 1893.

14. *Stockton Weekly Mail*, June 12, 1886.

15. *Stockton Daily Independent*, March 2, 1886. *Stockton Weekly Mail*, March 19, 1892.

16. *Stockton Daily Independent*, April 11, 1886.

17. San Joaquin County Assessor Poll Tax Roll 1874-1875, 1878-1879, 1880, 1884, and 1886, San Joaquin County Historical Museum. *Stockton Daily Independent*, August 16, 1893. In the tax ledgers, payments from the Chinese were separated from the rest of the roll. Their names, collectors' names and the amount received appeared in the back section of the ledger. Reason for the different accounting system has not been ascertained.

18. *Stockton Weekly Mail*, November 21, 1885; December 19, 1885.

19. In a contemporary house a nine-foot by twelve-foot bedroom with an eight-foot ceiling contains 864 cubic feet of air; however, older buildings and homes with the same floor dimension measured over 1,000 cubic feet because the ceilings were usually ten feet or higher. A common practice of the time was to suspend an artificial ceiling below the original height in winter to conserve on heat, and during summer the room reverted to the original height to make sleeping more comfortable on warm evenings.

20. *Stockton Daily Independent*, January 20, 1886.

21. *Stockton Weekly Mail*, December 19 and 26, 1885.

22. *Stockton Weekly Mail*, November 19 and 21, 1885.

23. *Stockton Weekly Mail*, August 22, 1885. *Stockton Daily Independent*, April 11, 1886.

24. *Stockton Weekly Mail*, October 10 and 31, 1885.

25. *Stockton Daily Independent*, October 15, 1885. J. A. Morrissey's relationship with the Chinese remained rather curious; in 1886 his public position was anti-Chinese; however, at the same time he was renting his property to Chinese.

26. *Stockton Daily Independent*, March 3 and 11, 1910.

27. *Stockton Daily Independent*, April 6, 1885; July 9, 1912.

28. *Stockton Daily Evening Herald*, August 14, 1878. *Stockton Daily Independent*, November 13, 1885; July 9, 1912.

29. *Stockton Daily Independent*, November 19, 1885; March 18, 1886; April 23, 1886.

30. *Stockton Daily Independent*, February 29, 1908; March 14, 1908.

31. *Stockton Evening Mail*, October 21, 1899; November 10 and 21, 1899.

32. *Stockton Daily Independent*, September 25, 1885.

33. *Stockton Daily Independent*, September 21, 1885; October 8, 1885.

34. Bill submitted to San Joaquin County dated February 22, 1864 by John F. Rathbone, M.D., and bill submitted to San Joaquin County dated May 10, 1864 by William Belville, M.D., both in author's possession.

35. *Stockton Daily Evening Herald*, October 3, 1878.

36. *Stockton Daily Independent*, April 1, 1886.

37. *Stockton Daily Independent*, March 25, 1886.

38. *Stockton Daily Independent*, April 16, 1886.

39/ *Stockton Daily Evening Herald*, October 3, 1878.

40. *Stockton Weekly Mail*, May 22, 1886.

41. *Stockton Daily Independent*, October 23, 1876.

42. Glenn A. Kennedy, *It Happened in Stockton 1900-1925* (Stockton, 1967), p. 39.

43. Stockton Rural Cemetery Plot Record, Book 13.

44. Helen Kennedy Cahill, "Captain Weber and His Place in Early California History," *Pacific Historian*, Winter 1976, pp. 431-36.

45. 1880 and 1900 Census. *Stockton Daily Independent*, January 12, 1876.

46. *Stockton Weekly Mail*, August 29, 1885.

47. 1870, 1880 and 1900 Census. Among other well-known individuals within the county are: Norman Alling, William Ashley, J. P. Austin, George Barber, Senator John Beecher, Louis Bixler, Thomas Buck, Joseph Budd, Thomas Clements, Rev. John Coyle, William DeVries, J. K. Doaks, Aldin Hammond, William Fairchild, Elias Hildreth, D. Kettleman, Victor Jahant, Isaac Leffler, Cyrus Moreing, Sidney Newell, Alfred Parker, William Nutter, A. V. R. Patterson, J. D. Peters, Samuel Ray, Jacob and Roswell Sargent, Wandon Shippee, Charles Sperry, Joseph Swain, John Thompson, James Welch, George West and Andrew Wolf.

The Years of Turmoil

5

In the 1850s the goldseekers' inability to cope with loneliness, competition, and the unfamiliarity they found in faces, cultures and conditions in the Mother Lode triggered many to lash out against their own miseries. While crying to heaven in frustration, they found an earthly scapegoat in the Chinese residents of the mining camps and foothill towns and soon vented their anger upon them. This xenophobic emotion, accompanied by physical manifestations, found vicious outlet in many northern California towns including Shasta, Yreka, Truckee, Dutch Flat, Bodie, Oroville and Placerville.

The violence and turmoil continued well into the 1890s with anti-Chinese meetings, riots and actual pogroms against Chinese residents. Even in the Central Valley, where farming provided an atmosphere of plenty, Chinese in Winters, Chico, Sacramento, Modesto, Merced and other towns in the San Joaquin Valley also felt the sting of the white man's anger.

Many factors combined to create this atmosphere of racial tension. In enumerating them, most historians agree that economic strife associated with the depression years encouraged the growth of trade unionism. In addition, the growing popularity of Social Darwinism, with its inherent ethnocentrism, also contributed to the violence against the Chinese.

Although the anti-Chinese movement was less traumatic here, San Joaquin County was not exempt from its turbulence. For more than thirty years Stockton's residents had been preoccupied with their own lifestyles and their own businesses. Yet when the dark clouds of sinophobia began to darken the skies of the valley these same citizens nearly forgot it was the Chinese who had contributed in great part to the good lives they enjoyed.

THE ECONOMIC PICTURE

Stockton's history reveals a half century of sustained growth. From a port city supplying gold miners in the Southern Mines, Stockton by 1854 had become the fourth largest town in California. During the city's first decade of development, it could look to a courthouse building, the first state insane asylum, streets, parks, public buildings and numerous schools as milestones.

In the 1860s growth became synonymous with civic improvement. An 1867 news article noted with pride that Stockton possessed ten schools, fourteen churches and three volunteer fire companies. One hundred fifty thousand dollars had been expended on public works such as graveling and grading city streets, and the estimated cost of the two new turnpikes leading from town was another $50,000. The local freight-forwarding business, so vital to the foothill and valley economy, thrived. In 1867 the Stockton harbormaster's annual log showed 619 steamers and 447 sailing vessels entering Stockton's port and carrying a total of 147,000 tons of freight and passengers. Copper from the mines just east of Stockton, grain and cord wood represented the bulk of the outgoing freight. As smaller towns and hamlets began to grow in the various townships they, too, showed signs of permanence. By the end of the decade sixty-eight county schools served the farming communities and more than four thousand men were listed in the Great Register as eligible voters.[1]

In the 1870s sounds of steel rails being spiked to wooden ties filled the air in many parts of the county as railroad lines connected remote communities to the Stockton hub. Wastelands and swamplands became agricultural bonanzas. Stockton catapulted into prominence as a city of farm implement manufacturers. In 1856 the Matteson Company began making farm plows at its plant on Main and Jose Jesus (Grant) streets. Local banks and investors with a hand on the pulse of progress gambled wisely with investments in innovative farm equipment patents, thereby helping revolutionize the agricultural industry. By the end of the 1870s six major implement manufacturing companies were rolling out reapers, harvesters, and gang plows. Houser, Haines and Knight Company, Pacific Agriculture Works, the H. C. Shaw Company, and the Stockton Combined Harvester and Agricultural Works preceded the Stockton Wheel Company, a johnny-come-lately formed in 1883. Today, old-timers remember the Stockton Wheel as the forerunner of the Holt Manufacturing Company (now the Holt Caterpillar Company).

An assortment of iron works, foundries and tanneries located themselves in the Stockton community. Two other plants began production south of the Mormon Slough at Lincoln Street, in the vicinity of the Chinese fishing village; Stockton Woolen Mills opened its doors in June 1870, and the California Paper Company built its brick plant diagonally across from the woolen mill. The paper mill began operations in 1878 and two years later it was producing enough newsprint not only for local demands but for San Francisco's *Chronicle, Call, Post*, and *Bulletin*. In addition, the company produced over a million tons of wrapping paper annually. The 1870s also saw four banks and three local newspaper companies vying for the 15,000 residents' patronage.[2]

In the 1880s the county's economic growth reached an even higher pinnacle as major reclamation projects in the Delta increased available farm

In the 1880s wheat was king as California led the nation in grain production. Stockton flour mills became the wheat processing center of the state. The double-stack, stern wheeler Centennial *is seen with its load headed for San Francisco and the international market.*

acreage. During that decade California led the nation in grain production, and Stockton's flour mills gained the coveted recognition as the wheat processing center of the state. The Sperry Flour Company on the embarcadero housed the largest mill in California. Large warehouses sprouted along the Stockton waterfront, and most were filled to the rafters with sacks of grain destined for the international market.

Stockton and the county's wealth exceeded all expectations; merchants filled most local needs, manufacturing companies competed in the larger state and national markets, and the farmers and flour companies answered the demands of this country and abroad. There was an abundance of job opportunities in the multitude of industries for those with semi-skilled abilities, and the blue-collar workers had the employment market to themselves. The unskilled or common laborer, interested in short-range or day labor work, focused on the readily available jobs found in railroad construction, reclamation, public works and farm labor work.

The 1880s were milestones in the history of the Chinese in San Joaquin County in that their population peaked during this period and, as a laboring force, they had become an integral part of the county. However, their social acceptance depended on individual circumstances, specific locations in the county, types of occupations and the tenor of the anti-Chinese tensions that began to drift into the Central Valley from San Francisco and neighboring towns which were suffering from the twin devils of the anti-Coolie pantheon, high unemployment and a correspondingly high Chinese visibility.

San Joaquin County residents were mindful of the arguments against the Chinese in California and other western states. Yet many citizens were ambivalent when it came to defining their own attitudes about the Chinese. After all, without these farm workers, brickmakers, levee builders and woodcutters, the county's agricultural industry would have been set back at least a decade or two. Unlike San Francisco, which had a large contingent of unemployed working-class Irish, this county had a need for men in the field which left few without jobs. Residents of the rural communities, mostly immigrant Germans or New England Yankees, conservative and, perhaps, provincial in their thinking, were more concerned with weather conditions, harvest, and the wheat market than with labor agitation. This is not to say they were unaware of the outside world, or that they lacked sophistication; rather, the citizens of the county simply put off taking sides for or against the Chinese. As early as 1854 when A. C. Bradford suggested the washing down of the Channel-Hunter Street Chinese quarters, racists' remarks were heard sporadically throughout the community. But, for every ill-remark, there were others who touted the Chinese and their contributions.

THE PRO-CHINESE BAROMETER FALLS

Dark clouds began to gather against the Chinese in the 1870s, and in 1871 citizens of Los Angeles saw the massacre of twenty-two Chinese following a day-long riot. In 1876, 4,000 Sacramentans, mostly members of the Sacramento Order of Caucasians, an organization dedicated to excluding Chinese labor and promoting white labor, met en masse.

However, the Sacramento group was small compared to the 10,000 who gathered in San Francisco on July 23, 1877, to hear speeches on the eight-hour day and nationalization of the railroads. Speakers at this meeting incited the masses to riot against San Francisco's Chinese, and after three nights of turbulence twenty-five Chinese laundries had been destroyed and an estimated $1 million worth of damage had occurred throughout the city. Denis Kearney, a local Irish businessman and property owner who claimed to be a working man, gave impetus to the growing popularity of the Workingman's Party of California through the violent demagogy of his notorious sandlot speeches. The anti-Chinese activities of autumn 1877 included demonstrations and mob activities in Courtland, Sacramento, Rocklin, and Santa Clara and in the torching of Chico's Chinatown.

The outlook for Chinese grew increasingly worse in 1878. By January the Workingman's Party had become a major political force in California. At the 1878 Constitutional Convention in Sacramento, members of that party garnered 51 of the 152 delegate slots. Their one-third control of the convention spelled disaster for the Chinese as the IWA introduced a series of anti-Chinese resolutions into the constitution. These resolutions included restrictions on Chinese immigration, delineation of Chinese neighborhoods in towns, and prohibition of their employment in state, county, municipal and other public works facilities. Major corporations with government contracts also were enjoined from hiring Chinese. Passage of the 1879 constitution incorporating these resolutions was clearly a setback for all Chinese in California.

In San Francisco the Chinese community fortified itself for the impending carnage by the victorious, power-hungry Kearneyites. However, less than a hundred miles away in Stockton, local officials soon learned how difficult actual enforcement of the new regulations could be. For instance, in keeping with the laws of the 1879 constitution, the city adopted an ordinance against use of Chinese labor on municipal projects. Street Commissioner C. W. Brunton, after but one attempt to enforce the new law, was forced to look the other way. In compliance with the law, he halted a street construction project midway when he discovered contractor William Alonzo had employed a Chinese work crew. Alonzo explained that he hired Chinese because he could not get white labor. As a result, the project actually remained suspended until Brunton rescinded his stop order. When work was finally resumed, the same Chinese crew was on the job. Interestingly, although the city ordinance technically prohibited construction of new roads by Chinese labor, it did not prohibit the use of Chinese prisoners on road maintenance details.

In another situation, local police officer Cohen was having difficulty corralling a stray cow when a Chinese on horseback rode by and offered his services in the situation; Officer Cohen agreed to pay him and the helpful Chinese quickly herded the animal into the compound. In submitting a pay voucher for the Chinese cowboy, Cohen found that he had violated the law. The last that the newspaper article reported was that Cohen's guilt would be resolved after a "judicial determination of the principle of the constitutional law." In essence, the Cohen case drifted into the abyss of the esoteric legal void.[3]

Two less intense anti-Chinese activities occurred closer to home. On the San Joaquin River the little settlement of New York Landing (now Antioch) publicly adopted a policy of prohibiting Chinese as residents. When one Chinese stepped off the steamer after it had stopped at that burg's harbor and was still on the pier when the ship pulled away, the town's people chased him and threw both him and his possessions into the river. In Linden, seventeen miles east of Stockton, hoodlums threatened to burn down a local flour mill if the owners did not discharge their Chinese workers. Although the owners refused to be intimidated, the Chinese were, and fearing for their lives, did not return to work.[4]

EXTRA! EXTRA! READ ALL ABOUT IT

Newspapers continually published stories of local Chinese activities which frequently highlighted the foreignness or uniqueness of the Chinese lifestyle. The consecration of the two-story, brick, Heungshan Joss Temple in 1882 and a colorful Chinese wedding drew the same amount of column inches as reports of Chinese attending Christian missions or Chinese activities that connoted assimilation of white customs. During a rare snowstorm in Stockton in January 1880 a friendly snowball fight got out of hand in the downtown area, and some young men began to use passing Chinese for targets. The ruffians descended on Chinatown the following day hoping to resume their sport, but found the Chinese armed with clubs, knives and iron bars, and dealt them "blow for blow." The *Stockton Daily Evening Herald* concluded its article on the incident with the following: "The Chinese are to be commended for their conduct as this is one instance they came out ahead."[5]

It seems clear that local editors began to categorize their opinions of the Chinese. Local Chinese, particularly those with whom newspaper reporters dealt in laundries and restaurants, were considered "inoffensive" and a "credit to the community." But when editors and reporters commented on articles from other newspapers or when they wrote about the Chinese as a distinct, faceless group, they applied the label "Heathen Chinese."

Stockton had several newspapers in the 1880s. The *Stockton Daily Independent*, a staunch Republican journal controlled by Joseph La Rose Phelps, towered over its competitors in both power and popularity. Editor Edward L. Colnon's *Stockton Weekly Mail* claimed to be independent in policy, but merely vacillated as it assumed the devil's advocate role against the *Independent*. The *Daily Evening Herald* folded in 1885, and the *Stockton Democrat* existed for only six months. The *Democrat* had hoped to reach the entire Democratic populace, but its zest for action against the Chinese, its leanings toward union and socialist-labor philosophies, and, at times, its promotion of anarchist activities repulsed the general readership. Thus, a Republican newspaper and an independent newspaper greatly influenced the county's reading public, and both made it virtually impossible for any idea or plan of action by Democrats or union leaders to succeed without either paper's endorsement. The jousting between these two papers actually tempered much of the citizens' ire against the Chinese, particularly when the papers took opposing views and each pointed out the other's foolishness in both reasoning and strategy.

ENTERING THE DECADE OF THE CRUCIBLE

Until 1880 most residents of San Joaquin County saw little reason to take sides on the Chinese issue, for their own experience with these people had been positive, and they were preoccupied with agrarian interests. But by March 10, 1880, the issue began to take shape when thirty men assembled at

Pioneer Hall in Stockton. The purpose of the meeting was to "wake up the working men of Stockton" and resulted in formation of a local chapter of the Workingman's Party. These men needed an issue to unite white workers and unanimously adopted the following resolution:

> That we, the Workingmen of Stockton, pledge ourselves anew to our principles—"The Chinese Must Go," and the Constitution [of California] shall be interpreted as was intended by its framers.

During the meeting Denis Kearney's name came up time after time. Although the ringleaders of the three-day pillage and plunder in the San Francisco 1877 riot had never been identified, the Stockton workingmen strongly suspected Kearney and his followers. Refusing to be linked to any acts of brutality or destruction, Billy Little, a spokesman in the Stockton group, suggested that the local chapter's philosophy and direction be less violent and aggressive than the Kearneyites'. The Stockton group also deplored use of vigilance committees to restore peace or rectify purportedly unjust competition from the Chinese. While each man agreed that the Chinese should be compelled to leave, they decided removal of the Chinese should be by "a war of intellect and brains and not by force." In agreement with Little's position, the group agreed the courts and police should be relied on to keep the peace. Appearing more timid than cautious, the Stockton chapter of the Workingmen's Party adopted a wait-and-see position; they decided to wait on the board of health to see about condemning Chinatown. This group's hesitation to act and its willingness to defer to the courts was very much in keeping with the reluctant attitude of Stockton's general population.[6]

Death came quickly to the Stockton Workingmen's Party; internally the group lacked drive, commitment and a plan of action to keep the organization alive. Foremost, however, was the fact that the Chinese in the area were not in actual competition with the white workers. Occupational parameters had been fairly well delineated. White machinists and laborers found employment in a multitude of foundries, tanneries, flour mills and farm implement manufacturing plants. The Chinese concentrated on laundries, restaurants, domestic work, farm labor and manual work, realizing that although they were working at jobs that paid less, they were in occupations that attracted little competition. It was to Stockton's benefit that instead of an atmosphere charged with antagonism, the two races were actually in a complementary situation.

Shortly thereafter, even San Francisco's Workingmen's Party lost momentum and the Bay Area union workers saw the anti-Chinese issue carried in quick succession by the Trades Assembly, League of Deliverance, Knights of Labor, and finally by Frank Roney's Federated Trades.

In the early months of 1882, as the Exclusion Act to limit Chinese

State Supreme Court Justice David S. Terry, a notable California figure, settled in San Joaquin County in 1850. In the late 1870s and early 1880s his public image was that of an anti-Chinese leader; archival records, however, suggest otherwise.

immigration and prohibit entry of Chinese laborers gained strong support throughout the western states and its passage through Congress was assured, San Joaquin County citizens were still uncommitted about the Chinese. Much to the consternation of local politicians, continued concern for the county's economy took precedence over support of pro- or anti-Chinese factions. County Republican and Democratic parties, in the guise of a community effort, jointly sponsored a public meeting in Stockton. Their purpose was to give citizens an opportunity to express their opposition to the Chinese as well as to pick possible leaders for the local anti-Chinese campaign.

H. O. Southworth, mayor of Stockton, presided at this meeting on March 4, 1882. Thirty of the most influential men in the county, from both political parties, were officially listed as vice-presidents of the occasion, and when called upon, most spoke publicly. Judge David S. Terry, the leading Democrat, who took a back seat to none, set the tone for his party's push to support the upcoming Chinese Exclusion bill. The basic theme was repeated by ten other speakers, and the meeting ended with the rousing sounds of a brass band and unanimous adoption of a resolution drafted by Superior Court Judges A. V. R. Paterson and W. S. Buckley. The resolution stated:

1. That we regard self preservation as the first law of nature;
2. That we as good, loyal citizens of the United States have the right to

Attorney James Budd, a Stockton-
ian, served in the U.S. Congress and
in 1891 as California's governor. In
the 1880s he gained political recog-
nition locally and statewide for his
anti-Chinese position.

protection of the Federal Government against the invading host of the Chinese empire and that we do hereby demand such protection by the speedy passage of such laws by the Congress of the United States as will effectually stop the importation of those hordes of Chinese; and

3. That the gratitude of our community is due and is hereby tendered to our Senators and Representatives in Congress for their untiring and earnest efforts to procure the long hoped for and much deserved legislation by Congress.[7]

This bi-partisan declaration served as the county's official position on the Chinese issue. In an analyzation of the resolution, its words appear weak but it was clearly a well-orchestrated political move. The resolution placed both parties in a safe position by shifting responsibility for the anti-Chinese legislation to their senators and congressmen. These crafty gentlemen were thus able to have their cake and eat it too. While they backed the anti-Chinese question of the hour in concept, they were not obligated to follow up with action.

Two months later, this bi-partisan committee held a second meeting to celebrate passage of the Exclusion Act. On May 9, 1882, Stocktonians enjoyed the fiery display of two bonfires in the public square on Hunter Street. The Dreyfus and Schmidt Brass Band provided suitably patriotic background music and the Stockton Guard, a local militia unit, performed an impressive drill routine. Judge J. H. Budd, father of future governor James H. Budd, shared the limelight with Judge Terry. The *Daily Independent*, in its coverage of the event, concluded: "Thus ended a grand demonstration at which no difference on the Chinese existed." The public stands of Judges Budd and Paterson (who drafted the original anti-Chinese resolution two months earlier) may well have been political gestures, for both employed Chinese cooks in their homes.[8]

One Chinese suffered some misfortune as a result of the Exclusion Act celebration. As the Stockton Guards were marching along Hunter Street near Channel, someone showered cobblestones on Sam Lee's Chinese laundry on Hunter Street and broke every pane of glass. While the vandalism distressed the laundryman, the sight of an armed military unit advancing from the celebration toward his shop clearly dismayed him more. According to the *Daily Independent*:

> The Chinese appeared to be of the inoffensive group who attend strictly to their business and enjoy the reputation of being excellent and reliable laundrymen. Such demonstrations of hoodlumism are deserving of condemnation of every law-abiding citizen.[9]

Clearly, the newspaper had yet to amalgamate the concept that the well-established local laundryman was of the same race of people that the exclusion law intended to eliminate.

From 1883 onward, newspaper editors realized that stories of anti-Chinese incidents in neighboring states, California counties, and in nearby communities attracted readers. Stockton's newspapers, initially slow to endorse the anti-Chinese position, found that biased reporting and strong anti-Chinese editorials increased circulation. Without exception the local papers began to malign the Chinese in distorted articles and malevolent editorials.

FUELING THE SPIRIT OF XENOPHOBIA

Normally, highly publicized political issues that reach a hiatus result in some type of legislative action, and the emotions and hoopla attached to the issues generally recede with the passage of a law addressing the problem. The Chinese Exclusion Act might have fallen into this pattern of outcry and resolution except for the westward expansion of labor unions. To foster their growth, the IWA, Trades Assembly and Knights of Labor kept alive the anti-Chinese issue to attract tradesmen and workingmen into their ranks. Union strategists realized eastern labor problems could not sustain western workers' interest but western workers could relate to the Chinese issue; so, highly visible, it became the symbolic red flag.

By mid-1885 a ménage à trois of union activists, politicians and newspaper publishers rallied around the anti-Chinese issue, each with great expectations. Unions wanted members, politicians supporters and newspapers readers. While each appeared supportive of the others, the relationships were tenuous, for deep philosophical differences divided the hierarchies of each group.

Anti-Chinese events in the west began to snowball by autumn of 1885. The massacre of twenty-eight Chinese in Rock Springs, Wyoming, and eviction of 200 others from the Puget Sound area by Tacoma's mayor, J. Robert Weisbach, triggered a West Coast alert. California was equally anti-Chinese; for example, in October 1885 in Folsom, Chinese residents were fingered in a double murder simply because the murder victims lived less than a hundred yards from Folsom's Chinatown. The revelation that the victims' son was actually the culprit was buried in the back pages of the newspaper.[10]

Without a doubt the sensationalism created in newspaper accounts hastened the anti-Chinese movement. Some people began to believe Kearneyite ideologies while others developed pronounced sinophobia. And like an epidemic sweeping into an area, for a brief period, politicians, civic leaders, newspaper editors and union leaders found themselves mouthing the same rhetoric from one end of California to the other.

Some county residents not only talked about California's Chinese problems, but planned action as well. Sometimes group plans were coordinated, but at other times people worked at cross purposes. Some of the agitators' activities were conducted as social and festive affairs. These occasions created a momentary sense of community spirit similar to the celebration of the Exclusion Act passage. Unfortunately, Chinese living in the immediate neighborhoods became the target of much abuse, particularly in the outlying towns of Linden, Farmington and Lockeford.

Superintendent May, director of the Stockton Insane Asylum, wanted to show his community spirit by playing an active role in the anti-Chinese movement. He wrote to Col. Frederick Bee, counsel for the Chinese in San Francisco, requesting to ship the asylum's sixty-five Chinese residents back to China. Colonel Bee promised to discuss the subject with San Francisco's Chinese Six Companies. Nothing came of the inquiry. It is worth noting that the 1880 census listed only thirty-seven Chinese inmates but five years later, at the height of the anti-Chinese movement, the number of Chinese committed to the asylum had almost doubled.[11]

The first major anti-Chinese meeting in Stockton was held on October 22, 1885, and drew 300 individuals to the German Turnverein Hall. Stockton Mayor Joseph Fyfe called the meeting to order, and City Councilman William Inglis was elected chairman. A resolution drafted by six citizens, including Mayor Fyfe and ex-Congressman James H. Budd, set the political tone for the upcoming local election and, more importantly, outlined new city mandates against Stockton Chinese. Budd defined concise areas of

The Stockton Police Department in 1886 with Police Chief Benjamin F. Rogers seated in the center. Although professing to be anti-Chinese, Rogers was exposed as having a Chinese cook in his employ during the heat of the 1885-86 Chinese boycott.

responsibilities within federal, state and local governments' jurisdictions which could systematically remove the Chinese. In his view:

> It was the duty of the federal government to see that no more Chinese were permitted to come to America and it was the duty of local government to "make it so devilish uncomfortable for the Chinese who were already here that they would be only too glad to leave."

Budd suggested the local strategy would essentially "throw the Chinese to the other side of the Mormon Slough." Once again, those in attendance agreed that removal of the Chinese must be accomplished only by legal means. While the group may be commended for their propriety and civil obedience, such direction also indicates a passive approach, one devoid of violence.[12]

In the ensuing weeks aspiring politicians used the anti-Chinese forum to enhance their visibility. Fading political leaders gained another opportunity to gather luster in the public's eye by supporting the anti-Chinese issue.

If one did not share this popular sentiment, his absence from the public forum drew much disdain. Often, when a person refused to join the anti-Chinese wagon, his standing in the community was questioned. Consequently, when asked to sign petitions or called upon to add comments at public meetings, these community leaders obliged. Only a few took the initiative to instigate or solicit outright public support against the Chinese.

When union leaders asked businesses to fire their Chinese help, they initially sidestepped cooks and servants working in white homes. Many prominent residents did not concede. One such was Sheriff Thomas Cunningham, who kept a Chinese as a cook at the county jail and one at home to watch over his children. And it became almost a game for the newspapers to expose those who employed Chinese servants. For example, a *Daily Independent* reporter discovered Democrat Police Chief Benjamin F. Rogers employed a Chinese domestic. In the November 1885 elections, incumbent Chief Rogers was opposed by William M. ("Pony") Denig and W. H. Woodbridge. During the campaign, the *Daily Independent* accused Rogers of taking bribes from Chinese gambling houses. Rogers denied the charges and claimed it was not his fault that the city could not successfully close down Chinese gambling. The *Independent*, a Republican newspaper, supported Rogers' opponents and sought to use the Chinese issue against him. At the local Democratic convention in October 1885, candidate Rogers convinced his audience he was anti-Chinese. Unwilling to lessen its pressure, however, the *Independent* tried another tactic and exposed the fact that Rogers employed a Chinese cook. Under the headline "Rogers' China Boy, Ah Jab" the article stated:

> For elasticity of tongue and conscience, and for infinite variety of the statements made to cover a single issue, Chief of Police Rogers is one of the most remarkable men in the political history of Stockton. He makes frequent occasion to point with pride to his career as a member of the Workingmen's Party, when he was one of the loudest of all declaimers against the Chinese in the face of the notorious and effectual use of the corruption fund of the Chinese gamblers in preventing the police department under him from abating the evils in Chinatown. Rogers addressed the anti-Chinese meeting in Turn Verein Hall last week, declaring that he was opposed to the employment of Chinese labor and that he was anxious to drive every Chinaman out of the state . . . For the benefit of the laborers and mechanics of this city who have been disposed to favor Rogers because of his anti-Chinese speeches . . . the Independent presents the fact that until within less than a month ago Rogers has had in his employ a Chinese servant . . . named Ah Jab. About three weeks ago Rogers told the Chinaman an election was coming on and he could not afford to keep a Chinese servant during the campaign. As a result Ah Jab was sent into the family of one of Rogers' relatives with the understanding that he should be taken back into Rogers' employment as soon as the election was over . . . [13]

The *Independent*'s campaign went for naught, as Rogers carried every ward in the city and presumably also got his cook back.

Toward the end of 1885 the county's Democratic Party adopted an anti-Chinese resolution, although the Republicans did not. However, during personal interviews, three leading Republican candidates attempted to convey their anti-Chinese posture to voters. Incumbent Mayor James Welsh, also the superintendent and owner of the Crown Flour Mill, stated:

> I don't like anti-Chinese agitation when sprung just before elections for political effect but as to the Chinese themselves, I think my position is pretty well understood in this town . . . As a matter of course Chinese nuisances should be abated. It is possible that some day I may be forced to employ a Chinaman but I hope that day will never be seen in America.[14]

Incumbent City Attorney Frank S. Smith said:

> If you want to know how I stand I am strongly in favor of using every lawful means to get the Chinese out of Stockton's limits . . . the city has and will continue to have my best efforts toward that end.

Street Commissioner C. W. Brunton, nominated for the office of city collector, gave the following statement:

> One of the most ridiculous stories I have heard this week was that [as street commissioner] I had employed Chinese on the streets. I say the story is ridiculous because every man in town ought to know that the Chinese would have been out of Stockton long ago if my wish would have made the Chinese go.

Campaign rhetoric was indeed in full bloom, and these three candidates must have said the right things for they were all elected that November. Yet there are some embarrassing postscripts which might be appended to these men's statements. The records show that Street Commissioner Brunton, in violation of the 1879 State Constitution, did allow the Chinese to work on municipal projects. As city attorney, Frank Smith eventually produced a laundry ordinance which upon court challenge was declared unconstitutional. And Mayor Welsh, when called upon to sign into law that same ordinance, refused to do so.

In the 1885-86 period strong anti-Chinese editorials created a colorful newspaper war between the *Stockton Weekly Mail* and the *Stockton Daily Independent*. Editors attempted to rouse what they saw as citizen apathy to a crucial issue and gave extensive coverage to news of Chinese expulsion everywhere, even in such small communities as Santa Rosa and Lincoln. They emphasized areas that were similar in environment, population and

STOCKTON DAILY INDEPENDENT. FRIDAY, OCTOR

THEY MUST GO.

The Chinese Must Not Remain Within the City Limits.

AN ANTI-CHINESE MEETING.

A Pledge for City Candidates—Permanent Organization to Be Effected.

In Turn-Verein hall, last night, was a large gathering of citizens to express an opinion in favor of removing Chinatown from within the city limits. The meeting was called for the city hall, but the room was insufficient and Turn-Verein hall was adjourned to. The meeting was attended by some of the best citizens of Stockton, and was enthusiastic. The attendance numbered about 300. The meeting was called to order by Councilman Joseph Fyfe. William Inglis was elected chairman, and Councilman John Doyle secretary.

EX-CONGRESSMAN BUDD

Was called for and responded with a speech in which he expressed himself in favor of the objects of the meeting—to devise means to move the Chinese beyond the city limits. He said the Chinese ought to be driven out of town, and he considered it was time for the state and nation to expel them from the country. He mentioned the fact that in 1882 congress passed a law which it was then thought would be a barrier against the influx of the Chinese. Unfortunately for the success of the scheme, the law was overridden by the tricks of shrewd lawyers. During the last session of congress the members of the California delegation met, at the instance of Senator Miller, to consider some means of keeping the Chinese out of California. The delegation secured the passage of an act that it was thought, would be effective. There were some points in the act that speaker did not like, but, taken all in all, it was a good law, and if enforced would have stopped the Chinese influx reason the coming of Chinese was stopped, was not because of any defect the law, but by reason of the power almighty dollar over federal office.

NOT A PARTY QUESTION.

The anti-Chinese question was question. In California all agree Chinese were a detriment to th that they were eating up the s ought to go to the workingma ly. The object of the meetin the opinion of the people of

---

The Weekly Mail.

SATURDAY .... JUNE 19

PUBLIC SENTIMENT DIVIDED.

As soon as the boycott is decently buried, let the real anti-Chinese sentiment of the State be enkindled. We cannot afford to let it come to pass that an idea shall prevail that any number of people in California want to tolerate the coolie evil in this Sta——usa Sun.

It would be intere—
Editor Green of t—
anti-Chinese sent—
We must confes—
what it is unl—
found express—
ment. But if—
and "real" a—
what has it—
what is it—
future ?—
of him p—

The chairman introduced Mrs. Laura De Force Gordon, who delivered an earnest and interesting address on the Chinese question. The speaker thought that a large majority of the people, in this vexatious Chinese—failed to appreciate Chinese affairs produce—the Chinese—convin—

ANTI-CHINESE

Last Night's Meeting at Ma—sonic Music Hall.

MRS. DE FORCE GORDON'S SPEECH

Some Trouble Experienced in Organizing an Anti-Chinese League.

A meeting was held at Masonic music hall last evening to organize a non-partisan anti-Chinese association in this city. The attendance was not as large as was expected. It was announced that N. F. Ravlin, the state organizer appointed by the executive committee of the Sacramento Anti-Chinese convention, would be present, but the gentleman was unable to fulfill his engagement. He was represented by Captain Hunt of Oakland, assistant organizer. A. O. Warrington was chosen chairman of the meeting and Mr. Ferguson secretary. A letter was read from Judge W. S. Buckley regretting his inability to be present on account of sickness, and assuring his one—his sympathy with the cause.

---

and those who have the issue is: An effort on one side one's own, and an e sistent effort on th which belongs to an

This is the industr dition which oversh Salisbury's remedy gration. Gladstone' land manage her ow —o an American —ance and —o h —lion —the —o, the —phenor —rn civil g

LAUNDR —am laundry —n of the Chi —ught to be. T —ee, but could n —ut charging con —s than the Chin —do not know whet —y is in operation the —eno one was establis —closed, because, as t the customers would n In Carson they have a pany running one of t ing establishments, b far has been only a the stock. The truste held a few days a turn the outfit ov Francisco man wh know how to run it if keep the thing going similar to those have l State. The trouble ap those who go into the business know nothing

---

Competing newspaper companies gave anti-Chinese meetings extensive coverage; however, other articles such as "Public Sentiment Divided" suggest the Stockton community was ambivalent on the anti-Chinese issue.

economic size to Stockton. They particularly applauded Fresno, Sacramento and Truckee leaders' efforts in their pleas for non-violent means to remove the Chinese; however, residents there felt no compunction to follow the advice of their local leaders and there were several violent incidents in those towns.

When the editor of the *Sacramento Bee* called for that city's ministers to mount their pulpits and denounce community members who defended the Chinese, Joseph La Rose Phelps did likewise in the *Daily Independent*. Through stinging editorials he stated that since the Sacramento clergy conscientiously and emphatically warned their congregations of the contagion of Chinese vices, Stockton clergymen should do no less.

Most anti-Chinese meetings in the county's small communities received coverage in local papers, as did a high school literary club's debate on the question "Resolved, That the Chinese should be expelled beyond the city limits." The article on this debate drew two long columns in the January 16, 1886, issue of the *Daily Independent*. Following a lively account of the debate, including commentary on points made, the article nearly failed to report the final result. With a dismissing sentence it said: "The judges retired for a few minutes and returned a verdict that the orators on the negative side of the question had won the debate."[15]

RESTLESSNESS LEADS TO ACTION

Stockton officials viewed the growing anti-Chinese tension throughout the state with mixed reaction. On one hand, the Chinese were still the main work force of the county—actually the backbone of the agricultural economy—and the various fees and fines they paid for business and illegal activities increased the city treasury substantially. Thus, it was in the best interests of most citizens not to purge either Stockton or the county of its Chinese.

Local government leaders, because of mounting tension, felt obligated to produce something substantial to placate some of their anti-Chinese constituents. The press and local enforcement agencies also received similar pressures. While other towns were actively driving the Chinese out of their communities completely, the more vocal Stockton residents did not insist on such drastic measures. They simply wanted their Chinese moved just across the slough—but still well within serving distance. A number of citizens recalled Charles Hubner's 1867 plan to remove city Chinese to the Mormon Slough area and suggested such an ordinance be passed. They truly believed if the Chinese left the North Hunter Street and Washington Street areas it would solve some of the health and fire complaints.

When pressured by moral and religious groups, the police, begrudgingly at times, raided gambling houses, even though they had learned that legal evidence was hard to obtain and convictions even more difficult. They did, however, increase harassment of the Chinese for even minor legal infractions. These instances also provided opportunity for those officers caught up in the anti-Chinese frenzy to ventilate their hostilities.

Local health and fire officials in Stockton also attempted to crack down on squalid housing conditions and places of business which were potentially hazardous. Many of the shanties had makeshift kitchens with little or no ventilation. Some laundries, particularly those with twenty-four-hour operations, heated water and boiled clothes in tubs over open fires in rooms with poor ventilation, and later dried the clothes over cans of burning charcoal.

Although the germ theory had been advanced by the 1880s, most people still believed that noxious-smelling vapors transferred communicable diseases. Unfortunately, each of the three Chinese settlements in town were in close proximity to an industry or condition which generated particularly offensive odors. For instance, the Heungshan Temple on Hunter Street was only four blocks from the Pacific Tannery on Oak and El Dorado streets. The tannery, at one time the largest in the state, employed forty men who tanned 1,500 hides a month, and the smells associated with its operation were truly atrocious. The Mormon Slough fishing village south of town emitted undeniably offensive odors, particularly when the fish dried in the hot summer sun, but the smells from the nearby paper and woolen mills added equally unbearable odors to the overall atmosphere. The main Chinese settlement on Washington Street in the heart of town was nearly free of nearby industrial odors. But it did lie in close proximity to many hotels and boarding houses, and its own high-density population and accompanying restaurants and stores taxed the already overloaded and inadequate sewer system.

Geographically, much of Stockton's downtown area rested on a pool of natural gas, and the city had a high ground water table. Gases frequently backed up in backyard underground vaults and, with poor drainage, as much as two feet of stagnant water ponded under wooden sidewalks in many areas of town. In addition, other serious health hazards plagued the city year-round; frequently winter floods caused raw sewage to seep into the streets, and during the rest of the year mosquitoes bred profusely under the seldom-drained sidewalks. The downtown area was a vision of mud, horse dung and cesspools.

Stockton's citizens were frustrated over all the unpleasant and unsanitary conditions. But the sight of the Chinese crowded into cramped quarters, the constant noisy street traffic in Chinatown, and the activity in all-night laundries became the displaced objects of their anger. Throughout the summer and autumn months of 1885 members of the city council, health officials, police, reporters, politicians and nearly everyone with vested interest in the situation conducted inspection tours of Chinatown. They obtained the names of property owners, measured the size of the lots, learned how much rent was charged and the types of businesses active in Chinatown. This parade of inspectors left little unturned in the Chinese quarter. As the inspections broadened to the block north of Washington Street, investigators found that in the areas occupied by whites the stench from the underground vaults was much stronger than from those in Chinatown. The most odiferous areas were near the Phenix Building, the Fountain Saloon and the backyard of the Wells Fargo Company office. Much to his surprise,

City Attorney Smith noted, following his obligatory tour of the Chinese quarter, that while abhorrent conditions were everywhere, "by far the cleanest places visited were the gambling dens, of which there were several on Washington Street."[16]

At the city council meeting of October 30, 1885, members passed a series of ordinances prohibiting gambling, open fires, opium smoking, and requiring 500 cubic feet of air per person during sleeping hours. All the new laws called for fines or jail sentences or both. Within these new edicts were also provisions to penalize police or other law enforcement officials who failed to enforce the new regulations. All ordinances contained the following standard phrase:

> Any person violating any provision of this ordinance shall be punishable by a fine of not more than $500 or by imprisonment not exceeding three months or by both.[17]

A second insertion regarding official enforcement read:

Punishment of Police for Neglect

It shall be the duty of the Chief of Police and of every regular and special police officer of the city of Stockton to see that the provisions of this ordinance are strictly enforced, and any of such officers who shall knowingly and willfully neglect or refuse to diligently prosecute any person violating any of its provisions or who shall neglect or refuse to diligently investigate any alleged violation which may come to his knowledge shall be punished by a fine of not less than $100 nor more than $500 or by imprisonment not exceeding three months, and shall be subject to removal from office.

The ordinance relating to gambling prohibited not only gambling paraphernalia, but the hanging of metal or steel doors and use of bars and bolts across the doors as well. Property owners who willingly and knowingly leased their property for gambling purposes were to be fined from $100 to $500, or remanded to the county jail for up to three months.

The opium ordinance was much more encompassing in regard to those who would be prosecuted. Owners, agents of owners, tenants, lessees, occupants of the premises, building, hotel, or a room where two or more individuals partook of opium, or even the sentry to a room where opium was smoked, were defined as offenders. Even those merely guilty by association were subject to fines ranging up to $500 or three months in jail, or both. In addition to the standard section on punishment of the police, two other sections of this lengthy ordinance underscore council members' intent to be thorough:

Section 6: It shall be unlawful for any person to aid, abet or assist another person in the smoking of opium or inhaling the fumes of opium.
Section 9: In this ordinance the singular number includes the plural and the masculine gender includes the feminine.

Thus women were clearly included in observances of the strict opium ordinance as were people simply breathing the same air as the opium smokers.

An ordinance to remove Chinese laundries beyond the city limits to the Mormon Slough section of town proved difficult to word and therefore was not adopted in this set of anti-Chinese laws.

WASHING OUT LAUNDRIES

One of the greatest manifestations of Chinese acumen was their monopoly of the laundry business. Keeping California in clean clothes without enough women to do this type of domestic work became a tranoceanic activity. Customers paid up to twelve dollars per dozen shirts washed and ironed by Hong Kong laundrymen. The lucrative laundry trade required the customer to wait at least four months for the return of his clothes. Soon, Chinese in Honolulu realized their geographic advantage and vied for the business; their price was eight dollars per dozen shirts. Astute Chinese coming to Caifornia took note of the washing need, and by the 1860s Chinese washhouses could be found in all major towns in the west.

In 1885 Stockton had twenty-four laundries, of which twenty-two were owned by Chinese. Only the French Laundry and the Stockton Laundry, owned by city councilman Lafayette Sellman, were white operated. None of the Chinese laundries was located in the Washington Street Chinatown, a fact which suggests that these laundries catered mostly to whites. In pinpointing the location of the Chinese laundries on the city map of Stockton, it is clear that the largest number of laundries were situated in areas easily accessible to people living in the downtown areas. Other laundries were located in close proximity to boarding houses and manufacturing complexes, which allowed working bachelors to drop their laundry off on their way to work.

A number of prominent citizens, such as former mayors B. W. Bours and J. K. Doaks, were on record as the property owners of the Chinese laundries. In fact, ex-mayor Doaks, former ferry operator, livery stable owner, and chairman of the county Republican Party in 1880, collected rent from three Chinese laundries in 1886: those operated by Feng Sing, Sing Wong Chung and Woo Lee.[18]

The Stockton City Council, in an attempt to adopt an out-of-sight, out-of-mind political philosophy regarding these laundries, ordered City Attorney Frank Smith to develop an ordinance which would limit Chinese laundries to the area around Mormon Slough. But Smith was faced with

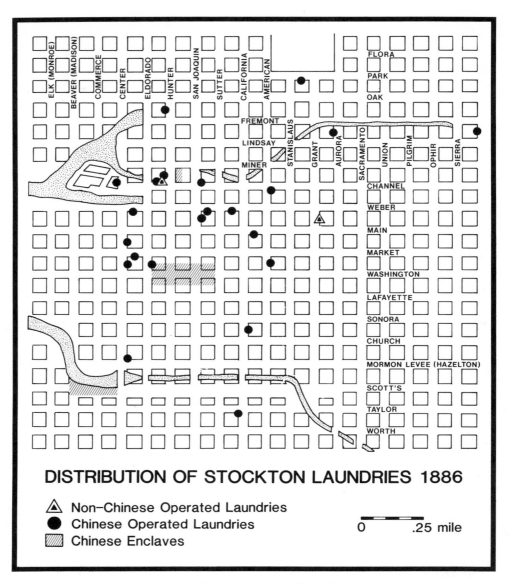

DISTRIBUTION OF STOCKTON LAUNDRIES 1886

△ Non–Chinese Operated Laundries
● Chinese Operated Laundries
▨ Chinese Enclaves

0   .25 mile

The January 22, 1886, issue of the Stockton Daily Independent *listed locations of twenty-four laundries in Stockton, two white and twenty-two Chinese owned. Diagonal lines indicate Chinese settlements. Map provides evidence that the Chinese laundrymen established their businesses downtown and in industrial areas about town.*

semantic problems—how to remove the Chinese without driving out the white laundries and how not to violate Chinese rights under the existing Burlingame Treaty.

The first proposed laundry ordinance, introduced with the other anti-Chinese laws in late October 1885, proved disastrous. Among other things, it required Chinese laundries to use only gas or electricity; however, neither utility was available in the region to which they were to be moved. Such a proposal was not only a hardship but an impossibility.[19]

A month later Smith attempted to write a second ordinance which did not include the utility restriction. The main features of this ordinance were:

> 1. All laundries were to be located west of Tule [Edison] Street and south of Mormon Slough. [This was a largely uninhabited area at the westerly leg of the slough as it entered the main channel, an area beyond the Chinese fishing village.]
>
> 2. Each laundry was to be connected to an underground sewer that discharged into a slough containing running or tide water.
>
> 3. Each laundry was to obtain a monthly health inspection certificate and a certificate from the fire department with receipt for appropriate fees paid.
>
> 4. There was to be no washing or ironing in the laundry between 10:00 P.M. and 6:00 A.M.
>
> 5. Enforcement of the ordinance included a penalty against violators and police who disregarded the law.

This ordinance was passed by the Stockton City Council on November 23, 1885.

Editor Phelps of the *Daily Independent* was elated despite the fact that the new ordinance required the mayor's signature and a five-week posting period before actually taking effect. In an editorial on November 25, he wrote: "The mayor will, of course sign . . . the mayor of no town in California would think of doing otherwise." Phelps was convinced that adoption of the laundry ordinance was the first step in the removal of the Chinese from the main part of town. However, despite Phelps' optimism, Mayor Welsh refused to sign the ordinance into law. He had conducted his own survey of the various laundry businesses, interviewed people who lived nearby, and concluded the laundries were neither dangerous to the public health or the general welfare of those living in close proximity. In addition, the mayor told reporters he found the condemned businesses generally clean and conducted according to the existing ordinance on proper drainage. Additionally, the mayor felt the new ordinance would prove a hardship on property owners who had been put through considerable expenses complying with recently revised requirements and that the new ordinance would drive their tenants away. The mayor's veto caught everyone by surprise, particularly the *Daily Independent*. Editor Phelps furiously lobbied the rest of the city elders and they soon overrode the mayor's veto with a vote of twelve to four.[20]

Confident that Chinese laundries within the city would soon close, the *Daily Independent* offered free advertising space to women, both white and colored, who wished to fill the washing void by taking in laundry or washing in others' homes. The newspaper also began printing instructions on how to wash and iron clothing. But only a week later, Phelps disgustedly lashed out at Stockton women, for his paper had not received a single response to the free advertisement offer. His scathing editorial purposely singled out white women who received aid from various city charity organizations, and stated that the "laundry business of this city is controlled by the Chinese but not denied to whites except by their own inaction."[21]

The Chinese themselves were also unhappy with the new laundry ordinance. Many gave no indication that they would move their place of business and when interviewed by reporters, they tried to point out the illogic in the law. For while the Chinese were prohibited from working in Chinese laundries, other Chinese washing in white-owned hotels and boarding houses were exempt. When asked if they would close their laundries, some responded by saying, "No, no close laundry. If arrested, will give bail and keep on washing."[22]

The Chinese laundrymen were aware that similar laundry ordinances had been adopted in other California towns. San Jose laundrymen, when arrested under the provisions of a similar city law, angrily retaliated by cutting the buttons off their patrons' clothing or closing their businesses in order to make it difficult for their customers to retrieve their garments. Stockton Chinese assured their own customers their clothes would not be damaged, and that they had no intention of acting like their San Jose countrymen.

As a group, Stockton's Chinese laundrymen decided to fight the ordinance through the courts. As a first step, they levied an assessment of fifty dollars per laundry to cover litigation costs. Even white landlords owning the buildings, such as Messrs. Bours and Doaks, also contributed toward the war chest. By January 15, 1886, the day the laundry edict took effect, this fund had already reached $5,000. Stockton Chinese hired attorney Lyman Mowry of San Francisco, who had an excellent reputation in the courts fighting problems facing the Chinese.[23]

On January 23, 1886, twenty-four laundrymen were arrested for violation of the new ordinance. Mr. Lafayette Sellman of the Stockton Laundry, and Mr. L. Luriette, manager of the French Laundry, were also arrested along with the Chinese. Expecting legal opposition to the ordinance, the county prosecutor and the various defense counsels had pre-arranged hearings of two test cases—one white, one Chinese—in order to prevent clogging the court calendar, minimize court expenses, and avoid inconvenience to businessmen who might be called as jurors.

Councilman Lafayette Sellman hired the firm of Terry, Campbell and Bennett to represent his business in the San Joaquin County Superior Court. The Chinese case involved the Tie Loy Laundry, whose hearing was placed on the U.S. Circuit Court calendar. All other cases were held in abeyance pending these decisions, and the rest of the laundrymen were released on their own recognizance and returned to washing.

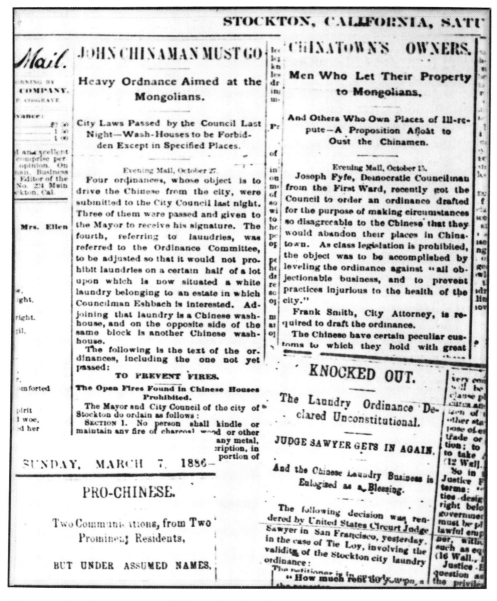

Mail.

JOHN CHINAMAN MUST GO

Heavy Ordnance Aimed at the Mongolians.

City Laws Passed by the Council Last Night—Wash-Houses to be Forbidden Except in Specified Places.

Evening Mail, October 27.

Four ordinances, whose object is to drive the Chinese from the city, were submitted to the City Council last night. Three of them were passed and given to the Mayor to receive his signature. The fourth, referring to laundries, was referred to the Ordinance Committee, to be adjusted so that it would not prohibit laundries on a certain half of a lot upon which is now situated a white laundry belonging to an estate in which Councilman Eshbach is interested. Adjoining that laundry is a Chinese washhouse, and on the opposite side of the same block is another Chinese washhouse.

The following is the text of the ordinances, including the one not yet passed:

TO PREVENT FIRES.

The Open Fires Found in Chinese Houses Prohibited.

The Mayor and City Council of the city of Stockton do ordain as follows:

SECTION 1. No person shall kindle or maintain any fire of charcoal wood or other any metal, ription, in portion of

CHINATOWN'S OWNERS.

Men Who Let Their Property to Mongolians.

And Others Who Own Places of Ill-repute—A Proposition Afloat to Oust the Chinamen.

Evening Mail, October 15.

Joseph Fyfe, Democratic Councilman from the First Ward, recently got the Council to order an ordinance drafted for the purpose of making circumstances so disagreeable to the Chinese that they would abandon their places in Chinatown. As class legislation is prohibited, the object was to be accomplished by leveling the ordinance against "all objectionable business, and to prevent practices injurious to the health of the city."

Frank Smith, City Attorney, is required to draft the ordinance.

The Chinese have certain peculiar customs to which they hold with great

KNOCKED OUT.

The Laundry Ordinance Declared Unconstitutional.

JUDGE SAWYER GETS IN AGAIN.

And the Chinese Laundry Business is Eulogized as a Blessing.

The following decision was rendered by United States Circuit Judge Sawyer in San Francisco, yesterday, in the case of Tie Loy, involving the validity of the Stockton city laundry ordinance:

"How much rest do'y. wpn, a

SUNDAY, MARCH 7, 1886

PRO-CHINESE.

Two Communications, from Two Prominent Residents,

BUT UNDER ASSUMED NAMES.

Pressured to drive out the Chinese, local officials scrutinized the Chinese quarters, investigated property ownerships and adopted a series of anti-Chinese ordinances. Much of their effort failed when the courts declared the laundry ordinance unconstitutional.

During the course of the two cases, several facts came to light which tended to debunk some of the reasons the ordinance had been written. For instance, Sellman's attorney proved that boiling the clothes and using strong laundry soap killed most of the germs before the wash water was emptied into the drainage system. The final decision on the new laundry law, however, rested on the Tie Loy case. Less than a month after the

Stockton laundry ordinance went into effect, on February 16, 1886, U.S. Circuit Judge Lorenzo Sawyer, who rendered the famous decision enjoining hydraulic mining in California, declared the Stockton laundry ordinance unconstitutional. According to Judge Sawyer, the intent of the comprehensive laundry ordinance was to move a business outside the city limits, which constituted banishment, and thus it was a total denial of the constitutionally guaranteed right to work. The *Daily Independent* published the full text of the court findings, but supplied truculent subtitles which left few readers ignorant of its beliefs in the matter: "Judge Sawyer Gets In Again," and "the Chinese Business Is Eulogized As a Blessing." Outraged by the court decision, Editor Phelps roundly attacked it and, with regard to Judge Sawyer, concluded: "Because of his jaundiced decision, he obviously would not even be qualified as a rural police judge."[24]

Another reason for the anger vented in the Stockton press against the court ruling was the fact that Modesto, a major town in Stanislaus County thirty miles south of Stockton, also adopted an anti-Chinese washhouse ordinance on July 2, 1885. Also tested in court, the Modesto ordinance was upheld. The major difference in the ordinances of the two towns lay in the fact that the Modesto ordinance allowed laundries within the city limits, whereas Stockton's was a prescribed banishment to a virtually uninhabited area outside the city limits. Stocktonians had always felt superior to Modesto, but, in this instance, the smaller city's ability to create an effective ordinance against Chinese laundries created a jaundiced attitude in the *Daily Independent*'s editor himself.[25]

OUTSIDE PRESSURE INCREASES

In the interim before publication of the laundry case decision, anti-Chinese activities continued to erupt in many parts of the state. The winter of 1885-86 was disastrous for many nearby Chinese communities. In November 1885, Merced and Fresno adopted a boycott policy against Chinese businesses, and in December Modesto's Chinatown was burned. The Chinese from the Florin area of Sacramento fled south to Elk Grove as that city's boycott achieved stranglehold proportions accentuated by numerous raids on its own Chinatown. Stockton became a refuge for many Chinese looking for relative safety, and by February 1886 Stocktonians noted an acute increase in the Chinese population, particularly in the number of men who were elderly and infirm.

Against this mosaic of statewide anti-Chinese activities, thirty-five communities reported evacuation of their Chinese between January and April 1886. Various state and local groups vied for leadership in this expulsion process. The national picture was equally bleak. Alexander Saxton, in his work, *The Indispensable Enemy*, stated: "The Rock Springs [Wyoming] catastrophe was part of a long continued and nationwide industrial conflict which reached a peak of intensity in the winter of 1885-86 . . . anger and discontentment building up among workingmen converted into anti-coolieism.''[26]

Until the winter of 1885-86, the anti-Chinese activities in San Joaquin County, and particularly in Stockton, had focused primarily on local election issues, local laws, and yellow journalism: all formal meetings had been strictly local affairs. This changed with the meeting of December 11, 1885, when Dr. C. C. O'Donnell, president of the Anti-Coolie League, arrived in Stockton to address a standing-room-only crowd at the Turnverein Hall.

Dr. O'Donnell, a deputy coroner in San Francisco, was noted for his anti-Chinese orations. Formerly Denis Kearney's lieutenant, O'Donnell received attention in the eastern press when he took the opportunity to distribute an anarchist pamphlet, *The Dynamite*. Instilling fear and building hysteria into his audience, O'Donnell ended the evening by administering a membership oath to 300 men who that night formed a local chapter of the Anti-Coolie League. Men nominated as officers of the newly-formed chapter were John P. Cosgrove, the local secretary of the International Workmen's Association, O. H. Warrington, also an IWA member and secretary of the Building Trades Union, Edward L. Colnon, editor of the *Stockton Weekly Mail*, J. J. Nunan and John Sexton. Cosgrove, Warrington and Colnan declined the nomination. Colnon felt his appointment might conflict with his business, and Cosgrove and Warrington claimed that as officials with the IWA their work on a union-sponsored anti-Chinese campaign would be more effective than any political effort.[27]

In an editorial on December 16, 1885, the *Daily Independent* skeptically advised those who had attended the meeting that "the great O'Donnell was losing his home reputation as an anti-Chinese savior," and further opined " . . . the great doctor is suspected of being a trifle loose in mental structure and one touch of nature makes the team akin."[28]

The *Daily Independent* was correct in its assessment of O'Donnell's fanaticism. On December 15, 1885, four days after the Stockton meeting, O'Donnell was publicly deposed as league president at the San Francisco German Branch meeting held in the Irish American Hall in that city. That same day, San Francisco police raided the headquarters of *The Dynamite* at 900 Montgomery Street, where they found a cache of "Hercules" dynamite and an assortment of chemicals and incendiaries. Several members of the anarchist-socialist organization were arrested, and authorities discovered in the group's minutes a plot to assassinate more than twenty prominent Californians, including Leland Stanford, Charles Crocker, Governor Stoneman, U.S. Judge Lorenzo Sawyer, and M. H. De Young.[29]

ACTIVITIES OF 1886

Statewide anti-Chinese activities quickly filled the calendar in the first two months of 1886. New chapters of the Anti-Coolie League were formed, and State Assemblyman C. F. McGlashan chaired a San Jose conference whose purpose was to formulate a plan for a statewide boycott of Chinese, their products and their white employers. Prior to adjournment the members agreed to reconvene in Sacramento on March 10 in conjunction with a convention of the Sacramento Mechanics' and Laborers' Anti-Chinese League. The goal of this convention was to create a bi-partisan, united front in the formation of a statewide organization, the California Bi-Partisan Anti-Chinese Association. Representatives at the Sacramento conference were committed, verbally at least, to the McGlashan boycott plan. In order to create the appearance of a semi-official status at the Sacramento conference, the board of supervisors of each county was asked to send delegates chosen from leaders of both political parties, local businesses and local government.

Numerous towns in San Joaquin County, under the guise of preparing for the upcoming convention, held anti-Chinese meetings and scheduled activities sanctioned by local officials. Lockeford held its first anti-Chinese meeting on February 5, 1886; the group adopted a constitution and bylaws similar to those of the Sacramento Anti-Chinese League and voted to become a branch of the state Anti-Chinese League. Yet the speeches at the Lockeford meeting still counseled against physical violence and urged strict adherence to the law. The members of the Lockeford group felt the only method by which to rid themselves of the Chinese was the boycott.

Tracy held an anti-Chinese meeting the following evening, February 7, 1886, and another on February 12. Town activists drew up their resolution to organize, voted to support other local anti-Chinese leagues, and pledged themselves to follow fair and honorable methods of accomplishing their desired purpose. Lodi followed Lockeford and Tracy's lead on February 11. In each town, however, the tone set by the meetings was one of non-violence in removal of its Chinese. By mid-February, County Clerk C. W. Yolland selected thirteen names as possible delegates from San Joaquin County to the Sacramento convention, and the following month the county board of supervisors approved the list, which included Joseph Phelps of the *Daily Independent*, John Cosgrove and James A. Morrissey. Morrissey, like Cosgrove, owned property in Chinatown and had Chinese tenants.[30]

The Knights of Labor, afraid of losing ground to competing unions, circulated a petition on February 11, 1886, to encourage legislation aimed toward changing the terms of the Burlingame Treaty with China in order to prohibit Chinese immigration forever. Many of San Joaquin County's foremost civic leaders, officers of the court and police officials signed the petition. One look at the names on the list suggests that the Chinese in the county had little chance for humane treatment, let alone fair trial under the law. Yet the appearance of the situation was much different from the reality. Many of those who signed the petition had Chinese employees or conducted business with the Chinese community—and continued to do so, a strong indication that some of these men signed strictly as a political gesture.[31]

Although the Knights of Labor solicited endorsement of local politicians, only the Federated Mechanic's Trades and Laborers' Union (Federated Trades), statewide and locally, gained the highly-coveted publicity. Leaders of the Stockton branch of the Federated Trades were A. O. Warrington, president; H. R. Starkhouse, recording secretary; John Cosgrove, corresponding secretary; and Henry Karsten, sergeant-at-arms.

On February 15, 1886, the Federated Trades launched its boycott against the Chinese by publishing the following resolution in the *Daily Independent*:

> RESOLVED:
> 1. Proprietors of hotels, restaurants, and lodgings are to discharge the Chinese in their employ by March 1, 1886 under penalty of boycott;
> 2. Chinese are to leave Stockton by March 1, 1886;
> 3. Anyone renting property to the Chinese is hereby notified that the federation will not be responsible for damages done to said property occupied by Chinese tenants after this date.[32]

The Federated Trades intended to take the leading position in the Stockton anti-Chinese campaign. However, to enforce their bold resolution, its members needed support of the community. In an attempt to woo public sentiment, they held a public meeting at Abbott Hall on February 19, 1886 and invited the Rev. N. F. Ravlin of San Jose, state organizer for the Anti-Coolie League, as guest speaker. At the podium, the former New York Baptist minister labored under the misconception that Stockton leaders wished his help in organizing an Anti-Coolie League. But to his surprise and that of his audience as well, the Federated Trades leaders declared Ravlin's role that evening was only that of a lecturer and not an organizer, and any effort on Ravlin's part would only duplicate the Federated's campaign to expel Stockton Chinese. However, before this became clear, the Rev. Ravlin, in fire-and-brimstone delivery, chastised Stocktonians for being behind the times. He believed his audience should take matters into its own hands and "shake the town from its center to its circumference." Ravlin further urged his listeners to arouse themselves, for

> "... there was doubtlessly many influential citizens and businessmen who wanted cheap labor and would not affiliate with the present anti-Chinese movement. They have not a particle of sympathy and incline to find fault with and throw cold water on the cause. Movement has gained popularity and has shaken Oakland and is now shaking San Francisco."[33]

The day after the spirited union meeting with Dr. Ravlin, Judge Lorenzo Sawyer handed down his historic decision in the Stockton laundry ordinance matter. However, rather than feeling the sting of defeat, local demagogues used the occasion to gather more support. Three days later some local businessmen signed agreements with the Federated Trades promising not to employ Chinese or purchase goods made by them. Included were Cox & Bros. Groceries; J. W. Bowers, vegetable dealers; the Union Restaurant; and the Commercial and Eagle hotels.[34]

During the next two weeks, the Federated Trades movement gained momentum and attracted many new members. Blacksmiths, machinists and patternmakers of the Iron Workers Union joined en masse, as did fifty other mechanics. The *Daily Independent* gave the campaign extensive coverage and encouragement. The editor reassured employers that if they discharged their Chinese employees, there would be many French, Italians and Germans willing to fill the vacancies. He also advised unemployed whites "not to assume an arrogant position." "Cooks and waiters," he continued in his editorial,

> "should not demand all the profits of the hotel or restaurant, with the privilege of getting drunk after each meal. Whites should be more sober, industrious, and reasonable in their demands; but, if they were the reverse, they cannot expect much sympathy, money or work."[35]

Activities of the Federated Trades Union were highly publicized, and the advertising section of the newspapers carried a list of all eating and lodging establishments supporting the boycott. As the boycott campaign progressed, local leaders became increasingly aggressive and demanding, and attempted to coerce employers into paying whites ten dollars more a month than Chinese workers if whites applied for the vacant positions.

To further their goal, the Union hired D. W. Allen to ride around Stockton on horseback and carry a banner listing restaurants that should be boycotted for not cooperating with the union. In at least two instances, restaurant owners, instead of complying with the demands, retaliated in kind. In one case, when Allen rode in front of the Independent Restaurant, proprietor M. Mitrovitch ran out with a hose and doused the rider like a fireman putting out an inferno. Police had to be called to restore order and disperse the more than one hundred persons witnessing the confrontation. In the end, Allen charged Mitrovitch with battery.

A second restaurateur relied more upon cunning than direct action. The owner offered to pay Allen an extra dollar if he promised to ride in front of the man's restaurant during the lunch hour. Allen, pleased with the promise of a bonus, showed up with his banner the following day. Soon a crowd gathered. During the morning the proprietor placed in his front window two platters of fried oysters. One looked doughy and weepy, the other a plate of golden delicacy. Beside the distinctly unappetizing oysters the owner laid a sign saying, "Cooked by a white cook," and, of course, the other platter had been prepared by the Chinese cook whose job the union was attempting to eliminate.[36]

When one reads the extensive newspaper coverage given the boycott, it would appear that the Federated Trades' campaign was an overwhelming success. Actually, however, it was shortlived. Many businessmen gave only lip service to the union's demands. Some hotels fired their Chinese cooks— but kept their Chinese laundry workers. Others, willing to give white cooks a try, discharged them as soon as union pressure on the restaurants lifted. Still others claimed they could not find whites willing to work the long, late shifts their Chinese cooks were accustomed to and thus felt justified in ignoring union demands entirely.

By mid-March, the *Daily Independent* ended its blissful relationship with the Federated Trades. Union leaders felt they were powerful enough to call a boycott against the local newspaper and its editor, Joseph Phelps. In a scathing editorial against the union on March 16, 1886, bold headlines proclaimed "Demagogues Must Go," rather than the usual "Chinese Must Go." The article stated:

> Weak-witted members of the Trades Federation called for a boycott of the Stockton Independent on the grounds that the Independent had failed to endorse everything the union had done. Most recognize the Stockton Independent as a sincere advocate of intelligent and reasonable agitation for the cause. Professional agitators must be tabooed and the resolution of the boycott killed. Several demagogues have tried to manipulate the federation for their own big advancement.
>
> Skilled, sober, reliable labor is too well treated in Stockton to willingly become tools of these men and unskilled labor by refraining from undue turbulence will get everything to which it is entitled. Demagogues must go!

Disgusted with the crude, boisterous union agitation methods, local political leaders stepped into the leadership void created by the downfall of the Federated Trades boycott and tried their hand at rousing the anti-Chinese movement. Unlike Stockton, other communities in the county were ready to purge their towns of all Chinese.

In the meantime, the March meeting of the Sacramento Anti-Chinese convention proved disappointing. It was controlled by the rowdy elements of the unions, and representatives of the counties found their attendance a waste of time. County resident Mrs. Laura De Force Gordon, although not a delegate, shared the platform with other anti-Chinese leaders.

Mrs. Gordon, one of the first women admitted to the California Bar, was an ardent suffragist and former editor of the shortlived *Lodi Valley Review* and the *Stockton Weekly Reader*. Her 1871 bid for a seat in the California Senate, although unsuccessful, gave her enough political expertise to spearhead the Non-Partisan Anti-Chinese League movement in San Joa-

Laura De Force Gordon, a lawyer, ardent suffragist and one of the first women admitted to the California bar, spearheaded the anti-Chinese political movement in San Joaquin County in 1885-86.

quin County. On March 11, 1886, the night following the Sacramento Convention, Mrs. Gordon, Dr. Ravlin and A. C. Cudner, a Lockeford delegate to the convention, addressed an anti-Chinese meeting held at Steacy's Hall in Lockeford to report on the convention's outcome. Other Lockeford anti-Chinese meetings were held on April 1 and 14. From mid-March to mid-April Mrs. Gordon and the Rev. Ravlin stumped through the county's small towns raising support for their cause. Tracy's anti-Chinese activists held a festive meeting on March 25. That same night, in the northern part of the county, the town of Acampo also held an anti-Chinese meeting and dance which featured Mrs. Gordon and Dr. Ravlin as the main speakers. For nearly an hour Mrs. Gordon told of the need for ridding California of its "hordes of Chinese filth and crime-breeding coolies." She explained that since Congress had ignored California's appeal for relief, the only legal way this goal could be reached was by giving the Chinese a severe "letting alone." Following this dynamic duo's stirring remarks, Acampo's citizens ratified the Anti-Chinese League's constitution adopted at the Sacramento Convention. With a social gala similar to that held under a tent the night after the Acampo soiree, the citizens of Lodi ratified the league's constitution on March 26. Both Lodi and Lockeford placed an April 1 moratorium on the presence of Chinese in their towns. Stocktonians witnessed the Ravlin-Gordon performance a week later, on April 2, 1886.

Until that time, Stockton had been the only town in the county which had not formed a Non-Partisan Anti-Chinese association. The Anti-Coolie League sworn into office by Dr. O'Donnell was now defunct, and the February appearance by Dr. Ravlin at the request of the Federated Trades Union did not result in league organization either.

Stockton's April 2 meeting, chaired by A. O. Warrington and held in the Masonic Temple, was much smaller than anticipated. Mrs. Gordon's speech that evening on the Chinese boycott was addressed principally to women of Stockton despite the fact there is no indication any women attended the meeting. She appealed to her feminine cohorts to discharge their Chinese help, claiming, "When I cannot get a white person to do my washing, I will lock up my law office, roll up my sleeves, and do it myself."[37]

At the close of the evening there were some difficulties in organizing the league and finding people willing to serve as responsible officers. Among those who were nominated but declined the honor were Justice Treadwell, George Leiginger and William ("Pony") Denig, the erstwhile candidate for Stockton police chief. At last Mrs. Gordon nominated Superior Court Judge W. S. Buckley, who had sent his regrets at being unable to attend the meeting but who had expressed sympathy with the cause. In his convenient absence, the judge was unanimously elected, and Denig was prevailed upon to accept the office of secretary pro tem. By the end of the April 2 meeting, the Stockton chapter of the Non-Partisan Anti-Chinese Association was officially formed and thirty members had signed the membership roll.[38]

In retrospect, the small number of people who attended the Stockton Anti-Chinese meeting suggests the effort to form a local branch of the league was a failure. In neighboring towns supportive audiences overflowed meeting halls, and previous anti-Chinese meetings in Stockton had drawn substantially larger crowds. For a variety of reasons, Stocktonians' interest in the Chinese issue had begun to wane. Many had been repulsed by the actions of union agitators, and others were bored with the continued anti-Chinese harangue in local newspapers. Some had placed trust in the anti-Chinese ordinances and become disenchanted when they proved ineffective. Stockton newspaper editors, while still anti-Chinese in sentiment, turned their attention to other issues such as the irrigation and free water problems beginning to affect the San Joaquin Valley.

The winter of 1885-86 had been harsh. Following record rainfall, the levees on several islands washed away and floodwaters devastated large tracts of farmland. Staten, Bouldin and Tyler islands were partially flooded,

Separation of labor between the white industrial worker and the Chinese day laborer/farm worker in the agri-economy town of Stockton curtailed trade unions' anti-Chinese efforts. These are employees of the Houser, Haines & Knight Manufacturing Company.

and when the levee on Roberts' Island broke, cattle had to be evacuated by steamboat to Stockton. I. B. Christiansen, a white engineer, and four Chinese workers drowned while repairing a portion of that island's levee. Near the city, 3,000 acres of Moss Tract were abandoned because of high water, and portions of Stockton, from Main Street south to the French Camp Slough, were flooded. More than three feet of water inundated the Chinese fishing village at Mormon Slough, and many citizens felt the floodwaters were comparable to those of 1861-62.[29]

By April the cold, wet, foggy weather which normally engulfs the Central Valley disappeared as spring began to warm the soil once again, and many citizens, particularly those who made their living from agriculture, turned their attention back to the land. Their energies were now devoted to spring planting and preparing their acres for another productive year. As Edward L. Colnan had predicted in a January 1886 editorial in the *Weekly Mail* during the height of the anti-Chinese campaign:

> The boycott of Chinese can only work if it is universal in Stockton . . . boycott feelings will not always be so intense as at present. When the next harvest comes people will be so busy with their work that they will not have much time to devote to the Chinese problem and if everyone boycotts the Chinese today from every avenue of employment or profit, he [the Chinese] would manage by slow degree to reinstate himself in six months or a year.[40]

Seeing the movement on the wane, the Federated Trades again attempted to re-establish itself in a leadership role. On April 30, 1886, at the Turnverein Hall with 125 people present, union representatives announced plans to take a more energetic stand. The boycott was to be aimed at employers who hired Chinese cooks and waiters, and they planned to publish a list of local saloon-keepers and grocers who hired Chinese. Ironically, the local Federated Trades was angered by the Cooks and Waiters Union because, as independents, they refused to join the Federated Trades despite the fact that the Federated Trades had spent more than sixty dollars in publicity attempting to gain employment for white cooks. During this rejuvenation period, the local Federated Trades also sought support from the White Boot and Shoemakers League of San Francisco, and lobbied San Francisco's Cooks and Waiters Union to exert pressure upon its recalcitrant brethren in Stockton. But once again, the ambitious plans of the union proved ineffective.

In May 1886, the Federated Trades Union, statewide, planned to sponsor a number of local gatherings to celebrate numerous purported union "victories." These victories ranged from a successful strike and boycott of the Printers' Union, to the anniversary of the Metal Trades Council. In San Francisco, a parade down Market Street followed by a public dance was attended by 10,000 people. In Stockton, union leaders and members of the Stockton Non-Partisan Anti-Chinese League co-sponsored a union picnic at Goodwater Grove (now Oak Park) on May 9.

Preparation for the picnic had a humorous side. The picnic committee requested bids for an ice cream contract and received two. Alex Gall, a local confectioner with a shop on Main Street, quoted a dollar and a half per hundred servings, and competitor John Gross bid one dollar per hundred. Gross, as lowest bidder, was awarded the contract. The picnic committee was unaware that Gall employed only white labor while Gross used Chinese workers. Gall created quite a stir when he questioned the union's action in light of their purported anti-Chinese stand, much to the committee members' embarrassment. In quick recovery they asked Gall to fill the order, which he refused, citing that he thought their actions inconsistent. Gross, meanwhile, demanded satisfaction of a contract legally entered into in good faith, on his part at least. The besieged picnic committee eventually paid Gross off, but refused to serve his product. As a result committeeman Pony Denig and a friend stayed up all night before the picnic to make the ice cream needed for 2,000 people. On the day of the picnic, Denig assured the reporter from the *Daily Independent* he could guarantee every dish of ice cream had been made by white hands. The Goodwater Picnic was the culmination of public activities by the Federated Trades and the Non-Partisan Anti-Chinese Association.[41]

DISSIPATING THE ILL WINDS OF DEMAGOGUERY

Until May 1886 the general trend of those who favored the Chinese was to keep their thoughts to themselves. However, on May 8, 1886, the day before the Goodwater Picnic, an Anti-Boycotters' meeting was held in Stockton, sponsored by Stockton Grange No. 70 of the Patrons of Husbandry. Grange members, in response to the anti-Chinese activities, adopted the following resolutions:

> 1. That we therefore, are opposed to the immigration of Chinese to this state or to the United States;
> 2. That we denounce the boycotts as UnAmerican, unjust, tyrannical, and opposed to our laws and free institution;
> 3. That we will use our influence to defeat all persons coming before the people for their suffrage who have made themselves prominent in the advocacy of the boycott;
> 4. That we deprecate the cause pursued by the press of the State as calculated to arouse the evil passions of the worst elements of society; and
> 5. Be it further resolved that the immigration laws of the United States should be amended as to prevent the immigration of the offscouring from any other country whatsoever.[42]

This declaration became the most powerful and effective means of ending the anti-Chinese scourge so rampant in the county. The grange's main thought was to prevent a loss to the local economy should the Chinese be successfully expelled from the county. There was, at that time, no other large group of laborers ready to work the fertile fields. While the anti-boycotters were not pro-Chinese, their threat to denounce and defeat those who initiated the boycott brought back some semblance of rational behavior.

In keeping with the onset of lethargy toward the Chinese question, Stockton's atmosphere was much less hostile too. This was particularly apparent by June 1886 when the rabid sinophobe Dr. O'Donnell returned to town and drew much criticism from former supporters. When he displayed large photographs of Chinese with leprosy at the Hunter Plaza, Police Chief Rogers ordered him to cover the pictures and move to a less conspicuous location.[43]

Coincidentally, boycott efforts of the state Federated Trades Union plummeted. The Stockton chapter, unable to function without support from San Francisco, announced the end of the overall boycott on Chinese except for the Chinese laundries. By 1887 even the union activities in this endeavor had ceased. The local grange stand caused many political leaders to abandon their anti-Chinese positions and frantically cast about for other causes.

Local newspapers removed their spotlight on the Chinese, and by 1887 there seemed, in the press at least, little outward indication that Stockton had experienced any anti-Chinese sentiment. For instance, local Chinese were mentioned in the papers only twice during the summer of 1887. One article reported an accidental fire that devastated the south block of Chinatown. The other article briefly mentioned a Chinese merchant who suffocated when a pile of sacked potatoes fell on him aboard the steamer *T. C. Walker*. This article concluded: "Ah Lee was a prominent Chinese commission merchant and was well known to steamboat men in this city." By the time this article appeared, the tone of reporting Chinese matters had altered dramatically from that of but twelve months earlier.[44]

WHEN THE DUST SETTLED

The anti-Chinese campaign was not without effect in San Joaquin County. By June 1886 Lockeford reported only one Chinese washhouse remained and that it was only a matter of time before it closed its doors. Lockeford landlords promised not to renew rental agreements with Chinese tenants. The boycott on potatoes and other produce raised and marketed by the Chinese remained in force. Lockeford's success in its anti-Chinese effort was echoed in Lodi. Laura De Force Gordon's efforts toward that end were more damaging to Chinese in both these outlying communities than in Stockton.

In the county seat itself, there was a decided alteration in mood, numbers, and ambience in the three Chinese quarters. Under the headline "Chinese Power Breaking in Stockton," an article in the *Stockton Weekly Mail* on

April 10, 1886, reported at least six Chinese shops had closed, gambling profits were down, and fewer Chinese were seen on the streets. One reporter surmised that more Chinese spent their hours smoking opium to pass the time and ease their disappointment. When confronted by reporters looking for a story, local laundrymen appeared hostile and suspicious. They were aware of the boycott of their businesses, and some commented that they had fallen upon hard times. Some Chinese laundries lowered their price to seventy-five cents per dozen shirts in hopes of enticing customers. Even at that price many whites withdrew their patronage. Local police reported half the activity of previous years in the Washington Street quarter. As a matter of self-preservation the police increased their arrests and raids in the Chinese quarters since the new anti-Chinese ordinances mandated their own punishment should they fail to enforce them. The woolen mill and paper mill south of Mormon Slough gave way to union pressures and discharged their Chinese help. The vacant positions were filled by women.[45]

Any assessment of the actual anti-Chinese sentiment in the turmoil years must be viewed in light of those citizens who refused to join the anti-Chinese campaign. Despite numerous editorial diatribes, these newspapers also published anonymous letters from local citizens calling attention to the dedication, hard work and frugality of the Chinese in their employ. Letters signed "Fair Play" and "Victor Ames" and others set forth rational arguments against the boycotts, and these articles appeared on the front page alongside articles on the anti-Chinese campaign.[46]

Both the *Daily Independent* and *Weekly Mail* were aware that public sentiment was acutely divided on the Chinese question. Many bankers and businessmen were accused of indifference to the issue. Ex-mayor Charles Belding, owner of the Belding Soda Water Manufacturing Company, totally rejected demands to discharge his Chinese workers. Rancher John Ladd, among others, adamantly refused to fire his Chinese cook even when whites applied for the job. While Laura De Force Gordon barnstormed the county against the Chinese, another woman, Rosanna Farrington, a Washington Street property owner, refused to bow to anti-Chinese pressure. Mrs. Farrington was gaveled to silence at a public meeting when she tried to tell the angry audience her Chinese tenants paid their bills on time and had never caused any problems. She also threatened legal actions against any who physically forced her Chinese tenants to move. And it was not just the wealthy or propertied who remained solidly opposed to the anti-Chinese issue. A *Weekly Mail* editorial chastised not only a clothier who refused to back the boycott, but a butcher who could not see how the Chinese hurt anyone, and a drygoods merchant who simply ignored the boycott.[47]

Even the actions of some union leaders and newspaper editors who most vociferously advocated boycott and expulsion were antithetical to their stated beliefs. At the height of the *Daily Independent*'s support of the Federated Trades boycott, the paper ran an advertisement for the Quong

Hing Lung, a local store, just two columns from a particularly scathing editorial diatribe. In another instance, an *Evening Herald* reporter spotted an active union leader exiting a Chinese butcher shop one Sunday afternoon. When queried about his purpose, the union leader remarked he did not have time to shop during the week, and also whispered to the reporter that the pork in the Chinese store was reasonably priced.[48]

The anti-Chinese feeling among single, white workers could not have been particularly deep. Many factory workers, machinists and tradesmen were bachelors and lived in boarding houses or other lodgings which employed Chinese as cooks, laundrymen or servants. While on the one hand these workers were supportive of the anti-Chinese campaign and attended union meetings, rallies and demonstrations religiously, they began and ended their day eating meals cooked by Chinese, wearing clothes washed and ironed by Chinese, and living in buildings cleaned by Chinese. In addition, because their landlords paid their Chinese servants less, the white lodgers or boarders paid less rent.

The decrease in the Chinese population of rural areas in the county can be attributed largely to the successful anti-Chinese campaigns of these small communities. Elliott, Elkhorn and Douglas townships, with their major population centers of Lockeford, Lodi and Farmington, managed to expel nearly their entire Chinese population. Even a hundred years later these areas remain locations where Chinese do not feel comfortable. But the acute sinophobia of the early 1880s did not reappear.

San Joaquin County's anti-Chinese campaign was not a total success— nor could it have been for many reasons. Foremost among them: the county lacked the manpower to replace the Chinese labor used in its agricultural system; weak-minded union leaders invariably deferred to or were upstaged by wealthy, strong-willed businessmen, farmers and politicians; the diverse positions of the two most popular local newspapers diffused whatever influences they may have had with the readership; and more importantly, many pioneer whites and Chinese had established a mutual dependency.

As time passed, two players in the county's anti-Chinese scenario moved up in the world. Ex-Congressman James H. Budd became governor of California in 1891, an astonishing feat for a Democrat from a staunchly Republican area. Edward Colnon moved to San Francisco after he became president of the Board of State Harbor Commissioners in 1896. And as for Laura De Force Gordon, probate proceedings following her death showed she leased one of her properties to a Chinese named C. G. Hung. While local histories tend to portray these hometown heroes as larger than life, the activities of all three during the anti-Chinese period amply demonstrate their weaknesses. One wonders if those whites who had some type of relationship with the Chinese and became involved with the anti-Chinese movement did so to guide and temper the forces into a non-violent direction or because they were just swept along by the forces of the turmoil years.[49]

The fact that Stockton did not undergo any sort of major physical violence is a credit to her community spirit and the wisdom of some of her leaders. Foremost in the thoughts of those deeply involved in the anti-Chinese activities was that any step taken must be legal. Adherence to that philosophy, despite an intensely racist context, demonstrated the basic integrity of the county's citizens and their overall respect for the law.

CHAPTER FIVE ENDNOTES

1. *Stockton Daily Independent*, January 1, 1868.

2. The California Paper Company was a twenty-four-hour operation and employed eighty-five men. During the 1880s this plant furnished much of the paper for the West Coast, but in the 1890s resource-rich mills of the northwest drove this mill out of business.

3. *Stockton Daily Evening Herals*, March 9, 1880.

4. *Stockton Daily Evening Herald*, July 11, 1878; October 3, 1878.

5. *Stockton Daily Evening Herald*, January 28, 1880.

6. *Stockton Daily Evening Herald*, March 10, 1880.

7. *Stockton Daily Evening Herald*, March 4, 1882.

8. *Stockton Daily Independent*, May 10, 1882.

9. *Stockton Daily Independent*, May 10, 1882.

10. *Stockton Daily Independent*, November 11, 1885; December 14, 1885.

11. *Stockton Daily Independent*, April 14, 1886.

12. *Stockton Daily Independent*, October 23, 1885.

13. *Stockton Daily Independent*, October 29, 1885.

14. *Stockton Daily Independent*, October 29, 1885.

15. *Stockton Daily Independent*, January 16, 1886.

16. *Stockton Daily Independent*, October 15, 17, 1885; February 25, 1886.

17. *Stockton Weekly Mail*, October 31, 1885.

18. *Stockton Daily Independent*, January 22, 1886.

19. *Stockton Weekly Mail*, November 14, 1885.

20. *Stockton Weekly Mail*, November 28, 1885; December 5 and 12, 1885; *Stockton Daily Independent*, November 27, 1885; December 1, 1885.

21. *Stockton Daily Independent*, January 15 and 20, 1886; February 25, 1886.

22. *Stockton Daily Independent*, March 2, 1886.

23. *Stockton Daily Independent*, January 1 and 15, 1886.

24. *Stockton Daily Independent*, January 24 and 28, 1886; February 17 and 19, 1886; March 7, 1886.

25. *Stockton Daily Independent*, March 25, 1886.

26. Alexander Saxton, *The Indispensable Enemy: Labor and the Anti-Chinese Movement in California* (Los Angeles, 1971), pp. 204-5.

27. Saxton, *Indispensable Enemy*, pp. 194-95. *Stockton Daily Independent*, December 12, 1885. Stuart Creighton Miller, *The Unwelcome Immigrant: The American Image of the Chinese, 1785-1882* (Berkeley, 1969), p. 164.

The IWA, organized in San Francisco in 1883 by Burnette Haskell, had socialist-anarchist leanings and was rumored to employ arson and dynamite when the occasions arose. IWA members included other anti-Coolie socieites such as Dr. O'Donnell's and loose groupings of trade union socialists.

John Cosgrove maintained a public anti-Chinese image; at the same time, however, public documents suggest he had extensive dealings and established close relationships with some of the Stockton Chinese. Cosgrove owned property in Stockton's Chinatown area and, in 1885, was renting to Chinese. In addition, a wedding license filed in 1882 listed Cosgrove and the then Chief of Police Orrin Langmaid as serving as witnesses at the marriage of Ung Gong and Ah Ham.

28. *Stockton Daily Independent*, December 16, 1885.

29. *Stockton Daily Independent*, December 17, 1885.

30. *Stockton Daily Independent*, February 5, 6 and 7, 1886; March 5, 1886. On March 5, 1886, the board of supervisors approved the following men to attend the Sacramento Convention as official delegates from this county: A. Leitch, banker and stock raiser; J. L. Phelps, editor of *Stockton Daily Independent*; C. W. Yolland, county clerk; James A. Morrissey; J. P. Cosgrove, union leader; E. J. McIntosch; Alex Chalmers, dry goods merchant; J. R. W. Hitchcock, Castoria farmer; D. A. Learned, farmer and fruit grower; T. J. Murray; W. L. Robinson; A. A. Cudner; and F. Green.

31. *Stockton Daily Independent*, February 12, 1886. The Knights of Labor petition was signed by C. H. Clements, police judge; John E. Budd and George A. McKenzie, receivers of U.S. Land Office; J. M. Caves, U.S. postmaster; J. W. Swinnerton and A. Van R. Paterson, judges of the superior court; A. B. Treadwell, county justice of the peace; F. H. Smith, Stockton city attorney; C. W. Yolland, county clerk; Thomas Cunningham, county sheriff; John C. Shelley, office court reporter; W. W. Cowell, city assessor; Wesley Minta, deputy district attorney; W. G. Bidwell, county auditor and recorder; and Benjamin F. Rogers, Stockton chief of police. The signers represented a bi-partisan cross-section of the top officials in the county.

32. *Stockton Daily Independent*, February 15, 1886.

33. *Vision*, First Baptist Church, Centennial Edition. *Stockton Daily Independent*, February 20, 1886. The Rev. N. F. Ravlin, a New Yorker, migrated to California in 1882 to accept the position of pastor of San Jose's First Baptist Church. During his short five-year tenure Dr. Ravlin's views of Christian faith split the congregation so severely that only after his departure did the two factions reunite once more. Ravlin left the San Jose Church in 1886, the year he campaigned heavily for the non-partisan Anti-Chinese League.

34. *Stockton Daily Independent*, February 21, 1886; March 7, 1886.

35. *Stockton Daily Independent*, February 22 and 23, 1886; March 2, 1886.

36. *Stockton Daily Independent*, March 11, 1886. *Stockton Weekly Mail*, March 13, 1886.

37. *Stockton Daily Independent*, April 3, 1886.

38. Denig, a colorful local personality, was a former pony express rider turned newspaper reporter. He ran against Ben Rogers for police chief in 1885 and during the anti-Chinese era remained an active figure well within the shadows of the movement. Denig later became the co-founder of the *Stockton Evening Record*, the only surviving major newspaper in Stockton today.

39. John Thompson, "The Settlement Geography of the Sacramento-San Joaquin Delta, California" (unpublished doctoral dissertation, Stanford University, 1957). *Stockton Daily Independent*, January 28, 1886; February 3, 1886. *Stockton Weekly Mail*, January 9 and 23, 1886. On January 24, 1886, the San Joaquin River burst in the Middle Division of Roberts Island. The damage to the island was estimated at $500,000 with $60,000 in crop loss. Other flooded areas included the Mokelumne mainland reclamantion near New Hope, parts of Stockton and its adjacent Moss Tract.

40. *Stockton Weekly Mail*, January 9, 1886.

41. *Stockton Daily Independent*, May 9, 1886.

42. *Stockton Daily Independent*, May 15, 1886.

43. *Stockton Evening Mail*, June 12, 1886.

44. *Stockton Daily Independent*, August 30, 1887.

45. *Stockton Weekly Mail*, April 10, 1886. *Stockton Evening Mail*, July 17, 1886.

46. *Stockton Daily Independent*, March 7, 1886.

47. *Stockton Weekly Mail*, October 31, 1885; May 22, 1886.

48. *Stockton Daily Evening Mail*, March 12, 1880. *Stockton Daily Independent*, October 12, 1876; December 20, 1885.

49. Before her death in 1907, Laura De Force Gordon was leasing one of her properties in Lodi to C. H. Gung, who transferred the lease to Tom Gee after March 1908. (Lease transfer agreement of the Laura De Force Gordon estate, March 12, 1908, Laura De Force Gordon Collection, San Joaquin County Historical Museum.)

Transition into the New Century

In San Joaquin County the rabid, often violent anti-Chinese period seemed to fade with the coming of spring 1886. The lure of the land and the drive to turn fertile fields into carpets of golden grain, lush green vegetable patches and vineyards of purple-hued grapes was stronger than hatred and racial discrimination.

The transition of this county's Chinese into the new century was similar to that of residents of other nationalities. They grappled with new inventions, changing economic times, and the general sense of moving ahead into the future. With the pragmatism and adaptability shown in earlier decades, the Chinese met and conquered new challenges in ways which had lasting impact on the future of both San Joaquin County and California itself.

The previous chapter indicated that not all white citizens of the county joined in the anti-Chinese movement. Many prominent citizens attempted to protect Chinese who were in their employ or were their tenants. Other citizens simply sat on the fence to see what would happen before casting their lot with the pro- or anti-Chinese forces.

One of the more interesting anomalies of the violent 1880s was the construction of a 39,000-square-foot agricultural pavilion on the edge of the Washington Street Chinatown. In spite of the tension demagogues created in 1885, local leaders felt no qualms about building an exhibit hall within arm's length of the Chinese quarters on Washington Square.

Washington Square, a public park, was exceedingly cosmopolitan in flavor. Immediately to the west was Chinatown and to the north was Saint Mary's Church, a religious center for the town's Italians, Irish, Mexican and other Catholics. Mexican residents also held many of their religious and secular fiestas in the park, and the Chinese used it as their commons.[1]

Plans for the District Agricultural Pavilion called for the occupation of the entire block bounded by Washington, San Joaquin, Lafayette and Hunter streets. Stockton architect Charles Beasley carried the neighboring Chinese influence into his wood and glass, three-story building which included upward-curved, pagoda-shaped rooflines on all four towers. The pavilion's front entrance faced San Joaquin Street, a logical orientation

San Joaquin Valley Agriculture Pavilion, built on Washington Square in 1887, was adjacent to Stockton's Chinatown. The mammoth exhibit hall was destroyed by fire in 1902 and the land reverted back into a public park.

since the streetcar line ran on that street; the rear of the building looked onto the south block of Chinatown.

THE FIRE OF 1887

Work on the agricultural pavilion had progressed well enough by the summer of 1887 to have a formal dedication scheduled for mid-September. On September 11, 1887, just a week before the scheduled opening, the pavilion almost succumbed to a fire that had started across the street in the Chinese quarters.

The blaze began in a wooden shed behind a brick building at the southwest corner of Hunter and Washington streets, where a Chinese delicatessen owner housed a large adobe and sheet-iron oven used to roast pig and barbecue slabs of pork. Unfortunately, on this Sunday, the cook tending the fire dropped a ladle of fat on the fire and an instantaneous surge of flame ignited a nearby barrel of lard. Within seconds the fire engulfed the shack and rushed to devour other nearby lean-tos. It licked its way ferociously up awnings and wooden balconies of neighboring buildings. The flames raced quickly down the south side of Washington Street and sought the inner sanctum of each dwelling as structure by structure the row of brick buildings surrendered to the heat and flames. Chinese onlookers quickly

formed bucket brigades to wet down the roofs of businesses, gambling houses and restaurants on the north side of the street.

The actual role of the Chinese in fighting this fire has been obscured by some local accounts of the incident. Chinese merchants purportedly blocked the firemen from gaining access to the burning buildings. A reporter covering the story suggested the merchants made no effort to rescue the goods from the buildings and surmised that "the Chinese knew a thing or two about 'Melican' ways and preferred to mulct the insurance companies for the value of their goods." While this speculation had validity, the Chinese possibly worried that the white firemen might abscond with some of their belongings. In addition, during the excitement sporadic explosions rent the air as the fire found caches of firecrackers and ammunition stored in the recesses of many basements and alcoves. The unpredictability of the explosions was reason enough for the Chinese to keep anyone from entering their premises.

As the fire spread from the Washington-Hunter southwest corner toward El Dorado Street, steady wind gusts from the Delta blew the flames and cinders high in the air. On three occasions the pavilion roof and second floor caught fire. Seeing their yet-to-be pride of the city threatened, the fire department turned all available equipment and men to saving the exhibition hall. As soon as one blaze was put out another section of the roof caught on fire. When the crisis passed, the department reported that there was little overall damage to the pavilion.

The Chinese block raged with the intensity of an inferno and after two hours the entire block was gutted. Among the charred rubble firemen found the remains of one Chinese. Most felt relieved that the fire did not jump to the north side of the street. Aside from the loss of one life, the total damage including buildings and stock was estimated at only $40,000. In retrospect, considering the intensity and duration of the fire, it was the only practical decision to make the Chinese quarter a secondary concern when the pavilion was threatened. No line of defense could have contained the fire when the row of structures and their contents were so flammable.

Unfortunately, local newspapers could not refrain from including a smattering of derogatory remarks regarding the Chinese; yet, in the same article, one newspaper also offhandedly gave credit to them for their attempt to contain the fire. One article noted: "The Chinamen were equal to the emergency . . . "[2]

The fire did not slow the pavilion's completion, and sixteen days after the fire, on September 27, 1887, residents celebrated its grand opening. Activities and exhibits in the mammoth pagoda-roofed building attracted over four thousand visitors in the first two weeks. Aesthetically, architect Beasley's eastern-influenced pavilion fitted well with the ambience of the Chinese quarters. Fifteen years later, in 1902, an electrical fire started inside the pavilion totally destroyed the structure, and city fathers decided not to rebuild. Washington Park reverted to its former use as a park for local residents.

HARD TIMES AHEAD

During the 1890s economic difficulties engulfed the nation. Gold and silver standard advocates fought to control the country's monetary system, each believing his economic theory would strengthen the declining value of paper currency. Adding to the ominous situation was agricultural competition from Argentina, Australia and Canada, who sought to usurp the United States' position as the major grain supplier of the world market. American wheat plummeted from a dollar and forty-eight cents a hundredweight to a mere ninety cents, a 40 percent decrease. Not unexpectedly, the nation sank into a severe depression.

A growing cry for political action to solve many of the nation's crises threw farmers and labor organizations into tenuous alliances while a populist agrarian movement gained wide acceptance in many sections of the south and west. The unemployed from the east as well as those leaving the declining wheat-producing midwest cut a deep path for California. Like a forceful wave pushed against a solid barrier, the migrational trek came to an abrupt end at the Pacific Ocean. Thousands of farm workers and other unemployed landed in the great valleys of California bewildered and embittered by their misfortune.

California's own economy at the time was equally unhealthy. By June 1893 twenty-seven banks in the state had failed, and more failures were expected. While the state as a whole floundered in turbulent economic waters, San Joaquin County initially appeared to be weathering the hard times comparatively well. A summary of Stockton's manufacturers in early 1892 suggests continued growth and vitality, the seeds of which had been sown during the 1870s and 1880s. Wheat was king in the county. While the market was depressed in other parts of the nation, the county's milling companies and transport lines were doing a thriving business. San Francisco docks served as the transshipping point to international markets, and all available watercraft loaded with wheat sailed there from the port of Stockton. Even light-draft steamers hauled as much as possible. The *Clara Crow* left Stockton harbor carrying 13,000 bags in one load, and other craft such as the *Leader* towed two barges of wheat at a time.

In a short time the rush to market turned into an oversupply forced by the lack of international buyers. As the farmers sat waiting for payment for their crops, the manufacturing companies also became hard pressed. A notice posted in the *Daily Independent* suggests the seriousness of the situation as the depression hit home for many.

> NOTICE: All farmers indebted to the Matteson & Williamson Manufacturing Company are notified that beginning August 17, 1892, for a period of one month, the company will accept from those unable to pay cash good milling wheat and barley to be delivered at the Union Milling Company's warehouse and agree to pay for the same five cents per cental above the regular quote price during the month.[3]

This notice, clearly an attempt by the Matteson and Williamson Company to recoup some of their losses, suggests that at this time a return to the old barter system was the only way to maintain some sort of sound financial basis.

Meanwhile many western legislators had not deserted their efforts to curtail further Chinese immigration. Although the 1882 Exclusion Law was in effect, the Chinese found other avenues of entry into this country, both legitimate and otherwise. Some came via Canada or Latin America. Others entered through the Gulf Coast states and the Caribbean. The quick and unexpected adoption of the Scott Act of 1888, a supplement to the Exclusion Act, completely denied re-entry of Chinese laborers to the United States. When the new law took effect at least twenty thousand Chinese were temporarily outside the United States. Under the provisions of the previous legislation, most carried documents certifying their right to return to America. Unfortunately, the change in the law affected them all. Within days of the Scott Act's passage, 600 returning Chinese were prohibited from landing in San Francisco even though they had families and businesses in California and carried valid certificates of residence.

As if things were not bad enough for the Chinese, in 1892 passage of the Geary Act extended the exclusion of Chinese for another ten years. Its provisions were even more stringent than those of the original Exclusion Act of 1882; in addition to the ban against naturalization of Chinese and immigration of Chinese laborers, the Geary Act required Chinese to carry residence certificates on their persons at all times. The law allowed only a one-year grace period for all Chinese to register as residents. Thereafter, all Chinese without appropriate certification were subject to deportation.

The Chinese Consolidated Benevolent Association, an influential San Francisco organization composed of all district and clan associations, advised its countrymen not to register, in defiance of the new law. According to its legal counsel, the arbitrary law did not separate those Chinese who were aliens and others who were citizens and entitled to the same rights and privileges as any other American citizen. Approximately 80 percent of the Chinese nationwide, therefore, did not register. This translates to 85,000 individuals who, by 1894, were subject to deportation. Immigration officials were not prepared to execute such a mass deportation plan and sought assistance from Washington. The McCleary Amendment was hastily adopted to extend the registration period another six months.

Not all Chinese followed the edicts of the family associations, however. Those Chinese who had worked and lived among whites for many years, particularly those in remote areas, weighed the injustice of the law against their own circumstances. One such individual was a cook working for state senator Ross Sargent in Elkhorn township. While the cook was aware of the non-conformance edict issued by the Stockton Chinese associations, his employer's influence appears to have been greater. Even though his job was secure, the cook was physically too far away to receive protection from Chinese counsel should immigration officials check the remote hinterlands. On January 22, 1894, the cook took a picture of himself to the courthouse and registered under the name of Koo Luke. Koo felt he had more to lose by not registering under the Geary Act.

Koo's action provides additional insight into the man and shows his desire to assimilate into the white society. When asked his name by the county clerk, Koo was unsure. He explained that Mr. Sargent had been teaching him about Matthew, Mark, Luke and John, the four apostles of the New Testament, and Koo assumed that there was a hierarchal order in these four names. He had originally been called John, a name commonly given to Chinese by whites. But Koo felt he had learned enough about western ways to ask his employer to call him Luke. Now, because of his action, he wondered whether he dared assume the name of Mark. The clerk convinced him to keep the name of Luke.[4]

A SECOND ALARM

In the summer of 1893 many unemployed whites migrating westward to California joined up with California's contingent of Coxey's army in a protest movement that sought to direct government leaders' attention to the plight of the jobless. Frustration and rage, natural emotions among the new arrivals, were vented as anger against the Chinese. Although their numbers were dwindling, the Chinese still remained the dominant workforce in the field. As in the early 1880s, California farmers and fruit growers refused to fire their Chinese labor at the demands of labor agitators. New anti-Chinese incidents, justified as efforts to round up unregistered, illegal Chinese immigrants, erupted in several agricultural counties. Violence flared in the vineyards and orchards of Fresno, Madera, Hollister, Redlands and elsewhere. Chinese fruit packers were expelled from Selma, and all laundrymen and peddlers of Fresno were given five days to leave that city. The *Daily Independent* reported all the anti-Chinese meetings and activities in Fresno and curiously concluded: " . . . Just why it was done is not known as none of the whites would work in the places where coolies vacated."[5]

The tone adopted by the *Daily Independent* was decidedly different from that of the Hanford *Sentinel*, whose vituperative editorial comments were directly responsible for at least three meetings of white laborers in Hanford and Lemoore. The *Sentinel* even admonished young Kings County women to learn the ways of the kitchen so it would be unnecessary to hire a Chinese cook. Yet the *Sentinel*'s cry kindled a feeling of *deja vu* as it echoed the diatribes so familiar to readers of the Stockton *Daily Independent* less than ten years earlier.

Stockton had been listed among cities with anti-Chinese pogroms, according to the *Los Angeles Times* and the *San Francisco Morning Call*. These reports were in error, for one local person's effort to arouse citizens' passions against the Chinese fell on deaf ears. No Chinese were expelled from the fields around Stockton or anywhere else in the county.

As the *Daily Independent* reported Chinese fleeing in terror in the southern San Joaquin Valley, it also alerted readers to the fact that Percy Cox planned to remove the Chinese in Stockton. Cox, a book agent, organized an anti-Chinese meeting in Hunter Square on the afternoon of August 18, 1893, which attracted some two hundred unemployed men. At that meeting Cox announced a second meeting, scheduled that evening, whose purpose was to organize a march on Chinatown "to tell the Chinese to leave Stockton." The *Daily Independent* could not understand this haste to expel the Chinese and speculated as to Cox's motives in taking the leadership position in this cause. Suspecting Cox had been goaded into his role, the paper reported:

> . . . It is said that what Chinese are at work in Stockton a white would not do. Most of them are domestic servants, gardeners or laundry workers, working for very meager wages . . .

The local police dismissed most of Cox's threats. However, as a precautionary measure, Police Chief Henery and his force, as well as Sheriff Cunningham and his deputies, placed their men on a standby basis. Henery prepared to cordon off the Chinese quarters to stop any demonstration from entering the area. Within Chinatown itself, the Chinese were celebrating the last of their three-day August Moon Festival. While many were aware of the Hunter Street gathering, most seemed unconcerned.

By evening a decidedly smaller crowd than that of the afternoon had gathered. Shortly after 8:00 P.M. Cox began the meeting. As reported in the following day's paper:

> The anti-Chinese agitation on Hunter Square last night did not amount to much, but there was plenty of wind . . . a pine table had been procured and the speakers mounted upon it, the candle which they tried to read by was repeatedly blown out . . . it was ludicrous and many a man had a hearty laugh at the speaker on the table reading by a candle half sheltered under a hat.
> The crowd of workingmen got together early but the Salvation Army marched into their midst with flags flying and drums beating and scared many of them into flight.

At the meeting, Cox reported 300 copper miners from neighboring Copperopolis and hundreds of men from Fresno, Bakersfield and Tehachapi were en route to Stockton to make the Chinese "git." At one point Cox saw ex-police chief Ben Rogers lingering in the background and called on Rogers to address the audience, but Rogers refused. When Cox persisted, the former chief turned and departed. Days after the meeting many Stocktonians still awaited for the arrival of Cox's mythical "army."

Union officials, fearing negative publicity because of Cox's unauthorized activities, immediately issued a press release. Under headlines announcing "Workingmen Stand Firm" the article read:

> Leading members of various workingmen's unions yesterday promulgated the following announcement:
> STOCKTON, AUGUST 19—Hearing that there is to be an anti-Chinese meeting of a violent nature tonight, we desire it understood that the various labor organizations of the city of Stockton are opposed to any and all violent measures of ridding the state of Chinese, believing that by intelligent, peaceful means we can accomplish the desired end and not bring discredit on the union laboring men of this City.

This pronouncement was signed by representatives of the Central Labor Union, Typographical Union, Molder's Union, Brotherhood of Carpenters and Joiners, and the Tailor's Union. Union leaders were clearly disassociating themselves from both Cox's anti-Chinese campaigns as well as any acts of violence which might occur. And although they did not discount the statewide effort to expel Chinese, Stockton union leaders had no plans to purge themselves of their own Chinese.[6]

Cox attempted a third public meeting but met with an even smaller audience. He had failed to arouse any excitement among the city's level-headed workingmen. Further, the unemployed who did attend would not contemplate any action that would garner them no benefit. They too may have realized, as did Cox and the *Daily Independent*, that: " . . . nine-tenths of the businessmen wanted the Chinese to remain here." At the heart of the matter, as the *Daily Independent* commented in a final report of the episode, was the fact that "no Chinese were taking jobs as in the Fresno vineyards."[7]

There were reasons why most white county residents lacked interest in the 1893 anti-Chinese activities. Only a week before the Cox incident, both the Crown and Sperry flour mills were in full production, preparing a 400-ton shipment of wheat to China. A local steamer was scheduled to leave with this cargo for the Far East on August 10. The international market, particularly during this depression, was important to the people of the county, who also remembered clearly all the unpleasantness and trauma associated with the anti-Chinese movement of seven years earlier. These people had sipped from the trough of racism, and its bitter taste still lingered. Additionally, the county's agricultural fields needed tending, and the Chinese were still their number one source of manpower. It would be another ten years before the Japanese would replace the Chinese in the fields.

Yet within the state's agricultural field the 1893 anti-Chinese activities were not without effect. According to historian Carey McWilliams, between the time the Chinese were driven out and the Japanese entered "over one half of one million acres of farmland was put out of cultivation in California."[8]

A POSITIVE ENDING

Resentment toward the Chinese in Stockton decreased rapidly as the nineteenth century came to a close, although some county residents still had difficulty resolving their personal feelings. The mood of the county's population was one of relief that the recent depression years had passed. Its people's optimism was further bolstered by the country's victory in the Spanish-American War. In 1898 with swiftness and minimal casualties the country became a colonial empire, taking in the Philippine Islands and Guam in the Pacific and Puerto Rico and Cuba in the Caribbean seas.

Thus it was with ebullience and pride that Stocktonians planned their Fourth of July parade in 1899, for that year also marked the city's golden anniversary. An extravaganza expected to eclipse all other past city celebrations was planned weeks in advance by the city council's Committee on Parades, and all city residents were included in the celebration. The Chinese community received an official invitation to participate in the parade, and

Lee Sing, a leading merchant and court interpreter, was asked to help arrange the details. Lee and the entire Chinese community could hardly contain their excitement. Lee told the *Evening Mail*:

> . . . I invited all the Chinese merchants to attend a meeting . . . not only the Chinese laborers but the merchants as well owe a great deal to the Americans, as without them the Chinese could not live here. I told them that the Americans have always been kind to us and that we ought to have something interesting in the parade and that it was our duty . . . [9]

Within two days local Chinese raised $200 for costumes and equipment, which they ordered from San Francisco. Some merchants donated as much as five or ten dollars for the cause. Hoping to involve as many Chinese as possible, Lee asked employers to release their Chinese help the day of the parade so they could participate. Yet the Chinese appearance in the great celebration was not without a touch of the old anti-Chinese resentment.

About a week before the parade, Ben Kohlberg, the former police constable responsible for arresting Chinese on Union Island in the 1870s and, at that time, president of the Exempt Firemen, protested the Chinese involvement. Kohlberg stated: "A few years ago we were trying to get rid of the Chinese, and now we are asking them to appear in our patriotic parades." Kohlberg claimed he was not alone in this feeling because " . . . yesterday when it became known what stand I had taken, people drove around my place to congratulate me and said I was right. Some of the best people in town, men like Jerry Robinson, Mose Thresher and H. C. Shaw . . . agreed." However, when Shaw, a local farm implement plant owner, found his name in the paper in such a context, he immediately called at the *Evening Mail* office to clarify his position and said:

> . . . No one would consider me such an ass as to take any such stand or endorse any such stand . . . I marched in a procession with Chinese fifty years ago in San Francisco on July 4th and the Chinese were the feature of the procession, they were cheered all along the route and made a mighty fine showing.[10]

C. T. Bender, a member of the parade committee, defended the city's invitation to the Chinese. He noted other towns had asked their Chinese to participate in similar parades, even in such locations as Hanford where anti-Chinese activity was but a five-year memory. When the railway line was completed in that town in 1898, the Chinese played a very prominent part in the celebration. According to Bender, "Kohlberg seemed to be trying to stir up discord. Chinese have appeared in public parades in various towns on the coast . . . The fact of their being in the procession does not make the parade any less American nor any gentlemen who appear in the same parade any the less American."[11]

COMPLIMENTS OF

Ben. F. Kohlberg,

Democratic Candidate

FOR SHERIFF.

Known to be anti-Chinese in philosophy, Ben Kohlberg tried to prevent their participation in the 1899 July Fourth parade. A public letter admonishing Kohlberg strongly suggested the anti-Chinese issue had finally been put to rest.

Under pressure from their president, the Exempt Firemen met and voted not to march in the parade unless the Chinese were excluded. The Stockton branch of the Butchers' Union, who planned to enter a float depicting American soldiers routing out the Spanish in Cuba, agreed to support the firemen's boycott. As the parade day approached those firemen who did not attend the meeting to sanction the boycott began to have second thoughts, particularly as their unit had purchased new uniforms and the opportunity to display their finery might elude them. A few nights before the parade, the Exempt Firemen held an emergency meeting and rescinded their plan to boycott the celebration. As member George Leiginger reported:

. . . That meeting [the first one] did not amount to much anyway. It was composed of a few who had been anti-Chinese all their lives and thought they should carry their dislikes of the Mongolians into a July 4th procession. I have fought the Chinese for many years and did so during the times of Denis Kearney, simply on the grounds that the Chinese were the enemy of white labor. But I don't feel that is any reason why I should not turn out in a procession where just a few Chinese were the feature. I might just as well refuse to turn out if there was a man in the procession I did not like, would there be any sense to that . . . We will be there alright, you may be sure of that.[12]

The parade was but one aspect of the great celebration, and as Independence Day grew closer, citizens became caught up in the spirit of the occasion. The length and breadth of Main Street was liberally festooned with bunting, and 150 red, white and blue incandescent globes brightened both sides of Main Street from San Joaquin to Sutter streets. Julius Cohn's Paradise Store did a thriving business selling endless yards of bunting, muslin flags and large historic posters. Firecrackers could be purchased in almost any store at a nickel for two packages while small paper flags were snatched up at five cents a dozen. Rosenbaum, a local clothier, gave away free firecrackers with the purchase of a boy's suit. Even Stockton's black citizens were excited for they too had been invited to participate in the parade and planned a float with a dozen riders.

On the last Independence Day of the nineteenth century, Stockton citizens anxiously waited along the parade route, many crowding the grandstand in front of the county courthouse. And nearby at the Hunter and Weber Avenue intersection a fireworks display area was set to go off as soon as the day's planned activities ended.

The parade began shortly after 10:15 A.M. and the forty-five marching units, which were divided into three divisions, took several hours to pass the reviewing stand. It was a universal experience and brought patriotic joy to both spectators and participants. The Chinese contingent consisted of two orchestras, one at each end of its parade section, a float, a cadre of Chinese dressed as ancient warriors, Chinese ladies in carriages, one Chinese woman dressed as a warrior on horseback, and a carriage carrying all the prominent merchants of the Chinese community.

The Exempt Firemen, in their crisp new uniforms and their red fire engines, marched proudly past the review stand as the fourth unit of the second division. The Chinese followed six units behind the firemen, in the same division. Unfortunately, the Butchers' Union had not changed its mind and was not represented.

Public response to the Chinese participation was overwhelming. The racial prejudice exhibited by Ben Kohlberg served as a relatively isolated example of an individual with deep-seated resentment. Time and conditions were different, and racists like Kohlberg were no longer in tune with public sentiment. On July 5, 1899, the *Evening Mail* published an open letter to Kohlberg from an anonymous businessman which summed up the change in attitude:

> My old friend Benjamin, did you see that and did you take to heart that the participation of the Chinese was a noticeable feature? The tom-tom and the dragon's head, the yellow banners and the generals on horseback, the barbaric splendor of the Orient, the feature of our highly civilized celebration with which we annually keep alive the illusion that we are free—did you see it all?
>
> And when they passed our public square what a fine scorn they must have felt for us, these yellow people when they remembered that it was but yesterday that thousands cheered until their throats were sore responsive to the cry, "The Chinese Must Go." And it was only yesterday, it seemed, friend Benjamin, that Democratic and Republican conventions in burning words denounced the "noticeable feature" as an accursed plague, a menace to our homes, our lives, our sacred institution. And it was only yesterday too, that Denis Kearney with the great public at his back, tried to drive the yellow men into the sea, even as the swine was driven in the olden time.
>
> ... Oh, Benjamin, my friend, you represent forty centuries of consistency in religious and social and racial customs, and you are sadly out of place where men change their fickle minds from day to day. And you are right and you are wrong, too, as many of us are. You are right when you refuse to admit by your actions, as so many others did yesterday, that when you denounced the Chinaman as an evil you were a demagogue. For he is as great an evil, as great a menace, as great a plague today as he ever was—if he ever was, and your course was consistent and manly in refusing to allow your manhood to be soiled by what you believed to be the contaminating contact of his touch.
>
> ... And you are wrong, friend Benjamin, when you fail to allow for the fickleness of our master, public sentiment ... [13]

The commingling of the entire population of Stockton at the great Fourth of July parade cemented an understanding between white and Chinese which transcended the confusion and frustrations of the anti-Chinese period of the 1880s. As 1899 ended both groups looked forward to closer and deeper relationships in the twentieth century—and they were not disappointed.

THE DELTA AND "'GRAS"

As Stockton continued along her course into the new century, a major change in lifestyle, agriculture and industry occurred which created new opportunities for the Chinese in the Delta region. While many locations in the county had struggled with the passion of the 1880s and 1890s, a quiet transformation occurred in the lives of those who lived in the islands and

Ushering in the new century, hundreds of electric light bulbs outlined the county courthouse. This city's message appeared over the building's east entrance in 1900. The Chinese experience in San Joaquin County was destined to be better in the twentieth century than in the previous one.

hamlets dotting the many Delta waterways. Although Chinese fishermen, by the late 1890s, no longer plied the waters with their large fishing nets, the river highway remained of prime importance, for it was still the cheapest and most reliable transport system linking remote island farms to river towns and giving access to the port cities of Sacramento and Stockton.

Four river towns in the Delta should be mentioned at this point. Although these towns—Walnut Grove, Courtland, Isleton and Locke—lie in

Sacramento County, their proximity to San Joaquin County and her Delta area was important to the Chinese. Each of these communities was well-established by 1900 with the exception of Locke, which dates only to 1912. Walnut Grove was founded in 1850, Courtland in 1870, and Isleton in 1878. Locke's Chinese community developed in 1915 after Walnut Grove's China-town burned and its Heungshan Chinese chose to relocate rather than remain in Walnut Grove with that town's Toishan population.

In each of these river communities the Chinese quarters consisted of an assortment of grocery stores, restaurants, rooming houses, theaters, laundries, barber shops, gambling houses and bordellos. These towns provided the services and ambience to satisfy the Chinese laborers' psychological and social needs. Some enterprising gamblers even outfitted boats with gaming equipment and brought gambling and prostitutes out to the laborers at the work camps.

However, for most visitors to the area, the Delta shoreline resembled the picturesque and rather idyllic Mississippi River in foliage and scenery. River traffic sounds and sailing activities enhanced the parallelism of the Ole Miss and the Delta lifestyle. Ships' captains alternated between blowing quick short toots or long mournful wails as barges, scows and steamers

Skyline view looking west over the Delta with a good view of the Stockton Channel and the courthouse in the left foreground, c.1925.

SAN JOAQUIN VALLEY

The Land of Great Promise

Special Round Trip Tickets

AT

REDUCED RATES

Commencing Tuesday, Sept. 20, and continuing every Tuesday thereafter until further notice, round trip tickets will be on sale at Los Angeles to the following San Joaquin Valley Points:

STOCKTON	-	$15.00
NEWMAN	-	15.00
MERCED	- -	13.50
FRESNO	- -	11.00
HANFORD	-	10.50
PORTERVILLE	-	10.50
BAKERSFIELD	-	8.00
MODESTO	-	15.00
TURLOCK	-	14.50
MADERA	- -	12.00
LILLIS	- -	11.00
VISALIA	- -	10.50
TULARE	- -	10.00

The Chinese used the major railroad lines and rural connectors as their principal mode of land travel. This turn-of-the-century rate schedule lists the important valley towns between Los Angeles and Stockton.

passed one another. As these watercraft dropped anchor at isolated river landings, passengers, mail and produce were loaded and unloaded according to schedule.

The independent steamboat operators first began to disappear in the early 1890s when the California Navigation and Improvement Company of the San Joaquin and the Southern Pacific Railway and California Transportation Company of Sacramento came to dominate river traffic. These carriers monopolized the trade, but they also provided dependable and timely services to hundreds of individuals in the Delta waterway.

Steamboats and other passenger vessels were a romantic aspect in the lives of the Chinese living along the inlets and tributaries. Old-timers today remember that as children raised in the Delta, they would scamper up the levee as soon as they heard approaching steamers blast the signal to bridge tenders to raise the drawbridges. As the ships sailed through, passengers and

By the 1920s wealthy Chinese had taken fondly to the large touring automobiles such as Franklins, Packards and the Reo pictured here driven by a Chinese youth.

land-bound children eagerly waved to each other. In the evening the large riverboats, with hundreds of incandescent lights strung from stem to stern, illuminated the river from bank to bank, while the sounds of calliope music and laughter cut through the still Delta nights. Yet few Chinese youngsters visualized themselves in the vessels, mingling in the brightly-lit saloons or partaking in the exquisite dining room. Nor could they imagine being served by Chinese waiters who were predominant among the service personnel.

It was the Chinese and, later in the 1930s, the Filipinos who provided the gracious amenities one could find aboard the steamers. Passengers on the *T. C. Walker, J. D. Peters*, or either the *Delta King* or *Queen*, could testify to the impeccable service provided by waiters dressed in stiffly-starched white uniforms. A fifty-cent fare for travel from Stockton to San Francisco included a berth and meals, and this price was not raised to a dollar until 1908. The pragmatic Chinese often used the riverboats to travel to San Francisco, but they usually opted for a lower-priced ticket. The twenty-five-cent steerage fee got the Chinese to the Bay city just as quickly as if he had paid twice the amount.

River travel remained popular until the advent of World War II; however, by the mid-teen years county residents saw improvements in hardtop levee roads, ferries and bridges. The arrival of the Model T, organized trucking services and the telephone in the 1920s gave many Delta towns better access to the modern world than they previously had.

*Founded in 1894, the Hickmott Company hired many Chinese from nearby
Terminous to work in the company's asparagus cannery on Bouldin Island.*

In the late 1890s major railway lines added spur tracks linking Delta
landings to the main network of rail arteries which formed the lifeline of the
county. One such water-rail connector, Holt Station, developed into a full-
fledged community. In 1900 the Atchison, Topeka and Santa Fe laid a main
line and whistle stop to this location just eight miles west of Stockton to
help insure their line got a share of the lucrative Delta crop transport
business. Holt Station was used by farmers on Roberts Island, Union Island
and others living on Upper and Lower Jones tracts. Skiffs and scows filled
with vegetables and grain sailed up Whiskey Slough and unloaded on the
bank. There stevedores hauled the produce a short distance to the railroad
loading platforms near the tracks. Other water-rail communities developed
along Middle River and at Orwood, Knightsen and Antioch. Holt Station,
with its close proximity to Stockton, took on special meaning for many
Chinese laborers when gambling houses located there. Although Holt
remained an entertainment center for the Chinese, few actually lived there.
Card dealers, money handlers and prostitutes commuted daily from Stockton by train to service the Chinese workers who came in from the outlying
farms.

While Holt Station's Chinese population was small, this was not the case
in the community of Terminous. Located at the junction of Potato Slough
and the Mokelumne River, the town's population in 1900 was over 750, all
of them Chinese. And by 1894, the lifeblood of this community was
asparagus.

Use of large Chinese bamboo baskets (foreground) eased the sorting and washing of asparagus in early day cannery production.

Bouldin Island, a 6,016-acre landmass in the Delta just west of Terminous, boasted the first county test field of asparagus to observe its adaptability to Delta conditions. The light peat dirt of the area produced delicate-flavored spears measuring as much as an inch and a half in diameter or about the size of a medium wrist. In 1901 the Stockton Chamber of Commerce cited Chinese expertise in horticulture and their numbers working the fields as key factors in the new crop's success, for it not only gained world recognition but also propelled the county's economy to greater heights.

The Chinese were not immediate experts in the new crop, but after the second year of production learned that if the plant were properly maintained, no replanting was necessary for seven to ten years. Harvest began as early as January, but adroitly the Chinese stopped harvesting the vegetable by mid-June in order to protect the plant and let nature take over, thus guaranteeing better results the following year. Stoop workers tended the crop daily, working each row until the entire field had been inspected and each foot-long, new sprout cut just below the soil line.

In 1894 the Hickmott Company built the first cannery on Bouldin Island to can "'gras," as the vegetable was called locally. By 1900 there were two

A Chinese cannery owner purchased a fleet of Model "T" trucks in 1927 to transport workers and produce. The Althouse-Eagal Fordson Company was on El Dorado Street in Stockton.

canneries on the island, the Hickmott facility, rebuilt into a larger structure adjacent to the Mokelumne River, and another located on the San Joaquin River side.

Few people other than the cannery owners understood that the Chinese were responsible for the success of this crop's growth and that they were also the backbone of the cannery labor force. Ordinarily, cannery owners did not hire workers for their canneries but rather contracted all operations to Chinese labor contractors, who provided the workers and furnished all benefits to the employees. During canning season hundreds of Chinese migrated to the island canneries to undertake the sorting, cutting, packing and cooking of the market-bound crop. Chinese workers often knew every phase of asparagus production including the manufacturing of tin cans and packing cases. From mid-March to mid-June the plant turned out as many as 625 cases—or twenty tons—of canned asparagus every day, an annual production of more than a hundred thousand cases. All of these cases were completely sold by the end of September each year. Asparagus canned locally was shipped all over the world, and local advertisers said, "Bouldin Island is specified on every can label and San Joaquin County stamped on all shipping cases. The asparagus from Bouldin has earned first place in the market and sells for the highest price."[14]

As new canneries opened in Isleton, Walnut Grove and Courtland, the Chinese still dominated the work force in asparagus cultivation and canning. By the 1920s Chinese entrepreneurs owned two major canneries in Isleton, the Bayside Canning Company and the National Cannery. Both specialized in canning asparagus, tomatoes and fruit. In later years Bayside

Many sons of the early Chinese pioneers, as first generation Chinese Americans, served the United States in World War I.

remained administratively Chinese but augmented its work force with Mexican, Italian, Portuguese and Japanese workers.

SECURE IN THE NEW CENTURY

The twentieth century brought on a new era for the Chinese living in Stockton and in the Delta. His innate talents, adaptability, perseverance and patience continued to guarantee him financial success. Frugality and communal resources assured his family's security. Undaunted in his dealings with the whites, the Chinese took to long-term investments in this country. The Chinese had come a long way; in his lifestyle he had amalgamated eastern and western ways. He prided himself as an American citizen, and with equal concern he continued to instill Chinese ways into his children.

In a matter of decades he built his legacy in the great Central Valley, concentrating on family and property. Great wars would interrupt his tranquility; his native country and his newly-adopted one would soon look to him for help and, without reserve, he would respond to both.

CHAPTER SIX ENDNOTES

1. A leading agricultural center, Stockton hosted its first and only state fair in 1857; civic leaders had hoped to have the event return in four years after Sacramento, San Francisco and Marysville had a chance to sponsor the fair in their cities. However, in 1861 the decision by state law makers to keep the annual activity in Sacramento greatly angered Stocktonians. Local leaders, not to be deterred, decided to sponsor a district fair and invited other valley counties to participate. The San Joaquin Valley District Fair became an annual event with eight counties actively involved. Although the district fair was a much touted affair, exhibits were housed at various locations throughout town, often times in makeshift buildings put up for the occasion. By 1880 members of the Agricultural Association decided to raise funds for a permanent exhibit hall and sought a location in town that was within budget. In 1885 heirs of Captain Weber offered Washington Park as a possible site.

2. *Stockton Daily Independent*, September 13, 1887.

3. *Stockton Daily Independent*, August 22, 1893.

4. *Stockton Weekly Mail*, January 22, 1894.

5. *Hanford Sentinel*, Special Edition, "The Immigrant: Chinese," March 1893. *Stockton Daily Independent*, August 12-18, 1893.

6. *Stockton Daily Independent*, August 19 and 20, 1893.

7. *Stockton Daily Independent*, August 23, 1893.

8. *Stockton Daily Independent*, August 8, 1893. Carey McWilliams, *Factories in the Fields* (Boston, 1940), p. 77.

9. *Stockton Evening Mail*, June 28, 1899.

10. *Stockton Evening Mail*, June 30, 1899.

11. *Stockton Evening Mail*, June 28, 1899.

12. *Stockton Evening Mail*, July 1, 1899.

13. *Stockton Evening Mail*, July 5, 1899.

14. *Stockton Daily Independent*, June 12, 1901.

East Washington Street: A Reconstruction

7

In the preceding chapters we have documented the arrival and settlement of the Chinese in Stockton and in the county. This and succeeding chapters will delve into the world of the Chinese living in Stockton, explore their activities, businesses, organizations, and religious and secular beliefs and practices.

A study of their physical bastion reveals a unique geographic sanctuary where ethnicity, language and cultural practices were held in common and where clothing, equipment, medication, entertainment and food could be obtained in commodious quantity and variety: Chinatown.

Stockton, the metropolis of San Joaquin County, was also the hub of Chinese economic and social life. Today, the three former Stockton Chinese quarters—the settlement on Hunter and Channel streets with the Heung-shan Temple its focal point, the fishing and industrial complex south of Mormon Slough, and East Washington Street—no longer serve as Chinese communities. A historic reconstruction of both the fishing village and the Heungshan Temple area have become virtually impossible. Sale of the Mormon Slough land in 1893 wiped out all physical traces of the fishing village. The only archival clues indicating anything of its physical appearance are a few old newspaper articles and some sketches done by Ralph Yardley, a local cartoonist of the 1940s who drew upon his own memories and those of others who remembered the settlement.

Some documentation of the Hunter-Channel settlement does exist, but the Chinese occupied only a few buildings near the temple, and their numbers were too small to declare the area a truly self-sustaining Chinatown. Thus, the Chinese complex on East Washington Street is the only ethnic Chinese site in Stockton which can lay claim to a solid hundred years of unbroken and documented history.

Careful scrutiny of the Washington Street quarters recaptures and reveals some sense of the life, color and action found within this once third-largest Chinese community in California (after San Francisco and Sacramento). Numerous sources hint at the earlier years' inner dynamics. Fire insurance maps accurately pinpoint building sizes, doorways, back yards and alleyways. Business and city directories document the growth of a self-sustaining

Looking east on Washington Street through Stockton's Chinatown. Structures in the background are Saint Mary's Catholic Church on the left and the San Joaquin Agriculture Pavilion on the right.

community, and from these resources one can almost visualize company signs hung over doorways and professional shingles dangling from second-story windows. News articles, assessors' plat books and oral histories fill in many details of the social and economic life—happy moments, disappointments, new and the everyday experiences of life along the one-block corridor of Stockton's Chinatown.

ON THE CITY MAP

East Washington Street lay midway between the city's two other Chinese quarters and was thus a logical place for settlement. Housing was available close to the business district, and more importantly, the land lay on higher ground and was not as susceptible to the winter flooding as the Mormon Slough settlement.

The East Washington Street quarters actually consisted of two city blocks bounded by Market Street on the north and Lafayette Street to the south. It was flanked by El Dorado Street on the west and Hunter Street on the east. When the Chinese first moved into the area they occupied both the north and south sides of Washington Street. As the population increased, they spread out to occupy the other six sides of the two city blocks. By the turn of the century, Stockton's Chinatown complex had radiated to the streets west and south of the original two blocks.

Each block was divided into sixteen lots. Study of the property assessment records from 1860 to 1920 indicate that for some unknown reason the value of the property decreased as one moved in a southerly and easterly direction, i.e., Market Street property values were higher than those of Washington Street, and Lafayette Street dwellers paid lower taxes than those who lived on either Market or Washington Street. Corner lots were assessed higher than mid-block locations. Illogical assessment practices were common in all areas of Stockton throughout the city's history, and study of assessment rate changes in Chinatown proved it no exception. The most striking rate increase occurred in 1920 when all property values in that two-block location increased three to four times the amount of the previous four-year assessment, and it may be of more than passing importance that this rate increase coincided with the period in which American-born Chinese began buying property in Chinatown.

Sanborn maps were originally prepared by the Sanborn-Perris Company to help fire insurance underwriters by providing evidence of the actual building layouts and types of construction materials used. An 1883 Sanborn map shows more buildings on the north block of Washington Street than on the south. On Washington Street proper, both sides of the thoroughfare were lined by a row of brick buildings covering five or six parcels and measuring sixty feet deep and fifty feet wide. On the ground floor, each parcel was divided two to four times so that the average business space alloted to stores was both narrow and deep, sometimes only a bit over twelve feet wide, yet sixty feet long. The second stories of each of these buildings were divided into only two sections. The remainder of the two-block area had a number of one-story, wood-framed structures whose sizes varied in relation to their use; i.e., boarding houses were much larger than single dwellings.[1]

CITY DIRECTORIES

Contemporary directories are compiled to serve the needs of a specific group, and early city directories were no different. Publishers of city/county directories, which were generally financed through subscription, annually amassed geographic and business listings to serve a particular community, in this case the dominant white society. Quite unerstandably these early directories often omitted areas of towns occupied primarily by non-white residents and businesses. They did, however, include Oriental establishments that catered to whites located in the main part of town.

Among the few Chinese businesses listed in early city directories, one particular store stands out. Located at 182 Levee Street, the cigar manufacturing outlet of Auck Gune & Company always had its name in large, boldface type positioned prominently in directories and local newspapers.

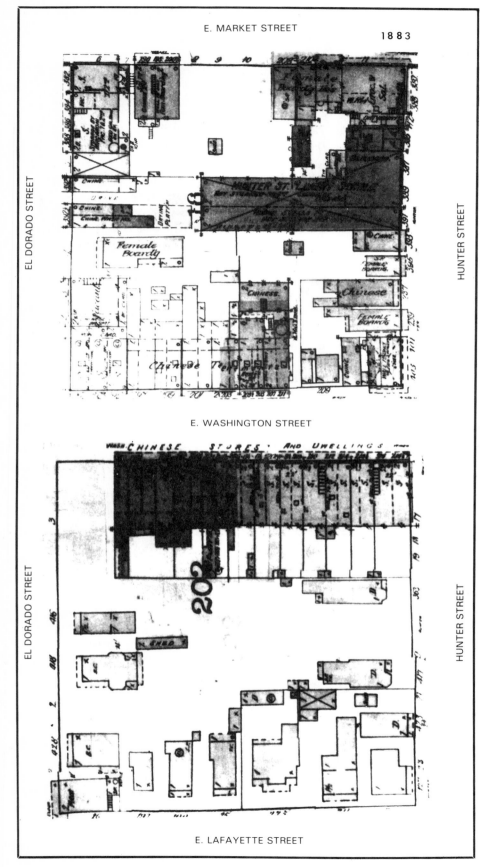

This Sanborn map shows five bordellos listed as "Female Boarding House" on the north block as well as a livery stable which was converted into a seventy-five-car garage and auto shop.

Toward the end of the nineteenth century the horse and buggy and drayage wagons were the only conveyance vehicles in Chinatown. This is an early photograph of On Lock Sam Restaurant (with men on the second floor balcony) which was founded in 1895.

A typical advertisement suggesting direct links to Chinatown reads:

AUCK GUNE AND COMPANY
Manufacturers and Dealers in the best Havana Cigars at the Lowest Wholesale and Retail Rates. Intelligence Office attached. Where the Best Help for Farms, Hotels, Private Families, Factories, etc. can be had.[2]

The Intelligence Office indicated was essentially an employment agency. Being conveniently located on the Embarcadero and conversant in English, owner Auck Gune turned a handsome profit as the go-between for Chinese labor contractors and white employers.

Some directory compilers saw Chinese businesses and residences of Chinatown as a separate world from their own. Washington Street addresses were rarely listed, and the 0-300 blocks of South El Dorado and South

Lee Yuen Merchandising Company stood on the northeast corner of El Dorado and Washington streets from 1878 when the company was founded. Lee Soon, a co-owner, is seen standing behind the counter of the store, c.1920.

Hunter and the 0-200 blocsk of East Market and Lafayette streets were totally ignored. In 1876 one conscientious agent made a concerted effort to list some Chinatown businesses in the directory and, accordingly, listed were seven grocery stores, a restaurant, two butcher shops, a general merchandise store, a drug store and the Tuck Fong Tai Kee & Company boarding house. It is difficult to know on which side of the street these businesses were located. Instead of actual addresses, the directory indicated only Washington or Hunter or on the corner of both.[3]

Wells, Fargo and Company directories also provide information on the Stockton Chinatown. In 1878 the company contracted with fifty-one Chinese businesses to handle its pick-up and delivery needs. Thirty-one of these clients were in Chinatown. Four years later, in 1882, its Chinese clientele increased to fifty-seven and the Chinatown trade grew to forty-three regular shops. Among these stores were eight general merchandise stores, three tailor shops, five grocers, four barbers, three restaurants, four butcher shops, three vegetable dealers, one physician and three opium establishments. Such a wide variety of businesses and professions suggests that business was booming in Chinatown around the time the anti-Chinese sentiment swept into the port city in the 1880s.[4]

Besides Wells Fargo several local steamers offered speedy and personalized mail service to the Chinese community. Immediately prior to a steamer's departure from Stockton harbor, a Chinese runner employed by the shipping line would scurry through the quarter picking up mail and small parcels destined for San Francisco.

REAL ESTATE INVESTMENTS IN CHINATOWN

Assessor's plat books indicate that all early property owners in the two blocks of Chinatown were white and mostly of northern Italian heritage. They bought these properties for rental purposes rather than for their own use. Changes in title for these Chinatown properties were the result of inheritance rather than sale or trade. The absence of active real estate exchange suggests these Italian landlords expected a long, profitable return on these investments. For example, two parcels on the northeast and southeast corners of Washington and El Dorado streets were purchased by the Bisango brothers in 1869 and remained a part of the L. Bisagno estate well into the 1930s. The building on the south corner, at various times, housed gambling enterprises, smoke shops, grocery stores and sundry other business enterprises during the Bisagno ownership. The north corner property had only one set of tenants during those sixty years.

The largest piece of property in Chinatown during the nineteenth century was owned by Zignego and Solari. The assessor's plat book for 1884 indicates these gentlemen purchased the back half of two parcels squarely in the center of the north Chinatown block. Over the years they increased their holdings until by 1916 their patchwork properties on this block equalled 27,500 square feet. At some point in their acquisition, the partners became the El Dorado Improvement Company, an unrealistic name, for according to subsequent Sanborn maps, neither improvement nor redevelopment occurred on the company's holdings.

No other section of Stockton has ever received as thorough an examination as Chinatown during the 1880s anti-Chinese period. Politicians, health officials and reporters, sometimes on official business but more often for self-serving purposes, marched into Chinatown and peered through windows, opened doors and climbed staircases to investigate conditions in the quarter. Systematic and meticulous documentation left no room for speculation; information on ownership particularly of absentee landlords, and building usages served as fuel for the anti-Chinese fire. Yet without these reports, initially damaging to the Chinese as they were, it would be impossible to reconstruct the heart of yesteryear's Chinatown.

One such investigative survey occurred October 15, 1885, and began at the southwest corner of Washington and Hunter streets in the building owned by C. I. Leach, a local banker. Leach had leased his property to Hong Fat, a Chinese merchant, for $100 a month. Hong, in turn, sublet the downstairs portion to two businesses and the proprietors of several small offices. A rooming house was located upstairs with a few apartments set aside for prostitutes. The roasting oven which triggered the devastating 1887 fire was located in back of this building.

Immediately west of Leach's property, V. Galgiani owned a somewhat narrower building which housed a clothing store and two rooms of gambling tables. Another Italian, A. Rossi, owned the land west of Galgiani, and the property, with a fifty-foot frontage, housed two stores, a barber shop and a restaurant with gambling tables located in the rear.

W. B. Johnson, who did not live in San Joaquin County, owned the next two lots totaling 100 feet of frontage, which he rented to five stores, a broker's office and two butcher shops on the lower floors, and a restaurant and boarding house in the second story. At the southeastern corner of Washington and El Dorado streets, the Bisagno building was used for a meat shop, a general store and a barber shop.

Across the street to the north, the other Bisagno property was leased to three Lee brothers who operated Lee Yuen, a merchandising store founded in 1878. Tenants of this building also provided shelter for members of the Lee clan. One partner, Lee Sing, served as an official court interpreter and led the Chinese contingent in the famous 1899 Fourth of July parade.

Adjoining the Bisagno corner lot was property owned by Mrs. Rosanna Farrington, an outspoken lady unafraid of defending her Chinese tenants at anti-Chinese meetings. Her tenants operated a gambling hall and a butcher shop on the downstairs floor and lodging rooms upstairs. Next door, Benjamin Gocke, an absentee landlord, rented his property to another gambling concern downstairs and a rooming house upstairs. Jean Catala, another owner who did not live in the county, owned the fourth parcel on the north side of Washington Street. Here, too, another gambling house doing active business could be found, but the property was also home to a store, a barber shop and an upstairs restaurant. In 1884 the two parcels on the east end of the block owned by partners Vizelich and Sanborn were sold to Zignego and Solari. The change of owners did not affect any of the businesses in the buildings; stores lined the lower floor and Chinese prostitutes occupied the upstairs.

Activities and color existed in greater number on the south side of the block than on the north side fronting Market Street. Peter Musto owned a two-story brick building on the southeast corner of Market and El Dorado where he operated a grocery store and a macaroni factory. The rear of Musto's building was used as a warehouse. Adjoining the Musto property on the east, the Stockton Bank-owned, two-story building was occupied by

Chinese prostitutes. An empty lot stood between the bank's property and L. Basilio's building, which was also used as a brothel. In the building at the end of the block, on the corner of Market and Hunter, a good-sized grocery store was located on the street level with a rooming house upstairs. Around the corner on Hunter Street, the predominant building was a large livery stable.[5]

The location of prostitute housing, first noted in local newspapers, was confirmed in the Sanborn map of 1883, which pinpoints at least five "female boarding houses," a more genteel term than "bordello" or "house of ill-repute." The Market Street bordellos appeared to be larger than those facing Hunter Street. However, the largest area populated by prostitutes was in the middle of the block, its property owned by Zignego and Solari. A wood-framed, one-story unit sat about twenty-five feet from the street near the El Dorado Street side. In later years this wooden structure was replaced by two one-story brick buildings, and the entire complex overlapped the adjoining lot. One could enter this area from either Hunter or El Dorado streets. This rather notorious entertainment center became known as the "bull pen" or Stockton's "cribs."[6]

Property listings indicate nearly one-third of the Washington Street owners were absentee landlords whose interest centered more on rents remitted on a timely basis than on their tenants' housing conditions. In their various inspection tours, health officials reported a scarcity of windows, which restricted both ventilation and light in the often smoke-filled rooms, and particularly in crowded sleeping areas. Fire officials shuddered at the sight of cooking areas; instead of stoves, bricks laid to about two feet high and four feet long, resembling outdoor barbecue pits, served as ranges in housing units without kitchens, stovepipes or vents. In buildings with kitchens, cooking smoke habitually permeated the interior of the buildings and blackened kitchen walls, and escaped only through windows and doors. Police considered the gambling halls the cleanest of Chinese businesses; however, the doors to these establishments hindered their sporadic raids. The doors were made of heavy wood about four inches thick and held shut by a stout wooden bar fitted into strong iron hasps bolted to the door casing. Many Stockton city ordinances adopted in November 1885 relating to gambling, fire, and minimum space standards were directed specifically at these conditions in Chinatown. And while angry white citizens berated the Chinese for these conditions, it was the landlords who were legally and morally responsible for such problems.[7]

THE SOJOURNER'S HOME

Chinatown as rebuilt by using public documents and newspaper files connotes a negative and sterile image. Even though the businesses were built and owned by whites, the businesses, interior furnishings, occupants and overall ambience more closely resembled bits and pieces of the village life these Chinese had left behind. The essential "Chineseness" of the area was obvious, the store signs suspended or nailed over doorways in pictographic calligraphy etched in black or gold ink. Like flags on foreign soil, these signs boldly proclaimed CHINESE even to those who could not read the hieroglyphics. When written in English, the names of many business houses, such as Kim Kee, Lung Hop or Gun Wah, tell us little about the business or its owners. But in Chinese, a simple message such as the name of the company written in two or three characters can identify the type of business, clan affiliation, and even the owner's euphemistic expectations for the business. In this regard, the store Lee Yuen when translated from Chinese characters reads "source of profit." Similarly, On Lock Sam, a popular restaurant on Washington Street, means "contentment" or "satisfied heart."

To the residents of Washington Street, Chinatown was a citadel surrounded by a sea of foreign influences, a warm refuge in which to kindle one's native spirit. Here, Chinese immigrants conversed in their own tongue fluently and rapidly with any and all. Hundreds of transient workers picked up letters from home and learned of news elsewhere. And here both Chinese and whites enjoyed cheap but good food or indulged in ten-course banquets.

There were simple pleasures within the magic boundaries of the East Washington Street Chinatown. A visit to a bordello could deaden the ache for one's wife or sweetheart left behind in the Toishan mountains. Intense concentration at the gambling tables could rejuvenate one's desire for instant wealth, a jarring recollection of the original dream to make it big in Gum Shan, the golden mountain. To these early Chinese, Washington Street represented cultural continuity and helped satisfy their intrinsic need to belong. Hundreds of bachelor sojourners called it home—to some, maybe for a few days out of the year; to others, the residence of a lifetime.

TWENTIETH CENTURY CHANGES

The year 1899 represented not only the end of the nineteenth century but a milestone in the legacy of Stockton Chinese as well. During the last decade of the old century, Chinatown had been geared to the needs of aging bachelor sojourners. Social activities such as visiting prostitutes and indulging in opium still existed, but they were clearly on the decline. Gambling operations continued to be a major industry, but all these businesses rode the roller coaster of economic change.

Washington Street in the early twentieth century still looked very much like the old Chinatown. Stores replete with work tools, utensils, bamboo baskets and hats, an assortment of practical western and Chinese clothing, notions and hardware were still the favorite one-stop shopping emporiums of visiting field hands. Tin cans of preserved duck, dried salt fish, imported mushrooms and dried delicacies in large wicker containers partially blocked

Earl Jann, pictured here at age four in 1914, is a third generation Stocktonian. His grandparents lived in the Mormon Slough fishing village. Following the sudden death of his grandfather, Jung Yee, the family moved back just south of Chinatown. Jann, following in his father's footsteps, made his career in the merchandising business.

the entrances to grocery stores, while baskets of fresh vegetables stacked on wooden crates formed an aisle on the sidewalk but remained well within the merchant's view should quick hands attempt to snatch an apple or other edible. In delicatessen windows, strong black iron hooks suspended mouth-watering slabs of barbecued spareribs, golden-hued ducks, roast pork and sausages to whet the appetites of passersby.

Yet with each passing year, those with keen eyes saw that the residents of Chinatown were following an assimilation course that befell thousands of Chinese across the United States. Little by little, Chinese residents discarded the traditional, loose-fitting, pajama-fashioned work clothes for western pants, shirts, and hard-soled leather shoes. Elaborately embroidered slippers, mandarin robes, and pillbox hats no longer indicated affluence. Merchants now preferred three-piece, pin-striped suits, conservative neckties and classic fedoras. Long queues worn tightly coiled about the head began to disappear as western hair styles were adopted to indicate support of the revolutionary movement against the ruling Manchu dynasty in China. English words, both written and spoken, slowly crept into daily conversations and business dealings.

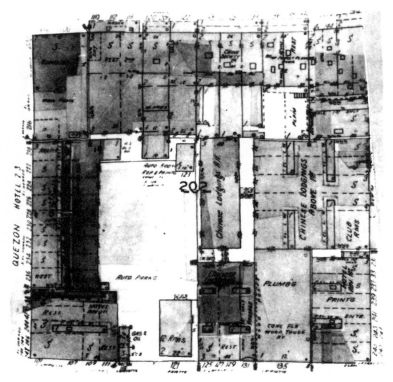

E. MARKET STREET

1917

E. WASHINGTON STREET

E. LAFAYETTE STREET

EL DORADO STREET

HUNTER STREET

Sanborn map showing changes in Chinatown. The north block shows a walkway around the two single-story bordello buildings. Narrow passageways between buildings were used as escape routes in and through the center of the blocks.

While a few die-hard drayage companies continued to haul goods in the horse and wagon, Chinese merchants, vegetable dealers and peddlers soon discovered gasoline-powered automobiles and trucks were more practical and economical. Cannery owners discovered trucks could be used for the dual purposes of hauling produce and transporting workers. Cases of canned goods and crates of vegetables stacked easily in the hull of the truck and, during commute hours, portable benches bolted to the truck floor turned the vehicle into a bus. In time, Model T's, Packards, Patriot trucks and Franklins hogged both sides of Washington Street where once the horse and wagon prevailed. With the gradual changeover to combustion engines, the large livery stable on Hunter Street was converted into a seventy-five-car garage and auto shop.

Chinatown changes were not limited to people and conveyances. The vacant land and space between buildings on both blocks of Washington Street seen on early Sanborn maps had disappeared by 1900. A turn-of-the-century picture of the same area shows densely impacted brick buildings flush against each other. Party wall agreements between adjacent land-owners allowed each building to straddle property lines.

On the north block, buildings facing the streets formed a peripheral protective wall and concealed the paths leading to the bull pens from public view. A long walkway surrounded the prostitutes' work area; on the north side the walk measured eleven feet while the south side had only a five foot clearance. Traffic entering and exiting the red light area could be observed from several back upstairs windows of adjoining boarding houses and restaurants. Two narrow entrances into the inner sanctum of the block and its maze of passageways existed on El Dorado Street, three each on Washington and Market streets and one on Hunter Street, all suitably obscured. In some instances the Chinese connected the second and third floors of adjacent but separate buildings by simply using the exterior walls of both structures, adding a front and back wall, subflooring and a ceiling. This construction covered the street-level passageways, which were no longer light and airy, and now resembled dark, dingy tunnels—a condition which piqued the imagination and curiosity of many white Stockonians. Raids into Chinatown became increasingly difficult as police found basement doors led to passageways, to other basements, and into rooms of other buildings. One could literally burrow into the heart of the block, and the alternate routes in and out were particularly convenient for those evading the law or escaping a vengeful countryman.[8]

In addition to the seasonal workers who annually trekked into the valley for agricultural or cannery work, in the early years of the twentieth century Chinatown received an infusion of new immigrants. Large groups of Japanese began to appear in San Joaquin County seeking employment in the fields. Because of their similar appearance, these new arrivals found lodging, similar food products and a modicum of cultural acceptance in the

Chinatown neighborhood. Within a short span of time, Japanese businesses could be found interspersed with those of the Chinese, although the main Japanese settlement was actually located just west of Chinatown on Washington Street between Center and El Dorado and on El Dorado Street itself. The Japanese frequented Chinese restaurants and gambling halls in the 100 block of East Washington; however, this block and the 100-300 blocks of South Hunter Street remained purely Chinese.

Chinatown absorbed a second population influx in 1906 immediately following the San Francisco earthquake. Untouched by the holocaust, Stocktonians organized relief efforts which sent food, money and medical supplies to the devastated city by the bay. Thousands of San Francisco Chinese fled that city following the fires which destroyed the greater part of its Chinatown. Oakland became the major Chinese evacuation center, and overcrowding became an immediate problem. Shortly, many fled the impacted east bay town and headed toward the Central Valley. The *Evening Record* estimated that 5,000 Chinese sought refuge in Stockton, while uncounted numbers opted for the safety of the Delta hinterlands. After a few months, when they felt it was safe to return to their city, many of the San Francisco Chinese left. Others migrated south, even to Los Angeles. Those who left may have felt cramped in the already crowded Chinatown; they also may have found the summer months in the San Joaquin Valley much too hot. Those who had been employed in urban occupations were unable to adapt to farm labor or cannery work, the only industries able to absorb the large number of unemployed. Relatives in Stockton helped those who were willing to adjust from a hectic urban lifestyle to the more leisurely pace of an inland valley community.[9]

HOUSING FACILITIES AND RECREATION SITES

The ever-increasing population of Japanese, the surge of earthquake refugees, and the accordion trek of seasonal workers put great demands on Chinatown. In 1926 the city directory listed only twelve rooming houses, but maps and oral testimony indicate at least twice that number of lodging places existed within the area. The second and third floors of multi-story buildings were often rented for short periods of time as well as for permanent residence. At 115½ East Washington Street, the Roosevelt Hotel occupied the entire second and third floors of the building, which extended the full length of the property that measured fifty by one hundred feet. There were forty rental rooms in this building, and next door the Wah Yick Hotel, with a gambling hall on the street level, was of similar size.[10]

All these hotels and rooming houses in the Chinatown area would be considered second rate by today's standards, but at least one attempt was made in the early twentieth century to offer more luxurious accommodations. In 1912, City Councilman Frank Madden, owner of two adjoining parcels on Hunter Street between Washington and Lafayette, announced construction of a large three-story housing unit which would be available for fifteen-year leases to Chinese companies. Madden stated that the first floor would be sublet for stores, and the upper floors would contain lodgings "equal in every respect to apartment houses built for white people." Madden intended to rent his apartments to wealthy Chinese farmers who wanted first-class accommodations whenever they visited Stockton. His plans called for suites of two or three rooms, some with housekeeping units, with the rest set aside for transient customers.

Fifty years later, the state highway department built a cross-town freeway through Chinatown during the course of which they bought and demolished Madden's building. Right-of-way records show that Madden's complex, known as the Kwong Chow Hotel at 223 South Hunter Street, did in fact house six shops on the ground floor. The second and third floors were separate hotels and each of their managers paid different rents. Each floor of the building had 9,260 square feet. Only fifty-four of the sixty rooms on the second floor were available for rental; the remaining six served as the manager's office, his private quarters, a store room, and a community kitchen area. There were only two bathrooms on the second floor for the occupants' use. Arrangements on the third floor were similar, although here some of the rooms had been converted into additional storage areas so that only fifty-one rooms could be occupied. Again there were only two bathrooms for the entire floor. Obviously, Madden's apartment building did not offer quite all the luxuries—let alone necessities—he claimed.[11]

Apparently when Madden built his complex the ordinance on the necessary minimum standard of cubic feet of air per person was no longer enforced, for individual rooms averaged only twelve feet by nine feet. Overcrowding, however, was a way of life in Chinatown. Bunk beds were stacked to the ceiling; each room was crowded, uncomfortable, unsanitary and hot. But it was a place for the single men to sleep and it was cheap. As deplorable as these lodging facilities appeared when compared to western standards, the tenants became accustomed to them, for they were similar to those provided in agricultural labor camps.

Housing for prostitutes became difficult to detect in the new century. The 1917 Sanborn map listed the "bull pens" and other brothels on the north block of Chinatown as merely "rooms" or "lodgings." The relabeling and obscuring of bordellos coincided with the disappearance of prostitutes in the occupation column of the 1900 census. Apparently, enumerators realized the notoriety of the area and attempted to obscure the facts. Additionally, they were trained to survey only those buildings facing the street with addresses, and may have been unaware that bordellos were located deep within the block; or even if they knew, the census takers may have been unable to gain access to these cribs. However, local citizens still recall when prostitutes were residents of the north block inner sanctum. Other places prostitutes frequented in the Chinatown area included the Kwong Chow

Hotel and the Juliana and Palace hotels. These two latter lodgings on the south block of Chinatown were built in tandem on Charles Hubner's old property at 125 East Lafayette Street. Although the bordellos were less visible, they remained an integral part of the teeming life of Chinatown.[12]

Opium dens also retreated from the public's eye. With the loss of legal status in 1908, state and city officials carried out raids to eradicate areas where opium smokers might congregate. These raids continued well into the 1930s. Known opium haunts were hidden behind a row of brick buildings on the northeasterly end of the Washington Street block. Stockton opium "dens" were actually separate sheds attached to the buildings, many of them adjoining drug stores or herb shops. Bow Tsee Tong, an herb shop at 141 East Washington, and Num Ning Tong, a drug store at 139 South Hunter Street, shared a common corner in the rear of their establishments and the backs of these two shops provided access to the same opium den.

The phrase "opium den" has in the twentieth century conjured up pictures of mystery and debauchery. But it should be remembered that local police found that the opiate was being smoked in downtown hotels and other locations outside Chinatown, indicating some popularity as a pastime among white citizens. It was unfortunate for the Chinese, whose own rooming facilities were so limited, that to find an area where he could partake of a mild stimulant, he was required to hide in an inner alcove appended to the back of a building. Descriptions of opium dens in China, San Francisco and other locations are quite similar to descriptions of those found in Stockton and suggest Stockton's hideaways may only have been in keeping with the nature of the now-illegal opium trade.

To the innocent passerby some entertainment centers in Chinatown were virtually invisible. Yet, when the right sign, question or gesture was given, one easily gained admittance. Gambling halls, however, were less easy to disguise nor were they meant to be totally obscured. As the 1917 Sanborn map indicates, gambling halls lined the westerly end of the block. Some used stores as fronts and vendors as lookout men. The You Lun Company, a small cigar stand at 104 East Washington, for example, served as the front for the Tai Sang Choy gambling house. Gambling halls which were not hidden behind other businesses were otherwise disguised by a play on words. As an example, the E. K. Lum & Company at 120 Market Street, and Chang Wah Company, 133 South El Dorado Street, were both listed as men's furnishings. The front section of the stores did contain a small show area displaying men's handkerchiefs, neckties and other haberdashery items, but most of the square footage was devoted to gambling. Gamblers knew Yet Quong & Company at 1 East Washington had fair gaming tables, but few realized the city directory listed it as a general store. Other gambling places were less inventinve and were simply listed as "Oriental" establishments. Chinese names for these gambling houses at 111, 117 and 121 East

Washington were Ng Woo Tong, Tong King and Chung Toh, respectively.[13]

Gambling houses frequently changed their names to attract a particular segment of the foreign population or as world conditions changed. Ng Woo Tong was once known as the "Berlin Company" but was changed to "New World." Tong King was called "Tokyo." The Yokohama, a Chinese gambling house on the northwest corner of El Dorado and East Washington streets, attracted Japanese patrons more than did the other houses. When whites and Filipinos began patronizing this establishment, proprietors renamed it the American Company. While some of the gambling houses accepted whites and non-Chinese patrons, most preferred to keep their businesses strictly for the Chinese trade.

Not all the Japanese living in the Chinatown area appreciated the Chinese gambling houses. In 1908 a group of Japanese businessmen filed a petition with the county board of supervisors asking that the Chinese gambling activities at Holt Station be closed. Among eleven of the Japanese petitioners were editors of two local Japanese newspapers and the minister of the local Buddhist Church. The petition stated:

> ... the Chinese gambling dens are kept open in Holt to the detriment of the community, especially those who being forced by unfortunate circumstances frequent these places ... [14]

The petition was received and filed on November 2, 1908, but the local law enforcement agencies may not have acted on the request for there was no appreciable increase in gambling violation arrests at the end of 1908-09.

DISTRICT ASSOCIATIONS AND TONGS

Three district associations maintained special facilities for the homeless, elderly, sick and dying members. The Heungshan facility was in the temple on North Hunter Street, the Sam Yup Association was at 19 East Washington Street, and the Sze Yup occupied a building at 216 South Madison Street. None of these facilities was actually within Chinatown, but all were near enough so the sick could walk easily to the herb shop, find assistance from nearby relatives, or make final arrangements and give instructions to family association officials for his eventual demise.

Family and clan organizations maintained their headquarters on Washington Street. Many of the buildings occupied by the associations were large enough to serve also as recreation halls where members could visit, read, play friendly cards or share an evening meal with kinsmen and friends.

Several tongs also maintained headquarters on Washington Street, for Stockton's many gambling establishments had attracted these organizations to the area to compete for a cut of the gambling pie. Anger, revenge, vendetta, bloodshed and ambush were but a few of the emotions and actions

The Sam Yup District Association building at 19 East Washington Street was one block away from the hub of Chinese activities. The organization's shelter provided temporary housing and social needs for people from the Sam Yup districts of the Guangdong Province in South China.

seen in these group headquarters, and not infrequently they spilled out to the public corridor. While a later chapter will detail Stockton's tong activities, it is important to note that all the tong offices were on the East Washington artery: the Suey Sing Tong was located at 137½ East Washington and the Bing Kung Tong sat across the street at 126 East Washington. During the local tong wars of the teens and twenties newspaper editors and citizens encouraged the police to cordon off Chinatown in order to let the tong members have at each other and "to kill off all the hatchetmen and put a stop to all the wars." However, press sensationalism created the opposite effect. Whites, curious about Chinese wars, ventured into Chinatown and stood just beyond the roped off area hoping to witness some action. Between 1910 and 1920 there were times when Washington Street served as a macabre tourist attraction.[15]

Gambling halls, bordellos, tong headquarters and opium dens spiced the Chinese community with excitement and color. These businesses were only one part of the Chinatown story, and yet an extremely important part, for each contributed to the economic health of the whole.

A NEW GENERATION, A NEW PLATEAU

Many first-generation Chinese, as aliens, had difficulty purchasing land; only second-generation Chinese, by right of being American citizens by birth, were eligible to own property. While laws acted as legal barriers to prevent Chinese from buying land, white property owners who contemplated selling to Chinese had to contend with other white social pressures. In the case of Chinatown property, the income derived from rent was both steady and profitable; some white owners felt no urgency to sell. In 1913, the first white-Chinese Chinatown property transaction occurred, almost fifty years after the Chinese first began occupying this particular part of the city. Heirs of Benjamin Gocke sold their lot on East Washington to Mar, Jan, Lew, et al. This particular lot had been in the Gocke family since its acquisition in 1869. Only one building stood on this parcel, and records indicate Mar and Jan owned two-thirds of the property, while Lew, et al., held the other one-third. In 1920 half of Lew's share was acquired by Mar, Jan and another party, Mrs. Wong Yau.[16]

A common practice among Chinese was to solicit a number of participants in major investments, not only to amass sufficient funds but to generate a spirit of cooperation as well. In this particular sale, the investors represented several major clans in Stockton. Names of the individuals listed on the deed may not necessarily have put up the money but were chosen by the clans because they were American born and thus eligible to purchase property. Mar Poy, listed as property owner for the Mar family investors, apparently was not even in Stockton at the time of the purchase, for county records show that in 1911, Mar, an employee of a local gambling house, was in El Paso, Texas, being held there for a murder investigation.[17]

Another anomaly to this property transaction was the involvement of parties other than those on the deed of purchase. A party wall agreement, signed May 27, 1913 showed Lem Sing, Lew Yuen and Lew Sheung Chuck, none of whom is listed on the deed, as responsible parties in the agreement with C. M. Jackson, owner of the adjoining property to the east: In 1963 when the Stockton Redevelopment Agency bought the property, acquisition files show that sales proceeds went to six individuals, including the earlier part-owner, Mrs. Wong Yau, who by now had acquired a three-fifths interest in the property.[18]

In its heyday, this first Chinese-owned building at 117-123 East Washington housed two gambling halls, Chung Toh and See Sing Loung, as well as the Mah Family Association office on the ground floor. All the units were

美國加省士作頓湘黃章弟兄合建之林肯酒店撮影

The Lincoln Hotel on South El Dorado Street, built in 1920 by the Wong brothers, was the pride of Chinatown. The five-story hostelry's interior and amenities equalled those of the other first class hotels in Stockton. The hotel was demolished in the late 1960s as part of the city's redevelopment project.

linked by connecting doors. The upstairs was occupied by the Wah Yick Hotel.

In 1919 a second piece of Chinatown property in the same block fell into Chinese hands when Wong Kee purchased land on the El Dorado Street side from the El Dorado Improvement Company (formerly Zignego and Solari). In 1920 Wong and his two brothers built a five-story hotel on the site complete with a full dining room, spacious lobby, damask-upholstered furniture and basement parking. Old-timers remember the Lincoln Hotel as "so fancy it was as beautiful as other first-class hotels in Stockton and it was the pride of Chinatown."

When the hotel was under construction, one brother, Wong Mow, an astute businessman, noted that the building on the adjoining property, still held by Zignego and Solari, laid seven inches into Wong's property. Wong insisted that a party wall agreement be filed whereby the former agreed to pay a dollar a month for the seven-inch infringement.[19]

During the 1920s and 1930s more Chinese bought property. As family, district and fraternal organizations matured, they bought real estate to increase their association's income. Merchants and individual families also turned to real estate investment and began to buy homes south of Washington Street. Some families invested their life savings in single dwellings built from Lafayette south to Charter Way and beyond as the city limits crept southward. These multi-ethnic neighborhoods in south Stockton were filled with first- and second-generation immigrants and all shared similar acculturation experiences. Families, no longer isolated in their own enclaves such as in Chinatown or the Mormon Slough area, noticed that they, like their foreign neighbors, were still steeped in their own cultural practices. In the ensuing years these residents felt their outlooks changing as they watched the western world enfold their children in the Americanization process.

Residential areas in north Stockton were not as receptive to Chinese occupants as the downtown and south areas, and when opportunities arose for the Chinese to buy, the neighbors' clamor was usually enough to discourage the Chinese. As late as 1936, Jim and Ruth Chew, an American-born couple, were forced to produce their birth certificates before a Stockton real estate agent would process the sales transaction for a home on Commerce Street north of Harding Way.

A LITTLE WESTERN ACUMEN

Optimism, a secure sense of their place in the community, and the ever-watchful eye for economic opportunities encouraged some Chinese merchants to seek parity with white businessmen. In the nineteenth century, white community and business leaders merely tolerated Chinese businesses in their midst, but as the twentieth century progressed they actively pursued

E. MARKET STREET

EL DORADO STREET · HUNTER STREET

BLOCK 20 · 1930

102 SAKIYAMA CO
108 PALACE RESTAURANT
110 CARUSO Boot Black
112 EL DORADO ROOMS
116 LINCOLN PHARMACY

112 114 116 118 120 124 126 130 132 138

HORN FOOK
112A ACME ROOMS
LIGHTNING CAFE
LEE BARBER
TAYLOR MEN'S FURNISHINGS
BALTIMORE HOTEL
HETCHY HETCHY Lunch Counter
MOSCOSA TAILOR
BALTIMORE HOTEL
TAYLOR FURNITURE STORE
VACANT

VACANT 103
PALM ROOMS 107
SHELBY ROOMS 113

117

120 LINCOLN HOTEL

GUYMAN & VASSAR GARAGE

125

124 ROMA LUNCH
124½ KUOMINTONG
126 FUJI ROOMS
128 WONG CHING BARBER
130 FUN KEE JEWELERS

NUM KING 129½
VACANT 131

136 ALTA ROOMS Above
138 T C SUIT CLEANERS
140 SANTIAGO Boot Black
142 NAKASHIMA BARBER
144 OSHIKA RESTAURANT

115½ HOTEL ROOSEVELT
119 WAH YICK Furnished Rooms
125 ON LOCK SAM

MIN ON CO 133
LUM JEW ROOMS 135
TIN SANG TONG Herbs 139

137½

LEE YUEN
BERLIN CO Ng Woo Tong
WONG WING BARBER
TOKYO CO Tong King
CHUNG TOH
SEE SING LOUNG CO
VACANT
VACANT
SUEY SING TONG
KWONG TUCK WO
BOW TSEE TONG
LEE ON CO Cigars
BOCK CHY TONG
WAH KEONG CO

101 105 107 109 111 115 117 121 123 127 131 137½ 139 141 143 145 147

E. WASHINGTON STREET

104 110 112 116 114 120 122 126 128 134 136 138 142 144 144½ 146 148

TAI SANG TAY Tai Fat Choy
YOU LUN CO
HAN HING CO
FOO LUNG
CHEW YING CHONG Groceries & Meats
CANTON LOW Restaurant
QUONG WAH YUEN Groceries & Meats
FOOK CHONG
BING KONG TONG
QUONG FAT CHONG Herbs
MAH HING CO
HEE CHONG Meats
KWONG JAN & CO
BOW NING TONG Herbs
WING WAH LUNG
SUEY QUAN TIN CLUB
CHII CHONG
KOO CHONG

128½ SUEY YIN TONG
134½ HEUNGSHAN BENEVOLENT ASSN

TSUE LOCK TING 213
YEE LEE RESTAURANT 215

216 WONG CHONG CO

BLOCK 29 · 1930

218 HASEGAWA CLOTHING
222 KAMBARA SHOES
224 NIKONIKO TEI CAFE

ORIENTAL HERB CO 217
BING KEE 219
GOLD STAR RESTAURANT 221

PASSAGE

JULIANA HOTEL AND APARTMENTS

223 QUONG CHOW HOTEL 2nd & 3rd Floor

226 TUCK HING CO
228 HOTEL FUKUOKA 1st & 2nd Floor
230 NAKAMORI BARBERS

JONES MARKET 225
YICK LUNG CO 227
VACANT 229

PASSAGE

232 LOS FILIPINOS Tailoring
234 TSURUMOTO Soft Drinks
236 MANILA GROCERY
238 HOTEL AMERICAN 2nd Floor
240 BILLONES PHOTOS
242 MYAN RESTAURANT
244 INOSHITA RESTAURANT
246 FILIPINO TAILORING
248 TOYO GENERAL MERCHANDISE

FILIPINO COMMUNITY CENTER
LIGHTHOUSE MISSION
MIUZUNO
TSUKAHARA Beancake Factory
SANFUKU RESTAURANT
PALACE HOTEL 2nd Floor
FUKAMI SIGNS

231 NEW VENICE HOTEL
YICK LEE BARBER 233
WING HING CO 235
NING YEUNG ASSN 239
SEE HING 241
SUN SUN Lunch Counter 243

PASSAGE

109 111 117 119 121 125 127

E. LAFAYETTE STREET

R.L. POLK & CO. 1930

Based on the 1930 city directory, these are the businesses listed for the two Chinatown blocks. Missing from the directory were the interior bordello businesses that could be found in Sanborn maps.

the Chinese trade as an integral part of their own business community. City directories now included a complete and reasonably accurate report of Chinese businesses. As the Chinese continued their low-key advertisements in local newspapers, white businessmen realized a virtually untapped market of potential customers lay in their midst. The Stockton Fire Department was one of the first organizations to tap that resource. A 1908 history of the fire department notes that twenty-seven Chinese merchants had contributed to the book's publication cost. Six were laundries; two businesses operated out of the Heungshan Temple building on North Hunter Street, Dr. Chong Juyan, an herbalist, and Tam Chong Yuen, a sewing factory. The remainder of the advertisers were businesses on Washington Street: Tuck Wo, Bing Kee & Company, Sun Fook Chong and Hung Far Low, a popular restaurant. Two historic businesses still operating today also subscribed, Lee Yuen & Company and On Lock Sam Company.[20]

The push to commingle their businesses with Stockton's more successful companies induced Sun Fook Chong, Tuck Wo, Wah Hing, Nim Sing, Lee Yuen and Woo Kee & Company to join the Stockton Chamber of Commerce in 1912 when membership in that organization totaled 135. In typical pragmatic Chinese manner, the merchants dropped their membership in the city organization when they felt it brought neither the prestige nor customers they had anticipated. In ensuing years other Chinese businesses continued to flirt with the chamber of commerce or other civic organizations they thought might serve their purposes.[21]

Family and district associations also began to manifest western processes. As a matter of practicality these family/clan offices consented to be part of the local listings in the city and telephone directories. Even their office methods began to reflect the western mode.

Assessors' plat books, Sanborn maps, city directories, newspapers and public documents give facts and dates on East Washington Street; Glenn Kennedy's memoirs provide the precious recollection of the sights and sounds of the once-thriving Chinatown in the era from 1900 to 1925:

> In the store windows were backscratchers, vases of sheerest porcelain, teakwood chests, brass candle snuffers, mandarin robes with gold brocade, jade goddesses, cinnabar boxes, and many, many other things of interest. On the sidewalk in front of the markets were open cases of steel-gray squid, and alongside was usually a bloody-aproned butcher, haggling over the price of dried fish or some other items. There were also live rabbits, quacking ducks and squawking chickens all in wire pens. In the windows of Chinese delicatessens were platters of crooked ginger root, green mongo beans, candied melon rinds, lichee nuts, and pressed smoked duck and barbecued spareribs on iron hooks. Herb shops displayed bottles filled with preserved snakes or dried sea horses.

Washington Street looking west. The On Lock Sam Restaurant at the far left end was relocated to Sutter and Sonora streets in the 1960s. This picture was taken just prior to redevelopment.

Chinese music came from an open window somewhere above, striking of wood on wood, music of fiddle and reed, and someone singing in a minor key. Old Chinese in black suits, black hats, and tieless shirts stood gossiping on street corners or sat in their association rooms playing cards.

At night, joss sticks burned and paper lanterns glowed on second and third story wrought iron ornamental balconies, with the gust of sound of weird and alien music from clashing cymbals, flute, mood fiddle and butterfly harp. This was Chinatown.[22]

CHAPTER SEVEN ENDNOTES

1. *Insurance Map of Stockton* (New York, 1883 revised to 1890), Map No. 202, Haggin Museum. Unfortunately, not all agencies or businesses share the same key system as the County Assessor's Office. The Sanborn Co. referred to the Washington Street blocks as #16 and #202 respectively; whereas the Assessor's plat books have the blocks listed as Block 20 and Block 29.

2. *Stockton Daily Independent*, May 10, 1882.

3. The city directories for the following years: 1856, 1873, 1878, 1883-88, 1895, 1900, 1901 and 1915 showed very few Chinese listings; however, the directories for 1876, 1910, 1915, 1926 and 1930 provided most of the information on Chinese businesses.

4. Wells Fargo and Company Express, *Directory of Chinese Business Houses for San Francisco, Sacramento, Marysville, Portland, Stockton, San Jose, Virginia City, Nevdada,* 1878 and 1882. Wells Fargo History Department, San Francisco.

5. *Stockton Weekly Mail*, October 17, 1885.

6. *Minimum Rates of Board of Fire Underwriters of the Pacific for Stockton, California* (New York, 1898), p. 408. Sanborn Map 1883, Map 16. Plat Book 1901, Block 20.

7. *Stockton Daily Independent*, October 15 and 29, 1885.

8. *Insurance Map of Stockton, California* (New York, 1917 revised to 1946), Map 16. *City Directory 1926*, p. 437.

9. *Stockton Daily Evening Record*, July 27, 1906.

10. Parcel No. 20-11 Mar, Nee, Jeung, et al. Parcel 20-12 Wong, William et al., Stockton Redevelopment Department.

11. *Stockton Daily Independent*, March 10, 1912. Addendum Sheet, Property File, Right-of-Way Department, CalTrans, District 10, Stockton.

12. Sanborn Map 1917. Interview with Harry Chin (1980, 1984), Earl Jann (1981-82), Lily Chin (1981), Ken Chinn (1981).

13. *City Directory 1926*, pp. 376, 401, 437. Interviews with Harry Chin (1980, 1984), Earl Jann (1981), Ken Chinn (1981), Don Lee (1981-83), Robert Mah (1983).

14. Board of Supervisors, San Joaquin County, Petition of Japanese to have Chinese Gambling Houses Closed, November 2, 1908. The action of the Japanese business community deserves further consideration. The wording of the petition implies that men who frequented gambling houses, particularly the Japanese customers, were at a psychological and social disadvantage as unwitting victims. While this may have been a legitimate social concern, the timing of the petition coincided with the growing anti-Japanese movement in California's history which resulted in the passage of the Gentlemen's Agreement in 1908 and the Alien Land Law of 1913. Directing others to the social ills of the Chinese may have been a diversionary tactic by local Japanese to take the pressures off themselves.

15. *Stockton City Directory 1926. Stockton Daily Evening Record*, January 15, 1915. Interview with Harry Chin (1983).

16. Plat Book 1916 and 1920, Block 20. Interview with Robert Mah (1981).

17. Official Records, Book I, p. 11, San Joaquin County Historical Museum Archives. County documents show that in 1911 Mar Poy was detained in El Paso, Texas on a murder charge. One local Chinese speculated that Mar may have gone to El Paso to help his employers settle a gambling debt. Texas officials apparently had insufficient evidence to hold Mar on the murder charge but while he was still in their custody they initiated deportation proceedings against him as persona non gratis. However, Mar filed an appeal claiming he was born in the United States and could not be sent to China. Mar's appeal was upheld in the higher court in 1925.

18. Parcel 20-11, Mar Nee, Jeung, et al., Stockton Redevelopment Department.

19. Parcel 20-14, Lot 13, Schoenig, Herman A. and Martha; Parcel 20-6, Lot 14, DeLucchi, Laura. Party Wall Agreement of Wong Mow and S. Solari and Louisa Zignego dated March 21, 1921. Stockton Redevelopment Department.

20. Allen M. Robinette, *History of the Stockton Fire Department 1850-1908* (Stockton, 1908), pp. 86 and 88.

21. *Stockton Daily Independent*, January 20, 1912.

22. Glenn Kennedy, *It Happened in Stockton 1900-1925* (Stockton, 1967), I, pp. 40-41.

Influences, Pressures and Consequences

8

The Chinatown which existed in Stockton during the late nineteenth and early twentieth century is now but a memory for it was swept away in the 1960s by freeway construction and city redevelopment projects. Yet another facet of the Chinese story comes into focus by probing into the lives of the Chinese and examining some of the pressures they faced, decisions they were forced to make, and even the consequences of their actions.

Before the Chinese left their homeland, most knew their destination, at least the town. Their choices were predetermined in family council based on advice from those who had emigrated before and who were a part of the mutual aid network. In San Francisco the Sam Yup, Sze Yup and Heung-shan district associations had temporary housing available for all new arrivals, and they retained smaller facilities in inland communities. Yet, even within these district shelters, immigrants were often lonely. Many were strangers to each other and, except for distinctive dialects and regional folkways, had little in common with their fellow lodgers.

The young Chinese did find other places where he could feel at home; after all, the custom of making room for one more in China also applied in America's Chinese communities. Stashed in the back of the traveler's mind were other names and locations of relatives, distant kin or clansmen, even businesses owned by men who shared last names. The Chinese pioneers who preceded the flood of new arrivals established businesses and prospered, and were now in a position to help others from their natal villages. Through experience the business pioneer learned that by sending for and sponsoring brothers, nephews and cousins, his business flourished with their help. They were kin, less apt to cheat him, and were, of course, willing to work for less money. The offer of aid tended to bind incoming Chinese to a place where money, supplies and food were available—to say nothing of fellow-ship and similar language. The prosperous pioneer also displayed an altruistic bent, offering use of his facility openly and generously and going well beyond the simple proffer of a cup of tea, a meal or a bed in the store-room.

In such places where pioneers and subsequent immigrants gathered, bonding and kin ties were renewed. While some were related by blood,

Within the Chinese community an individual could seek aid, shelter and resolutions to problems from his district, clan and fraternal organizations. Representatives of these associations meet as a council of elders known as Chung Wah (Chinese Association of Stockton). These are Chung Wah members in 1943.

others claimed only clan relationships and traced their geneaology back to an obscure or even mythical ancestor. Still other men casually or informally formed loosely-knit bonds. Soon long-term personal relationships developed. Custom and courtesy dictated that younger men address a member of the generation past as uncle and those two generations away as grandfather or granduncle. Other men were casually referred to as cousins, godfathers or goduncles. While the titles may seem somewhat artificial, the relationships were based upon respect and had a "family" touch.

Communal sites—such as the back of a laundry, the corner section of a Chinese restaurant or even the stoop in a recessed alcove of a store—became educational centers for new arrivals. Here the young immigrant learned the ways of the network and how best to profit from his Chinese heritage. Through conversation the young man was reminded to pay his family association dues, attend the annual clan spring banquet, and live frugally. Here the literate wrote letters for those who could not, and the storekeeper processed remittance money for wives and relatives in China. The young learned of the Chinese welfare system as well as how to fend for themselves in the white world and how to depend upon each other to make their way.

Old-timers served as role models in place of fathers, brothers and uncles at home. They also taught skills that would enable the young to make something of themselves and apply Chinese know-how to western techniques.

The younger ones also learned about the pitfalls of living among whites, gained knowledge of local laws and what to say when questioned by authorities. Among the difficult lessons they learned were whom to trust, what areas to avoid, which towns were anti-Chinese, where to find work,

民國卅二年十二月十七日作市頓作中華會館

which work sites were controlled or managed by other Chinese district groups (a situation which made job opportunities nonexistent for non-members), how to solve transportation problems, and how to acquire clothes, food and medicine in isolated locations.

When a man planned a brief trip back to his homeland, he was advised to place his belongings and assets with one whom he trusted; in getting his travel documents together, he was told to seek out witnesses to verify his tenure in this country; and, finally, he learned how to go about paying the exit fee imposed by the Chinese community. As part of the Chinese mutual aid system each returnee was assessed an obligatory twelve-dollar contribution. Nine dollars went to the Chinese Benevolent Association and three dollars to his own district association. (This amount covered both administrative and shipping costs to have remains of all Chinese who died in America returned to the homeland.) All homebound Chinese knew this fee was paid in the San Francisco headquarters of his association. The receipt for the sum paid was collected by an association official at the pier.

The young learned one method of circumventing the exclusion laws—by investing in local trading companies he could upgrade his occupational status, thereby allowing him and his family to travel more freely. The system was rather clever as explained by the late Louie Yee Pai.

Louie Yee Pai was born in China in 1891. His three older brothers had journeyed to California earlier, and when he was eighteen, Louie Yee Pai joined them. His father, Louie Seun Hawk, had lived in Stockton in 1882, but returned to his native village to retire. As each of the Louie boys reached manhood, he followed his father's footsteps into the San Joaquin Valley.

Many of the early Chinese pioneers were young and single and immersed themselves in a bachelor-sojourner society. Some sent photographs home to impress their kin with their well being.

Yee Pai arrived in San Francisco in 1909 and was taken by company wagon to Suey Sang Lung, a local store on Grant Avenue, where the young man reported his safe arrival to his sponsor, the owner. Yee Pai then headed for Stockton, where his older brothers operated a truck garden plot on land leased from the Vignolo family across from the campus of the present-day University of the Pacific. Yee Pai applied himself in his brothers' fields and also peddled the vegetables they grew.

There was one problem which increasingly concerned Yee Pai: his entry papers indicated he was single when he had, in fact, married a year before his departure. Quite naturally, he not only missed his homeland, but his bride as well.

Listening to the advice of old-timers, he frugally saved $1,000, then took the money to the Shanghai Bazaar, a trading company located at 645 Grant Avenue in San Francisco. The money was used to buy shares in the company, for which investment he received a receipt and a stock certificate bearing his name. He waited and waited for the company to declare a dividend, but none ever arrived. For a time he believed he had thrown his hard-earned savings away, but eventually realized the wisdom of the counsel given by the elders. The bonafide shareholder's certificate had elevated Yee Pai into the merchant class, for he now had shares in a company. By moving from the laborer to the merchant classification he was legally qualified to return to China and bring his wife to America. In 1912 he returned to China and sired two children who, with their mother, joined Yee Pai in California in 1928 with no immigration difficulty. Such a financial transaction as this was a legitimate maneuver, and several other trading companies in San Francisco performed similar services for many others in the same position as Yee Pai. Yet the importance of the story lies not so much in Yee Pai's success as in the wisdom he showed in listening to his elders' counsel. Such advice helped cushion America's rocky roads for many young Chinese who came before and who were yet to come.[1]

THE LUCKY AND THE LESS FORTUNATE

With a similar quest as the young white men Horace Greeley told to go west, when the Chinese argonaut left his homeland he experienced a wide spectrum of living conditions and job situations. He developed skills and gained a sense of well being. His lot was, perhaps, easier than that of his white counterpart because of the extensive Chinese and institutional aid available. There seemed little chance an individual Chinese could fail. But measuring success is subjective, and while some use such factors as wealth, prestige, family name, recognition and reputation, others prefer the more qualitative measures such as the health and welfare of one's children or even the ability to live a quiet, unobtrusive life.

One example of a flamboyant, successful businessman is Charles Ar Showe, a Boston tea merchant who visited Stockton in 1878. Although his stay was short, his life story enhances our knowledge of the Chinese American experience elsewhere.

The editor of the *Stockton Daily Evening Herald* was quite taken with Mr. Ar Showe and ran a feature article on him—this in itself quite extraordinary. During the interview the seemingly modest, unassuming but intelligent businessman spoke fluent English, although he had a decided Chinese accent. Showe stated he became a naturalized American citizen in 1860 and lived in Boston for thirty-two years. He had been married to an American woman for twenty-eight years and had three sons who, Showe proudly proclaimed, were "full-blooded Yankees." The oldest, age twenty-five, had married an American girl and worked in Showe's business. His second son was away at school, while the third still lived at home. Following the recent death of his wife, Showe decided it was time to visit his homeland and he was here on the West Coast to reacquaint himself with the Chinese lifestyle and language before actually making the journey home.

Showe reported many details about himself such as the fact he was a member of the Episcopal Church and he knew six other Boston Chinese who were also American citizens, three of them married to white women. It is interesting to note that the article indicated Showe's company hired both Chinese and white workers. The editor noted: " . . . Showe would have forgotten his native language to a great extent if it were not for these Chinese . . . As it is, in his conversation with other Chinese he drops off into the English language about every ten words. He apparently does his thinking in English and translates his thoughts into Chinese."

Politically, Showe and his Chinese friends were registered Republicans. He expressed great contempt for Denis Kearney, whom he once saw at Faneuil Hall in Boston, and as to his opinion on the purported California Chinese problem, Showe said he would prefer to see a better class of Chinese come from China instead of the laborers. Because he saw himself relatively well-integrated into the white culture he felt other Chinese could find more opportunities in the farms and factories back east where there was less hostility.

Showe attended the interview armed with documents showing he had traveled in Europe. He had attended the World's Fair in London in 1850, and among his possessions was a letter from Queen Victoria with a British seal affixed. Showe also possessed letters from Secretary of State William Maxwell Evarts and Mayor Pierce of Boston. While displaying these papers may seem a bit ostentatious, the editor pointed out: "With these documents he will have no difficulty in making his American citizenship understood and respected."[2]

Without a doubt, Showe's life was impressive, and beyond the personal data he provided, Showe demonstrated good planning by immersing himself back into the Chinese culture before he returned to his homeland.

In contrast to Charles Ar Showe, most Chinese in the United States earned a reputation as quiet achievers: the special care Tom Wah Att gave the Asa Clarks, his surrogate family, and the fact that love was reciprocated when the Clarks laid old Tom to rest in their own family plot, symbolizes a life-long story of love and respect. Koo Luke's courage, demonstrated by ignoring the instructions of his district association and registering under the Geary Act, was that of a man displaying a sense of self-preservation and an unobtrusive but deeply-felt belief in law and order.

In the annals of the Chinese community, men who made favorable impressions on the white community, those who aided their fellow clansmen and others who raised their children honorably were unequivocally regarded as successful individuals. Among this number, several Stockton

Chinese merit special notice: Lee Yuen and Lee Sing, both court interpreters, storekeepers and Chinese community leaders at the turn of the century, clearly distinguished themselves. Other businessmen such as Wong Sai Chun, Billy Wong and, of course, Louie Yee Pai, must also be mentioned.

For centuries Chinese have lived, worked and functioned as closely-knit groups, and the traits of sharing and giving have become normal practice. Yet, there are always those in any society who flow against the cultural grain of their ethnic group. And, in Stockton, there were some who, for one reason or another, retreated from kin and family responsibilities, ultimately withdrawing from both the white and Chinese societies.

One such individual was Ah Tat, a hermit. For several years, Ah Tat lived in a small hut on Sargent Tract in the northwest part of the county. The local Chinese wanted nothing to do with the old hermit for he carried a keen-edged hatchet and preferred to beg for rice money rather than work. In addition, Ah Tat ate roots, wild grass and Chinese tuber potatoes he harvested from the river banks. Ah Tat came to the attention of authorities in 1899 when the sheriff was informed a vagrant Chinese who appeared to have leprosy and other ailments had been seen. Upon investigation, Ah Tat was found to be in good health, but quite eccentric. Because he was both physically and mentally competent, the court charged and convicted him of vagrancy and he was sentenced to ninety days in the county jail. Yet once he had served his time, Ah Tat resumed his reclusive lifestyle.[3]

Chinese inmates at the Stockton Insane Asylum, by virtue of their incarceraton, tell of those who were banished from society because of mental illness. Some, when given the chance to return from this purgatory, preferred not to, as was the case with Lung Foy, mentioned in a previous chapter.

Among immigrants who found their stay in this country less than propitious, the least fortunate were those who, because of circumstances and tragedies, could no longer tolerate the pressures of life nor life itself. Yook Sung, a twenty-two-year-old who died by his own hand in 1876, experienced a depth of loneliness and mental anguish that beset not only Chinese but individuals in other societies whose dreams of fortune and fame became disillusionments.

Yook Sung was imprisoned in the county jail for allegedly robbing another Chinese. During his trial, the non-English speaking Sung apparently did not get his side of the story across to the authorities. According to one cellmate's testimony following Yook's death, Yook told him he did not know why he was in jail. There had been little communication among the four cellmates. A major factor was dialect differences, and also, each was deeply engulfed in his own misery.

As Yook awaited transfer to San Quentin the three cellmates noticed that the young man grew increasingly despondent. Once, Yook made a gesture that he was thinking of committing suicide, but a second cellmate motioned him not to do it. In the early evening of January 11, 1876, Yook gave the jail trustee some money, a letter of instructions and a bone ring which he asked be given to a Chinese prisoner on another floor. The trustee forgot the letter in his possession until the following morning when he found the young man had hanged himself by his own queue which was wrapped around the upper bars. The suicide letter was immediately translated for prison officials; while it does not give great insight into Sung's reason for suicide, it is poignant in its forthrightness:

> I die tonight, no more see you. Got five dollars in my pocket. I going to hang myself. Tung You You is my father, he lived in Soi Hong Kong, China. Tell Jim Edmunds Ah Chuck is no good man and to tell the lawyer so. He wants to get money and go back to China. I die at 2 o'clock tonight. Tell all my friends to make some money and go back to China. Tell Bow Long Sah Company I die and they give you ten dollars to bury me with. I was born August 18 and am 22 years old. Give ring and money to Ah Fook.[4]

Taking his own life was Yook Sung's ultimate solution when he saw no hope for his future. His suicide note summed up concisely his knowledge of the Chinese burial system and his attempt at clearing his name.

Jail officials were surprised his cellmates did not try to stop him or alert the jailer immediately of his death. However, since his mind had been made up they felt they were in no position to interrupt the course of fate. Yook Sung may be an extreme case; nevertheless, his outlook on life and death does reflect a particular segment of the Chinese American experience.

SELF-PRESERVATION AND SAVING FACE

As part of their group-centered philosophy, Chinese pride themselves on conformity rather than individuality. The examples of Lung Foy, Ah Tat and the tragic end of young Yook Sung suggest, however, that life in the predominantly male society was not easy even with advice from elders and assistance from the family-clan mutual aid network. A psychological profile of the average young Chinese of the period shows that within their own community, men without the tempering influences of women and family exhibited anger when frustrated. They took cues from their peers and, at times, reacted rather than reasoned. It is important to note a cultural caveat: Asians place great importance on face-saving. Situations and incidents must therefore be scrutinized carefully because of this particular trait.

In definition, "face" is a perceived image, a visage one wants to project—mostly of wealth, prestige and integrity. Maintaining one's face is a primary responsibility learned in early childhood. A loss of face results in bringing dishonor to one's family. Causing someone to lose face is to create a doubt about that person's character. In the Cantonese language, when one person

According to the county "mug" book, Ah Ching was convicted of assault with a deadly weapon and sent to Folsom State Prison. An entry to the left of this photo states: "DEAD— Suicide at Folsom June 26, '86." Although the circumstances which caused him to break the law are unknown we can nevertheless sense his feeling of desperation and hopelessness.

accords another respect, he is "giving face." Hence, face encompasses many dimensions. For some, face formed the basis of one's purpose, decisions and actions in life. At times, face guided motivation, and at other times gave an excuse for vendetta and retaliation by instilling courageous feelings, loyalty and purpose to the defense of honor.

Chinese convicted of criminal activities also were concerned about their self image. In the courts judges normally handed out three types of sentences: straight county jail time, commitment to the state prison at San Quentin, or public works details. In San Joaquin County the Chinese preferred Sheriff Cunningham's hospitality, they feared San Quentin, and they didn't "like the idea of being herded with white vagrants and forced to work on the streets with a ball and chain attached to their ankle, particularly when there was an off chance they might be recognized by their friends." To the Chinese, the crime or the punishment was not as important as a public loss of face.[5]

Both individually and as a community the Chinese have often been portrayed as weaklings who would rather flee than fight when threatened, and at times, their defenses appeared non-existent. Unlike westerners, however, the Chinese abhorred direct confrontations and opted instead for indirect methods which centered about pre-planned strategies for dealing with unpleasant situations. While on the surface they seemed tolerant of white harassment, in reality the Chinese were demonstrating extreme patience. Among themselves, their tolerance levels were very low; where the white man's ignorance could be excused, insults by fellow countrymen could not be. The Chinese believed in fair play and self-preservation. Sometimes, however, their concern for face-saving forced them into acting rashly.

White pioneers who understood the Chinese after decades of contact saw the oriental demenaor as quiet, serious and non-malevolent. Yet these people also knew the Chinese were neither simpletons nor pushovers. Some who employed Chinese praised the industrious, tolerant and somewhat pacificist nature of the uncomplaining workers, but others learned that these hard-working men from the East would explode quickly when ired. The Chinese expected decent wages for an honest day's work, and when they felt they were not treated fairly they had little compunction about expressing their feelings, particularly when group solidarity and numerical strength bolstered their cause. This was essentially the situation in which 2,000 Chinese tunnelers found themselves when they struck against Central Pacific in June 1867. The Chinese learned that the railroad's white laborers received forty dollars a month for an eight-hour day in comparison to the thirty dollars and ten- to twelve-hour days worked by the Chinese on the same project. They demanded equal compensation. Charles Crocker, of course, was not one to let little details slow him down and he brought in strikebreakers. The strike did last a week, but the presence of scabs was enough to make the Chinese reconsider their position, particularly in light of possible total employment loss. Even though their efforts went for naught, the fact that these Chinese asserted themselves gave others the inspiration to express their concerns.

On August 15, 1867, two months after the unsuccessful railroad strike, nineteen Chinese employed on the Stockton-French Camp gravel turnpike project arrived at the job site an hour late. The contractor, a Mr. Stanley, angered because of their tardiness, announced that he was going to deduct nineteen hours' pay from the group's total wage, one hour for each worker, more than two work days' worth of money. This arbitrary decision infuriated the Chinese, who, after a few words with the contractor, retired to their nearby tent. Stanley then moved to demolish their tent, but the Chinese armed themselves with cleavers, firearms, shovels and clubs. The following day Stanley convinced the police to round up the angry workers and brought charges against them. Two days later the court judge dismissed Stanley's case because of conflicting testimony. Although they had been tardy, the Chinese were quick to spot Stanley's ruse to save himself some money.[6]

As a rule the Chinese did not believe in instigating trouble, but when pushed to the limit or physically threatened, they stood as tall as any man. As an example, after an unusual snowstorm one January day in 1880, citizens found sport in friendly snowball fights. A number of rowdy individuals decided to use Chinese passersby as targets. One suggested that they go to Chinatown for more action. The Chinese braced themselves for the impending onslaught. According to the *Herald*, as the young whites entered the Chinatown neighborhood they found their intended victims armed with clubs, bars of iron and knives, and the Chinese dealt blow for blow. To sum up the incident the *Herald* concluded: "The Chinese are to be commended for their conduct as this was one instance where they came out ahead."[7]

Newspaper clippings help explain how individual Chinese handled situations involving face-saving and self-preservation. Their racial pride moved a few to correct misinterpretations made about them in local papers. For instance, in 1852 when the Chinese presence was still a novelty, a news article suggested they were being brought to California as slaves. A Chinese restaurant owner marched into the *San Joaquin Republican* office and demanded that the paper print a retraction. The following day an item appeared which refuted the editor's initial statement: "John wanted to set the record straight that the Chinese are not slaves and not under contract."[8]

As taxpayers, the Chinese also felt they were entitled to the same police services given white citizens, and were not adverse to expressing their position. One afternoon in 1928 a Chinese peddler reported to the police that his horse and cart had wandered away while he was buying vegetables at the waterfront. Later in the day he called back at the station to see if his horse had been located and became angry when he was told it had not. He stated: "G_ _d_ _ _policeman sit on chair all time. No go lookie." A police reporter who overheard the comment was surprised at the outburst but agreed there were citizens all over Stockton who could fully appreciate the comment.[9]

In another incident, a young stevedore known as the bully of the Stockton waterfront, thinking to entertain the crowd by tripping a passing Chinese, thrust out his foot. His intended victim, seeing the trap, stopped short of the foot and quickly kicked the stevedore's other foot from under him, sending the man sprawling onto the concrete. According to the witnesses, "as the Chinese walked away he was cheered by a number of men standing about while the toughy, embarrassed by the coup, hurried into a nearby saloon."[10]

The young of any culture are often tempted to settle their problems by fighting, and the Chinese are no different. When anger went beyond the fist-swinging stage, knives, hatchets or guns became part of the action. One mishap caused an explosive situation between young Chinese which could be called the story of the aimless spit.

Quite often in this day and age one can still see a passerby expectorate in public. While it may be disgusting to witness, the act itself is a reflex action that men seem to execute easily, regardless of place. One morning Ye We Hack, who lived on the second floor of the northwest corner building on Hunter and Washington streets, woke up, stumbled out onto the balcony, stretched his limbs and, as part of his normal waking ritual, cleared his respiratory passages. However, as Ye expectorated a large glob of phlegm from his throat landed on the face of Quong Ah Sung, who happened to be walking by. Greatly angered and insulted, Quong pulled out a pistol and shot at the overhead offender. Luckily the gun was old and rusty, and the bullet went astray. Immediately both gentlemen were on the street corner engaged in more than just a heated argument. Insults accompanied physical blows. When the police arrived and the matter was sorted out, Ye returned to his morning routine. But Quong was arrested for carrying a concealed weapon without a license and discharging it in public. He paid his fine, and eventually the Ye-Quong conflict was resolved when both family associations looked into the dispute.[11]

Feuds also provided another arena of warfare in Chinatown, for the roots of antagonisms often went beyond the family and clan and disappeared into the mists of history. Like the Hatfields and McCoys, the Heungshan and Sze Yup Chinese have historically been at odds with one another, and historians have yet to find the origin of the dispute. The Sze Yup-Yeong Wo (the official name of the Heungshan Association) War of 1854, which occurred in Weaverville, California, showed that such feuds could easily be rekindled far from home. Participants in this particular confrontation prepared for the pitched battle an entire week and used a variety of weapons in the sortie, including tridents, shields and swords. On July 4, 1854, the two groups assaulted each other in an open field. Accounts vary as to how many Chinese were involved and range from two hundred to six hundred. Eight died in the conflict and an unknown number of individuals were wounded.

Locally, the separation of the Heungshan colony on the Hunter-Channel Street section of town and the Sze Yup on Washington Street three blocks to the south may have prevented hostilities between the two groups. In 1881-82, however, a couple of shooting scrapes between individual Chinese from both districts refueled antagonism. During this period Dr. John Ho, court interpreter, herbalist and caretaker of the Heungshan Temple, was charged with fraud and made a quick exit from town. In court cases involving individuals from the Sze Yup group and Heungshan group, the good doctor's translation tended to favor his own countrymen. Dr. Ho was succeeded by Je Jen, another Heungshan, and he, too, was accused of being biased.[12]

Lee Yuen, a Sze Yup who became the official court interpreter in 1894, did not allow his loyalty to interfere with accurate translations. Even though his reputation was impeccable, he still carried a gun for self-protection. Yuen had no difficulty obtaining a permit to carry a concealed weapon, but other Chinese without such permits were fined twenty-five dollars when charged and convicted. Much of the firepower in Chinatown during the years of the tong wars, however, was unlicensed and used by tong members for self-protection.[13]

THE AMBIENCE OF THE GAMBLING HALL

In a society where men spent their recreational hours confined to a small area, tempers would flare and injuries followed on the heels of insults. The Chinese spatial environment was limited and they were not welcomed elsewhere than in Chinatown. They could not afford leisure travel, a change

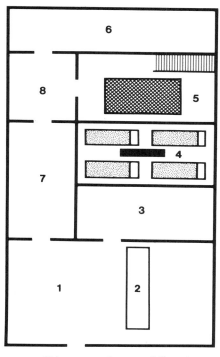

CHINESE BUSINESS AND GAMBLING HOUSE

1 Store   2 Counter

3 Small room with box window from which cigars and opium are dealt out

4 Tiers of bunks and opium table

5 Tan room with stairway

6 Kitchen and eating room

7-8 Corridors

ADAPTED FROM THE <u>STOCKTON</u> <u>WEEKLY</u> <u>MAIL</u>
February 6, 1892

Diagram of a gambling house and opium room from a Chinese New Year article of 1892. Reader was left wondering how one entered the opium smoking room and where the stairway led to from the Tan room.

of scenery or to become involved in sports. A few Chinese did relax by flying kites on Washington Square, but that activity was as rare as the leisure time others used to ride bicycles when the two-wheelers were introduced at the close of the nineteenth century. Some Chinese had the opportunity to witness local fiestas at the nearby green when the Mexicans held their religious and secular celebrations, but neither group would intrude on the other's cultural activity nor would they have been welcomed. Only the whites had the audacity and curiosity to dabble in the affairs of other cultures.[14]

So the Chinese looked within their own community for conversation, companionship and moments of excitement, often in the gambling halls. Even those living on the farms along the river anticipated Saturday night gambling in Stockton's Chinatown, Holt Station or in the river communities of Isleton, Walnut Grove or Locke. As they rode into town, jammed into flat-bottom horse-drawn wagons, their minds were recalling gaming rules and envisioning or reviewing betting strategies conceived during working hours while stooped over the rich brown soil. They were anxious to try out their system at fan tan, a button elimination game; pai gow, also known as Chinese dominoes, which used both red and white dotted tiles; marking off their favorite characters in the eighty-character poem lottery; or other games such as dice and poker. Gambling charged the workers' spirits, sharpened their minds, and deadened their loneliness. For many, gambling was a social outlet, and, as with opium, the Chinese indulgence was moderate—few ever became addicts.

In Delta towns, to find a game was just a matter of walking through the front door of the gambling house, where a plethora of gaming tables beckoned. Stockton's welcome mats, however, were much less visible. Unwanted guests were blocked in many ways: by a lookout running a cigar stand, a series of thickly-hasped wooden or iron doors bolted with stout timber, or an isolated foyer with a door encasing a grilled peep window. Inside, the large gaming rooms were smoke-filled and poorly ventilated. Various sounds assaulted the visitor: the slamming down of chips, a cuss word or two as unlucky cards were slapped on the table, the din of the hopeful standing three and four deep around various gaming tables. At one end of the room the cashier, in his cage, counted out money as fast as dealers raked in the cash; the lottery operation also claimed a section of the room as runners brought in customers' tickets and clerks transferred the marked characters onto the official house forms. Twice daily the proprietors randomly selected twenty winning characters from the esoteric poem.

On a table or small stove near the kitchen, an urn filled with steaming hot tea welcomed customers and visitors. As an added enticement, most of the gambling halls also offered free meals. Shortly before the scheduled repast, these halls were filled to capacity. In the Delta three meals were served daily. Breakfast was at eight in the morning and consisted of rice gruel, doughnuts, and coffee or tea. At noon a lunch of chow mein, soup, rice, a combination meat-vegetable dish and tea appeared. Around five in the afternoon another substantial meal was served. At ten in the evening coffee and bread were offered. The city gambling houses offered only two meals a day, at four in the afternoon and ten in the evening, although free tea was available throughout the day.

Those who enjoyed a purely Chinese ambience patronized gambling houses where dealers called out numbers and winners only in the Chinese language. In other establishments, when sufficient numbers of whites, Japanese and later Filipinos showed consistent interest in gambling, investors set up separate halls and operations geared to the foreign clientele. English was spoken in these places, and lottery forms used eighty numbers for the eighty characters. White were hired as bouncers and watchmen to keep customers in line.

Generally gambling concerns pooled their resources and hired their own white security personnel in addition to the usual city policeman assigned to the Chinatown beat. In the 1880s Orrin Langmaid, a retired police chief, was hired by the local Chinese businessmen as Chinatown's peace officer. Langmaid's knowledge of the law and the ties he had formed during his years on the Stockton police force proved extremely beneficial to his employers. After an 1885 raid of Stockton's gambling houses, Langmaid charged, before the district attorney and city council, that Police Chief Ben

Top: These are posted announcements of lottery drawings. Major gambling houses ran from two to four daily lottery games, and each drawing was identified by name and drawing time.

Right: The eighty-character Chinese poem on the lottery ticket evolved into an eighty-number form when whites and Filipinos took an interest in the game.

Rogers' forced entries into the gambling halls were illegal, and he took issue with the chief's clean-up campaign.[15]

Part of Langmaid's duties included making bail arrangements for arrested dealers. City officials and newspaper editors knew Langmaid was on the Chinese payroll and suspected the city policeman who patrolled Chinatown and the police chief were having their palms greased by Langmaid's employers as well. At one point reporters discovered evidence that Je Jen, the court interpreter, and a Chinese doctor on El Dorado Street were collecting monthly assessments from the gambling houses for contribution to a special police fund. One article reported twenty-seven fan tan tables assessed seven dollars per table and five lottery companies who anted up seven dollars each. The total collection approximated $224 a month. Expenditures included twenty dollars each to the two collectors and $184 for the police and incidental protection.[16]

Payoffs, disposing of evidence before police broke through gambling room doors and hiring lookout men were only a few of the methods proprietors used to cover all the bases. Yet, these schemes also were employed in other Chinese gambling houses in America.

Out-of-town gambling investors periodically tried to gain a foothold in Stockton; but since the Wongs and Mahs, two of the three major families in town, already controlled a good portion of the business, newcomers' efforts were quickly discouraged. Yet try they did. For instance, on December 17, 1878, police were called to Washington Street to break up a fight between Stockton gamblers and gamblers from San Francisco who had attempted to set up a bank game in the den operated by the Stocktonians. The Stockton group resented the intrusion into their territory and at least one hundred men from both groups were battling each other when the police arrived. When push came to shove, however, the Stocktonians refused to identify or press charges against the invaders. Only one Chinese from San Francisco was arrested, for carrying a concealed weapon. The newspaper article reporting the incident ended with sound advice to those who would attempt to muscle in on the Stocktonians' action: " . . . San Francisco gamblers must not interfere with our local institutions.—Never!"[17]

TONGS AND TONG WARS

Chinese tongs or secret societies have existed in California since the early 1850s. Some historians claim that young immigrants who, for various reasons, were disenchanted with their own family-district associations or were unwilling to abide by their rules set up fraternal organizations for mutual aid, socializing and protection. Other historians believe that men from smaller, weaker clans started tongs as a reaction against the powerful families, such as the Wongs, Lees, Yees and Chins, who controlled the Chinese Benevolent Association and among whom the leadership position rotated.

This view of the Stockton "cribs," heart of the city's prostitution area, was taken from the walkway in the interior of the north block of Chinatown.

One must understand the differences between the family-district organization and the tongs. The former, as torchbearers of cultural continuity, administered burial needs and provided guidance, a variety of welfare services and shelter. The tongs, on the other hand, were interested in control of the social activities: gambling, prostitution and drug operations.[18]

Young men who were easily influenced, those who enjoyed the camaraderie of peers, and others who were impressed by the power tongs held over recreational outlets made prime candidates for the tong organizations. However, some old-timers reported they joined the tongs because such memberships offered excellent employment opportunities in the gambling houses and other businesses where tong influence was strongest.

Many tongs resorted to violence to settle disputes among themselves, and there were many reasons for such disagreements: drug trafficking problems, theft of another's prostitutes, disputes over organizational territories, insults, or lies—yet the violence could also be touched off simply by hot tempers or too much to drink. Also, the fear of losing face often signaled the opening charge of full-scale war. Feuds erupted in various communities, and it was often impossible to trace the misunderstanding back to its point of origin.

In the late 1800s tong wars involved individual killings, and revenge was sought on a personal level. Tong members used knives and hatchets to carry out their assassinations. After the turn of the century, they resorted to revolvers, rifles and even bombs. In this later period the killings became indiscrimate, as long as the victim was a member of the opposing tong. For lack of better terminology, whites generally referred to the particularly vicious tongs as fighting tongs and their hit men as highbinders.

In singleminded pursuit of their purpose, tongs often offered rewards for the elimination of an enemy. During the First World War and into the 1920s, the going rate was $500 per dead opponent, although local leaders or presidents of opposing organizations commanded a higher price, as much as $2,000. Notices in Cantonese, called "chun hung," were posted on the tong bulletin boards, and if an individual in the hiring tong cared to do the job, he would post a reply notice. This reply did not necessarily identify the acceptor but simply let others know the assignment had been taken. When the job was completed, the reward money was placed in an envelope, posted on the same bulletin board, and discreetly collected. Yet the chun hung served a double purpose—in addition to soliciting a hit man, it informed the intended victim his time was short, and he immediately went into hiding or left town.[19]

Most of the Chinese gambling establishments were syndicated tong operations. In Stockton's family gambling concerns, at least one partner in any given business was a tong member, and that tong served as that establishment's protector. Unfortunately, Stockton's Chinese social history is tainted with a high number of tong incidents, as far back as 1876 when two San Francisco tong members were killed and two others wounded in Stockton.[20]

Of the twelve groups operating in the Bay Area, only three—the Suey Sing, Bing Kung and Sen Suey Yin tongs—rose to prominence in Stockton. Two others, the Hop Sing and Suey Ong, achieved some sense of notoriety for a short time. The Bing Kung Tong, an offshoot of the Chee Kung Tong, was particularly strong. In fact, this organization controlled most of the gambling operations in the Central Valley and north to the Canadian border, and it was extremely difficult for other tongs to establish themselves in the smaller communities, the Delta or even Sacramento.

From 1902 to 1924 at least thirty-five tong-related incidents occurred in Stockton, episodes which virtually terrorized the other inhabitants of Chinatown. Chinese not associated with tong activities watched in silent horror as a small number in their midst were stabbed, shot or murdered by strangers, or sometimes by acquaintances. The Chinese code of silence hampered police investigation time and again, although when a tong realized that it was being overwhelmed by an opponent's numerical strength, it did not hesitate to ask for police protection.

Depending on the circumstances of the conflicts, alliances between strong and weak tongs lasted only until that particular dispute was resolved. Subsequent flare-ups saw different sets of liaisons. As a rule, however, in Stockton the Bing Kung Tong was often supported by the Sen Suey Yin Tong, and the Suey Sing Tong was generally allied with the Hop Sing Tong. All of the groups were quartered in the heart of Chinatown. The Bing Kung facilities were on the south side of Washington Street, at 126 East Washington, and its ally, the Sen Suey Yin, was located at 128½ East Washington. The Suey Sing headquarters lay almost directly across the street, at 137½ East Washington Street.[21]

Local tong incidents were singular in nature, generally ambushes. While not all tong violence resulted in death, the following accounts give ample evidence of the pressures tong members, local police and the Chinese community itself faced during the period of greatest tong violence, 1912 to 1924.

During the two-month period of March and April 1912, four Chinese died of gunshot wounds. After the murder of Wah Lee, a hotel keeper, on March 11, tensions deepened in the quarter. Compounding the problem was a gambling dispute which developed between two other local men—one a member of the Suey Sings and the other a Bing Kung. Aware of the situation, police expected the other shoe to drop at any moment, and it was not long in coming. On the afternoon of April 23, a shot was fired from the Bing Kung Tong headquarters into crowded Washington Street, apparently aimed at some Suey Sings on the north side of the thoroughfare. A burst of gunfire answered. In the ensuing panic two white men who were working on the cobblestones of the street dropped flat into the shallow excavation of some removed cobblestones with bullets flying over their heads. A woman ran from a store during the battle, stumbled and fell into the gutter; a merchant ran out and grabbed her, pulling her to safety. Others sprawled face down in the street where they had been standing. People inside adjacent buildings retreated to the deepest recesses of those structures and hoped the bullets would not penetrate the walls. About 150 shots were fired, and as quickly as the incident had begun, it was over. One man had been shot in the throat, one through the lungs, five others were hospitalized and thirteen arrested. The police immediately cordoned off Washington Street from El Dorado to Hunter. Two officers were assigned to cover the area, and all gambling establishments were closed. Pan Lun Man, a tailor; Lun Louie, a cook; and Kew Louie Jok, a merchant, all died from wounds received that deadly Saturday.[22]

By the end of May 1912 the *Stockton Evening Record* noted that from this particular local incident a series of vendettas and retributions occurred all along the West Coast, resulting in the deaths of twenty and the attempted murder of yet another twenty. The paper also noted how brazen the hit men were, for all the victims had been killed in broad daylight.[23]

Stockton's gambling houses were closed for almost five months, and the ban was lifted only when the Chang Wah Company, a dry goods store fronting for a gambling establishment, protested that many local business-men were beginning to feel the financial pinch as whites, Japanese and many Chinese were staying away from Chinatown.[24]

Less than a week after the gambling ban was lifted, the Suey Sing Tong held an elaborate banquet for 300 members and friends at the Canton Low Restaurant, just three doors down from the Bing Kung Tong headquarters. Suey Sing membership was estimated at 400, and this banquet seemed not only fraternal but a display of strength as well. Among the many guests were officials from the coroner's office and the sheriff's and police departments. The guests, apparently all men, were escorted to the banquet in limousines provided by the hosts. As an article described:

> Seated at the sides of each of the guests were the most exquisite young Chinese maidens from San Francisco. The coy maidens with their faces hidden mostly behind fans were attired in the height of Chinese fashion in the costliest of silk gowns, wearing jewelry that would make the average white society woman green with envy. Some of the fifteen young women wore bracelets from elbows to their wrists, brooches, pins and hair ornaments that were most elaborately patterned. It was estimated that each was bedecked with gold and jewelry valued at not less than $2,000 per woman.[25]

Through means such as this banquet, local Suey Sing leaders managed to convince city officials of their goodwill, although the other tongs remained vigilant, for no tong ever took an opponent at face value.

Three years later, in San Francisco, a tong war suggests the heavy-handedness of the Suey Sing. In the early evening of January 24, 1915, the heads of the Sen Suey Yin and the Suey Sing met at a summit meeting on Waverly Place in the bay city. The two groups planned to discuss a series of disputes which had occurred the preceding year between their members in Chinatowns from Marysville south to Monterey. During the course of the conference differences of opinions turned into heated arguments and, suddenly, Quong Quock Wah, president of the Sen Suey Yin, was fatally shot. Joe You, also a Sen Suey Yin, standing in front of his tong's headquarters, was gunned down only moments after Quong's murder. Across the bay in Oakland's Chinatown, Cheung Leung, another Sen Suey Yin member, was attacked by four gunmen and shot twice, in the shoulder and hip. In Stockton that same night at 7:30 P.M. two men walked into the office of a gambling house at 103 East Washington Street and emptied their gun into the proprietor's son, who was sitting at his father's desk. The victim was Yee Gim, a twenty-eight-year-old bookkeeper and a member of the local Sen Suey Yin. The gunmen quickly left the premises, dropped their Colt revolvers on the sidewalk and fled west on foot down Washington Street. Although the police recovered the revolvers, no one was arrested, for none admitted seeing anything.

Meanwhile, to add fuel to the night's excitement, Ah Wah, a Suey Sing member, was struck by three bullets in a shootout at Holt Station, eight miles west of Stockton. A saloon keeper testified he saw the gunmen get into a taxi headed for Stockton after the shooting.[26]

The Sen Suey Yin Tong charged that the murder and wounding of their members in San Francisco, Oakland and Stockton were premeditated by the Suey Sing Tong, who, they suspected, never intended a peaceful accord. The simultaneous attacks certainly did not seem coincidental. Locally, the Suey Sings were so fearful that they asked for police protection and requested Chinatown be closed. The incidents, however, continued.

On January 27 funeral services for Yee Gim were held. The family ordered the casket placed on Washington Street in front of the Suey Sing head- quarters and held the services outdoors. A score of deputy sheriffs and policemen patrolled the area to prevent any outbreak. The idea of conduct- ing the funeral in front of the rival tong's headquarters, of course, was to "flaunt the deed in the faces of the enemy." Because of Yee's personal popularity and the sensationalism which surrounded his murder, hundreds of white and Chinese spectators crowded onto Washington Street to witness the funeral in macabre fascination. Yee had recently married, and his young bride threw herself on top of the coffin and had to be pried off by members of the mourning party. The funeral procession to the cemetery took place under heavy guard. This murder had a bizarre twist: Yee Gim had been a Sen Suey Yin, but his father was a member of the Suey Sings who had murdered his son.[27]

Yee Gim's murder was avenged two months after the funeral. At twelve o'clock on March 6, 1915, Sue Yip, a fifty-five-year-old cook and a Suey Sing, was sitting inside a store at the northwest corner of Washington and Hunter when two young men gunmen appeared at the entrance and opened fire. A month later, a Suey Sing cook was pursued by five Chinese hit men as he returned to his employer's house at the southwest corner of Acacia and San Joaquin streets. The pursuers, reportedly under twenty years of age, were Sen Suey Yins anxious to collect the $500 bounty on the cook. The cook's employer, William Buckley, heard the commotion outside, armed himself with a revolver and ran out to help. Together Buckley and his cook routed the hit men, but the cook did not leave the Buckley home for several weeks.[28]

The discord of 1915 continued through the following year. In 1917, in the month of May alone, a total of five Chinese were laid to rest in the Stockton Rural Cemetery, all killed by bullets. Death took a toll from the membership rolls of all the tongs, but the futility of these vendettas was lost on those bent on settling scores and others enticed by the bounty money.

Although the Suey Sing Tong was involved in most of Stockton's tong problems, its members were generally older men, at least a generation older than most Sen Suey Yin members. In fact, the growth of the Sen Suey Yin was attributed to younger Suey Sings ousted from that group for one reason or another. Once they became Sen Suey Yins they vowed to kill members of their former tong and split the bounty money with members of their new ally, the Bing Kung Tong.[29]

Patterns did develop following tong violence. When retaliatory pressures reached the explosive stage, Stockton tongs not only sought police protection but they also hired white men to help guard their headquarters, and most stayed close to their own facilities, believing there was safety in numbers. One other pattern emerged among the hit men: after making a kill the highbinders got rid of their guns and left town. While the police had little difficulty locating the weapons, they could not connect the weapons to any individual. Lacking today's sophisticated fingerprint identification procedures and hampered by Chinatown's code of silence, the police rarely made any headway in apprehending the tong killers.

Chinatown's code of silence deserves a word in itself. Among the Chinese, news of tong incidents spread quickly via the telephone, telegraph and word of mouth. More often than not Chinese communities got wind of disputes long before the police, the newspapers or the white community. Almost everyone in Chinatown remained close-mouthed, and only when an innocent bystander became the victim of foul play did the family and district associations press the police for investigation.

The burial records at the Stockton Rural Cemetery list a total of twenty tong-related killings between 1912 and 1921. It is not known how many were wounded in these incidents during this nine-year period. Data on the deceased shows they were relatively young, between twenty-two and fifty-five. Most were bookkeepers, merchants or cooks, although one was a hotel keeper and another a tailor. All were employed in urban occupations, which left plenty of free time for tong activities, as opposed to the farm laborer who spent his hours toiling in the fields from sunup to sundown.[30]

By 1924, disputes among tong members were dwindling, and in 1925 there were no local tong killings. Some old-timers believed the tongs had "buried the hatchet." Because of what we now know regarding the extensive and wanton stabbings and killings associated with this period of Chinese American experience, we must empathize with those who were then young and impressionable and also those who made the fatal decision to enter a tong brotherhood in those days.

Tongs today in no way reflect their colored past. The tong-active period, however, cannot be excused or ignored in Chinese American history, and it also must be placed in context with other violent activities within our nation's history. The twenties also ushered in the period of prohibition, bootleggers, racketeers and gangsterism. Race was the major difference between the white gangsterism, with its Saint Valentine's Day Massacre and similar incidents, and the tong wars.

The presence of the very few children in the Chinese community, such as this young boy in 1897, reminded many single men of their financial obligations to their families in the homeland.

AN UMBILICAL RESPONSIBILITY

A great many young Chinese heeded the advice of their elders. Not all became involved with the tongs and not all gambled away their hard-earned money at the gaming tables, although the temptation to do both was tremendous. Young men like Louie Yee Pai and Wong Sai Chun were fortunate that their lives became filled with family and work. Their responsibilities were immediate for their families lived in this country. Other Chinese felt their parents' needs in China were long-termed and superseded their own desires and ambitions. Yet, as time went by, conditions for the Chinese in America and in San Joaquin County changed while the wants and needs of a family in China did not. A letter preserved in the Haggin Museum gives insight into the dilemma and futility of one Chinese male whose story was, perhaps, the story of countless others. The letter was written to Cheong Jim Low in 1935 by his older brother in Canton:

> You left home at the age of twelve, you are now forty-four years old. You
> have left home for thirty years and have never returned home. You have
> been lazy as a young man which is the reason for your wasting life in a
> foreign country. You are hurting yourself if you do not mend your
> backward ways. If you do not save while young, old age will become
> miserable for you. Your mother is sixty-seven years old and cannot do
> any work, when she is ill she cannot cook for your father and herself.
> Come home and care for them.

A reader of this letter might be inclined to believe its recipient a lazy ne'er-
do-well, and if such searing criticisms were not enough, the writer continued:

> We received your hundred dollars remittance in early September. The
> house repairs required two to three thousand dollars. You promised to
> send the money for repairs. The balance of $1,000 is still outstanding. If
> you have money send some home to clear the bill.[31]

This last was not a request, it was a demand, and it seems evident that
Cheong's family could not begin to fathom his life in the United States.
Although they were experiencing hardships in China, their pressure on
Cheong, even from afar, made life difficult for him as well. No matter how
frugal a life he lived, no matter how much money he saved and sent home, it
would never be enough, and the demands and criticisms would never end.
The fact he had arrived in 1904 at the age of twelve and, without parental
guidance, managed to feed and clothe himself was in itself a miracle. During
the tong war era Cheong was in the prime of life, and he managed to avoid
falling victim to tong violence. The money he sent home expressed the
depth of his filial piety even when work and money were almost non-
existent for him during the Depression years.

Like other young Chinese immigrants, Cheong felt his obligatory ties to
his parents. His reluctance to return to his homeland may have been that he
had spent the greater part of his life in the United States and decided that this
country would be his permanent home. Cheong's life, like many others,
became a culmination of both Chinese and American influences and
experiences.

CHAPTER EIGHT ENDNOTES

1. Interview with Louie Yee Pai, Stockton, 1981.

2. *Stockton Daily Evening Herald*, November 20, 1878. Evarts served as attorney general for President Johnson.

3. *Stockton Evening Mail*, June 27 and July 1, 1899.

4. *Stockton Daily Independent*, January 12, 1876.

5. *Stockton Daily Independent*, December 6, 1886.

6. *Stockton Daily Independent*, August 15, 1867.

7. *Stockton Daily Evening Herald*, January 28, 1880.

8. *San Joaquin Republican*, April 28, 1852.

9. *Stockton Daily Independent*, January 28, 1928.

10. *Stockton Daily Independent*, March 31, 1908.

11. *Stockton Weekly Mail*, December 19, 1885.

12. *Stockton Daily Evening Herald*, February 2, 1882; *Stockton Daily Independent*, September 12, 1885. Many of today's second and third generation Chinese Americans can still recall being forewarned as young adults that they should not marry a mate from another district. This societal taboo was largely ignored by those whose upbringing became more Western than Chinese in later generations.

13. Documents: Permit to Carry a Concealed Weapon 1897-1905 and Certification of Chinese Interpreter 1894, 1897, possession of Esther Lee Fong, Stockton.

14. *Stockton Weekly Mail*, July 17, 1886; August 8, 1891.

15. *Stockton Daily Evening Herald*, February 17, 1885.

16. *Stockton Daily Independent*, September 14 and 15, 1885.

17. *Stockton Daily Evening Herald*, December 18, 1878.

18. The word "tong" means hall or great chamber in Cantonese. The title used by organizations suggests not only a meeting place but also the people who are members. There is a vast difference between gambling tongs and other Chinese associations which also used the name tong; i.e. Suey Sing Tong was a gambling tong but the Bow On Tong was a charity unit attached to the Kong Chow Association. In Cantonese, Sunday School is referred to as "Ly Bai Tong" or rather the gathering place where one meets on Sunday.

19. Glenn Kennedy, *It Happened in Stockton* (Stockton, 1967), p. 54. Interview with John G. Wong, Stockton, 1980.

20. *Stockton Daily Independent*, September 11, 1876.

21. Stockton City Directory, 1926.

22. *Stockton Daily Independent*, April 25, 1912. Kennedy, *It Happened in Stockton*, p. 53. Stockton Rural Cemetery, Death Register, Book "C."

23. *Stockton Evening Record*, May 28, 1912.

24. *Stockton Evening Record*, July 7, 1912.

25. *Stockton Daily Independent*, July 13, 1912.

26. *Stockton Evening Record*, January 25, 1915.

27. *Stockton Evening Record*, January 28, 1915.

28. *Stockton Evening Record*, March 7, 1915; April 19, 1915.

29. *Stockton Evening Record*, January 25, 1915; March 7, 1915.

30. Stockton Rural Cemetery, Death Register, Book "C."

31. Letter to Cheong Jim Low, October 7, 1935, Haggin Museum, Stockton.

Women and the Institution of Marriage

9

The bachelor society dominated most of the Chinese history in this county from the days of early settlement to almost the turn of the century. Life was bleak for hundreds of single Chinese living an almost celibate existence. Those who emigrated as young men soon realized that while they were of marriageable age, finding a mate was as difficult as finding a large gold nugget, for Chinese women were a rare commodity. Married men who came to this country alone saved their money until they could be reunited with their families. These reunions often were delayed for several decades. Some continued to work here and sent money home to support their families. For them the warmth of family life with the laughter of their children under the ancestral roof eluded them.

Even though the story of these men is one of bravery, sacrifice and loneliness, the true builders of the Chinese legacy in this country were the family units. The topic of Chinese women comes at a late point in this book, but it is placed here for the sake of spatial development. And as we attempt to understand the parameters of their lives within the context of the total Chinese story, we are overwhelmed at the magnitude of their contributions.

Chroniclers of the mid-nineteenth century focused primarily on the arrival of Chinese men in California. The arrival of their women was almost totally ignored. The few Chinese women here did not fit a preconceived image found in books and described by visitors to the Far East. Western travelers were in awe of the Chinese women of the Imperial Court; tales of their small, bound feet became stereotypical descriptions of women in China, at least ladies in high society. Women with big, unbound feet were thought to be from the lower class and certainly were not considered ladies.

The thousand-year-old practice of binding the tender young feet of girls began in the royal houses. It was the court women's attempt to imitate the willowy and graceful glide of dancers and courtesans. Scholars and poets applauded this bizarre custom as women's ultimate sacrifice to mutilate bodily parts into love fetishes for their men. In Chinese literature these deformities were described as "golden lilies" and "orchid hooks." In reality, bound feet only rendered a woman's movements virtually impossible, and, in her old age, servants were necessary to aid her in dressing, walking and so

A Chinese wife traditionally remained in China to tend the family hearth and care for her husband's parents while he sought his fortune in the new world.

forth. Parents continued to bind their daughters' feet as a sign of their own wealth and in order to help assure marriage. A young lady's helplessness indicated she was so well off she need not tax herself by any sort of work. The white Victorian mentality of the period apparently placed Chinese women with bound feet on the pedestal with white "ladies."

THE COUNTY'S FIRST CHINESE WOMEN

During the gold rush, an enormous imbalance of men and women occurred within all ethnic groups. Stockton's early censuses show that here, as elsewhere, men outnumbered women by more than ten to one; the count was even higher among the Chinese. Thus the appearance of the first Chinese women in Stockton warranted not only some excitement but news coverage as well. The headline of the *Stockton Times* for March 12, 1851, read, "Distinguished Arrival From the Celestial Empire" and detailed the fact that when the steamer *Mariposa* sailed into Stockton harbor that day white men at the pier were astonished to see a Chinese woman disembark. According to the locals, "She created quite a sensation among our citizens being, we believe, the first celestial lady who has honored Stocktonians with her presence." Onlookers were unable to gawk for long, however, for the lady was rushed to the Chinese settlement a block away.[1]

This first Chinese woman may have been a prostitute; when ruffians attempted to wash down the same Chinese quarter in 1854, only three years after her arrival, another newspaper article mentioned Chinese gamblers and prostitutes running from a bordello. This second mention of Chinese women in the community suggests they had already been negatively stereotyped.[2]

Unlike many of their white female counterparts working in the saloons and dance halls, most Chinese females rarely chose either their profession or their location. Most came to America unwillingly. Chinese men whose business it was to obtain and import women considered it common sense to select prostitutes whose own backgrounds were compatible with those of their customers, mainly the laborers and farm workers. Only the peasant singsong girls from poorer wine shops in China and the less-than-attractive prostitues who worked in low class brothels were sent to California to serve the large number of unskilled laborers from Guangdong Province. In addition, many other young and inexperienced girls were bought or kidnapped and targeted for the "gold mountain" trade. While women were a reasonably inexpensive commodity in China, in America the price of a prostitute ranged from $175 to as high as $2,500, the price depending on beauty, the manner in which she was acquired and her potential earning capabilities.

Frequently traveling with only the clothes on their backs, these young women suffered seasickness, terrible anxiety and emotional grief throughout the duration of their long and arduous journey to California. Housed in the dirty, crowded steerage sections of the steamer for a voyage that often took three months, the young women could not even be guaranteed their safety aboard the ship.

Once in California they were sorted into groups; the prettiest were reserved for wealthy Chinese merchants in San Francisco; others were purchased by the various tongs and assigned to work in the mining towns of the Mother Lode or the various labor camp circuits in the Central Valley or Delta islands.

Previous historians have documented that some prostitutes willingly signed the seven-year indenture contracts which bound many of them. While this may be true, at the end of the contract period many women who had worked in the hinterland and had been traded among various tongs were unable to negotiate their freedom with the original contract owner and were forced to retain slave status until purchased as a wife. By that time, of course, they would have served many more than seven years in their forced profession.

While traveling her assigned circuit or even while working in a stationary location within the squalid Chinese quarters of a town, the prostitute was generally forced to live in dirty facilities and rarely received any sort of medical attention. These women rapidly fell victim to gonorrhea and syphilis or turned to using opium to relieve their many emotional and physical pains. Ironically, it may have been their husband's or father's addiction to opium and the need to support that habit in China which led their male kin to sell the women into prostitution in the first place. Stockton had at least one incident in which a prostitute, Chin Choy, died of an overdose of opium in 1878.[3]

FROM THE CENSUS ROLLS

A disparity in numbers between Chinese men and women was common; some historians have estimated the ratio to be as high as one female to twenty men in some California communities. In San Joaquin County the ratio was even greater; census rolls of the late nineteenth century show that Chinese females in this county remained a consistent 2 percent of the total Chinese population even during the peak population count in 1880.

The Chinese Population in San Joaquin County by Sexes

	1870	1880	1900
Males	1,579	1,930	1,833
Females	40	59	45
Total	1,619	1,989	1,878

Other data extracted from the censuses are helpful in developing an even clearer picture of a society almost devoid of women. One must also remember that included in the total female count are girl babies and children.

Chinese Female Population in San Joaquin County 1870 to 1900

By Age:	1870	1880	1900	By Marital Status:	1870	1880	1900
Under 5	--	6	7				
10-19	3	6	4	Single	--	18	17
20-29	32	19	12				
30-39	4	21	12	Married	--	22	24
40-49	1	7	6				
Over 50	--	--	4	Unknown	40	19	4

The ages of the females in 1870 were closely grouped. Of the forty females, the youngest was eighteen and the oldest forty-one. Thirty-two, or 80 percent of the women were between twenty and twenty-nine. Occupationally, thirty-six were listed as prostitutes. Two others described themselves as "keeping house," but may have been prostitutes as well, for they were of the same age as and resided with a group of prostitutes. Two females in this census were wards of the Stockton State Insane Asylum. While the 1870 census does not list marital status for the Chinese females, some of the women may have been married. An overall picture in this census is that of youthful women, undoubtedly brought to Stockton for prostitution.

These 1870 Chinese women resided in nine separate groups, ranging in number from two to five or six per housing unit. Only one group had a male in the household. Although all-female bordellos were not uncommon in those days, this same census noted five different groups of Mexican, Peruvian, and Panamanian prostitutes in Stockton, each unit having a Chinese male cook living with them and, presumably, attending to their meals and needs.

By 1880 there were only twenty-three Chinese prostitutes in Stockton, according to census figures, and they no longer lived by themselves but were in small heterogeneous groups. The 1880 era saw other changes in the Chinese female demography, for there were now twenty-two married women, all but one living in Stockton. In addition, two other women, a seamstress and a cook, were listed as gainfully employed.

A majority of the fifty-nine Chinese females in the 1880 census were between twenty and forty years old. The age span here was wider than in the previous decade. There were now infants as young as four months and several toddlers, and the oldest woman was forty-nine years of age. The relatively youthful age of the oldest woman and documentation of the newborns are added evidence that changes were occurring within the Chinese community.

TARGETS OF AN UNWITTING SOCIETY

The growing antipathy to the Chinese was noticeable by 1870 and applied to the women as well as to the men. Blanket judgments were made on both sexes, for now Chinese laborers were considered too industrious and their women only as prostitutes. The 1870 census enumerator may have reflected his own bias in listing prostitution as the sole female occupation. Yet he was not alone, for at the height of the anti-Chinese movement, the editor of the *Weekly Mail* suggested an ordinance be adopted to remove all houses of ill-repute in order to rid Stockton of its Chinese. His rationale was that without Chinese prostitutes the opium dens and gambling halls would have to close down. Less than two weeks following this suggestion in print, Stockton witnessed the first and only known arrest of a Chinese prostitute. Her name was Ah Toy and she lived in a semi-respectable part of town, according to the article. Her address was the block-long bordello on Zignego and Solari's property. The newspaper claimed she had been arrested for attempting to bribe a police officer. She may have been successful, for there were no other reports of Ah Toy in later papers.[4]

Chinese bordellos were seldom raided. One reason for this may have been the fact there were fourteen other known bordellos in nearby locations, some owned and operated by whites. As to Chinese bordello managers, the only known arrest and conviction of such a person was that of a blind Chinese man who, upon conviction, opted for 180 days in jail rather than pay a $360 fine.[5]

Chinese prostitutes were never streetwalkers and never had to advertise their presence. Research has not produced any evidence that Chinese prostitution in Stockton was either syndicated or considered the sole territory of one particular tong. In addition, although the information is inconclusive, housing patterns extracted from census studies suggest that prostitutes generally lived together in small groups, although some lived

Chinese women who lived in the Central Valley communities, like their men, fell victim to the anti-Chinese sentiments. Often they were labeled prostitutes without the opportunity to prove otherwise.

with groups of men. It is possible that in these cases such women might also have served as housekeepers.

Aside from the rare possibility of marriage, there were only two means of escape from the joyless existence of the prostitute: suicide or mental derangement. When a prostitute succumbed to mental illness, her owner usually got rid of her by placing her in a mental institution. The 1870 and 1880 censuses for San Joaquin County listed respectively two and five Chinese female inmates in the Stockton Insane Asylum, and the death records of the Stockton Rural Cemetery testify to the suicides among single, young Chinese women in the nineteenth century. A few escaped their misery with the help of Methodist and Presbyterian missionaries. Donaldina Cameron of San Francisco, famous for her "raids" to free Chinese girls from slavery in San Francisco's brothels and gambling establishments, came to Stockton on such a mission at least once.

THE INSTITUTION OF MARRIAGE

Chinese men who wanted to marry within their own race could do one of three things: return to China for a bride, buy a prostitute, or send for a mail-order bride. There was no guarantee that the mail-order bride would arrive a virgin, for conditions on the steamers were brutal. Whoever the bride was and however chosen, the groom was careful to select a woman who would be compatible with his own station in life. Most assuredly, her feet were not bound, particularly if the couple planned to live in San Joaquin County. While the women of many wealthy Chinese families in the Bay Area adhered to the tradition of footbinding, research has yet to discover any Chinese woman living in San Joaquin County who had bound feet.

Men who were married when they left their homeland continued the Chinese custom of confining their women under the familial roof. Additionally, social pressures within the Chinese society frowned on a woman's emigration. Also, because of the migratory nature of their work, men could not afford to burden themselves with extra mouths to feed in this country and still be expected to send money home to help extended family members.

Another problem lay in the path of those Chinese wishing to marry in California but unable to find a wife. In common with many southern states, California enacted miscegenation laws in the early 1850s which were primarily directed at non-Caucasians. According to the 1872 California Civil Code, all marriages of white persons with Negroes, Mongolians, members of the Malay race or mulattoes were illegal. This law was not rescinded until 1948. Official marriage records of San Joaquin County listed four marriages of Chinese men with non-Chinese women between 1857 and 1920, and in each case the county clerk, conscious of the miscegenation law, diligently noted the bride's race on the marriage certificate. Of these inter-racial unions, three brides were black and one was Japanese. In one case, that of Irene Wilson, who married Gun Chu in 1895, the clerk noted she was a mulatto from New Orleans.[6]

County clerks and judges were aware that Stockton had an active Society for the Prevention of Miscegenation. Acting upon advice of informers, the society, with police escort, raided private homes where children suspected of being Eurasian lived. One day society members broke into the back of a tavern and tore a Chinese baby from a white woman's arms. Upon further investigation, the Irish barkeeper explained his wife had befriended some Chinese ladies and one had approached him and asked if he would take her baby since she could not raise the child. The society's decisions for the child's future overrode those of the natural mother, and the child was placed in the custody of a local Chinese merchant.[7]

As cautious as the county was to prevent miscegenation, it did not prosecute a Chinese doctor and his white wife who moved to Stockton in 1886. They had been married in Wisconsin, a state without miscegenation laws, and their presence piqued the curiosity of Stockton society. A reporter interviewed the pair in their home on Main Street, where part of their house was used as the doctor's office. A shingle hanging in the front yard stated:

"Dr. Wee Lee. Chinese Drugs and Medicine—No Queue, Wears Western Clothes." During the interview Dr. Lee told the reporter he and his family had been well received in other white communities, and he produced letters from the mayor and other citizens of La Crosse, Wisconsin. The Lees' two children, the reporter noted, exhibited no trace of Chinese blood except for their skin tones. Dr. Lee was apparently not of Cantonese descent for he spoke harshly about West Coast Chinese and admitted that the Chinese in Chicago did not like him. His arrogance was further demonstrated when he emphatically said that he did not allow Chinese women to visit his house and family for he felt the local Chinese women were "dirty and immoral." Stockton Chinese, like Chicago's, quickly sized up the doctor's pompous attitude and isolated the couple, as did the rest of Stockton's citizens. Dr. Lee did not remain in town long.[8]

Information on Chinese marriages in the county was obtained from one major source, the San Joaquin County Marriage Records. While they are the best archival evidence, there were occasions when Chinese couples, out of ignorance of the law, exchanged vows but did not apply for a marriage license. Between 1857 and 1880 county records listed seventeen Chinese marriages, but from 1881 to 1895, no marriages were recorded. The anti-Chinese tension of the period and the exclusion laws against Chinese laborers, while not directly affecting Chinese women, had severe implications on their immigration and marital status.

Changes in the community from the bachelor society to that of family units became apparent after 1900. From 1900 to 1924 forty-three marriages were recorded, a 72 percent increase over the previous fifty years. Information on the licenses reveals most brides were about twenty-one years of age. Many of the grooms listed their occupation as farmer or merchant. The men usually stated they were from the Delta islands or from other parts of the county, and the women often said they came from San Francisco or smaller communities such as Sonora, Ione, Placerville and Fresno. Seldom did either marriage license applicant list China as his or her place of origin.

Prior to the twentieth century the justice of the peace performed most of the marriages, with his employees serving as witnesses. In other cases it was the Chinese court interpreter or a prominent merchant who signed as witness on the marriage license. In one wedding, the bride appeared to know the importance of the marriage license. When Get Gam, age twenty-seven, married Fook Chung Wong in January 1898, the county clerk wrote "Bride Requested Recording" in the comment section of the license in large, bold print. At another Chinese wedding solemnizing the union of Lew Wing Chew and Miss Koo Shee, a photograph of the young couple was pasted to the back of the marriage certificate. The groom explained that the bride's parents were planning a visit in the near future and the photo gave conclusive evidence that their daughter's wedding complied with all the American rules of propriety.[9]

Research shows that in the relatively small number of marriages that occurred prior to the twentieth century the bride averaged twenty-one years of age and most often was married to either a merchant or a farmer.

By 1920, friends or relatives were signing the marriage license rather than court employees, and with growing affluence in the Chinese community, many young couples opted for weddings in San Francisco rather than locally. San Francisco, with its far larger Chinese community, had more banquet facilities to handle such celebrations, and more people were able to attend. In addition, a ceremony in the city was considered prestigious.

For the average Chinese man, the process of acquiring a wife entailed far more complicated procedures and negotiations than the western traditions of asking the girl's father for her hand or of two consenting adults falling in love. Within the Chinese community arranged marriages were not the exception, they were the rule. The Chinese custom of comparing family backgrounds, economic status, the couple's respective temperaments and physiognomies and their astrological compatibility made good sense. Matching young couples required judicious consideration, for marriage was a union not only between two individuals, but included their families and clans as well. Those families who were wealthy, traditional and cautious went so far as to research the entire family background of the prospective bride or groom to at least three, and often five, generations, looking for signs of mental illness or questionable characteristics of family members.

Some bachelors dutifully returned to their home village to fulfill marriage contracts arranged by their parents. The few American-born Chinese men also were expected to return to their parents' village to wed a local girl. In contrast to the laws of the United States, monogamy was not the rule in China but a condition guided by the man's economic state. Although it was rare, it was not unknown for a man to return to China several times and marry several women and yet still have a wife here. While the man was polygamous, his marital attachments were legal as long as he lived with only one wife in this country.[10]

CHINESE WEDDINGS AND MOTHERHOOD

The first Chinese weddings in San Joaquin County were usually not elaborate due to the strained finances of the young couple, who nonetheless tried to retain many of their cultural traditions. In some cases, the festivities could be opulent. In March 1882, a newspaper article recounted the spectacular wedding of Hong Fat, a prominent Washington Street merchant, at which local citizens were provided a rare opportunity to witness part of the activities. According to the article, a crowd gathered to await the bride, who journeyed to Stockton by train from San Francisco. When she arrived at her new home in a rented carriage, she was welcomed by a burst of firecrackers. The bride's face was half-concealed behind a tasseled headdress, and the fan she carried covered the rest of her features. To the disappointment of the crowd which had gathered to catch a glimpse of her, she was hurried into the building. A Chinese priest performed the ceremony, and the bride retired to her apartment while the groom entertained his friends at a festive banquet the bride was not permitted to attend.[11]

A second brief account of a large wedding appeared in the newspaper a year later. The wedding party arrived at the California Steam Navigation Company shed at Stockton's embarcadero in three hacks, the first of which carried the bride "with her head in a bundle of bright-colored Chinese silk which concealed every feature." The carriage was flanked by boys on foot

Raised in a Christian home, Ruth Chew chose the Chinese Congregational Church in San Francisco for her wedding to James R. Chew in 1923. Often couples preferred a western ceremony followed by a Chinese banquet celebration.

carrying long candles and incense. Two other vehicles contained a number of Chinese women, some of whom were to be attendants at the wedding. The bride was quickly whisked aboard the steamer *Mary Garratt*, and the party left for Bouldin Island where the ceremony was to be held. The bride was from Sonora and had never seen her future husband, who was a farmer on the island and had bargained for her with her father. She was now being sent to him according to the contract.[12]

Wealthy local Chinese followed many of the old customs associated with marriage agreements, including the bride price paid by the groom's family. While there was no actual monetary transaction, large baskets of bride cakes, pastry, a whole roast pig, several cooked chickens and ducks, candy and other food items were sent as gifts to the bride's family prior to the wedding. The groom's parents also gave the bride jewelry for her personal dowry—a gold bracelet, jade pendant or earrings. In addition to the groom's family's, her own family and other close relatives added to her cache of jewelry. By the turn of the century it was customary to see the bride at the wedding banquet wearing all her valuables; the more she wore, the more it demonstrated both families' wealth.

Except for weddings and minor mention of Chinese prostitutes, Chinese women in San Joaquin County were seldom seen or heard. Few people realized the married Chinese woman, like other early pioneer wives, faced loneliness and many hardships. For the Chinese wife, there were few with whom to share her thoughts and burdens. If her husband took in male boarders, as many living in Chinatown and in nearby labor camps did, the wife's weary round of cleaning, cooking, washing and sewing increased proportionately for each additional male.

When children were to be born, she delivered at home without a doctor, but with the help of a friend or midwife. If she had been well coached on pregnancy, the expectant mother attempted to follow cultural practices and traditions to keep her healthy and make the delivery less difficult. An important feature in the months before and after childbirth was the abstention from certain foods: shrimp, crab and other crustaceans were toxic to the system, and deep-fried foods created an acid imbalance harmful to both fetus and mother. If time and money allowed, the expectant mother entered a period of confinement. She limited her bathing as she was susceptible to drafts.

After childbirth, both mother and child lived as shut-ins for thirty days, again exposure being the danger factor. During this time, the new mother subsisted on a traditional diet of pigs' feet cooked with black vinegar and chicken wine soup. Filled with nutritious ingredients such as fresh ginger, mushrooms, fungi and herbs, these two dishes helped rebuild the mother's stamina. The gelatinous substance of the pigs' feet helped replace her loss of calcium and increased lactation. Chicken and herbs cooked in a broth and mixed with white wine served as an anti-coagulant elixir to eliminate blood clots and other debris remaining in the womb.

After the child had survived a full month the proud parents threw a Full Moon party to welcome the child. The celebration also ended the mother's confinement and allowed her to resume other pressing chores.

There is no data on how many Chinese women gave birth in this county prior to the twentieth century. One way of estimating the number is to scrutinize data on Chinese Americans. A listing of second-generation Chinese Americans in the 1900 county census showed fifty Chinese males and sixteen females. In this group three men and one woman were over forty and were probably the earliest offspring among Chinese pioneers, for computation of their birth years indicates they were born during the 1850 decade. There is, however, no evidence these Chinese were born in this county; most of them, if not all, must have migrated here. Sixty percent of the American-born males were between fifteen and thirty years old, and the dates of their births coincide with the height of immigration by Chinese males between 1870 and 1885.

The ratio imbalance between the American-born adult males and females raises questions for which there are few explanations. Perhaps, due to the shortage of females in California, parents preferred to marry their daughters to more prosperous Chinese in the Bay Area. Another less pleasant specu-lation is that female infanticide may have been practiced here, as in China.[13]

American Born Chinese — 1900 Census		
	Males	Females
Under 5	6	6
5-9	4	1
10-14	3	3
15-19	13	1
20-29	17	2
30-39	4	2
40-49	3	1
	50	16

THE LIFETIME CAREERS

In addition to her household duties and raising the children, the Chinese wife was also expected to share her husband's work. Division of labor placed men outside the home and women inside. Yet, for the peasant woman, who was a part of the majority in the first-generation immigrant community, work in the field was part of the familial domain. She unabashedly worked as a farmhand alongside her husband when needed. Even though she was exhausted from such demanding physical labor, she also cooked for the entire work crew and dispensed medical attention to those in need. The daily rounds of her life were as closely bound to the rhythms of the land as those of her husband, the farmer.

If the immigrant couple belonged to the merchant class, the young wife was expected to help in her husband's store, laundry or restaurant to avoid the cost of hiring additional help. Women were generally kept out of view until the 1930s, relegated to washing dishes and helping the cooks in the restaurant, or washing, ironing and folding clothes in the back of the laundry, or preparing vegetables and other produce for the display cases in the store. It is only within our own lifetime that the proprietor's wife appeared publicly as the cashier, busboy or waitress in the restaurant, or the clerk in the store or laundry. The high visibility and ease of interaction with customers now seen on the part of Chinese women in family businesses was nearly unknown prior to the 1940s.

Women whose husbands were neither merchants nor farmers found work elsewhere to help augment the family budget. Some became seamstresses working for other women, including prostitutes. These women adapted easily to cottage industry, and many spent countless hours stamping lottery company names on the preprinted lottery tickets, working late into the night marking and bundling the forms for the following day's delivery to the various gambling houses. Some women earned extra money during

Through the mother-daughter relationship, customs and traditions are passed from one generation to the next, and after the daughter's marriage, from one family into another.

special holidays preparing moon cakes for the Moon Festival or hom tsung, a tealeaf-wrapped rice dumpling filled with sweet glutinous rice, sausage and egg, for the Dragon Boat Festival. In addition, some sold these home-made delicacies to local grocery stores.

FEMALE INFLUENCES IN THE CHANGING SOCIETY

With more women in the community, holidays took on new emphasis and reached greater heights of enjoyment. Where once men spent their holiday gambling, drinking and indulging in opium, it was now a time spent with the family—a time to appreciate the rewards of one's efforts and a time to enjoy specially prepared cakes and traditional edibles which male cooks seldom found time to prepare. Some of the intricate holiday fare required extraordinary time and effort for soaking, dicing and slicing procedures usually not involved in ordinary food preparation.

Chinese homes also began to show the women's touch. Interiors were no longer stark, with simple make-do plank beds and rickety furniture. Under the women's critical eyes, comfortable sofas, bedroom furniture and refrigerators began to appear in the homes. Mother-of-pearl inlaid and carved screens, camphor chests and teak tables, as well as scrolls and porcelain vases, once considered the pride of wealthy whites, became common adornment in Chinese households.

Since their workload limited their free time, Chinese wives seldom frequented the joss temple. Yet this aspect of life was not neglected. To fulfill her spiritual needs, she often built her own small shrine for ancestor worship in a recessed niche or closet. The altar pieces were simple: bowls and vases held incense, flowers and candles. The focus of the altar was a picture or inscription of a deity, often that of Kwan Yin, Goddess of Mercy. Some wives even had a small shrine devoted to the kitchen god, the altar sitting high out of harm's way in the kitchen.

The frugality and tenacity Westerners admired in the Chinese laborers was also found in the Chinese women. Few whites realized that behind her quiet, unassuming and sometimes unattractive demeanor, the Chinese wife and mother was an able administrator, strict teacher and the family's pillar of strength. On the rare occasions they appeared in public just prior to and following the turn of the century, Chinese wives were seen walking behind their husbands wearing formless tunics over shapeless, dark-colored pants; their jet-black hair was worn in a tight bun tucked in at the nape of the neck. Unlike their husbands, who had adapted to western clothing, short haircuts and hard-soled shoes by the 1920s, the wives' clothing showed little change.

They may have appeared submissive in public, but within their own homes the Chinese females were strong-willed and exerted great influence over husbands and children. The Chinese mother rarely missed an opportunity to instill Chinese values and foster education in her children. The young learned the folklore of the twenty-four tales of filial piety and nursery rhymes about the August moon and the lunar new year. As purveyor of the traditional Chinese culture, the immigrant wife saw to it that her family's daily life incorporated all the religious and folk practices, including food preparation and traditions which had formed a part of her own childhood.

Many in today's Chinese community recall with fond memories their own upbringing and particularly the role their mothers played. While these patient and overworked women realized they and their men had been victims of prejudice, they neither dwelt on mistreatment nor discussed discrimination with their children. Instead, they diverted the intense energy of what might otherwise have been a subjectively ingrained hatred into a

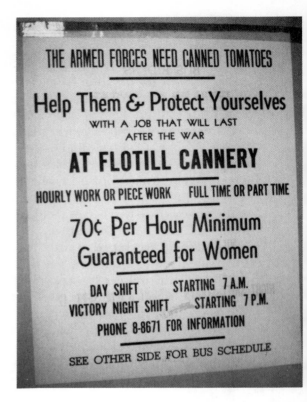

THE ARMED FORCES NEED CANNED TOMATOES

Help Them & Protect Yourselves
WITH A JOB THAT WILL LAST
AFTER THE WAR

AT FLOTILL CANNERY

HOURLY WORK OR PIECE WORK   FULL TIME OR PART TIME

70¢ Per Hour Minimum
Guaranteed for Women

DAY SHIFT   STARTING 7 A.M.
VICTORY NIGHT SHIFT   STARTING 7 P.M.
PHONE 8-8671 FOR INFORMATION

SEE OTHER SIDE FOR BUS SCHEDULE

A large contingent of Chinese house-wives went into cannery work during World War II when Stockton's white female work force filled jobs in the local naval shipyards and nearby military bases, c. 1940.

positive, competitive spirit in their children. Only in passing or in school did the children experience firsthand a fraction of the prejudices suffered by their fathers and grandfathers.

As in China, the Chinese families in America tended to be large, often from eight to ten children. Sons were more favored than daughters, since male heirs guaranteed continuity of the family name. Yet girls often felt as loved as their brothers in other ways. For instance, Chinese mothers never encouraged their daughters to dress in the old-fashioned clothing they themselves wore and often even permitted them to wear western clothing and fashionable hair styles. Only on special holidays did the young don Chinese dress. It was the second generation Chinese women who first became accustomed to wearing western clothes.

During the years following her marriage, the immigrant mother acquired a cache of expensive jewelry—perhaps as a hedge against starvation in old age, a trait learned from older women who had suffered hard times in the homeland. Their daughters also came to cherish and enjoy jade, pearls and twenty-four-carat gold jewelry handed down as valuable heirlooms and dowries from their mothers. A twenty-four-carat gold chain with a brilliant imperial or apple-green jade pendant, they were told, was a charm to insure good health. The Chinese preference for jadeite became universal, and wearing the talisman gave the female a sense of ethnic identity, setting her apart from the Japanese and other Asian women who did not place great emphasis on jewelry adornment.

As early as the 1910s Chinese women formed the greater part of the county's cannery work force. The seasonal work later provided these women health and union benefits, a social outlet with a high degree of psychological independence and, for many, their own retirement funds.

Between 1912 and 1930, garment factories were established in the China-town area, and Chinese females began working outside the home. From the sewing factory experience they moved into yet another type of work force—that demanded by the many canneries moving into the Delta and Stockton. At the height of the season, when canneries operated on a twenty-four-hour basis manned by three shifts, these women, with the talent to do piece work, adapted to canning and packing fruit. Those who stayed on the cannery premises during canning season lived in dormitories separate from the men. Others who could not leave their families for long periods were transported daily from designated locations in Chinatown and back again after their shift ended. The work outside the home and the wages earned gave the women a sense of self-satisfaction and personal independence. Personal relationships developed within the cannery walls which became the focus of

念紀影攝時會讌店酒肯林在軍將館廷蔡迎歡弟兄章湘黃墥作士省加國美

Women's involvement in community activities included their appearance at this Stockton banquet honoring General Tsai Tin Kai in 1934.

their social life. Even though they spoke little or no English, the cannery was the meeting place where the women exchanged news and gossip.

As they helped support their families, these women discovered that work allowed them to be less dependent upon their husbands. Yet while work outside the home certainly expanded their social horizons, the independence they felt was bittersweet, for too often they were exhausted and drained from the double burden of working and raising a large family.

Some immigrant wives found time for self-improvement. Records of Christian missions show that local churches made significant inroads into the Chinese community because of the women. They were attracted to the social services the missions provided, such as aid to widows, day care for children and English language classes. Although they would not try to speak English publicly, they knew the language well enough to comprehend their children's discussions. Many women became Christian converts out of appreciation.

Community activism among Chinese American women was a natural consequence of the independence gained from years of working outside the home. In 1911 the Women's Young China Society was organized to support Dr. Sun Yat Sen's revolution in China. These women related to the reforms

Dr. Sun wished to make, particularly the prohibition of footbinding and female infanticide. Many were on hand to hear his personal appeals during his visits to Stockton and other Delta communities, and they unhesitatingly rallied around his cause to overthrow the Ching dynasty.

During the 1930s the call for aid went out again when the Japanese invaded China. This time it was the aging immigrant wife and her second-generation Chinese American daughters who formed the local chapter of the New Life Movement to raise funds for the war victims in China. Their patriotic efforts continued through World War II, and when asked for their support, they threw their hearts and energies into activities sponsored by the Kuo Ming Tang Association, the political organization founded by Dr. Sun and later led by Generalissimo Chiang Kai Shek.

LEGACY OF THE FOUNDING MOTHERS

All communities have individuals who are recognized as founders; here, too, in Stockton there are a number of Chinese women who are considered founding mothers of the Chinese community. The oldest was Choy Won, who came to America in 1853 at the age of eleven. In the 1860s she married Jung Yee, a disillusioned gold miner turned jack-of-all-trades and, at one time, a handyman for Captain Charles Weber. Of Heungshan origin, the couple lived south of the Mormon Slough in the fishing village. It was in

Concerned with the turmoil in their homeland, the Chinese Patriotic Women Society of Stockton actively raised funds for the war victims of China during World War II, c.1940.

that location that all eight of their children were born. Jung Yee died in a freak accident in 1885 when he was hit by a runaway brewery wagon. Although her husband's death occurred during the height of the anti-Chinese tension, Choy Won decided she and her children would remain in Stockton rather than seek the security of the larger Chinese community in San Francisco, for she felt this valley community was already part of her children's roots. Her two older sons became peddlers during their teenage years and were grocers later in life.

When the family was forced to evacuate the old fishing village following sale of the land, the Jung family moved into the Chinatown neighborhood and lived at 337 South Center Street. In later years they adopted the name Jann and by pooling their limited resources not only survived but thrived. When her daughters reached marrying age, Choy Won arranged for suitable husbands to insure their security and to conform to tradition. As the matriarch of her sons' families, she guided the upbringing of her grand-children. After twenty-eight years as a widow, Mrs. Jann died in November 1913. Yet, even with her passing, the Jann legacy lives on. At least five generations of Janns live in Stockton.[14]

Choy Won was one among many who devoted their lifetimes to their children and to community service. Another was Mrs. Rose Wong Ah Tye, who was born in Red Bluff in 1887. In 1907, she married Dilly Ah Tye and the couple set up their first home in San Francisco. While there, Rose became involved in community work and helped at the famous Donaldina Cameron Home for Girls in that city. When the Ah Tyes moved to Stockton in 1918, Rose continued her civic activities and became the pillar of the Methodist mission on Hunter Street, later renamed the Chinese Christian Mission. The Ah Tyes raised fifteen children in Stockton, but watching their brood grow was apparently not enough to challenge the young banker's wife. During World War II she opened her home to many service men, and six of her own sons served in the armed forces. During the war years she also worked at the local Red Cross surgical dressing headquarters as well as at the mission. In later years, Rose continued her activities by helping the blind and elderly Chinese of Chinatown. Rose Ah Tye was honored as Chinese Woman Community Leader of the Year not once, but twice during her lifetime. Mrs. Ah Tye passed away in 1975 at the age of eighty-seven, yet her impact in the community was so extensive that even today when one inquires about prominent Chinese her name is among the first mentioned.[15]

THE SINGERS BECOME THE SONG

Many early Chinese women were considered only a commodity. After all, they were largely illiterate and came from low economic backgrounds. In America and faced with additional hardships, loneliness and despair, they discovered that by perseverance they could not only survive, but improve

Mrs. Rose Ah Tye, pictured here in 1963 at age seventy-five, was honored not once but twice as Chinese Community Leader of the Year, in 1963 and 1970.

their own lives as well as those of their children. As quick to learn as their male counterparts, Chinese women were equally able to learn new skills and techniques for a variety of occupations. With time and experience these women developed a dauntless outlook and healthy self-esteem. While they were restricted by convention from finding their own gold mountain, the wisdom and counsel they imparted gave their children the ability to perceive the winds of fortune. Despite all adversity and without others to show the way, these pioneering women became the role models for today's active Asian women.

CHAPTER NINE ENDNOTES

1. *Stockton Times*, March 12, 1851.

2. *San Joaquin Republican*, September 18, 1854.

3. Sue Gronewald, "Beautiful Merchandise, Prostitution in China, 1860-1930," *Women & History*, Spring 1982, pp. 5-74. Stockton Rural Cemetery Death Registers, Vol. B.

4. *Stockton Weekly Mail*, October 10 and 31, 1885.

5. *Stockton Daily Independent*, March 11, 1910.

6. San Joaquin County Marriage Book 6, p. 623; Book 18, p. 275; Book 21, p. 179; Book 23, p. 408. San Joaquin County Historical Museum.

7. *Stockton Daily Evening Herald*, January 20, 1885.

8. *Stockton Weekly Mail*, April 10, 1886.

9. Marriage Book 7, p. 281. *Stockton Daily Independent*, April 24, 1908.

10. This author knows of one particular situation in which a Sacramento truck farmer had three wives in China and yet married a Sacramento-born Chinese women who bore him three children in this country as did his other wives in China.

11. *Stockton Daily Evening Herald*, March 23, 1882.

12. *Stockton Daily Evening Herald*, March 27, 1883.

13. In China, the killing of baby girls occurred in many poor families. Unfortunately, the culture placed little or no value on females who, when grown, were destined to serve their husband's family. Boys, on the other hand, were favored because they carried on the family name and, in the agrarian society, they were valuable as extra hands.

14. Stockton Rural Cemetery Death Registers, Volumes B and C. 1880 and 1900 Federal Census. Interview with Earl Jann, 1984.

15. *Stockton Record*, February 11, 1962; April 11, 1970; May 8, 1975.

Community Living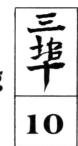

10

Although the first Chinese families were few in number, they brought about the development of certain institutions within the Chinese community. Education, religion and patriotism evolved from pure Chinese practices into amalgamated East-West expressions which their children and grandchildren later came to epitomize. To grasp both the Asian and western influences in many facets of the Chinese American experience and to understand their evolutionary processes, one must delve into each institution separately.

The masses of Chinese males who immigrated were thought able to read and were considered functionally literate. While this may have been true for the Chinese employed in urban occupations, such as merchants and businessmen, it was not always the case for the men in the laboring class. Pay receipts from Chinese workers on reclamation projects suggest a high incidence of illiteracy. Many signed their names with a simple "X" in contrast to those few who stroked their Chinese surnames onto paper.

The laborers and other urban workers who were illiterate were not particularly interested in obtaining a western education when they arrived. Most of them immigrated simply to make money and learned just enough English to carry on the most basic conversations. Any formal instruction they received in English occurred either because of their own ambitions or through their employer's influence. In hopes of converting the Chinese, Christian missionaries offered English language classes. The earliest known missionary school in Stockton's Chinatown existed in 1872, when the American Missionary Association sent two women from New England to teach Chinese adults. The curriculum offered by the mission included instruction in religion, spelling and penmanship, although there was no provision for courses in math or science.[1]

EDUCATING CHINESE CHILDREN

Public education is another story. In 1850 schooling for children was primarily the responsibility of parents, who sought private tutoring or private institutions. By 1853 the office of the state school superintendent had been established, and the city of Stockton passed an ordinance to form a school district headed by a city school superintendent and a three-member board of education. Stockton's first two public schools were divided by sex—one for boys and one for girls—white children only, of course. Black children's education began in 1859 under the religious auspices of the Ebenezer African Methodist Church. Four years later, black leaders petitioned and received the city council's permission to place black education under the same tax-supported system as white education. In 1868 a new facility for black children was built on Elk Street to replace their first schoolhouse, which was on the church grounds. The opening of the Elk Street school promised much advancement for black children when Jeremiah Sanderson of Massachusetts was hired to fill the teaching post. Sanderson, a compatriot of William Lloyd Garrison and Frederick Douglas, was well received. He had gained a national reputation in education and his teaching assignment here came shortly after the Civil War. Under Sanderson's six-year tenure, the black community's pride in its Elk Street school was comparable to the whites' pride in their children's education. Sanderson left Stockton in 1874 and was replaced by two female white teachers in succession.

School trustees had discussed integration of city schools. But it was not until 1877 that integration occurred in the previously all-white high school. Black admission to the high school was allowed some months after a Chinese child's hostile reception at the Elk Street school helped white educators see the fallacy of continued segregation in this relatively small community.

Chinese children were even more scarce than women between 1850 and 1880; thus the first attempt to place a Chinese child in a public school did not come until January 22, 1877, when a tea merchant obtained a permit from the superintendent of city schools to allow Ah Nam, his New Orleans-born child, to attend the Elk Street school. When Ah Nam appeared at the school on Elk Street near Washington Street, the teacher, Miss Susie Baxter, was nonplused. She asked that the boy return in the afternoon after she had time to check with the superintendent for further instructions.

The superintendent informed Miss Baxter that school regulations prohibited admission of colored children to white schools, but this policy did not provide for a separate school for every color. He then directed her to admit the boy. News of the Chinese child in the colored school angered many black parents, and as a group they besieged the superintendent's office the following day in an effort to block Ah Nam's admission. Although the superintendent turned down their request, the damage was done. Ah Nam's father decided against sending his son to the public school for fear the hostility felt by the black parents would be expressed by their children to the boy. His decision to give his son private tutoring after this incident was in keeping with the usual Chinese cultural practice of avoiding confrontation whenever possible.

Unable to understand the commonality of learned experiences and expecting the blacks to be magnanimous in this situation, the reporter who covered the incident wrote: "... as they [the colored] have suffered enough from color prejudice, unfortunately, yesterday they inflicted what they have felt."[2]

In the end, perhaps because of Ah Nam's experience, Stockton educators re-examined their segregation policy and by February 3, 1879, Stockton schools were completely integrated and the Elk Street school closed.

Thirteen years later, in 1892, the county school census reported that fourteen Chinese children were attending public schools in Stockton, eleven of them American born. In that same year three other Chinese living in the south part of the county enrolled in a Ripon school.[3]

The few Chinese children living in Stockton during the 1880s did not go to public school, for it seemed unsafe in the anti-Chinese climate of the decade. By the 1890s, however, when conditions had improved, Chinese children enrolled at the Franklin Primary School on Center Street, between Washington and Lafayette. Once in school, they demonstrated their diligence at learning, and before the end of the nineteenth century, western education had become an integral part of these children's lives.

The desire to assimilate can be considered one measure of educational success. In San Joaquin County this milestone was achieved by a young Chinese man eighteen months before the turn of the century. After attending public school, Joe Dye, a second-generation Chinese American, wished to fulfill his duties in the American political process. On July 24, 1898 he went to the county courthouse on Weber Avenue and took the test for voter registration. The test was rigorous: the twenty-one-year-old merchant read portions of the state constitution and answered questions based on what he had read. After further examination, County Clerk Otto Grunsky judged that Mr. Dye spoke fluent English and had demonstrated sufficient reading and writing skills to qualify. The following day, July 25, 1898, in a ceremony that made him the first Chinese in San Joaquin County eligible to vote, Joe Dye signed his name in the county's Great Register.[4]

In 1906, with tension mounting against Japanese immigration and Asian competition in general, San Francisco passed a local school ordinance excluding Japanese, Chinese and Korean children from neighborhood schools. Other California communities also adopted discriminatory school measures; however, there was no statewide pattern. For several years Stockton talked of isolating the Japanese and Chinese students, but community sentiment was mixed. At a public meeting of the school board on June 28, 1911, the issue of school segregation was killed. It had been buried in some complicated school bond act to build new facilities in north Stockton.

Chinese children in Delta communities, however, did not fare as well as those in Stockton. Separate schools were opened in Walnut Grove, Isleton, and Courtland for Chinese and Japanese, and remained in operation until the beginning of World War II. These Delta communities' form of segregation was rather peculiar. Chinese, Japanese and Filipino children were assigned to one school, while whites and blacks attended another. Both schools were side by side, separated only by a chain link fence. When the Japanese were sent to internment camps, only the Chinese and a few Filipino children were left, and the administrators realized that it was no longer economically feasible to maintain separate schools.

Until 1970 all children in Stockton's unified school district were educated in neighborhood schools. In that year, a cross-town busing policy was instituted, following civil rights activists' demands for ethnic racial balances in these schools. Their attempt to achieve representative percentage quotas of whites, blacks and Hispanics sadly ignored the needs of Asian students who were included in the mass treks across town. Because they were neither black nor Hispanic, and even though they were truly a minority, Chinese and Japanese children were lumped together as "other" in initial surveys and in the final tally, "other" was included in white totals. It was undoubtedly easier for administrators to ignore these students since they did not fit the criteria of the underprivileged or handicapped. And again, like their uncomplaining parents and elders, these Asian students managed to learn, persevered and rose above the politics of education.

RELIGION
A Host of Beliefs

The intellectuals and older people filled with worldly wisdom could furnish answers to the complexity of religion, philosophical ideals, and man's search for the meaning of life. However, it was doubtful if the early immigrant Chinese expended much time indulging in such esoteric questions. Yet, to understand the religious and philosophical outlook of these early gold seekers and reclamation workers, one must focus on the commonly followed traditions and folkways rather than attempt to define or categorize what was religious, traditional or even Confucian in practice.

As part of their culture, the Chinese placed their faith in a composite belief which combined elements of ancestor worship, mysticism and Taoist and Buddhist doctrines, as well as Confucian teachings. Folk tales and legends learned in their childhood humanized a pantheon of deities, but only those gods and goddesses which reflected the immigrant Chinese needs were worshiped. Among the most popular was Kwan Kung, the god of war and peace as well as of literature and valor. This deity is most often depicted as a fierce-looking man with a red face and a black beard holding either a book or halberd. Tien How, the queen of heaven, is noted for protecting travelers, sailors, actors and prostitutes. In the Buddhist pantheon she is the Bodhissattva Avalokitesvara, and in the Chinese, Kwan Yin, goddess of mercy. Other enlightenments of Buddha also were worshiped. Both Taoist and Buddhist deities, in pictures and carvings, stood enshrined on altar tables next to each other. In addition to the religious entities, Chinese adherence to Confucian ideology had mutated into a quasi-religious format. Confucius' precepts for an orderly state emphasized the importance of filial piety, and it is understandable that the obedience and respect given to living parents were to be continued upon their death in the form of ancestor worship. The veneration of deceased ancestors comes full circle; as the Chinese believes, those in the spirit world have the power to intervene and help in the affairs of the living. In addition, praying to ancestors created a sense of continuity, for through one's dead parents, grandparents, ad infinitum, a person could view himself as a direct link between the living and the spirit worlds.

The Chinese approached their worship pragmatically. There were no formal services to attend nor a specific time or day for worship. When a Chinese wished to communicate with the gods, asking for guidance or protection or in simple appreciation for good fortune, he visited the joss temple. Before the deity of his choice the supplicant burned incense sticks, candles and paper money as offerings. His rituals, offerings and religious outlook were similar to that of his Christian brother. When the joss temples were too far from his location, the Chinese prayed at makeshift wayside shrines or even erected his own homemade altar. The only difference between the personal shrine and those of the temples was that the temple artifacts and decorations were more elaborate; and the temple keeper, for a small fee, was available to tell one's fortune. Taking a canister containing thin bamboo sticks, the fortune-seeker prayed as he shook the can and stopped only when one or two sticks fell out; then he had the temple attendant interpret the signs and symbols on the sticks. One other method of obtaining a quick or simple answer from a divine being was to toss a small pair of pecan-shaped carvings or a pair of palm-size wooden blocks in the air and watch how the individual pieces landed. Both types of implements were flat on one side and curved on the other; having them land flat side down meant a "yes" as opposed to the two other possible answers of "no" and "maybe."

Not all Chinese were religiously inclined, but most were superstitious and, as in China, many followed traditional methods of warding off evil and insuring health and wealth. Moreover, common practices among individuals were an important indicator of conformity within the group-oriented society.

As added assurance of prosperity, the Chinese paid attention to the science of geomancy, the directional placement of structures such as houses and tombs. Temple priests or professional geomancers were consulted on the proper *Feng Shui* (literal translation is "wind and water")—the aligning of one's home or graves to mitigate environmental forces and capture the harmonious cosmic flow in the universe. The flow of waterways, wind directions and the topography were taken into consideration before actual sites were located and buildings positioned. In such planning, special attention was given to the placement of doors and windows, the angle of the rooms, and, in homes, even the position of the beds.

All Chinese communities commonly recognized a number of religious and festive holidays based on the lunar calendar. The lunar new year and the Harvest Moon Festival (fifteenth day of the eighth moon) called for great public celebration. Equally important was Ching Ming (Pure Brightness Festival); this day was also known as the Chinese Memorial Day or the day families devoted to the sweeping of the ancestors' tombs. Other holidays popular in America included the Dragon Boat Festival (fifth day of the fifth moon) and the Festival of the Winter Solstice (Tung Chih).

Regional differences among the Chinese resulted in subtle variations in the way holidays were celebrated and the foods associated with each. Some customs were commonly practiced and had universal significance, such as the burning of incense sticks, red candles, paper clothing and paper money. Burning these objects transmitted their usefulness to the spirit world and purportedly made them available to the ancestors. Firecracker noise created a din to chase away evil spirits, just as drums and gongs were used to awaken the gods and get their attention. During festive occasions, red was the favorite color in both public and personal decoration. Its color represents blood and therefore life and, symbolically, denotes happiness and prosperity. Placards and signs painted on bright red paper and pasted over doorways usually referred to wealth, longevity and many sons. Common phrases such as "may your entering and departure be peaceful" or "ten thousand generations and long duration" equated with the western felicitation of "happy new year" and "God bless." Signs and symbols enhanced holidays and special occasions: displays of quince, cherry blossoms and Chinese lily suggested signs of spring; peacock feathers symbolized wisdom; the five-toed dragon equated with the emperor or imperial family; and eight wands or spears represented the fabled eight immortals. White visitors learned that when candied fruit, sugared melon and melon seeds were offered, it was their Chinese host's way of wishing the visitors many descendants.

The Sze Yup Chinese in San Joaquin County never built their own joss temple, but each family and clan association maintained a family altar in its association headquarters. The Heungshan Temple at 120 North Hunter Street, built and supported by the Heungshan colony, was the only official Chinese house of worship in the county. The temple remained undisturbed throughout the nineteenth and early twentieth century. In 1923, when relations between the Sze Yup and the Heungshan had improved greatly, the Heungshan leaders chose to relocate their temple in the midst of Chinatown, and temple artifacts were transferred to 134½ East Washington Street, where the Yeong Wo Association (company name of the Heungshan district) found a new home. The new temple was on the second floor of the building, while company offices were found on the ground floor. Worshipers continued to frequent the temple until the 1960s when, because of redevelopment, the temple closed its doors and its artifacts were sent to San Francisco. Unfortunately, during the move a three-by-four-foot marble slab engraved with names of more than one hundred local contributors who had financed the 1880s temple on North Hunter Street was lost. The only Chinese houses of worship now in San Joaquin County are of the Christian variety.[5]

Soldiers of the Cross

Missionaries who taught English to the immigrants made the first attempts to christianize the Chinese. Far more successful conversion occurred when a few Chinese, fluent in both their own dialects and English, accepted the task of spreading God's words to others of their race. The California Chinese Mission, sponsored by the Congregational Church of San Francisco, accepted the responsibility of finding and educating Chinese candidates for its home missionary program.

One who was successfully converted was Yong Gim, who entered the United States in 1875 and worked as a miner and family servant. In 1879 he converted to Christianity and was paid thirty dollars a month by the California Chinese Mission for his evangelical labors. During an interview in 1883 with a reporter from the *Herald*, Yong, assigned to the Stockton mission at the time, said he had been in the Lord's service for two years and had preached in the streets of Oroville, Sacramento, San Francisco and other locations. Yong's salary was equal to that paid Chinese laborers at the time, and since he lived at the mission and paid no rent, he was financially better off than many of his fellow Chinese.

Yong claimed he had converted a few Chinese, but said he feared bodily harm from his fellow countrymen for his western beliefs. The day he decided to preach on Washington Street, he asked Police Chief Ben Rogers for police protection. Yong took a stool out onto the sidewalk, mounted it and began his sermon with a police officer nearby. A few Chinese stopped to listen to the young convert, some went about their business, and others stood in doorways to observe with indifference. To catch the audience's response, the reporter interviewed some passersby; they snickered, laughed and thought it ludicrous for Yong to feel he needed police protection when the ambience of Washington Street was one of live-and-let-live.[6]

The local Congregational Church opened a mission school at the corner of El Dorado and Washington streets in March 1880. Within two years this mission, funded by an annual budget of $520 donated by the San Francisco Congregational Church, had converted twelve Chinese and maintained another forty on the membership rolls. Shortly after baptism of the first Chinese, members of Stockton's First Congregational Church realized they were divided in their opinion about having the Chinese as full members of their own congregation. After much heated debate, however, the Chinese were accepted. Yet, in a final caveat, church members decided the Chinese

The Chinese Methodist Episcopal Mission was organized in 1895 and became connected with the College of the Pacific (UOP). Renamed the Chinese Christian Center in 1941, the center remained in the Chinatown area until 1954 when it combined with the Clay Street Methodist Church. Here members of the early mission are pictured in Washington Park in 1927.

converts would continue to worship at the mission and be allowed to attend the main church only once a year, on a special Chinese Worship Day. On these occasions, the Chinese were the main performers, demonstrating their ability to read scripture and sing hymns. At the conclusion of the service, white church members congratulated the Chinese on their progress and themselves on their broad-mindedness. Considering the anti-Chinese tenor of the 1880s, one should not be surprised that even Christians hedged on their religious convictions of brotherly love.[7]

In the 1890s the Methodist Church replaced the Congregational efforts to christianize the Chinese. A Methodist Mission opened in 1895 on South Hunter Street (the site of a former ice cream parlor) and was successful in its endeavors. During the Congregationalists' attempts the Chinese bachelor society still believed their sojourn was just that. But when the Methodists arrived, the community was undergoing a transition into a society of family units. To capitalize on these changing attitudes, missionaries focused their attention on the entire family with special programs for women and children.

In 1925 the Methodist Mission moved from the storefront property into space offered by the Chinese Benevolent Association at its new facility on Lafayette Street. Renamed the Chinese Methodist Episcopal Mission, this organization offered many activities for the young and sponsored a boys' and girls' program and a boy scout troop. Under the tutelage of Dr. George Colliver and other faculty members from the College of the Pacific, Chinese students attending the college served as student pastors at the mission. During this period, the Americanization process of young Chinese was greatly accelerated. These young adults attended Christian conferences at Zephyr Cove near Lake Tahoe and there found other young Chinese from different California towns with similar backgrounds and interests.

By 1941 the mission became the Chinese Christian Center, and on July 5, 1954, the center was combined with the Clay Street Methodist Church. Amalgamation of the center with an established church moved Chinese Christian influence from the immediate Chinatown sector. But as a neighborhood church, it continued to serve the majority of Chinese parishioners who lived between Chinatown and Charter Way. In 1956 the Clay Street church was renamed Saint Mark's Methodist Church. It continues to function today as both a community center and house of worship for third- and fourth-generation Stockton Chinese. Although the Chinese today are of various expressions of the Christian faith, those from Saint Mark's continue to play a prominent role in the affairs of the Chinese community.[8]

The Chinese approach to religion, like other facets of Chinese American life, has become one of interfacing and acculturation. As Christians, they find no conflict in participating in the traditional rites of filial piety and ancestor worship at the family association headquarters and at the Chinese cemetery. As Chinese, they feel obligated to carry on traditions, but as Americans they believe themselves free to worship in the religion of their choice.

SUPPORT ORGANIZATIONS

Almost as soon as the first handful of Sze Yup, Sam Yup and Heungshan Chinese settled in Stockton, they established district organizations to help

The congregation of Saint Mark's Methodist Church in the spring of 1957. Pastor Wilbur Choy (seated front center) later became a bishop and a member of the Council of Bishops of the United Methodist Church.

Members of the Toishan District Ning Yeung Association dedicate their new facilities at 239 South Hunter Street in 1928. Note the lion dance troupe in the front row.

future immigrants. Patterned after parent organizations in San Francisco, they provided five primary forms of aid: food, clothing, shelter, medical care and funeral expenses. Both food and clothing came from the generosity of fellow members who owned stores and restaurants. Chinese physicians and herbalists provided medical care at cost. Shelter proved to be the most important form of assistance, particularly for those who were broke, sick or unemployed.

The Heungshan, represented by the Yeong Wo Association, maintained their center at the temple on North Hunter Street until the mid-1920s when it was relocated to East Washington Street. Its activities have been documented elsewhere in this book. The Sze Yup organization, representing the majority of the Chinese in San Joaquin County, established its association shelter at 216 South Madison Street and in 1924 moved to 131 East Church Street. Until the 1960s the Sam Yup shelter remained at 19 East Washington, between Center and El Dorado streets. All these district centers were large enough to house their members for at least short-term stays.

The sojourners' dues by no means paid for the total organization budget. Exit fees charged departing Chinese, those who chose to return to the homeland, funded the bulk of the district association's operating costs, and gambling house owners generously augmented these funds periodically by donating a set amount of each table's profit toward this charity.

Even though these district associations were firmly established as permanent units, their functions were temporary measures to help the sojourner. There were other organizations in the community which were not for

the sole purpose of helping the common laborer or transient worker. Merchants and other businessmen formed loose alliances to solve pressing problems, such as funding legal defenses against anti-Chinese legislation and seeking the good wishes of the white public. Other Chinese in urban occupations, such as laundry workers, formed guilds for job protection and to further employment opportunities. In the early decades of the Chinese settlement there was little need or interest in family-clan units—the sojourner still equated family as those living in China and clan units as thriving organizations in his home village.

As time passed, families with definite stakes in the community became identifiable in prestige and by numbers. Family-clan associations developed in the same way; a large number of people with the same surname claimed ties to the enterprising settlers who had arrived first and induced their kin to join them. To those without actual blood relatives nearby, the family association gave a sense of belonging, a feeling of solidarity that the district associations never quite provided.

Each major city in California with an identifiable Chinese community has its own prominent families. The Delta communities are well populated with members of the Owyang, Au, Lim and Jang families. Sacramento is home to large contingents of Fong, Wong and Lee. Stockton's major families are the Lees, Mahs and Wongs.

Along with individual family associations, multi-clan organizations represent the smaller families so that they are not overpowered by the larger families in the community. The various families' alliances into clan units resulted from centuries of historic power struggle in ancient China, and these clan alliances have continued to the present. For example, the Lung Kong Tin Yee Association is for Chinese with the surnames of Low, Kwan, Chang and Chew, whereas the Soo Yuen Association represents the Louie, Kwong and Fong families. And even though the Fongs are many in Sacramento, they follow the dictates of the Soo Yuen Association rather than form a family association of their own.

Association headquarters in the various Chinese communities are supported by the individual familial groups. Only larger families and clans, because of their numerical strength, were able to finance and maintain separate facilities. For example, the Wong, Ong, Yee and the Soo Yuen associations have large, attractive buildings in Sacramento, as does the Lee in Stockton. However, the number of Lung Kong members in Sacramento are so few they have no facility in the capital city; but because they are of moderate strength in Stockton, this multi-clan group maintains an association headquarter above a restaurant on Washington Street which adjoins that of the Stockton Soo Yuen facility. In fact, the two organizations have restaurants on the ground floor with family offices, altar and meeting rooms above. The few Stockton Yees in the 1980s have experienced difficulty raising sufficient funds among themselves to build a local headquarters and have turned for help to neighboring cities with large Yee contingents.

Each organization is supported solely by family and clan members. Much of the money is donated annually, and fund drives are held around the time of Chinese New Year. On occasion the family associations sponsor gambling on their premises, and house profits are earmarked for the association operating expenses.

Part of the annual collection was at one time forwarded to San Francisco where each family/clan association had its main offices. In the early years the money was redistributed to smaller community groups needing financial support. Many of Stockton's organizations received their initial seed money through this system of redistribution. Through the years the local leaders' prudent use of funds and their extensive investment in local properties, particularly during the 1930s and 1940s, have placed Stockton organizations in financial condition equal to that of their San Francisco counterparts. Today, money received from rental units is the main source of financial support for the family organizations, and while money is still sent to San Francisco, the redistribution system returns little to San Joaquin County.

VOICE OF THE COMMUNITY

The multitude of organizations and their responsibilities were fairly well defined even though, at times, it appeared their duties overlapped. This system, which benefitted the individual Chinese, also relieved the financial burden on any one organization.

It became quite clear that a cooperative spirit between the various district associations, family-clan associations and merchants' guilds was needed not only within each town but between towns. San Francisco's Chinese Six Companies, a composite of the early district associations and merchants' guilds, served as the first unofficial voice of the Chinese in dealing with white society. When family-clan associations grew rapidly in the late 1890s, the disputes among various groups made it necessary to superimpose another group with the power to adjudicate over all organizations and at the same time serve as the unified voice of the Chinese community. In 1901 an umbrella organization known as the Consolidated Chinese Benevolent Association was established to succeed the old Chinese Six Companies. In Chinese it was called "Chung Wah" (literal translation: the center of the greater whole). Stockton's many Chinese organizations also combined under a parallel system in which the president of each family-clan group sat as a member of the Stockton Chung Wah Board along with representatives from the various district and fraternal associations.

While each organization mediated and arbitrated internal disputes among its own members, the Stockton Chung Wah looked to San Francisco to arbitrate local disputes. At times they were dissatisfied with the larger city's rulings. In a complicated murder case in Lodi in March 1910, the Stockton Chinese were divided into factions, one supporting the alleged murderer and the other the victim's family. To avert a possible tong war, the San Francisco Chung Wah conducted its own investigation and reached the same conclusion as the local police. It then posted placards on local bulletin boards warning Chinese not to protect the guilty or otherwise to take sides.

The situation became awkward when local leaders saw their own authority had been circumvented. Displeased by what appeared to be expanded authority from San Francisco, the Stockton Chinese formed the Oriental Independent Society in 1911. Its stated purpose was to settle all difficulties within Stockton and the county and to end San Francisco's jurisdiction over disputes initiated in the county. Some considered the move as local muscle-flexing; others interpreted it as an attempt to regain lost power. However, almost immediately after this announcement the active years of the tongs began. When tong-related incidents stretched beyond Stockton's social and geographical abilities, local leaders again were forced to ask San Francisco to arbitrate. Stockton leaders felt powerless as they were too close to the situation, both offenders and victims being members of the community. Moreover, a newspaper editorial had chastised Chinese leaders for their ineffectiveness following a 1912 tong incident. Surmising they had suffered a loss of face, particularly in the whites' eyes, the local Chung Wah leaders again sought aid from San Francisco as a solution to their helplessness and to relieve themselves of some of the pressures and responsibility of bringing peace into the community.[9]

Top: Children of several wealthy Wong families gather for the dedication of their family-funded, private enrollment language school on October 16, 1923. The Wong Edmon Private School was located on the corner of Monroe and Clay streets in Stockton.

世巡遊畢在公園之撮影

Except with regard to tong problems, a cooperative spirit generally prevailed at the local levels of Chung Wah. Elders gained power as they developed a holistic concern for the entire Chinese community. In addition to their responsibilities toward the sick, aged and dying, they began to address problems of the young. With the advent of the Chinese Christian Mission and western education, local leaders took note of the diminished interest in Chinese language and culture among the children.

Wealthy parents concerned with their offspring's departure from traditional Chinese ways often sent them back to their own home village for a few years to live among relatives and grandparents. For these youngsters, usually eight to ten years old, the experience of living in the village and studying reading and writing exclusively in Chinese remained permanently imbedded in their minds.

Parents unable to afford the expense of sending their children away sought other ways to reinforce Chinese tradition in the young. In 1912, a group of parents, spearheaded by poultry merchant Quong Kin Cherk, hired Fong Jook Ping to give private lessons in the Chinese language. The parents paid the teacher's salary and found space wherever possible to house the classroom, first in a small building on Parker Alley and later in a room on the second floor of Frank Madden's Kwong Chow building on South

Below: At Stockton's Washington Square, school children, leaders of Chung Wah and affiliated organizations turned out for the formal dedication of the Chung Wah Chinese Language School in 1924.

本 會 館 學 校 洌 幕 時 僑

Hunter Street. By 1917, when Chung Wah agreed to finance and sponsor the language school, the students literally moved under Chung Wah's roof, into its storefront facility at 123 East Market Street.[10]

In 1925 both the Chinese Christian Center and the Chinese Language School moved into the new Chung Wah building at 208 East Lafayette Street. The language school, covering eight grades, held sessions from 5:00 to 8:00 P.M. Mondays through Fridays and from 9:00 A.M. to noon on Saturdays. Since its inception, the school's average enrollment has been around one hundred children. Its most active years were between 1917 and the end of World War II. In the 1930s the language school sponsored a Chinese girls' drum corps which participated in Stockton community parades and competed with similar Chinese groups from Sacramento, Oakland, San Jose and San Francisco.

Stockton's Chung Wah elders were proud that they drew together under one roof religious, social and cultural teachings for their children. As Chung Wah's past president, Harry Chin, recollected:

> Since Chinatown existed as a closed entity, we youngsters had no place for play and recreation so the school served both as a center of learning and the focal point of socialization and recreational activities. Washington Park, across the street from the school, was our playground.[11]

PATRIOTIC RESPONSES TO THE MOTHERLAND'S PLEAS

Chung Wah leaders created an interest in events occurring in China among Stockton's Chinese Americans and the Stockton community as a whole. At the turn of the century, Chinese Americans across the United States began to realize the homeland was in the midst of a political struggle between the forces of the decadent Ching government and the Kuo Ming Tang, the revolutionary party headed by Dr. Sun Yat Sen. Dr. Sun realized that the Chinese in America had the wealth and the influence to make a major difference in the outcome—whether the imperial government or a democracy would be the victor in China, the largest country in the Far East.

Traditional loyalty to the Chinese emperor had diminished greatly as Chinese in America found the Ching government unable or unwilling to solve many of the racially-rooted inequities affecting them in America. The imperial government was far more concerned with trade and diplomatic problems than issues that affected what they considered "coolie problems of the Cantonese."

That Dr. Sun was a Christian Heungshan native of Guangdong Province, and educated in the United States, were endearing points which made him popular among Chinese Americans. In addition, Dr. Sun's Three Principles of the People—Nationalism, Democracy and People's Livelihood—had the same familiar ring as the tenets of the United States Constitution. Thus,

In the 1930s Chung Wah sponsored a girls' drum corps. Here the girls are shown warming up for a city parade in 1934.

while the Chinese in China looked to him as one with revolutionary vision, the Chinese in America viewed him as a compatriot.

The Chinese in Sacramento, the Delta and Stockton knew Dr. Sun years before he gained international recognition. Following one of his several attempts to overthrow the Ching dynasty, Dr. Sun and many of his followers retreated to the backwaters of the Delta to escape the price on their heads. Many old-timers remember how, as children, they saw Dr. Sun in Courtland visiting his friend and secretary, Loo Hou Tung. Many also claim Sun wrote portions of the Chinese constitution at the Bing Kung headquarters on I Street in Sacramento. At least one local elder noted Dr. Sun often slipped in and out of Stockton, staying at the Kwong Chow Hotel on Hunter Street or sleeping above the Canton Low Restaurant on Washington Street. His visits, of course, remained known only to his most trusted followers.[12]

Dr. Sun's tour of northern California in the spring of 1904 resulted in large monetary pledges and a great deal of enthusiasm among local Chinese.

During one particular Stockton stop on a Sacramento-to-Modesto tour, Chung Wah elders gave him their wholehearted support and mobilized the community into hosting a rousing reception for him. When Dr. Sun made his rounds again in 1910 seeking money for the revolution, Stockton Chinese were prepared with money, moral support and organizational means. Chung Wah honored him with a large banquet held at the Canton Low Restaurant.

Stockton Chinese were elated by the success of the October 10, 1911, Wuchang Uprising which was followed by the fall of other Ching strongholds. Before the end of the year China was freed from imperial rule and Dr. Sun declared the father of the new republic. He was sworn in as the president of the Provincial Government of the Chinese Republic at Nanking on January 1, 1912.

Five days later, on January 6, 1912, Stockton Chinese threw a community-wide celebration to toast the birth of the new government in their homeland. They had reason to celebrate: the Chinese revolution had been financed by Chinese Americans, and Stockton Chinese had done their fair share. The jubilation on Washington Street resembled the atmosphere of Chinese New Year. Public stands were erected at both ends of the 100 block of East Washington Street, where massive fireworks displays continued on into the wee hours of the morning. Three leading restaurants hosted one huge banquet for Stockton's proud sons, and barber shops were kept busy for

San Joaquin citizens, both Chinese and white, filled the Civic Memorial Auditorium at a banquet honoring General Tsai Tin Kai in 1934.

General Tsai Tin Kai, commander of China's Nineteenth Route Army, is greeted by Stockton city manager Walter B. Hogan (left) and mayor Con J. Franke. The general arrived on November 17, 1934 while on a goodwill tour to raise funds for China's war victims. Activities associated with the general's visit remain a highlighted memory among the Chinese.

weeks as the Chinese lined up to have their queues cut off, symbolically casting off the yoke of the Manchu dynasties. There were, however, no special activities planned at the Heungshan temple, nor was the traditional dragon parade included in the celebration, for Chung Wah officials felt both were reminders of the imperial government. To demonstrate their deep attachment to the father of the republic, those who hailed from the Heungshan district, as he did, began to identify themselves as people from the Chungshan district, for Dr. Sun's Chinese name was Sun Chung Shan.[13]

PATRIOTISM AND CARING NEVER DIE

The patriotic fervor displayed under Chung Wah's leadership during the independence struggle was not a one-time affair. Money continued to be collected on behalf of the new government, despite Dr. Sun's untimely death in 1925.

In the 1930s, Japan's invasion of China caused another great alarm among local Chinese, who were worried about the safety of their relatives still living in the villages. The Japanese drive southward through Manchuria routed much of the Chinese forces. However, when they attacked Shanghai in early 1932, they were repelled by the Nineteenth Route Amry led by General Tsai Tin Kai. The general's force was actually a warlord army composed mostly of Cantonese fighting men.

Two years later when General Tsai, dubbed the "Defender of Shanghai," toured America raising funds for China's defense, Stockton's citizens proudly rolled out their red carpet. On November 17, 1934, almost everyone in the Chinese community was at the Southern Pacific Depot to receive the military hero. Mayor Con J. Franke and city manager Walter B. Hogan led the city delegation. When the tall, handsome soldier, dressed in formal morning attire, stepped off the train, he was greeted by two young, attractive Chinese women armed with large bouquets of flowers. The Chinese Drum Corps, decked out in new white uniforms purchased just for the occasion, performed in his honor at the depot and again in front of the Chung Wah headquarters. The official reception was held at the Memorial Civic Auditorium with hundreds of Chinese and whites in attendance. An immense flower backdrop ordered from a San Francisco florist covered the length of the auditorium stage. The floral arrangement, reportedly costing several thousand dollars, was donated by the Wong brothers, owners of Chang Wah and the Lincoln Hotel. Many old-timers vividly recall the events of that day; some believed it a significant historic event wherein they too were the players.

The Battle of Shanghai slowed the Japanese war machine only briefly. By 1935 they controlled five provinces, and on July 7, 1937 they captured Peking, the nation's capital. By then the Nationalist and Communist Chinese forces realized the war with Japan was a life-and-death struggle, far more threatening than their own ideological-philosophical differences. When the Japanese marched on Shanghai again in August it signaled the start of a full-scale war. Local Chinese and those in every major Chinatown across America immediately launched a campaign to raise money for the China War Relief Fund. The fund-raising spanned a nine-year period, and between 1937 and 1946 more than five million dollars was collected from

Top: *War bonds to support the China War Relief funds were sold in $5.00 to $5,000.00 denominations. Amortized for fifteen years and yielding 5 percent interest per annum, the bonds, backed by the Central Bank of China, were bought as a patriotic gesture rather than for the investment value.*

Bottom: *Leaders of the Stockton Chinese community responsible for the fund drive for the 1940 July 7 anniversary of the Japanese invasion of Shanghai. In nine years of fund raising for China war relief the Stockton community raised over $400,000.*

Among the many fund raisers was this event held at the Haggin Museum in 1939. The jade exhibit in the background is now housed at the Oakland Museum.

Chinese across America. The Stockton community alone contributed $411,132.42.[14]

The campaign was a broad-based community effort. All Chinese gave generously to aid war-torn China, particularly during Chinese New Year and on the birthday of the republic (October 10). On the anniversary of the attack on Peking (July 7) each person was expected to donate one day's wages to the cause. There were other special drives, often earmarked for specific funds such as "winter clothes for the front" or "air to save China," and three Chinese war bond drives. Even children were expected to donate their nickels and dimes, and for their contributions they were given lapel pins citing their patriotic deed. War bonds were sold in both large and small denominations, but most individuals bought the one hundred-, fifty- and twenty-five-dollar issues. Collection boxes were placed in stores, restaurants and even at the Pioneer Museum-Haggin Galleries, where a few fund-raising events were held. Women went beyond wrapping bandages; they staged "rice bowl" parties and performed skits to raise money. Not surprisingly, the most generous individual donors were the gambling houses.

Edward Ah Tye, number three son of Mrs. Rose Ah Tye, served as a top gunner on a B-17 in World War II European Theater. The Ah Tyes had five sons and one son-in-law serving their country while their mother actively participated at the surgical headquarters of the local Red Cross.

Often it was Billy Wong, an enterprising local mogul, who led the way. During the first drive he gave $6,000 and another $5,000 a few months later. The American Company gambling house donated $1,500, and all the other gambling houses followed suit in the same amount. Chinese merchants also matched each other's pledges.

The most remarkable aspect of this China War Relief Campaign was that it occurred at a time when many were without jobs or money, in a time of national depression when thousands desperately sought food and a roof over their heads. The Chinese were also affected by this economic strife, but the needs of the homeland overrode any local considerations. San Joaquin County Chinese gave until it hurt and convinced many of their white friends to do the same. No other Chinese community could have been more patriotic and dedicated to the Nationalist Chinese cause than the Chinese Americans of Stockton.

Chung Wah's importance continued well through the 1940s. In 1949 the organization incorporated under the name of the Confucius Church, so named because Chung Wah's overall responsibilities for the teaching and preservation of the values of Chinese culture reflected the main tenets of Confucianism.

Chung Wah remained a strong bonding agent until the 1950s, serving and guiding its people, the young and old, families and remnants of the bachelor society, the affluent and the indigent. The elders were proud of what they had achieved in America but remained concerned about conditions in China and hardships faced by relatives. And wisely, the Chung Wah leaders eased the acculturation process of the children, demonstrating it was possible to think and act both as a Chinese and as an American.

CHAPTER TEN ENDNOTES

1. *Stockton Daily Independent*, August 13, 1872.

2. *Stockton Daily Evening Herald*, January 23, 1877.

3. *Stockton Weekly Mail*, June 25, 1892.

4. *Stockton Evening Mail*, July 25, 1898.

5. Interview with Horace Loo, who aided in the dismantling of the Heungshan temple and shipment of artifacts to San Francisco, 1981.

6. *Stockton Daily Evening Herald*, August 27, 1883.

7. *Stockton Daily Evening Herald*, November 5, 1880; June 20, 1881; June 19, 1882.

8. *St. Mark's Methodist Church 1849-1968* (Stockton, 1968).

9. *Stockton Daily Independent*, July 12, 1911. *Stockton Evening Record*, May 28, 1912.

10. Interviews with Don Lee, 1981-86.

11. Harry Chin, presentation on "The Chinese Benevolent Association of Stockton," before the San Joaquin County Historical Society, February 24, 1986.

12. Henry Shih-Shan Tsai, "The 1911 Revolution and the Chinese Americans," *Chinese Historical Society Bulletin*, Vol. I, pp. 2-3; Vol. II, pp. 2-8. *Sacramento Bee*, special edition, "Chinatown, Sacramento," January 17, 1971. Interview with Louie Yee Pai, 1981.

13. *Stockton Daily Independent*, January 7, 1912.

14. *The Statement of Nine Years (1937-1946) Contributions to the Anti-Invasion and Relief Efforts of the Chinese Association of Stockton, California* (Stockton, 1937).

Toward the Final Rest

This study of the Chinese cannot be considered complete without a review of the end of their life cycle. While the records of the Stockton Rural Cemetery verify actual death and interment of those who once built the levees and tilled the valley floor and who are remembered today as the first generation of many Stockton families, these records should be analyzed within their appropriate context. That context is an overall view of the final phases of Chinese life, closely associated with folk medicine and other, more professional medical services available within the Chinese community. And inevitably, our attention also must turn to the funeral rites which once piqued the curiosity of many westerners.

The funeral rite followed by burial was but another step in the final journey for many. It has been only half a century since Chinese bones were last exhumed and shipped to China, and a look at this element of cultural continuity, the ultimate wish of thousands of Chinese sojourners in America, must be included in this review.

A CURE FOR EVERY AILMENT

The Chinese were steeped in traditional methods of home remedies and holistic medicine when they arrived in the western world, and they saw little need to change their practices.

At the first sign of pain or discomfort, most Chinese turned to the numerous home remedies and native products available to them. Perceptive merchants in mining communities and local Chinatowns imported large supplies of popular Chinese medicines used in various ways for a variety of ailments ranging from upset stomachs to liver disorders. For instance, continual massage with tet dah jow, a brownish tincture in an alcohol solution which smelled pungently of benzoin, relieved pains from sprains, strains, bruises and even broken bones, although the liniment did not claim actually to heal the break. Tiger Balm, white flower oil and wind extraction oil (similar to Mentholatum or Vicks) cured headaches, dizziness, insect bites and other external ailments. Aromatic oils containing elements of menthol, eucalyptus, camphor, fennel, anise and cinnamon came in both liquid and salve forms and were used as both an analgesic and an anesthetic. Drinking a few drops purportedly cleared the sinus passages and relieved asthmatic conditions.

Chinese pills came in all sizes, from small vials filled with tiny pills the size of beebee shot to large, individually wrapped medication as big as a golf ball. One particularly large white pill resembled a wax-textured ping pong ball and, when steamed with pigeon meat, melted into a medicinal broth especially good for women with menstrual problems. A poultice composed of mud and grass, used to heal open sores, cuts and wounds, was a popular first aid among laborers and ranch hands.

Teas such as Oolong, Wo Hop, jasmine and chrysanthemum flower were good for many minor ailments. The extremely bitter herbal teas which took many hours to brew cured constipation, diarrhea, rheumatism and circulation problems. Melon and herbal soups and juices steamed from lean beef were credited with increasing the body's red blood cells, while eating mushrooms reportedly helped ward off cancer.[1]

When self-medication did not solve a particular health problem, the Chinese sought the services of an herbalist. For 4,000 years Chinese have practiced holistic medicine in the belief that the human body is a complete organism. In common with American Indians, they used natural herbs, animal parts, roots, flowers and insects to restore their health and increase their strength and male potency. They believed by eating animal organs the transference of organ for organ enhanced their agility and prolonged life.

Herb shops proliferated in all Chinese communities. Some in smaller communities, such as the Chew Kee store in remote Fiddletown, became the gathering center where the old Chinese socialized and obtained medical advice. Stockton had herb shops in both the Washington Street Chinatown and the Hunter-Channel complex. In his office on the ground floor of the Heungshan joss house, Dr. John Ho, the herbalist and court interpreter, attended to Chinese patients as well as to some whites who sought eastern remedies when western medicine proved ineffective.

Herb shops had a wonderfully warm and mysterious smell of mustiness combined with the faint scent of dried herbs. Most appeared similar to typical western apothecary shops, for there was the usual long counter uncluttered except for a hand-held scale, a mortar and pestle, stone grinder, a stack of square wrapping paper and twine. Behind the counter stood a large cabinet extending from floor to ceiling along the length of the wall, containing many, many drawers. Each drawer was divided into four compartments for greater storage capacity. Most herb shops carried at least five hundred to as many as three thousand popular items of plant, mineral and animal parts. Ingredients such as bark, a variety of roots, branches, shells, fungi, seeds, flowers, dried seahorses, small antlers and horns served as standard inventory. Among the herbs was usually found ginseng, a root which is grown in the mountains and whose shape is often nearly human. This herb was considered helpful in increasing circulation and male potency. Fook sang, a curative similar to Indian Snake Root, contained serpentine and was believed to calm nerves, and herbalists often prescribed it as a sleep tonic. Another popular herbal compound, ma wong, contained the drug ephedra and was prescribed for asthma sufferers to dilate the bronchial tubes and for others with constriction problems.[2]

Herb practitioners believed illnesses stem from body dysfunctions and healing could only occur when the balance in the body was restored. The dysfunction or disharmony often were caused by man's greater environment, elements which included pollution, lifestyle, parasites, insects and extremes in climatic conditions. Most knew standard formulas but mixed special concoctions for customers with unusual ailments. Often when an herbalist's prescription proved effective he safeguarded the formula, since there was no patent protection, and competition in the trade was fierce. A patient's improved health lent credibility to the herbalist's skills and reputation, thereby increasing his business.

After hearing his customer's complaints, the herbalist gathered and prepared the necessary ingredients, weighed and divided the portions, folded the herbs into a square of white paper, and wrote instructions for their use on the package. Prescriptions took various forms: pills, pellets, powders, ointments or brews which called for simmering for several hours. Some brews or teas were served cold, but most were consumed while hot in the belief the warm liquid increased the speed of absorption into the bloodstream.

The Chinese knew that acupuncture was an alternative to medicine for correcting a disorder and also was a method of alleviating pain. While some herbalists had knowledge of acupuncture, the sick more often sought Chinese doctors who were noted for their skills in acupuncture treatments.

The theory behind acupuncture is that electrical energy flows throughout the body; there are eight meridians or networks of energy lines. Within these web-like networks lie more than two thousand energy points which correspond with nerve junctions. Piercing a particular network of points overrides the pain signal and restores the electrical balance in the body's energy system. In recent years, western doctors have looked with interest at the use of acupuncture in lieu of anesthetic, as it is used in China.[3]

CHINESE FUNERALS

Seldom did the early Chinese seek western doctors or use the county hospital because of language barriers, costs and their unfamiliarity with western medicine and practice. Many moved into the district shelters to live out their last days, when their illnesses became terminal. Those with contagious diseases and those in the last phases of life were cordoned off from the rest of the lodgers in these houses. And after the Chinese drew his last breath, the shelter caretakers notified the coroner, mortuary and cemetery officials to handle the immediate arrangements.

In our present society we have come to identify certain funeral practices with various ethnic groups. The lively party atmosphere with the dead body on display amidst the participants suggests the makings of an Irish wake; the slow, mournful march of musicians, family members and friends that changes to a quick-stepping, lively parade immediately after the burial, evokes a sense of the New Orleans custom. Funeral traditions and burial practices other than those of one's own culture have always piqued curiosity. From time to time, newspaper articles tell of white interest in Chinese funerals. Whites who stood along the streets watching Chinese funeral processions make their way to the local cemetery estimated the deceased's wealth and community standing by the activities and length of the procession. For instance, in 1881 a reporter reasoned an influential member of Chinatown had passed away, for the procession included six hacks and a fiddler which sounded like Scottish bagpipes to him.[4]

The funerals of early Chinese pioneers, particularly in outlying regions of the county, were often swift and simple because of limited funds. A few friends followed the coffin to the cemetery and, at intervals, firecrackers and the metallic clanging of a gong would interrupt the mournful silence of the cortege. Mourners scattered mock paper money along the route in the belief that it would bribe evil spirits from harming the deceased. The noise of the gong and fiddle was to prevent such spirits from following the entourage. The grave markers were usually inexpensive boards. Chinese inscriptions written with an oil-based black ink lasted for many years despite inclement weather. In addition, each burial was duly recorded in the district association's ledgers for future reference.

As Chinese communities gained permanence, numbers and wealth, Chinese funerals became more attuned to traditional Chinese practices of the homeland. The elaborateness was dictated by the age, sex and status of the deceased, with the least attention given to a girl child and the most to a wealthy merchant or community leader. If the family was particularly well off, they might arrange for shipment of the deceased's body to China for funeral rites and burial; otherwise it took place in the community. A death notice written in Chinese calligraphy on white paper was usually posted on the front door of the deceased's home and served the same purpose as the black wreath hung on American doors. Obituary announcements, placed in local Chinese and American newspapers, extolled the dead person's achievements, affiliations and family ties. These notices often exaggerated the deceased's age by a few years to increase his importance in the spirit world.

Many aspects of family mournings were strictly regulated, although family attire and behavior and the length of the mourning period varied according to different districts and regions. Daughters could not cut their hair and sons were not allowed either to cut their hair or shave. Family members remained sequestered during the mourning period except for gravesite visitations.

Prior to the funeral, the deceased lay in state at the family home. At times the deceased would be wrapped in four blankets (or thin cloths in lieu of blankets), representing the four seasons. The Chinese believed the spirit world also underwent seasonal changes, and the blankets were for the deceased's use in the afterlife. In some instances the children supplied the blankets as a gesture of their concern and devotion. In other cases friends supplied the blankets in lieu of flowers or other expressions of sympathy. It was also acceptable for friends to give "white gold" (envelopes filled with cash) to help defray funeral expenses, rather than send flowers or contribute to a charitable organization in memory of the deceased.

At the head of the coffin there was a makeshift altar on which vases and urns filled with flowers and incense surrounded a large picture of the deceased. At the foot of the coffin a low table held offerings to the deceased: large platters of roast pig, a whole chicken, a variety of food, fruit, wine and tea. Visitors who paid their respects bowed three times before the coffin while family members looked on in stoical silence. Their own grief was interpreted by the loud laments and sobs of professional mourners.

On the day of the funeral, female family members donned burlap hoods which covered most of their faces, and the men wore armbands as well as long burlap sashes around their waists. The coarsely-woven burlap was not unlike the western sackcloth and ashes. The officiating Buddhist priest chanted sutras while the mourners gave their final performance. The funeral procession began after wagons loaded with food, incense, paper furniture, some of the deceased's personal belongings and flowers were assembled for the trek to the cemetery. Family, friends and musicians (replaced by marching bands in the 1920s) followed behind the hearse. As in earlier times, the funeral procession of a particularly wealthy individual was often accompanied by two or three hired bands. Long strips of red paper, or in some cases, small circular papers in the shape of Chinese coins were scattered along the route to bribe the evil spirits.

At the cemetery, the food was unloaded and spread on a concrete feast table. Paper models, money and the deceased's belongings were placed in a nearby incinerator and burned, enabling the deceased to use them in the spirit world. After the coffin was lowered into the grave, everyone threw a handful of dirt upon it and, as each left the cemetery, he received a small package containing a piece of candy and a coin—either a nickel or a dime— as a token of the occasion. The sweetness of the candy was to evoke pleasant memories of the deceased, and the coin was to be spent on something equally pleasurable in order to recapture good thoughts of the dead.

Following the burial, friends joined family members for a meal at a local restaurant. Food at this dinner was similar to everyday fare and contrasted sharply with the gastronomic delights served at Chinese banquets. The meal, intended to exemplify the routine of daily life, served as an occasion for the family to thank friends for their kindness. The dinner took on a superficially lighthearted atmosphere indicating that life does go on.

Formal mourning by the family members did not end with the funeral

In the late 1920s the Chinese community built a private cemetery for permanent and temporary burials on Matthews Road in French Camp. Twice a year the leaders of Chung Wah attend "tomb sweeping" rites according to traditional dictates.

dinner. Every seventh day for forty-nine days, the family paid a visit to the grave, taking food, tea and incense. Some families even took wine and cigars. The visits and offerings were symbolic acts to assure the deceased that even though he was no longer part of the present world, the family had not abandoned him. Such grave visitations also served as an adjustment period for the living and helped them accept the finality of death.

In time, even the most fundamental funeral practices were affected by western acculturation and practicality. In China and Southeast Asia, white had generally been the mourning color. Now, at Chinese American funerals, the wearing of white has given way to the darker colors traditional in western cultures.

CHING MING

Each spring, Chinese around the world celebrate *Ching Ming*, the Pure Brightness festival, the Chinese version of Memorial Day. Ching Ming occurs 105 days after the winter solstice, a time when nature unfolds the fresh green fields, birds shake off their winter lethargy, and a sense of vitality and rejuvenation fills the air. Springtime for the Chinese is a period of new beginnings, and it is particularly at this time that their minds come full circle in contemplation of their ancestors, themselves and their own children in the plane of life. On this occasion, families gather at the cemetery to clean the graves, clip the grass, pull weeds and clean the monuments. When the cleaning tasks are completed, a feast is laid before the graves, wines poured into the ground, candles and incense lit and paper money burned for use in the spirit world. Each family member kowtows before the grave, the oldest first. When this simple rite has been completed, the families spend the rest of the day feasting and visiting with each other. In addition to the traditional Chinese dishes, soft drinks and hamburgers now have been added to please younger family members.

In Stockton Chung Wah leaders, representing all the family clans, are responsible for the community-supported annual Ching Ming ceremony which includes one large feast in the cemetery for all participants. Frequently such items as a whole roasted pig and other dishes are placed on the ceremonial table in the cemetery. Following speeches extolling the history of various prominent ancestors, the food is divided among the families present. To underscore the importance of Ching Ming, one local elder stated that the Ching Ming rites would be performed at the cemetery as long as Chung Wah existed.[5]

THE FINAL JOURNEY HOME

The Stockton Rural Cemetery, where Chinese in Stockton were buried for many years, was founded in 1861 on land once owned by city father Charles M. Weber. This non-sectarian cemetery, located at the end of Cemetery Lane, just north of Harding Way, served outlying communities and the Delta islands as well as the city of Stockton. In May 1862 the trustees of the cemetery designated the northwest corner of the facility, far removed from the main burial location, for the exclusive use of the Chinese. This isolation proved advantageous for both Chinese and whites, for the Chinese had little wish to disturb white resting places when they exhumed the bones of their own people for shipment to China. At one time a fence within the Chinese area isolated the Heungshan from the rest of the Chinese.[6]

In contemplation of the practice of exhumation and shipment of one's bones to China, there is an important Chinese philosophy, especially to the Cantonese, to be considered—that of "falling leaves returning to the root." The Chinese feared that when they died their spirits would not rest until their remains were in a proper grave at home. The early years in the United States were a particularly worrisome period for most Chinese, as many feared their graves would be unattended without clan or family members in the vicinity. If their bones were returned to the homeland there would always be somebody, some blood relative, to perform the Ching Ming rites over their graves. As stated in the previous chapter, the twelve-dollar exit fee collected from sojourners returning to the homeland, and in later years the annual dues to the associations, funded this final trip home. Details of the exhumation, bone-packing and shipment process were uniformly carried out by district association leaders and cemetery officials. Each association established its own charitable units to handle the physical details.[7]

For the most part the exhumation and repacking was done en masse, and the costs were quite high. Shipping a box of bones was five dollars; reburial expense was seven dollars. In the 1880s, a ten-dollar public health permit for each grave exhumed added to the cost. The fee came about during the heat of the anti-Chinese period with the state legislators granting the San Francisco Public Health Board authorization to levy the assessment. In March 1885, a Dr. Phillips, secretary of the San Joaquin County Board of Health, informed the board of supervisors that Santa Clara County in the previous year had collected $500 in additional revenue because of exhumation permits and, as a new way to generate additional income for sanitary purposes, he proposed a similar ordinance. He estimated approximately forty to fifty permits would be issued to the Chinese annually.[8]

Phillips's estimate was quite accurate, for in the first two months of 1858 521 boxes of exhumed bones had been shipped from California to China on the French ship *Asia* and the clipper ship *Flying Cloud*. In 1861 one small article noted that the steamer *Eureka* had just left Stockton with twelve boxes of bones and headed for Sacramento to collect more before depositing its load in San Francisco. The small ship had transported 197 such boxes already that year. In 1863 a shipment of 258 boxes to the homeland cost $20,500. This large amount included traveling expenses for four supervisors who accompanied the shipment as well as a payment to Tung Wah Hospital in Hong Kong for transshipment to the correct family plots.[9]

No religious rites were attached to the exhumation process, which was performed by Chinese men from San Francisco with expertise in the task. Depending on the soil condition, a grave was usually opened between seven and ten years after burial. The initial step in the process was to locate a brick or bottle buried with the deceased, which served as a means of identification. The deceased's name would be painted on the brick, and the surname identified his clan and lineage. Other information might also be included, such as his root village and district. The bottle contained a piece of linen bearing the same sort of information. There was no particular significance to the size or shape of the bottle.

When identification was completed, a white cloth was laid in front of the grave to hold the bones. As each bone was removed from the coffin, it was carefully scraped clean, dipped in a bucket of brandy and water, then polished with a stiff brush until it almost shone. The bones were then laid in such a way as to reconstruct the skeleton, and an account was made of every bone. Should one be missing, care was taken to resift the loose dirt until it was located. The carpal, metacarpal and phalanges of each hand were placed in a small bag, and the bones of the feet were similarly separated and bagged.

Upon completion of the laying-out process, the bones were carefully packed in a tin can or wooden box lined with an oil cloth or heavy canvas. The femur, being the longest bone, regulated the height of the box to be used, but the box's width was a standardized eighteen or twenty-four inches. The bones were then placed in the can in a tight fetal position with the skull resting on top and the brick atop the skull or the bottle inserted somewhere in the can. After the tin was soldered shut, designation labels were affixed to the outside. Several tins were then packed into shipping crates and sent to the main collection point in San Francisco.

Without a doubt there were major philosophical differences between

In the rear section of the Chinese cemetery this marble tombstone marks a large common grave where lie boxes of individuals' bones. Because of Japan's invasion of China, they were not returned to China for the final rest.

Chinese and white funeral and burial customs, and that contrast extended to the actual grave digging and exhumation practices. One news article in the Hanford area of the San Joaquin Valley mentioned that a few Chinese grave diggers assigned to exhume some bones were heard grumbling as they worked. They could not understand why the whites had such stringent rules about burying their dead six feet deep when people in China dug their graves to a depth of only two feet. In another unfortunate situation farther up the Central Valley, some careless Chinese grave diggers angered the residents of Merced, a town sixty miles south of Stockton. In their haste to complete their exhumation chores and leave town, they abandoned the coffins they had unearthed and left clothing in which the bodies had been attired strewn about the local cemetery. Merced officials were further infuriated when they inspected the particularly shallow abandoned graves, for none was more than eighteen inches deep.[10]

Mass exhumations occurred at the Stockton Rural Cemetery nearly every year during the latter part of the nineteenth century. In the twentieth century they occurred in 1903, 1925, 1928 and 1932. Final removal of all bodies from the Chinese section occurred in September and October 1936. At that time 518 graves were exhumed, although not all were returned to China. Some were re-interred in a new Chinese cemetery on Matthews Road in French Camp, built in the 1920s. Chung Wah elders chose this particular site because of its sandy soil, for they believed its porosity aided in hastening decomposition of the bodies.

The practice of re-interment in China ended in 1937 with the Japanese invasion of China. Any additional hope for reburial in China was further dashed by subsequent events in China—the turmoil of World War II, the internal Communist-Nationalist conflict, and the closing of China to the western world by Mao Tse Tung. The last group of Chinese bodies removed from the rural cemetery was placed in the back section of the Matthews Road cemetery, where all burials are permanent and not subject to exhumation.

Early Stockton Rural Cemetery Record of Burials lists the interment and exhumation of 1,387 Chinese from 1863 to 1935.

STOCKTON RURAL CEMETERY DEATH RECORDS

Little remains of the Chinese section of the Stockton Rural Cemetery, and the area now included people from all races. Although all physical evidence is gone, the death records of the facility retain the names and some of the history of those who were buried there. Census materials, maps, newspapers, official documents and oral tradition provide valuable clues to help reconstruct the history of the Chinese. The death records serve as an additional resource to verify their existence and societal dynamics. These burial records are untainted by prejudice for the most part and tell of the vitality of these people who met death by violence, illness, accident and the inevitable aging process.

The first Chinese buried at the Stockton Rural Cemetery was a male laid to rest on January 13, 1863 and identified only as "Chinaman." On February 1, 1935, the last to be buried and later exhumed was a premature baby girl named Joy Go Lee. During the seventy-two-year span of the records, 1,387

Chinese were buried and exhumed: 1,290 males, 96 females and one whose sex was not stated. The few women and children found in the death records correspond to their small numbers in the census, and there is minimal information concerning their deaths except that most died at a very early age (as infants). Consumption (tuberculosis), while prevalent among whites, was particularly endemic among the Chinese. One of its victims was Mow Jew, a Chinese woman who died in 1869 at the age of twenty-five. Other women who met death at an early age were Tee How, who was only twenty-four when she drowned in 1867. Sui Hi was twenty-eight when she died of venereal disease in 1876. Both Sui and Tee were unmarried. Oy Mui May, a seventeen-year-old housewife, died from septicemia at childbirth in 1925. Yet by 1925 there were indications some women were living to a mature age, for Shee Chin died of arteriosclerosis at age sixty-three. Women were listed as either single or married, and with but one exception "housewife" was the only recorded occupation. That exception was the fifty-eight-year-old widow Ah Hoe, a seamstress, who died of consumption in 1905.

Prior to 1901 eighty-eight males out of 419 were married. The lack of Chinese women and the early deaths of those who were in Stockton obviously created a void in the men's total outlook on the purpose of life and progeny. This changed with time. By 1920 the death records show an increasing number of married men, more than 18 percent over earlier years, and by 1935 there was another 25 percent increase.

Occupation trends for the 1,290 males are divided into two time periods, before and after 1900. The majority were laborers, and some died from drowning around Holt, Bouldin, Sherman and other islands in the Delta region. Repairing a levee break in the cold and rushing water accounted for many of these work-related drownings. Many of the Chinese from Guangdong area did not consider swimming a recreational activity, and few had ever learned to swim.

The second largest number of Chinese burials according to occupations was that of cook, although their count was far less than laborers. Again, the peak of this employment corresponds to their peak in the federal censuses.

As the Chinese population leveled off to a fairly constant figure, the number of deaths among the laundrymen and merchants increased. Prior to the twentieth century only nine laundrymen had died, but between 1902 and 1921 eighteen laundrymen met with death. Five of these men died in an early morning fire in February 1904. They perished inside their crowded living quarters in the back of a laundry on South Hunter Street. The other deaths might be attributed to the aging of these men who were no longer employed but still living in the Stockton area.

Only ten deaths among the many merchants of Stockton were recorded prior to 1899. Yet, between 1902 and 1920 sixteen merchants died. This increase was a result of several factors, among them the aging of the many merchants who had arrived during the peak immigration years of the nineteenth century, the increase in the number of merchants in the community, and the fact that some were the victims of tong wars. By the turn of the century the death registers also indicate Chinese working in such modern positions as bookkeeping and engineering.

There was also an indication of improvement in economic status, leisure time, and perhaps, fulfillment of life's ambitions: by 1925, three men were occupationally-classified as "retired."

While suicides were numerous among the Stockton Chinese, it is difficult to arrive at a precise figure because most suicides occurred during the time of the greatest population in Chinatown and also during the peak years of tong activities. The ages and occupations of those who may have committed suicide were similar to those of murder-by-gunshot victims. Additionally, one suicidal method employed, that of cutting one's throat from ear to ear, suggests it was a suspiciously dubious way to depart this world considering other simpler alternatives. Other accidental deaths also must be considered carefully. Among them were five cases of fractured skulls among men between forty-seven and fifty-eight years of age, all of whom died between May 1919 and November 1921. The ages and occupations of these men were similar to those of tong war victims, and one cannot help but wonder if the fractured skull individuals should not be included with the tong war casualties. Other accidental deaths are less suspicious, such as the victim of a runaway brewery truck, a man hit by a Santa Fe train, one kicked by a mule and another killed in a cave accident.

Changes in the causes of death during these seventy-two years reflect increased medical awareness and advancement. As with murder cases and accidental deaths, a coroner's inquest was conducted when the cause of death was unknown and was thereby diagnosed through autopsy. Perhaps influenced by Dr. C. C. O'Donnell, the fanatical racist who at one time served as deputy coroner in San Francisco, the local coroner's main fear was a spread of leprosy among the Chinese. No case of leprosy was ever discovered in the death registers; however, the outward symptoms of syphilis resembled those of leprosy, and many Chinese died of syphilitic conditions. Their autopsies uncovered cases of cerebral syphilis, syphiloma of the brain and syphilitic endocarditis.

Consumption and liver disease were other common causes of death. Some of the natural deaths in the early days can be blamed on inadequate medication. The most effective medical preventative used today, but a scarce commodity then, is soap. Cancer, although considered a fairly modern killer, was found in a variety of diagnoses. They ranged from carcinoma of the lower intestine, stomach, rectum and groin to cancer of the larynx.[11]

By the 1920s the main cause of natural deaths seemed to be the various forms of pneumonia, myocarditis, pulmonary tuberculosis, nephritis, pericarditis, valvular and heart disease and dropsy. Older classifications of ague, apoplexy, hard work, "exhausted" and plain "worn out" were replaced by

Within the grounds of the sixty-plus year Chinese cemetery the permanent burials serve to remind the community of its legacy.

more sophisticated terminology. Occasionally humor could be found in the records, perhaps to bring the overpowering thought of death down to a level of human control such as in the comment on Dr. Ho Hoom, who died in April 1877 at the age of sixty-eight of "old age and whiskey."

Autopsy reports of later years indicate the Chinese suffered from diseases common among the aging, a clear indication that diet, living conditions and general health were much improved. Within fifty years, between 1870 and 1920, the average life span of the Chinese increased more than eleven years, from an average age at death of 57.5 to 68.6 years.

CONCLUSION

The use of death records is significant when it supports or refutes the findings of other documents. The Stockton Rural Cemetery death records bear mute testimony to the basic history of the Chinese in this country. Early registers show most of the sojourners were single, but later records also show that, within their own community, the Chinese displayed elements of violence and hostility, traits seldom recognized by the white community. Victims of tong wars are evidence of the energy and aggressiveness found among the young and also among the more affluent members of the Chinese community. At the turn of the century the increased numbers of deaths suggest that the aging Chinese, once employed in this area, remained here. New types of occupations indicate that the second generation Chinese Americans were coming of age and felt America was their home. Where most had been agricultural laborers there were now more landowner-farmers. Another sign of this upward mobility was the decline of field hands and an increase in white collar workers.

By the 1930s all the Chinese buried in the Chinese section of the Stockton Rural Cemetery had been exhumed and removed. The land has been designated as additional burial sites for the ever-expanding cemetery. While their physical remains are gone, their names in the death registers remain as vital evidence of their colorful existence. The Chinese Cemetery at French Camp is now the final resting place for those who have spent their lifetime in this community.

Chinese in San Joaquin County
Death Totals by Sexes from Death Register

	No. of Deaths	Male Deaths	Female Deaths
Volume A (1862-1876)	140*	127	13
Volume B (1877-1901)	315	292	23
Volume C (1902-1921)	616	581	35
Volume D (1922-1936)	316	290	26
Totals:	1,387	1,290	97

*In one death the sex was not recorded.

Occupations of Chinese Males Listed in the Death Register

	Volume A (1862-1876)	Volume B (1877-1901)	Volume C (1902-1921)	Volume D (1922-1936)
Laborer	45	109	336	78
Cook	8	16	44	14
Miner	5	--	5	--
Fisherman	8	4	3	--
Domestic	4	4	5	--
Laundryman	2	7	18	3
Merchant	1	9	16	14
Doctor	1	4	--	--
Farmer		1	54	10
Bookkeeper			6	5
Engineer				1
Retired				3

CHAPTER ELEVEN ENDNOTES

1. Interview with Edward Chew, 1986.

2. Dr. Paul K. Yee, address to Docent Council of Haggin Museum, 1983.

3. During examination Chinese doctors frequently apply pulse diagnostic techniques to ascertain the total state of the patient's being. Through observation, the doctor examines the color of the patient's tongue, his energy level and the aura in his eyes. With the patient's wrist resting on a pillow the doctor measures the pulse rhythm at three points on the radial artery of both arms, as each pulse position has a direct correlation to a particular body organ.

4. *Stockton Daily Evening Herald*, June 15, 1881.

5. Harry L. Chin, "Ching Ming—Ancestral Worship Day," pamphlet prepared for Stockton Unified School District, no date.

6. Delmar M. McComb, *The City of the Great Peace; An Historical Study of Stockton Rural Cemetery* (Stockton, 1961), p. 53. Interview with Don Lee, 1981.

7. The ten charity units established by the district associations represented most of the geographical districts within Guangdong Province. They were Fook Yam Tong of Nam-Hoi, Cheong Hou Tong of Poon-Yue, Hang On Tong of Shun-Tak, Bow On Tong of Tung-Koon, Yue Hing Tong of Sun-Ning (Toishan), Fook Sien Tong of Heungshan, Tung Tak Tong of Sun Wui, Yang On Tong of Tseng-Shing, Tung Fook Tong of Yan Ping and Hoi Ping and Kwong Fook Tong of Shui Hing and Hop Wo.

8. *Stockton Daily Evening Herald*, March 3, 1885.

9. *Stockton Daily Independent*, December 28, 1861. Pei Chi Liu, *A History of the Chinese in the United States of America* (Taipei, 1976), p. 164. Francis L. Hsu, *American and Chinese* (New York, 1972), p. 2.

10. *Stockton Daily Independent*, December 21, 1885. *The Hanford Sentinel*, Special Edition, "The Immigrant: Chinese," March 1983, p. 19.

11. Cancer of the larynx may be due to extensive consumption of preservatives, particularly saltpeter, used in barbecued pork. Another possible reason for the numerous cases of cancer of the esophagus and larynx was the heavy smoking done by many Chinese men.

Epilogue

A de facto housing practice existed in Stockton until the mid-twentieth century. Real estate agents and developers refused to sell new homes in the north section of town to the Chinese in the belief that Japanese and Filipinos would follow and neighborhood property values diminish as yards and homes deteriorated. However, many white homeowners selling their homes had fewer qualms about selling to the Chinese, particularly after they learned the Chinese did not quibble about the price and frequently paid in full or made sizable cash down payment. Once Chinese moved into a neighborhood, people who had had doubts soon realized that their concerns had been groundless.

By the late 1950s, Chinese families began to move into the more exclusive Caldwell Village and Riviera Cliff neighborhood, and when housing tracts mushroomed north of the Calaveras River, they bought into the Weberstown, Sherwood Manor and Mayfair subdivisions. This had a great impact on the surrounding shopping areas, for rather than make the long trek downtown to Chinatown to buy tofu, bok choy and other ethnic food products, the Chinese Americans living in these neighborhoods patronized the nearest supermarkets. Soon other services offered in Chinatown were also found in the suburbs. Thus, a majority of the second- and third-generation Chinese Americans reached the apex of the assimilation pendulum: they lived among white; they spoke, read and thought almost exclusively in English; and their primary entertainments were American movies and music. They were truly Americans of Chinese ancestry.

THE END OF CHINATOWN

Without the patronage of their own group, store owners on Washington Street suffered economic hardships, and their changed personalities reflected their demoralized state. They no longer dusted the shelves, washed the grime off the floors, or introduced new wares; they just let their stock dwindle and food quality deteriorate. City officials saw the time had come for improvement, and the bulldozer seemed the only way to cleanse the inner city rot. Once redevelopment and freeway construction plans were approved, many Chinatown property owners privately prayed for sizable

Second- and third-generation Chinese Americans have fully acculturated their eastern and western heritages. These young people are enjoying a church picnic in 1959.

condemnation prices for their holdings. During the twelfth hour, souvenir hunters scurried to salvage the last few items in the Chinese buildings before the wrecking ball struck its first blow, but no one cried "stop," least of all the Chinese.

To commemorate the Chinese past, city fathers erected Chung Wah Lane, a twenty-five-foot wide, one-block-long walkway in the middle of the block bounded by Washington, Market, El Dorado and Hunter streets. At each end of the promenade stands a brightly painted arch supported by two round pillars, closely resembling tori gates. The path is delicately laced with inlaid stone motifs of Chinese dragons and lucky symbols. Except for an occasional wino squatting near the bushes and one or two elderly Chinese men taking in the sun, it is difficult to imagine this was once the heart of Stockton's Chinatown and the site of most of Stockton's red light establishments. One look at this airy, yet strangely desolate, area might prompt the knowledgeable visitor to wonder if the redevelopment bulldozer destroyed not only the edifices of the Chinese, but their spirit as well. The area exhibits some artificial-looking oriental structures with pagoda-shaped, red-tiled roofs. While the buildings may be modern and antiseptic, they seem to have sprung from an architect's drawing board without a hint of humanity or history.

A few still call the area Chinatown, for four family associations and five

restaurants still exist on the block. Lee Yuen, the old Lee stronghold, still
sits at the same northeast corner of Washington and El Dorado streets as it
did in 1878. But the store is now housed in a modern building and its name
has been changed to Lee's Liquor and Hardware. Recently the Stockton
Chamber of Commerce honored the store as a Stockton heritage business,
thus acknowledging its continual existence for over a hundred years. Few
other businesses in town have thus far shared that honor.

A few Chinese stores and restaurants are scattered just south of this block,
but most are struggling to stay in business, with the exception of On Lock
Sam, the 1895 restaurant that has now become an institution among white
and Chinese devotees throughout the San Joaquin Valley. In its cocktail
lounge there are a few pictures of the restaurant as it stood on Washington
Street during its heyday. Aside from these old black-and-white photos, only

*A 1963 view of Stockton with Washington Square and its pedestrian paths in the
shape of an X. Stockton's Chinatown is to the left. This photo was taken prior to the
city's crosstown freeway construction and Stockton's redevelopment projects.*

Recreation for the young included this bird hunting trip on the outskirts of town. They are (left to right) Robert Mah, Charles Low, Haye Chan, Lawrence Lee and Art Chan, c.1940.

a small permanent herb shop exhibit in the basement of the Haggin Museum serves as a public reminder of the Chinese past.

INSTITUTIONS

With the sights, sounds and smells of that once-thriving Chinatown buried under tons of dirt and concrete, one would assume the Chineseness of the people might also have disappeared. Yet, even if one were fully accultur-ated into mainstream America, there is no escaping from one's heritage. There will be certain biological and psychological reminders of ethnicity which will periodically disturb the human soul. Obviously, the Chinese cannot change the color of his skin and, once in a while, he will crave the type of ethnic food on which he was weaned. And as mid-life and the twilight years glimmer on the horizon, his longing for definitive answers to his roots and cultural heritage may grow increasingly stronger. Moreover, by tradition, the Chinese are a tightly-knit, group-oriented society and they tend to seek the familiarity and reinforcement of their own people.

Institutional systems and networks continue to thrive. Family and district associations which bind together Chinese of the same clans and surnames have undergone changes only in keeping with the times. It would be unthinkable for the Chinese to cast aside these inherited institutions; to do so would be to turn one's back on his own roots. Clan-family associations continue to hold an annual Spring Festival dinner. From late February until the end of April, family associations alternate hosting an annual banquet to which family members, friends and influential white civic leaders are invited. Of course, a little friendly gambling occurs afterward, in keeping with custom.

Stockton Chinese Americans, today, have the time, interest and funds to enjoy sports such as golf, bowling and fishing and have formed clubs to pursue these recreational activities. There are similar Chinese clubs in other communities, and periodically the local Chinese sponsor invitational competitions and statewide tournaments which bring in participants from Sacramento, Oakland, Los Angeles and other far-flung communities to Stockton.

The Stockton Cathay Club, formed in 1946, lists many Stockton-born Chinese on its membership rolls. The club's stated purpose is to promote civic and social betterment of the Chinese community and to provide recreational outlets for its members. Since its inception, the Cathay Club has been the primary force helping second- and third-generation Chinese straddle their bifurcated world. Most of its members were raised in older, traditional Chinese households, but their education, work and residence patterns have been among the whites. Some individuals recognize there is still an identity conflict, particularly when they see they have not achieved social equality and total acceptance by the dominant society. For these people, the closeness felt in Cathay Club activities, attended almost exclusively by Chinese, satisfies their social needs.

An influx of new Chinese immigrants from Taiwan, Hong Kong, Mainland China and Southeast Asia has created a second type of Chinese presence in the Stockton community. Initially a disparity existed between the native-born of Cantonese descent and the new immigrants, who, even though clearly Chinese, have decidedly different backgrounds and histories. The Chinese Cultural Society of Stockton(CCSS), founded in 1976, mostly by newcomers, was organized to cultivate and perpetuate the entire Chinese heritage, not just the cultural customs particular to Guangdong Province. CCSS sponsors a Chinese folk dance troupe and a lion dance group and

To commemorate the bi-centennial of the United States the Chinese community gave this Confucius monument to the city of Stockton. Located across the street from City Hall, it generates a feeling of tranquility in an otherwise bustling thoroughfare.

hosts performing artists and musicians who visit Stockton occasionally. In 1978 CCSS launched a public Chinese New Year celebration which has now become an annual event held at the Civic Memorial Auditorium. Stocktonians of all ages and colors, not just Chinese, put the festival day on their calendars. Working participants in this yearly event include all major Chinese American groups in Stockton, such as the Christian churches, Asian educators and students of various high school Asian clubs—even those Chinese not active in any particular organization lend a hand. By its tenth anniversary, the Chinese New Year festival had evolved into a dichotomous affair of history and heritage reminiscent of Chinese New Year activities of the late nineteenth and early twentieth century. One individual claimed that a Chinese can act and feel like an American every day of the year except the festival day, for on that day he immerses himself physically and mentally in the spirit of his heritage.

The Stockton Cathay Club, Chinese Cultural Society of Stockton and Saint Mark's Methodist Church are all represented in the inner circle of Chung Wah's nineteen associations' membership. Presidents of these contemporary organizations are seated among family and clan association representatives on the Chung Wah Board. Assimilation is pervasive even among these traditional bastions as almost all are incorporated and have non-profit organization status.

公曆一九七八年元月
八日本埠四邑會館會
務結束將全部存欵會
萬零陸佰元陸亳陸仙
捐助本孔教堂指定為
青年奬坽塲老人福利
中華僑衆坽塲等項用途及
邑尚資刻銅牌永留紀
嘉並資鳴謝牌永留紀堪
念斾鞸中華孔教堂誌

BE IT RESOLVED THAT THIS PLAQUE BE DEDICATED IN
PERMANENT MEMORY TO THE SEE YUP ASSOCIATION IN
APPRECIATION OF ITS NOBLE GESTURE OF DONATING
ITS RESIDUAL FUND OF TEN THOUSAND SIX HUNDRED
DOLLARS TO THE CONFUCIUS CHURCH UPON THE
ASSOCIATION'S TERMINATION, JANUARY 8, 1978. BE
IT FURTHER RESOLVED THAT THIS FUND WILL BE USED
EXPLICITLY AS A SCHOLARSHIP FOR THE STUDENTS OF
THE CHINESE LANGUAGE SCHOOL, FOR THE WELFARE
OF THE CHINESE SENIOR CITIZENS AND FOR THE
BIANNUAL MEMORIAL CEREMONY AT THE CHINESE
CEMETERY, AND FOR THE CEMETERY'S MAINTENANCE.

THE CONFUCIUS CHURCH OF STOCKTON
JANUARY 1978

*In 1978 the local Sze Yup Association dissolved and, according to
state law governing non-profit organizations, the elders transferred their association funds to Chung Wah for the perpetuation
of certain community activities.*

The newer organizations have superseded much of Chung Wah's early
influences. And while Chung Wah is not as active as it was forty years ago,
its elders are still dedicated to Confucian teachings and the principles of Dr.
Sun Yat Sen.

Today, Chung Wah still oversees the Chinese cemetery at French Camp
and conducts the annual Ching Ming memorial rites there. Years ago bones
of deceased Chinese were returned to the homeland, but the practice ceased
some fifty years ago. There is an ironic postscript to that practice—recently
two shipments of Chinese bones arrived for interment in the French Camp

The Ah Tye Brothers service station on El Dorado and Sonora streets began in 1931. The brothers later had stations at two other locations. Obviously the Chinese were involved in other businesses besides restaurants, laundries and groceries, c.1950.

cemetery. These were bones of Chinese who did not live in America during their lifetime but requested that their bones be shipped here so their immigrant relatives could tend their graves during Ching Ming.

The Chinese Language School, under Chung Wah's auspices, has operated for over seventy years, although its enrollment has decreased as families have moved from the old Chinese neighborhood. Classes are now conducted on Saturday mornings and are not as long or demanding as those of the past. The school will, however, remain in existence as long as there are parents who wish to see their children educated in the rudiments of the Chinese language.

Adjoining the Chung Wah building on Lafayette Street is Jene Wah, a Chinese Senior Citizen Center, where older community members can participate in federally subsidized luncheon programs. After their meals, they stay to socialize, talk over old times, see Chinese movies, and play mah jong and other games.

While these older citizens enjoy their twilight years, their children are at work in all facets of the city and county's economy. A hundred years ago most Chinese labored in the fields and worked in service-oriented occupations in urban communities. Once merchants and storekeepers were numerous in Stockton, and the community leaders rose from their ranks. Today few stores are owned by the Chinese and there are perhaps less than a hundred others employed in local restaurants. Unfortunately, only two or three Chinese families are involved in local farming enterprises. By far the

Jung Yee settled in Stockton in the 1860s following a short stint as a gold prospector. Together with his wife, Choy Won, he established a five-generation legacy which continues to the present.

Louie Yee Pai at age ninety. In his lifetime he spent seventy-two years in San Joaquin County, fathered five children, and served as president of his clan organization, the Soo Yuen Association. He also was a member of the Chung Wah Board of Directors. He began as a vegetable peddler's helper, became an entrepreneuer and later owned a delicatessen.

largest percentage of the Chinese work in the medical, dental and professional fields and many other are employed in civil service occupations, but few have risen to managerial ranks in the latter field.

A COMMENTARY

While Chinese civil rights and affirmative action groups in San Francisco and Los Angeles have forged ahead on a direct but often rough and confrontational course, and the Sacramento Chinese have developed an awareness of their own potential political clout, Stockton's Chinese are less active in the political and civic arenas and seem unconcerned that this is so. Within their own community the Stockton Chinese are dynamic, but within the context of the dominant society, they seem to exhibit many of the same symbiotic relationships as those established by their forefathers. It is unnecessary, of course, that one Chinese community closely follow the example of another, for within each of the major cities are different sets of civic leaders, community temperaments and economic climates. More importantly, their individual histories have established unique Chinese-white relationships.

While it is possible to interpret the actions of the San Joaquin County Chinese as slower and more circuitous, in the end they have received what they asked for and, without making demands, they have been accorded recognition as important contributors to the county's economy and history. In 1986 the San Joaquin County Historical Society instituted an award recognizing contributions of pioneering families in the county. Among the first five accorded this honor was the Jung Yee or Jann family, whose legacy has stretched back five generations. Unlike the other four, all white families whose histories included land ownership and commercial enterprises, the

Jann argonaut came as a gold seeker and never rose above the status of a handyman for city founder Charles Weber. Yet today this man is recognized as a pioneer of San Joaquin County. His contributions and those of his descendants have gained the respect of the entire community.

It is clear that the history of the San Joaquin County Chinese is unique and will continue to evolve in its own way and time, despite the fact that this community lies geographically only a mountain away from the teeming coastline of California and the pervasive influence of other major Chinese communities there. And while some would demand that final conclusions be drawn in the study of a people, we live in a complex and transitional world and cannot arbitrarily say that such a history is complete and the conclusions clear and unalterable.

The Chinese of San Joaquin County have held steadfastly to their heritage but have in their forthright manner adopted western philosophical beliefs and lifestyles. Yet even today their world is a dual one, and total reconciliation of the Chinese and the American world may be possible only within the individual. As a people we are at a crossroad, and the continuing influences of both Chinese and white America upon our bifurcated world can only enhance the future of Chinese Americans in years to come and further change what seems clear today.

Bibliography

Primary and secondary materials are alphabetized together.

An Illustrated History of San Joaquin County, California. Chicago: Lewis Publishing Co., 1890.

Armentrout-Ma, L. Eve. "Chinese in California's Fishing Industries, 1850-1941." *California History* 60 (Summer 1981): 142-57.

Augusta, Dorothy. "Locke." *Golden Notes* 16 (October 1970). Sacramento Historical Society.

Baltich, Frances. *Search For Safety: The Founding of Stockton's Black Community.* Stockton, California: Cottage Creations, 1982.

Barth, Gunther Paul. *Bitter Strength: A History of the Chinese in the United States 1850-1870.* Cambridge, Mass.: Harvard University Press, 1964.

Be Dunnah, Gary P. *A History of the Chinese in Nevada 1855-1904.* San Francisco: R and E Research Co., 1973.

Bloch, Louis. *Facts About Filipino Immigration Into California.* California Department of Industrial Relations Special Report. California: Department of Industrial Relations, 1930.

Bloodworth, Dennis. *The Chinese Looking Glass.* New York: Dell, 1966.

Bonta, Robert and Horace A. Spencer. *Stockton's Historic Public Schools.* Stockton, California: Stockton Unified School District, 1981.

Boyton, Gladys R. "Brick Making in San Joaquin County." *San Joaquin Historian* 4 (March 1968): 1-3.

Brienes, West, and Schulz. *Overview of Cultural Resources in the Central Business District, Sacramento, California, 1971.* Report for the Sacramento Museum and History Department. Sacramento: n.p., 1981.

Browne, Juanita Kennedy. *Nuggets of Nevada County History.* Nevada City, California: Nevada County Historical Society, 1983.

Buffum, Edward Gould. *Six Months in the Gold Mines: From a Journal of Three Years' Residence in Upper and Lower California 1847-8-9.* Philadelphia: Lea and Blanchard, 1850.

Bulosan, Carlos. *America Is In The Heart.* New York: Harcourt, Brace and Co., 1946.

Burkhardt, V. R. *Chinese Creeds and Customs*. Taipei, Taiwan: Caves Book Co., 1970.

Cahill, Helen Kennedy. "Captain Weber and His Place in Early California History." *Pacific Historian* 20 (Winter 1976): 425-60.

California State Board of Controls. *California and the Orientals: Japanese, Chinese and Hindus*. Sacramento, California: State Printing Office, 1920.

Carpenter, Frances. *Tales of a Chinese Grandmother*. Tokyo, Japan: Charles E. Tuttle Co., 1973.

Carson, James H. *Recollections of the California Mines*. Stockton, California, 1852.

Caughey, John Walton. *The California Gold Rush*. Berkeley: University of California Press, 1975.

Chamberlain, Jonathan. *Chinese Gods*. Taipei, Taiwan: n.p., 1983.

Chan, Anthony. *Gold Mountain: the Chinese in the New World*. Vancouver, British Columbia: New Star Books, 1983.

Chan, Donald P. Interview with Author, Stockton, California, 1980.

Chan, Mabel. Interview with Author, Folsom, California, 1983.

Chan, Sucheng. "Chinese Livelihood in Rural California: the Impact of Economic Change, 1860-1880." *Pacific Historical Review* 53 (August 1984): 273-307.

_____. *This Bittersweet Soil: The Chinese in California Agriculture, 1860-1910*. Berkeley: University of California Press, 1986.

Chang, K. C., ed. *Food In Chinese Culture: Anthropological and Historical Perspectives*. New Haven, Connecticut: Yale University Press, 1977.

Chen, Jack. *The Chinese in America*. San Francisco: Harper & Row, 1981.

Chen, Ta. *Chinese Migrations With Specific Reference to Labor Conditions*. New York: Paragon Book Gallery, 1923.

Cheung, Lucia Yim San, Eric Ray Cho, Tze Yu Tang, and How Boa Yau. "An Exploratory Descriptive Study of the Low Income Chinese Elderly in Sacramento and Their Family Health Care System." Master of Social Work, CSU-Sacramento, 1978.

Chew, Edward. Interview with Author, Sacramento, California, 1983 to 1985.

Chew, James R. Interview with Author, Stockton, California, 1976 to 1982.

Chew, Ruth Pon. Interview with Author, Stockton, California, 1976 to 1985.

Chin, Dorothy. Interview with Author, Stockton, California, 1979.

Chin, Harry. Interview with Author, Stockton, California, 1979 to 1985.

Chin, Harry. "Ching-Ming-Ancestral Worship Day," pamphlet prepared for Stockton Unified School District, n.d.

_____. "The Chinese Benevolent Association of Stockton," talk delivered before the San Joaquin County Historical Society, Micke Grove, Lodi, California, February 24, 1986.

Chin, Lily. Interview with Author, Stockton, California, 1981.

Chinn, Kenneth. Interview with Author, Stockton, California, 1981.

Chinn, Thomas W., H. Mark Lai, and Philip P. Choy. *A History of the Chinese in California: A Syllabus.* San Francisco: Chinese Historical Society, 1969.

Chiu, Ping. *Chinese Labor in California 1850-1880: An Economic Study.* Madison, Wisconsin: State Historical Society of Wisconsin, 1967.

Chu, George. "Chinatown in the Delta: The Chinese in Sacramento-San Joaquin Delta 1870-1960." *California Historical Society Quarterly* 49 (March 1970): 22-34.

Clappe, Louise A. K. S. *The Shirley Letters,* introduction by Richard Oglesby. Santa Barbara, California: Peregrine Smith, Inc., 1978.

Cole, Cheryl L. "Chinese Exculsion: The Capitalist Perspective of the Sacramento Union. 1850-1882." *California History* 57 (Spring 1978): 8-31.

Colville, Samuel. *Sacramento Directory,* volumes V and VI. San Francisco: Monson, Valentine & Co., 1856.

Coolidge, Mary E. *Chinese Immigration.* New York: Henry Holt, 1909.

Cormack, J. G. *Chinese Birthday, Wedding, Funeral and Other Customs.* Peking, China: China Booksellers Ltd., 1927.

County Probate Receipts Collection. Petsinger Library, Haggin Museum, Stockton, California. Reclamation receipts from Roberts Island, Catalog no. LB80-8523-2039 through 2035, October 1884.

Cronin, Kathryn. *Colonial Casualties: Chinese in Early Victoria.* Carlton, Victoria: Melbourne University Press, 1982.

D. M. Bishop and Company. *Stockton Directory of 1876-1877.* Stockton: B. C. Vandall, 1876.

De Carli, Dean. *Holt Station, Holt School, Patterson School.* Stockton, California: n.p., n.d.

Department of the Interior, Office of the Census. Ninth, Tenth and Twelfth Censuses of the United States. San Joaquin County, California. Population Schedule: 1870, 1880 and 1900. U.S. Archives, Washington, D.C. (Microcopy, CSUS-Library).

Development of Yee Fow Chung Wah Headquarters. (Author unknown) Hong Kong, 1963.

Dillon, Richard. *The Hatchet Men: San Francisco's Chinatown in the Days of the Tong Wars 1880-1906.* New York: Ballantine Books, 1962.

Directory of Stockton City and San Joaquin County 1926. Sacramento: R. L. Polk & Co., 1926.

Directory of Stockton City and San Joaquin County 1930. Sacramento: R. L. Polk & Co., 1930.

Dobie, Charles Caldwell. *San Francisco's Chinatown.* New York: D. Appleton-Century Co., 1936.

Eberhard, Wolfram. *Chinese Festivals.* New York: Henry Schuman, 1952.

Egan, Ferol. "River People." *Motorland* 102 (Nov./Dec. 1981): 20-21.

1850 Census of San Joaquin County. Stockton: San Joaquin Genealogy Society, 1959.

Fisher, C. E. *San Joaquin County-California: California Fruit for Health, California Lands for Wealth*. Stockton, San Joaquin County, California: Sunset Magazine Homeseekers Bureau for the Board of Supervisors, circa 1915.

Fisher, Lloyd H. *The Harvest Labor Market in California*. Cambridge, Mass.: Harvard University Press, 1953.

Fong, Esther Lee. Interview with Author, Stockton, California, 1981-1985.

Fong, John. Interview with Author, Stockton, California, 1981-1985.

Fong, S. L. Interview with Author, Stockton, California, 1980.

Franklin, William E. "Governors, Miners, and Institutions: The Political Legacy of Mining Frontiers in California and Victoria Australia." *California History* 65 (March 1986): 48-57.

Free China Weekly, Taipei, Taiwan, April 8, 1979.

Gilbert, F. T. *History of San Joaquin County, California With Illustration Descriptive of Its Scenery 1879*. Oakland: Thompson & West, 1879. Reproduced by Howell-North Books, Berkeley, 1968.

Gong, Eng Ying. *Tong War*. New York: Nicholas L. Brown Co., 1930.

Gronewald, Sue. "Beautiful Merchandise: Prostitution in China, 1860-1936." *Women & History* 1 (Spring 1982): 1-110.

Haggin Manuscript Collection, Petsinger Library, Haggin Museum, Stockton. Letters to Cheong Jim Low, in care of Poo Woo Tong Co., 1935 and 1937. Catalog No. 71-120-6A and 71-120-6B.

Hanford Sentinel, Special Edition, "The Immigrant: Chinese." Hanford, California, March 1983.

Hammond, George P. *The Weber Era in Stockton History*. Berkeley: The Friends of the Bancroft Library, 1982.

Hemminger, Carol. "Little Manila: The Filipinos in Stockton Prior to World War II." *Pacific Historian* 10 (1980), Part I (21-34); Part II (207-220). County 1850-1920." Master of Arts, CSU-Sacramento, 1983.

Hirata, Lucie Cheng. "Free, Indentured, Enslaved: Chinese Prostitutes in Nineteenth-Century America." *Signs* (Autumn 1979).

Hoexter, Corinne K. *From Canton to California: Epic of Chinese Immigration*. New York: Four Winds Press, 1976.

Hom, Gloria Sun, ed. *Chinese Argonauts*. Los Altos Hills, California: Foothill Community College, 1971.

Hoy, William. *Chinese Six Companies*. San Francisco: Chinese Consolidated Benevolent Association, 1942.

Hsu, Francis L. K. *American and Chinese*. American Museum Science Books Edition. Garden City, New York: Doubleday Natural History Press, 1972.

Insurance Map of Stockton, California. New York: Sanborn Map Publishing Co., 1883 revised to 1890 and 1917 revised to 1946. Petsinger Library, Haggin Museum, Stockton.

Jann, Earl. Interview with Author, Stockton, California, 1981-1985.

Jenkins, John C. "Sutter Lake or China Slough." *Golden Notes* 13 (December 1966).

Jones, J. Roy, M.D. *Memories, Men and Medicine.* Sacramento: The Sacramento Society for Medical Improvement, 1950.

Kao, George. *Chinese Wit and Humor.* New York: Sterling Publishing Co., 1974.

Kaptchuk, Ted J. *The Web That Has No Weaver: Understanding Chinese Medicine.* New York: Congdon & Weed, Inc., 1983.

Kennedy, Glenn A. Interview with Author, Stockton, California, 1979-1985.

Kennedy, Glenn A. *It Happened in Stockton 1900-1925.* 3 volumes. Stockton: Kenco Reproduction Service, 1967.

Kemble, Edward C. *A History of California Newspapers 1846-1858.* Los Gatos: The Talisman Press, 1962.

Kingston, Maxine Hong. *Chinamen.* New York: Alfred A. Knopf, 1980.

Kingston, Maxine Hong. *The Woman Warrior.* New York: Random House, Inc., 1975.

Knoll, Tricia. *Becoming Americans: Asian Sojourners, Immigrants, and Refugees in the Western United States.* Portland, Oregon: Coast to Coast Books, 1982.

Kroupa, B. *An Artist's Tour.* London: Ward and Downey, 1890.

Laura De Force Gordon Collection. San Joaquin County Historical Museum, Lodi, California. Lease transfer agreement of the Laura De Force Gordon estate dated March 12, 1908.

Lee, Calvin. *Chinatown U.S.A.: A History and Guide.* New York: Doubleday and Co., 1965.

Lee, Donald. Interview with Author, Stockton, California, 1981-1985.

Lee, Lily. Interview with Author, Stockton, California, 1981.

Lee, Rose Hum. *The Chinese in the United States of America.* Hong Kong: Hong Kong University Press, 1960.

Li, Dun J. *The Ageless Chinese, A History.* Third edition. New York: Charles Scribner's Sons, 1978.

Liang, Edna. Interview with Author, Sacramento, California, 1983.

Life, Influence and the Role of the Chinese in the United States, 1776-1960. San Francisco: Chinese Historical Society of America, 1976.

Limbaugh, Ronald. "Yee Ah Chong Remembers Vacaville's Chinatown." *California History* 63 (Summer 1984).

Lip, Evelyn. *Chinese Geomancy: A Layman's Guide to Feng Shui.* Singapore: Times Books International, 1979.

Liu, Pei Chi. *A History of the Chinese in the United States of America.* Taipei, Taiwan: Li Ming Cultural Enterprises, Republic of China, 1976.

Lodi Sentinel, Lodi, California. May 21, 1968.

Loo, Horace. Interview with Author, Stockton, California, 1981.

Lord, Paul A., ed. *Fire & Ice: A Portrait of Truckee.* Truckee, California: Truckee Donner Historical Society, 1981.

Louie, Yee Pai. Interview with Author, Stockton, California, 1981.

Low, Leslie. Interview with Author, Stockton, California, 1981.

Lydon, Sandy. *Chinese Gold: The Chinese in the Monterey Bay Region.* Capitola, California: Capitola Book Company, 1985.

Lyman, Stanford M. *Chinese Americans.* New York: Random House, 1974.

Ma, Ching. *Chinese Pioneers: Materials Concerning the Immigration of Chinese to Canada and Sino-Canadian Relations.* Vancouver, British Columbia: Versatile Publishing Co., 1979.

Mah, Robert. Interview with Author, Stockton, California, 1981-1984.

Mah, Rose. Interview with Author, Stockton, California, 1981-1984.

Mar, Dave, ed. *I Am Yellow (Curious).* Davis: Asian American Research Project, University of California, Davis, 1959.

Mar, Timothy T. *Face Reading: the Chinese Art of Physiognomy.* New York: Dodd, Mead & Company, 1974.

Martin, V. Covert, R. Coke Woods, and Leon Bush. *Stockton Album Through the Years.* Stockton: Simard Printing Co., 1959.

McCollum, William S. *California As I Saw It: Pencillings by the Way of Its Gold and Gold Diggers! and Incidents of Travel by Land and Water.* Edited by Dale L. Morgan. Los Gatos, California: Talisman Press, 1960.

McComb, Delmar, Jr. *The City of the Great Peace: An Historical Study of the Stockton Rural Cemetery.* Stockton: n.p., 1961.

McCunn, Ruthanne Lum. *Thousand Pieces of Gold.* San Francisco: Design Enterprises of San Francisco, 1981.

McDonald, Douglas and Gina McDonald. *The History of the Weaverville Joss House and the Chinese of Trinity County, California.* Medford, Oregon: McDonald Publishing, 1986.

McLeod, Alexander. *Pigtails and Gold Dust.* Caldwell, Idaho: Caxton Printers, 1947.

McWilliams, Carey. *Brothers Under the Skin.* Boston: Little, Brown, and Co., 1946.

_____ *California: The Great Expectation.* Santa Barbara, California: Peregrine Smith, Inc., 1976.

_____ *Factories In the Fields: The Story of Migratory Farm Labor in California.* Boston: Little, Brown, and Co., 1940.

Melendy, Howard B. *The Oriental American.* New York: Hippocrene Books, 1972.

Miller, Stuart Creighton. *The Unwelcome Immigrant: The American Image of the Chinese 1785-1882*. Berkeley: University of California Press, 1969.

Minimum Rates of Board of Fire Underwriters of the Pacific for Stockton, California. New York: Sanborn-Perris Map Co., 1898. Petsinger Library, Haggin Museum, Stockton.

Minnick, Sylvia Sun. "A Demographic Analysis of the Chinese in San Joaquin County 1850-1920." Master of Arts, CSU-Sacramento, 1983.

———. "Chinese Funeral Customs." *Golden Notes* 27 (Fall 1981), Sacramento County Historical Society.

Minske, Pauline. *Chinese in the Mother Lode 1850-1870*. San Francisco: R and E Research Associates, 1974.

Nee, Victor G. and Brett De Bary Nee. *Longtime Californ': A Documentary Study of an American Chinatown*. New York: Pantheon Books, 1973.

Osios, Camilo. *The Filipino Way of Life*. Boston: The Boston Company, Inc., 1964.

Ow Wing, Horace. Telephone interview with Author, Stockton, California, 1983.

Owyang, Katharine. Interview with Author, Stockton, California, 1983.

Paul, Rodman W. *California Gold: The Beginning of Mining In the Far West*. Lincoln, Nebraska: University of Nebraska Press, 1947.

Pen Pictures from the Gardens of the World: A Memorial and Biographical History of Northern California. Chicago: Lewis Publishing Co., 1891.

Praetzellis, Mary and Adrian Praetzellis. *Archaeological and Historical Studies of the IJ56 Block, Sacramento, California: An Early Chinese Community*. Sonoma, California: Sonoma State University, Cultural Resource Facility, Anthropological Studies Center, 1982.

Raven, Ralph S. *Faith of Our Fathers: A History of the First Congregational Church, Stockton, California*. Centennial Edition 1865-1965. Stockton, California, 1965.

Reed, Karen Lea. "The Chinese in Tehama County: 1860-1890." Association for Northern California Records and Research, No. 6, 1980.

Renewal Division. Parcel Records. Stockton Redevelopment Department. City of Stockton, Stockton, California.

Right-of-Way Department. Property Files. District 10, CalTrans. Stockton, California.

Robinette, Allen M. *History of the Stockton Fire Department 1850-1908*. Stockton, California: n.p., 1908.

Rodescape, Lois. "Celestial Drama In the Golden Hills: The Chinese Theatre in California 1849-1869." *California Historical Society Quarterly* 23 (June 1944).

Rohe, Randall E. "After the Gold Rush: Chinese Mining in the Far West, 1850-1890." *Montana, The Magazine of Western History* (Autumn 1982).

St. Mark's Methodist Church 1949-1968. Stockton, California: n.p., 1968.

Sacramento Daily Union, Sacramento, California, November 1852 through February 1876.

Sacramento Guide Book. Sacramento: The Sacramento Bee, 1939.

Sacramento's Chinese Directory. (Author unknown) Chinese Publishing House, circa 1960.

San Joaquin County Assessor. Poll Tax Roll: 1874-1875, 1878-1879, 1880, 1884, 1886. San Joaquin County Historical Museum, Lodi, California.

San Joaquin County Assessor. Stockton City Plat Books: 1869, 1871, 1877, 1884, 1901, 1906, 1911, 1916 and 1920. Petsinger Library, Haggin Museum, Stockton, California.

San Joaquin County Marriage Licenses. Volumes 1 through 54. San Joaquin County Historical Museum, Lodi, California.

San Joaquin County Official Records. Book I. San Joaquin County Historical Museum, Lodi, California.

San Joaquin County Road Overseer of District No. 32 to Board of Supervisors of San Joaquin County, May 1878. San Joaquin County Historical Museum, Lodi, California. (Material uncataloged) Copy in author's possession.

San Joaquin Historian. San Joaquin County Historical Society Quarterly. Vols. 13-17.

San Joaquin Republican, Stockton, California, May 1851 through October 1855.

Sandmeyer, Elmer Clarence. *The Anti-Chinese Movement in California*. Urbana, Illinois: University of Illinois Press, 1939.

Saxton, Alexander. *The Indispensable Enemy: Labor and the Anti-Chinese Movement in California*. Los Angeles: University of California Press, 1971.

Schwarz, Henry G., ed. *Chinese Medicine on the Gold Mountain: An Interpretive Guide*. Seattle, Washington, 1984.

Schweitzer, Jeffrey. "Afloat to Stockton," *Pacific Historian* 20 (Spring 1976).

Shepherd, Charles R. *Ways of Ah Sin: A Composite Narrative of Things As They Are*. New York: Fleming H. Revell Co., 1923.

Sing Lim. *West Coast Chinese Boy*. Montreal, Quebec: Tundra Books, 1979.

Starr, Neal L. "Stockton State Hospital: History and Development," *exChange* 1 (June/July 1974):8-14.

Steiner, Stanley Fusang. *The Chinese Who Built America*. New York: Harper & Row, 1979.

Stockton City and San Joaquin County Directory 1910. Sacramento: Polk-Husted Directory Co., 1910.

Stockton City and San Joaquin County Directory 1915. Sacramento: Polk-Husted Directory Co., 1915.

Stockton Daily Argus, Stockton, California, September 20, 1854.

Stockton Daily Independent, Stockton, California, February 1867 through July 1912.

Stockton Daily Evening Herald, Stockton, California, January 1877 through March 1885.

Stockton Evening Mail, Stockton, California, May 1886 through January 1900.

Stockton Daily Evening Record, Stockton, California, November 1956 through 1975.

Stockton Record, Stockton, California, November 1956 through 1975.

Stockton Rural Cemetery. Death Registers. 4 volumes. Stockton Rural Cemetery, Stockton, California.

Stockton State Hospital 1968 Fact Sheet. Stockton, California.

Stockton Times, Stockton, California, March 1850 through March 1851.

Stockton Weekly Mail. Stockton, California, January 1885 through January 1892.

Sun, Patrick Pichi. *Recollections of a Floating Life*. n.p., 1972.

Sung, Betty. *The Story of the Chinese in America*. New York: Collier Books, 1967.

Supernowicz, Dana. "The Ubiquitous Celestial: The Impact of the Overseas Chinese in the Mother Lode Region of California." Paper presented at the Society of Historical Archaeology Conference on Underwater Archaeology, Sacramento, California, January 8, 1986.

Tachiki, Eddie Wong, Franklin Odo, and Buck Wond, eds. *Roots: An Asian American Reader*, a project of the UCLA Asian American Study Center. Los Angeles: Continental Graphics, 1971.

Taylor, Clotilde Grunsky. *Stockton Boyhood, Being the Reminiscence of Carl Ewald Grunsky Which Covers the Years from 1855 to 1877*. Berkeley: Friends of the Bancroft Library, 1959.

The Statement of Nine Years (1937-1946) Contributions to the Anti-Invasion and Relief Efforts of the Chinese Association of Stockton, California. Stockton, California: n.p., 1947.

Thompson, John. "The Settlement Geography of the Sacramento-San Joaquin Delta, California." Ph.D. dissertation, Stanford University, 1957.

_____. "The People of the Sacramento Delta." *Golden Notes* 28 (Fall/Winter 1982).

Thompson, Thomas H. and Albert Augustus West. *History of Sacramento County, California-1880*. Berkeley: North-Howell Press, 1960.

Tinkham, George H. *History of San Joaquin County, California With Biographical Sketches*. Los Angeles: California Historic Record Co., 1923.

Trauner, Joan B. "The Chinese as Medical Scapegoats in San Francisco, 1870-1905." *California History* 57 (Spring 1978): 70-87.

Tsai, Henry Shih-Shan. "The 1911 Revolution and the Chinese Americans," Part I. *Chinese Historical Society Bulletin* 16 (October 1981): 2-3.

_____. "The 1911 Revolution and the Chinese Americans," Part II. *Chinese Historical Society Bulletin* 16 (November 1981): 2-8.

Vallanga, Roberto V. *Pinoy: The First Wave (1898-1941)*. San Francisco: Strawberry Hill Press, 1977.

Walker, Henry Townsend, Jr. "Gold Mountain Guests: Chinese Migration to the United States, 1848-1882." Ph.D. dissertation, Stanford University, 1976.

Weinstein, Robert A. "North From Panama, West to the Orient: the Pacific Mail Steamship Company." *California History* 57 (Spring 1978): 46-57.

Weiss, Melford S. *Valley City: A Chinese Community in America*. Cambridge, Mass.: Schenkman Publishing Co., 1974.

Wells Fargo & Co. Express. *Directory of Chinese Business Houses for San Francisco, Sacramento, Marysville, Portland, Stockton, San Jose, Virginia City, Nevada*. San Francisco: Wells Fargo Co., 1878.

Wells Fargo & Co. Express. *Directory of Chinese Business Houses for San Francisco, Sacramento, Marysville, Portland, Stockton, San Jose, Virginia City, Nevada*. San Francisco: Wells Fargo Co., 1882.

Weys, Ernest. Interview with Author, Stockton, California, 1979.

Williams, C. A. S. *Outlines of Chinese Symbolism and Art Motives*. New York: Dover Publications, Inc., 1976.

Williams, Stephen. *The Chinese in the California Mines: 1848-1860*. San Francisco: R and E Research Associates, 1971.

Willis, William L. *History of Sacramento County, California With Biographical Sketches*. Los Angeles: Historic Records Co., 1913.

Wilson, Carol Green. *Chinatown Quest: One Hundred Years of Donaldina Cameron House, 1874-1974*, rev. ed. San Francisco: California Historical Society, 1974.

Wong, John G. Interview with Author, Stockton, California, 1980.

Wong, Jade Snow. *Fifth Chinese Daughter*. New York: Harper & Row Publishers, 1950.

Wong, Sam, compiler. *An English-Chinese Phrase Book, Together with the Vocabulary of Trade Law, etc*. San Francisco: Dubery & Co. Books, 1875.

Wolff, L. *Little Brown Brothers*. Garden City, New York: Doubleday, 1961.

Wood, R. Coke and Leonard Covello. *Stockton Memories: A Pictorial History of Stockton, California*. Fresno, California: Valley Publishers, 1977.

Yee, Herbert. Interview with Author, Sacramento, California, 1983.

Yee, Paul K. Interview with Author, Stockton, California, 1981.

Yep, John. Interview with Author, Stockton, California, 1980.

Yip, Christopher L. "A Time for Bitter Strength: The Chinese in Locke, California." *Landscape* 22 (Spring 1978): 3-13.

Yip, Rose. Interview with Author, Stockton, California, 1981.

Index

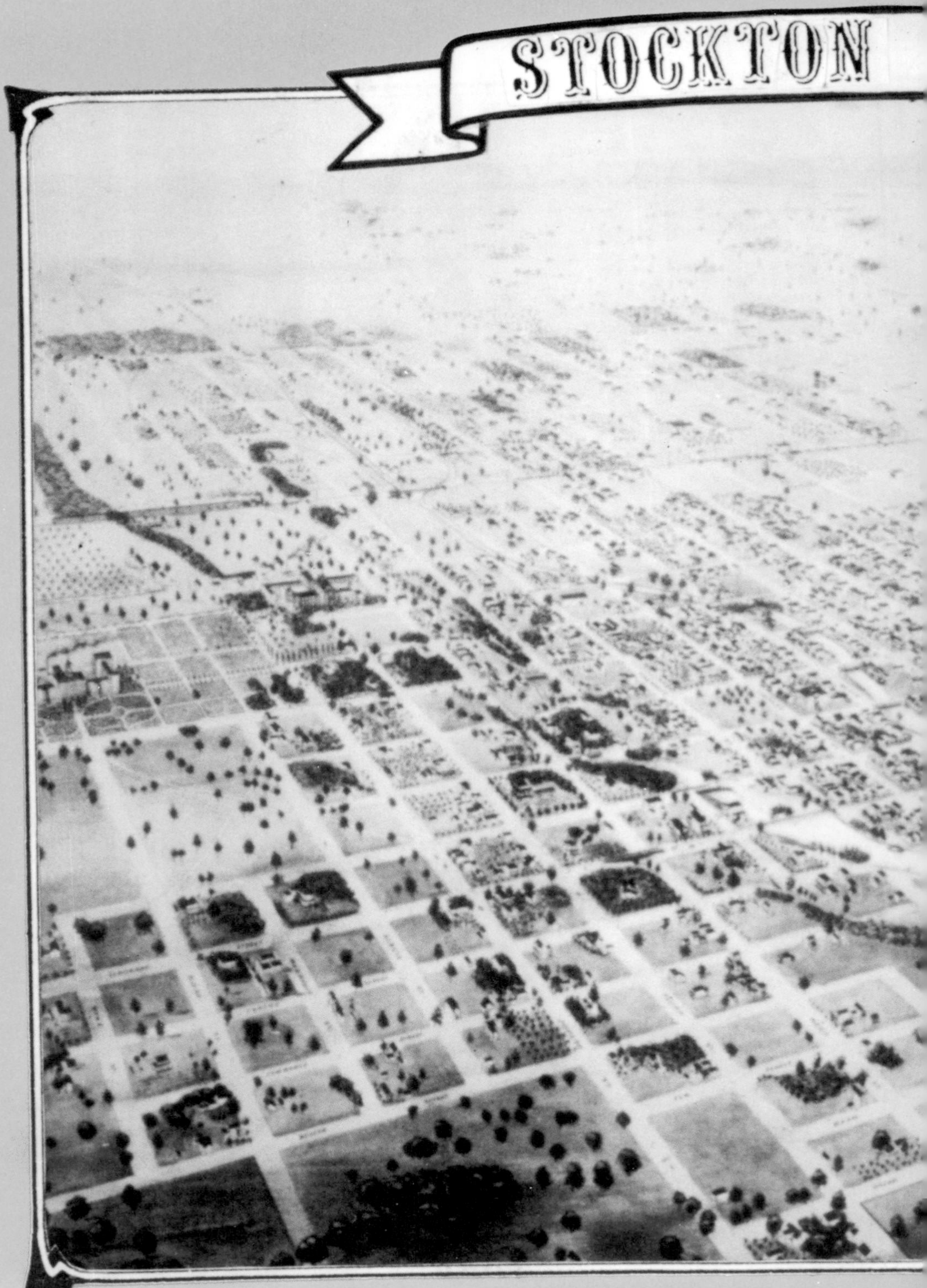
STOCKTON